THE LOST GOLD RUSH JOURNALS

DANIEL JENKS 1849-1865
UNTOLD TALES OF GOLD RUSH ADVENTURE

TRANSCRIBED AND ANNOTATED
BY LARRY OBERMESIK

Library of Congress Control Number: 2021901887

Printed in the United States of America

Published by Larry Obermesik

ISBN: 978-1-7365299-2-8

10 9 8 7 6 5 4 3 2 1

COPYRIGHT © 2021 Larry Obermesik

All Rights Reserved

Table of Contents

Table of Contents iii
Author's Note 1
Daniel Jenks Gold Rush Journal Volume 1: 1849-1851 3
   Barque Velasco ~ Boston February 11, 1849 4
   Our Crew 8
   Take A Balloon - 3/9 12
   Pico ~ Azores Islands - 3/11 13
   Faial ~ Azores Islands - 3/11 14
   The Consul's Garden ~ Orto, Faial 16
   Faial Crater 19
   Cape De Verdes Island ~ St. Vincent, Porta Granda - 3/30 20
   Crossed The Equator - 4/11 21
   Drinking Poisoned Water – 6/15 23
   Diego Ramirez Island – 6/17 30
   A Funeral At Sea - 6/18 31
   Goodbye Cape Horn - 6/30 33
   The Glorious Fourth - 7/4 35
   Becalmed Off Talcahuana - 7/6 36
   Talcahuana, Chili ~ South America - 7/12 38
   Concepcion City - 7/13 42
   Crossed The Equator - 8/16 48
   A No Confidence Vote - 9/7 52
   The Doomed Velasco - 9/17 55
   Dos Amigos Hard Ship - 9/17 56
   Square The Yards - 10/2 60
   Long-Nosed Weather Dogs - 10/4 61
   San Francisco Bay, California - 10/7 62
   San Francisco - 10/13 65
   Her Great Bereavement - 10/25 67
   Crowded Star - 10/30 67
   Stockton, California - 11/4 68
   Branch Hotel ~ Stockton City, California - 11/5 71
   Chinese Camp - 11/18 74
   My Birthday ~ Chinese Camp December 2, 1849 78
   Happy Hungry New Year - January 1, 1850 79
   $1 Per Bite ~ Chinese Camp - February 1850 79
   I Must Succeed 80
   Varmint Companions 81

Taint Thar ~ Chinese Camp - March 1850	82
White Indians	83
Swamped ~ Mouth of Sullivan's Creek - April 1850	84
Chilean Camp	85
Humbug Creek, Tuolumne Co. - May 1850	86
Savage's Camp or Garrote - June 1850	88
Meet Judge Lynch	89
Big Oak Flat ~ Garrote - July 1850	90
Chief Cyprianna	91
Prospecting Tuolumne and Merced	92
Standing Guard	94
Where White Men Never Tread	96
Back To Garrote, Poorer	97
Jacksonville - August 1850	98
The Burns Affair	99
Letters From Home	102
Don't Insult The Lady	102
River Company Setbacks	102
Meet Mrs. Bruin	103
A Miner's Sabbath	104
History Of The Mines ~ Jacksonville - October 1850	105
Rhode Island Bar ~ Jacksonville - November 1850	109
Lucky Strike ~ Jacksonville - December 1850	110
I'm Blessed ~ Jacksonville - January 1, 1851	111
I'm Less Blessed	112
Our Daily Murder Bread	112
Divine Deaths	114
Duly Elected Desperados	116
Societal Restraints	118
Elusive Ditch Piles - February 1851	118
Savage On Savage	120
The Two-Year Itch	121
Kanaka Creek - March 1851	122
Bible Bowl	123
Forgotten Victims	125
The Black Legs	125
He's Just Foolin'	127
Big Baby Business	128
How Do I Look?	128
Kanaka Creek - April 1851	129
Breakin' Bullies	130
Texian Renegades	132
The Bar' Hunt	133
Lovely Jacksonville - May 1851	136

Dollar Buckets - June 1851 136
The Boling Incident 137
Clerk Dick's Rage 138
Killing Snow 139
Burglin' Mardis 140
Vigilante Justice 140
Don't Mess With Sonora's Marshal 142
The Vigilance Committee 143
Life In San Francisco - July 1851 143
No Hope For Sinister Charlie 145

Daniel Jenks Gold Rush Journal Volume 2: 1852-1856 148

    Marysville, California - January 1852 148
    Marysville, California - February 1852 150
    Sacramento Valley Flood 151
    Marysville, California – Broken March 1852 153
    California Has Rats!!! 154
    Marysville, California - April 1852 156
    Tanner's Gauntlet 157
    Off To Oregon – Glorious May 1852 158
    Sacramento Valley - 5/11 159
    Old Settler's Ranch - 5/12 159
    Private Sanctum 160
    Miserable Hovel – 5/12 162
    Shasta City 163
    The Road To Yreka - 5/16 163
    Gary's Ranch - 5/17 165
    Martin's Ranch - 5/18 166
    Yreka - June 1852 167
    Prospecting Salmon River Mountains 168
    Leonard's House ~ Yreka - July 1852 169
    Rogue River Valley War ~ Yreka - August 1852 169
    The Destitute & Sick - September 1852 170
    The Yreka Fire - October 1852 170
    Callahan's Ranch - 10/28 171
    Shasta - November 1852 171
    Marysville - 11/3 172
    Take The Stage 172
    Shasta - 11/11 174
    Gary's Ranch - 11/13 175
    Fouch's Hacienda ~ Long Gulch - 11/14 176
    The Grand Opening – November 25, 1852 176
    The Grand Closing - December 25, 1852 176
    Trapped, Sick & Starving - January 1853 177

Feeding On Air	178
The Dying - February 1853	179
Blue Flour Train - 2/28	180
Unfit For Duty - March 1853	181
Broke, Sick & Alone - April 1853	181
I'm Cursed - May 1853	182
Saved By An Englishman - June 1853	182
Rogue River Valley Indians	183
Ravaging Rogue River	185
Hiram Woods' Ranch - August 1853	186
Shasta Indian Medicine	187
The White Wolves	189
Modoc Indians	191
'Attack' On Woods' Ranch	192
2-Cent Diggin's - September 1853	193
3/4 Froze In Yreka	194
Mule Train To Crescent City - October 1853	196
Waggoner's Ranch - 10/27	197
Jacksonville, Oregon - 10/28	198
Ambush Swamp - 10/29	198
Smith's River Mountain - 10/30	199
Cold Springs House - 10/31	199
Mule Road To Hardscrabble Creek - 11/3	201
Unbelievable Redwoods	203
Crescent City	204
Back To The Mines - 11/7	205
Redwood Swamp - 11/9	206
Fording The Mule Train	207
Clark Ranch - 11/12	209
Slippery Hardscrabble Mountain - 11/13	210
Bar Fight	211
Big Bar on Smith's River - 11/29	212
Here Comes The Sun - 11/30	212
Camp Foot Rock - 12/4	213
Elk Camp House - 12/5	214
Gates' Ranch - 12/6	215
Deer Creek - 12/9	216
The Hornets' Nest - 12/10	218
Our Indian Chief - 12/11	218
Table Rock Mountain - 12/13	219
Jacksonville - 12/14	220
Worse Than A Dog's Life	221
No Show Yreka - 12/19	222
Long Gulch - December 25, 1853	223

THE LOST GOLD RUSH JOURNALS

Unhappy New Year - January 1, 1854 223
The Mines Owe Us $39 224
Brass Bed 225
Dirty Long John 226
My Long Gulch Claim - 1/22 226
A Miner's Life 227
Waterless Claims - February 1854 229
An Eternal Fool 229
All Work And No Pay - March 1854 230
The Innards Win - April 1854 231
Job Never Mined For Gold 231
Unworthy Claims - May 1854 233
Old Channels Pay - June 1854 233
The Glorious Fourth - July 1854 234
Yreka's Aristocrats 234
Jack Barker Was From Holt's Bottom 236
Rebuilding Yreka - August 1854 237
Gulch Claim Business - September 1854 237
Diggin' The Gulch - October 1854 238
Still No Water - November 1854 238
What A Charming Life - December 1854 239
A Long Gulch New Year - January 1855 239
Don't Make It Worse - 1/31 240
No More Townsmen - February 1855 240
Yreka's Weather 241
Rockin' The Gulch - March 1855 242
Chinaman Game 242
What Are They? 243
Strippin' The Gulch - April 1855 244
The Yreka Ditch - May 1855 245
Get A Mess - June 1855 246
The Nation's Sabbath - July 4, 1855 246
Driftin' The Gulch - August 1855 248
Beware, The Poor Indian - September 1855 248
The Indians Prepare For War - October 1855 249
War In Oregon! - November 1855 249
Where Are Cooper's Indians? 250
It Never Rains In California - December 1855 251
Deadly Business: Squaws For Guns 251
My Folly - January 1856 253
Experience Is A Stern Teacher – 2/16 253
My Only Friend - March 1856 254
Blackfeet Attack Seattle 255
California Justice 255

Rogue River Massacre - 3/9	256
Broken Promises & Lies	257
Yreka's Grand Highway Robbery - 3/16	258
War In Oregon Rages On	258
My Disappointing Results – 3/26	259
It Rained! - April 1856	262
There's Fighting Everywhere	262
It Sure Smells Like War	264
Blockhouse Last Stands	265
More Indian Troubles - 4/13	265
Torching Cascades	266
Alarm & Confusion	267
Indian Bill	268
Dry Ditches & Highwaymen	268
What A Miserable Life	269
Golden Era Poetry - May 1856	271
Sick And Alone In The Wilderness - 5/5	271
Two Totally Different Wars - 5/7	273
The Poor Indians' Plan	275
Who Has The Rights?	276
James Beaufort – Eye Witness	277
War Doesn't Pay	278
Wise Media Solomons	279
Yreka's Dry Ditch	280
The Vigilance Committee Reorganizes	280
Election Fraud Exposed	281
Captain Smith Sees The Light?	282
You No Payee - 6/26	283
The Vigilants Take Control - 6/26	284
Yreka's Ditch Is Wet - 6/27	285
Vigilance Committee: The Rest Of The Story	285
Fireworks: Millhouse & Blunt - July 4, 1856	289
Miner Street Mob - 7/5	291
I'd Like A Shot At Taylor	292
Subpoenaed As A Witness	293
The End Of War In Oregon	293
My Best Friend Is Gone - 7/9	295
A Perfect Slave	295
California Riots - 8/7	297
More Modoc Mischief	298
My Log Cabin Home - 8/10	299
My Desperate Hope - 8/17	300
Highwaymen, Politicians & Indians - September 25, 1856	301

Daniel Jenks Gold Rush Journal Volume 3: 1857-1859.................303

  Remember Me...306
  Happy Holidays? - January 1, 1857..307
  Slavery Schemes 307
  Merry With Who?..308
  The Longest Day - January 2, 1857 310
  The Beauties Of Solitude 312
  Cut Off From All Creation 315
  Workin' The Gulch - 1/16 317
  A Miner's Funeral – 2/3 318
  Scarce Wood ~ Massacres A Plenty – 2/5 319
  Lockhart's Ferry Massacre 319
  Chief Lalakes 320
  A Night At The Yreka Theatre - 2/12..321
  Lantern Thin 323
  Sickly Again – 2/16...324
  My Upside-Down Chimney - 3/6 325
  A Miner's Spring – 5/5 326
  Massacre Of The Filibusters - 5/24..327
  Yreka Canal Script – 5/31..327
  Ready To Vamoose – 6/14...328
  Sellin' The Gulch 329
  Homeward Bound – July 6, 1857 330
  Dog Creek House – 7/7 330
  Shasta City - 7/8...331
  Marysville - 7/9...331
  Sacramento City – 7/10 331
  San Francisco - 7/11 332
  Time And Fortune – 7/13 333
  The City Life ~ San Francisco – 7/14...333
  Neptune's Tribute ~ Onboard John L. Stevens...................................334
  Acapulco, Mexico – 7/30 335
  Panama – 8/3 335
  Aspinall – 8/3..336
  Steamer Central America – 8/ 10 337
  New York - August 12, 1857 337
  Home Again - August 15, 1857 338
  Pawtucket - September 1st 338
  The U.S. Economy Collapses 339
  Long Gulch Is Payin'? 341
  First Baptist Sewing Circle 341
  A Pawtucket Sunday – 12/20...342
  The Unemployment Crisis 342

An Irish Christmas	343
Protect Yer Pile!	343
Enjoying Society	345
Troublemakers	346
Weather & Correspondence - January 17, 1858	346
Sleighing Pawtucket Pike	347
Pomfret, Connecticut	348
The Weather & Economy Begin To Thaw	349
Fouch's Lazy Fortune	350
Sacred Sticks & Stones	351
My Last Resting Place	352
Pawtucket Weather	352
This Rainy Hole	354
Having Regrets	354
Drizzle Town	355
Oregon - The New Eureka?	356
The Beginning Of Hostilities	357
I'm Lost	361
Atlantic Telegraph & News	362
Dexter Brothers Explosion	363
Slatersville	363
Conquering Self-Doubt	364
Autumn Blues	365
Discontented Wanderers	365
Blackstone Bridge Jollification	366
Society's Luxuries	366
The Providence Fire	367
My Birthday ~ December 2nd	368
Pike's Peak Or Bust?	368
There's No Going Back	369
Praise The Living - January 3, 1859	370
Blew, Snew & Stuck	370
Shoveling For Dollars	371
Old Bill & My Cousins	371
Mysterious Undergarments	372
Drawings For My Friends	372
Tolerably Coolish	373
Who's Next?	374
Lonesome Wanderers	375
I Must Go	377
Thackery's Virginians	378
Being Content	380
I Dreamed Of A Different Life	381
About My Journal	383

Goodbye Pawtucket 384
Daniel Jenks Gold Rush Journal Volume 4: 1859-1860 385
  Pawtucket 386
  St. Louis 387
  Onboard Steamer Carrier 389
  Kansas City 390
  Colonel Milton McGee 393
  Camp 1: Shawnee Springs - March 26, 1859 395
  Camp 2: Cedar Creek - 3/30 399
  Camp 3: Hickory Point - 3/31 399
  Camp 4: Willow Spring Creek - 4/1 400
  Camp 5: 110 Creek - 4/3 400
  Camp 6: Burlingame - 4/4 402
  Camp 7: Dragoon Creek - 4/5 402
  Camp 8: Elm Creek - 4/6 403
  Camp 9: Council Grove - 4/7 403
  Camp 10: Prairie ~ West of Council Grove - 4/8 404
  Camp 11: Cottonwood Creek - 4/9 405
  Camp 12: Turkey Creek - 4/11 407
  Camp 13: Little Arkansas Creek - 4/12 407
  Camp 14: Chavis Creek - 4/13 408
  Camp 15: Plum Butte - 4/14 411
  Camp 16: Arkansas River Great Bend - 4/16 411
  Camp 17: Arkansas River - 4/17 412
  Camp 18: Pawnee Fork of Arkansas River - 4/18 414
  Camp 19: Chief Little Mountain - 4/19 415
  Camp 20: Desert between Arkansas & Pawnee Fork - 4/20 416
  Camp 21: Arkansas River - 4/21 416
  Camp 22: Arkansas River - 4/22 418
  Camp 23: Arkansas River - 4/23 419
  Camp 24: Arkansas River - 4/24 420
  Camp 25: Arkansas River - 4/25 421
  Camp 26: Arkansas River - 4/26 422
  Camp 27: Arkansas River - 4/27 423
  Camp 28: Aubrey's Crossing - 4/28 424
  Camp 29: Arkansas River - 4/29 424
  Camp 30: Cold Spring Camp - 4/30 425
  Camp 31: Arkansas River - 5/1 426
  Camp 32: Bent's Fort - 5/2 427
  Camp 33: Chief Ten Bears - 5/3 429
  Camp 34: Arkansas River - 5/4 430
  Camp 35: Arkansas River - 5/5 431
  Camp 36: Handcart Man & Boney - 5/6 432

Camp 37: Charley Autobees' Trading Post - 5/8 435
Camp 38: Arkansas River - 5/9 436
Camp 39: Fountain Creek 5 Miles North of Pueblo - 5/10 436
Camp 40: Fountain Creek 10 Miles North of Pueblo - 5/11 438
Camp 41: Independence Camp ~ Fontaine qui Bouille - 5/17 438
Camp 42: Jim's Camp - 5/18 439
Camp 43: O'Falley's Grave - 5/19 440
Camp 44: Head of Cherry Creek - 5/20 440
Camp 45: Lying Speculators - 5/21 441
Camp 46: Cherry Creek - 5/22 442
Camp 47: Cherry Creek - 5/23 443
Camp 48: Denver City - 5/26 443
Camp 49: Dry Gulch - 5/27 445
Camp 50: Mountaineer Creek - 5/28 446
Camp 51: Frosty Creek - 5/29 446
Camp 52: Cache La Poudre Creek - 5/30 447
Camp 53: Camp Windy - 5/31 448
Camp 54: Hunters Camp - 6/1 449
Camp 55: Laramie Valley - 6/2 450
Camp 56: Laramie River Valley - 6/3 450
Camp 57: Pretty Creek - 6/4 451
Camp 58: Muddy Creek - 6/6 452
Camp 59: Cherokee Pass of the Rocky Mountains - 6/7 453
Camp 60: North Platte - 6/8 454
Camp 61: Mud Creek North Platte Valley - 6/10 456
Camp 62: Pine Grove Creek - 6/11 457
Camp 63: Summit Camp - 6/12 458
Camp 64: Desolation Camp - 6/13 460
Camp 65: Alkali Camp ~ Valley of Desolation - 6/14 461
Camp 66: Bitter Creek ~ American Desert - 6/15 461
Camp 67: Bitter Creek - 6/16 462
Camp 68: Bitter Creek - 6/17 463
Camp 69: Bitter Creek - 6/18 463
Camp 70: Green River - 6/19 464
Camp 71: Hams Fork of Green River - 6/20 465
Camp 72: Black Fork of Green River - 6/21 466
Camp 73: Black Fork - 6/22 467
Camp 74: Bridger Fort - 6/23 468
Camp 75: Silver Creek - 6/24 469
Camp 76: Head of Echo Canyon - 6/25 470
Camp 77: Echo Pass - 6/26 470
Camp 78: Dry Camp - 6/27 471
Camp 79: Dragoon Camp - 6/28 472
Camp 80: Salt Lake City - 6/29 473

Camp 81: Salt Lake Valley - 6/30 475
Camp 82: Salt Lake Valley near Weberville - 7/3 478
Camp 83: Salt Lake Valley - 7/4 480
Camp 84: Salt Lake Valley near Willow City - 7/5 480
Camp 85: Brigham City Box Elder Creek - 7/6 482
Camp 86: Warm Springs - 7/7... 483
Camp 87: Blue Springs - 7/8 484
Camp 88: Deep Creek - 7/9.. 485
Camp 89: Pilot Spring Camp - 7/11... 485
Camp 90: De Casure Creek - 7/12... 486
Camp 91: Mountain Spring ~ Goose Creek Mountains - 7/13......................... 487
Camp 92: Goose Creek - 7/14... 487
Camp 93: Rock Spring ~ Thousand Spring Valley - 7/15 490
Camp 94: Thousand Spring Valley - 7/16.. 490
Camp 95: Thousand Spring Valley - 7/17.. 490
Camp 96: Head of Thousand Spring Valley - 7/18 491
Camp 97: Head of Humboldt Valley - 7/19... 491
Camp 98: Humboldt River - 7/20.. 492
Camp 99: Humboldt River - 7/21.. 493
Camp 100: Humboldt River - 7/22.. 495
Camp 101: Humboldt River - 7/23.. 496
Camp 102: Gravelly Ford Humboldt River - 7/24 496
Camp 103: Humboldt River - 7/25.. 497
Camp 104: Humboldt River - 7/26.. 498
Camp 105: Humboldt River - 7/27.. 499
Camp 106: Humboldt River - 7/28.. 499
Camp 107: Humboldt River - 7/29.. 500
Camp 108: Humboldt River - 7/30.. 501
Camp 109: Big Bend or Lassen's Meadows - 7/31 503
Camp 110: Antelope Springs - 8/1.. 503
Camp 111: Rabbit Hole Spring - 8/2 504
Camp 112: Warm Spring - 8/3 505
Camp 113: Granite Creek - 8/4... 506
Camp 114: Wall Spring - 8/6... 508
Camp 115: Smoky Creek - 8/7 509
Camp 116: Honey Lake Valley - 8/10.. 513
Camp 117: Honey Lake Valley - 8/11.. 514
Camp 118: Susanville - Honey Lake Valley - 8/12... 514
Camp 119: Mountain Camp - 8/13 515
Camp 120: Eagle Lake ~ Summit of Sierra Nevada - 8/14 517
Camp 121: Indian Battle Camp - 8/15 518
Camp 122: Spring Camp - 8/16... 519
Camp 123: Pit River ~ Mouth of Willow Creek - 8/17 520
Camp 124: Fall River ~ Opposite Fort Crooks - 8/18 521

Camp 125: Near Fort Crooks - 8/19 521
Camp 126: McCloud's River - 8/20 522
Camp 127: Near Pilgrims Camp - 8/21 522
Camp 128: Mountain House ~ Shasta Butte - 8/22 523
Camp 129: E. Herd's Ranch ~ Shasta Valley - 8/23 523
Camp 130: Shasta River California - 8/24 524
Yreka City ~ Siskiyou County California - 8/25 525
Pike's Peak Expedition Mileage Chart 527
Pike's Peak Expedition Summary 529
California Expedition Mileage Chart 531
California Expedition Summary 533
Yreka - 9/12 535
Yreka - 10/27 535
Yreka - 12/2 536
Yreka - 12/24 536
Long Gulch ~ Near Yreka - January 1, 1860 537
Long Gulch ~ Near Yreka - 2/1 538

Daniel Jenks Gold Rush Journal Volume 5: 1863-1865 541

Yreka - September 23, 1863 543
E. Herd's Ranch - 9/24 544
Grass Lake Valley - 9/26 545
Bob's Camp on Butte Creek - 9/28 548
Little Klamath Lake - 10/1 549
Lost River - 10/3 550
Chief Jacks of the Klamath Lake Indians - 10/5 551
Yarnee Lake - 10/6 553
Martin's Fork of Klamath - 10/8 553
Old Jones the Santa Fe Ox Driver - 10/11 557
Trout Creek - 10/11 558
Beautiful Meadow Valley - 10/12 559
Licam Creek - 10/13 559
Spring Creek - 10/15 560
Silver Lake - 10/16 560
Snake Indians - 10/17 561
Tornado Lake ~ You All Will Die - 10/18 563
Arctic Plains - 10/20 565
Chalk Springs - 10/21 565
Dog-Gone Mountain Springs - 10/22 567
The Wagon Rescue - 10/24 569
Crooked River Valley - 10/25 570
Harney Lake Valley - 10/28 570
The Dead Sea - 11/1 571
Camp Five Shirts - 11/3 572

Emigrant Trail Junction - 11/4	573
The Cattle Heist - 11/8	575
Cattle Rustlin' Indians - 11/9	576
George Wasson's Grave - 11/13	579
Lost In Indian Country - 11/15	580
Owyhee River - 11/16	581
Camp Lost Hope - 11/19	584
This Infernal Hole - 11/22	586
Here Again Canyon - 11/26	588
Dorris' Drovers from Siskiyou - 11/29	589
The Indians Pick A Fight - 12/4	591
Out of The Wilderness - 12/7	594
Old Fort Boise - 12/10	595
Junction House ~ Boise Valley - 12/15	596
Junction House - January 1, 1864	596
Boise City - 3/17	598
The Horse Chase - 3/24	600
Wood Creek Hotel ~ Road to South Boise - 3/28	603
Happy Camp - 3/30	606
Rocky Point - 4/1	607
Syrup Creek House - 4/3	608
Boise City - 4/6	608
Shaffer's Ranch - 4/21	611
Placerville - 4/24	612
Pioneer City Idaho - 6/1	613
Hog 'em - 7/1	615
Hog 'em - January 1, 1865	621
Idaho City - 7/11	622
Placerville ~ Idaho Territory - 7/15	624
Weather Record - Winter 1864/65 Pioneer City Idaho	626
Umatilla Landing - 7/18	632
Dallas - 7/20	633
Portland Oregon - July 22, 1865	633

Author's Note 635

Acknowledgements 636

Dedication 638

Annotation Notes 639

Index 640

Author's Note

"If there is a book that you want to read but it hasn't been written yet, then you must write it." Those words are attributed to Toni Morrison. And so it was with me, when I happened upon the gold rush journals of Daniel Jenks. This started from wanting to learn more about the little-known history of Independence Camp, a site in southern Colorado near my home. The camp had been a way station for gold-seekers during the 19th century gold rush.

Yet my digging led me to the travels and travails of Jenks, who threw caution and a comfortable life to the wind in search of gold half a world away. It seemed as though I was sifting the soil, mining dim shafts of history in search of an interesting nugget or two. And in that deliberate excavation of the past, I struck a gleaming vein of gold in the dark. That treasure was Daniel Jenks' journals, and what could one do but dig and delve deeper?

I never aspired or thought myself to be an author, but rather was inspired by Jenks' journey and his persistence in putting it to paper. He was no geologist, seafarer, or outdoorsman either - far from it. Yet Jenks learned as he went, summoned resolve and resourcefulness, and made do. I took keen interest in and courage from his faith in what's possible, and trust I've done justice to his tale.

Larry Obermesik

Daniel A. Jenks
1827-1869

Daniel Jenks Gold Rush Journal
Volume 1: 1849-1851

Pawtucket January 1, 1849 - I am now 21 years old, my 21st birthday being the 2nd of December last. Although but just arrived at man's estate, still I have already learned that disappointment is the lot of all. Many causes have conspired to make home (i.e. Pawtucket) disagreeable and I am about to leave it for a far distant country. It would be useless to say what these causes for my present discontent are. My friends all know, and others may judge from the lines on the opening page. Suffice it to say that where once all was right, is now darkness. And hope has made way for, shall I say, despair? No. I am bound for California and the Gold Regions.

1/5 - Joined the Narragansett Mining and Trading Company. This company, consisting of 86 members, was organized in this town. We have bought the Barque Velasco of Boston, fitted her out for a two-year cruise with ample supply of provisions, water and so forth for the trip around Cape Horn to California. Where we intend to follow gold mining, trading, etc. God knows I am not so anxious to dig gold. May God preserve my dear kind parents and sisters during my absence.

2/8 - This cold icy day is my last day at home, it may be for many years. God only knows. What changes may take place ere I return? And what may my fate be abroad, in this wild and unsettled country I am about to visit? Aye, it may be my fortune to lay my bones in this strange land. Maybe we will never reach there. For we have many a thousand miles of the wide ocean to cross before we are through. But we are all in God's hands, whether at home or abroad. And if we are to die, it matters but little whether we are at home or not, so we are prepared for the change. This life is but a dream, at best. May we all meet at the grand awakening after death.

Barque Velasco ~ Boston February 11, 1849

Today we dropped out from the wharf and came to anchor out in the stream. We are all ready now for our long voyage around the Horn. I left home on the eighth and have been in Boston ever since, I feel that now the last tie is indeed severed. And tonight, as we lay out here in the stream, I heard the chime of bells on one of the city churches tolling out that old familiar hymn Old Hundred. Every note seemed to strike a nerve leading to my heart and I never, in all my life, felt so solemn. All around us was hushed in the stillness of night. Naught else could be heard, except the splashing of the water against the sides of our barque. It was indeed a solemn hour to me.

2/14 - Since the 11th we have been froze in. But about 2:00 PM we got under way and crowded our way through the drifting ice and at dark we discharged our pilot and stowed out to sea. Goodbye my native land. Fare thee well my childhood's home, parents, sisters dear. Farewell. May the supreme ruler of the seas, as well as the land, watch over and protect you and guide me.

~~~~~~~~~~~~~~~~~~~~~~~~~~~~~~~~~~~

Author's note: The text in the following paragraph is partially obscured, some words are not readable. Here's what I think Daniel wrote:

"And Sarah dear, although we may never again meet here on earth, may your life be one of happiness, may you never know what it is to feel as I now do, so utterly bereft of friends and bourn down by sorrow, so broken."

~~~~~~~~~~~~~~~~~~~~~~~~~~~~~~~~~~~

2/17 - Sails Ho is the cry this morning. But little care I for the cry. I would not go on deck to hardly save a universe, for I am sick. Yes seasick, heartsick and homesick, and if that is not enough to make a man desperate, what is? The morning after we left Boston, we all awoke to find ourselves in the worst gale that many of us had ever experienced. The old barque rolled and tumbled about, utterly regardless of our feelings. And most of us Greenhorns were soon glad enough to crawl back to our bunks, where we lay. A sicker mess was never seen. And as to that, we as yet are not much better off today.

2/18 Latitude 36° 51' Longitude 62° 54'
2/19 Latitude 36° 21' Longitude 59° 48'
2/20 Latitude 36° 0' Longitude 57° 4'
2/21 Latitude 35° 0' Longitude 55° 40'
2/22 Latitude 33° 28' Longitude 55° 2'
2/23 Latitude 32° 22' Longitude 54° 25'
2/24 Latitude 31° 16' Longitude 53° 51'
2/25 Latitude 31° 47' Longitude 53° 7'
2/26 Latitude 31° 27' Longitude 52° 17'
2/27 Latitude 31° 26' Longitude 49° 40'

"Sail Ho, Sail Ho," is the cry. "Where away? Two points off the weather beam," is the reply and we could see afar off in the distance two sails. But oh, what weather we have had for the past week, such a miserable set as we are here. Cooped up in our miserable quarters between decks 5 feet in height. No fire and cold as blazes, all seasick and the ship layed too most of the time, unable to make sail in this gale.

2/28 - Neither of the sails are in sight this morning. I am beginning to recover from my fit of seasickness and will endeavor to write a little today and firstly, let me describe our vessel and her accommodations for her 86 owners. The Barque Velasco is an old-fashioned tub of about 250 tons burthen, formerly in the East India trade. She has a small cabin on deck with 14 bunks. The officers of the ship occupy this cabin and the balance of us are stowed away between decks.

Here we have a sort of a rough cabin fitted up for 72 of us. This cabin is but 5 feet in height. Consequently, we cannot stand erect nor walk about without stooping nearly double. Add to this the double row of bunks around the sides of the ship, another double row fore and aft amidship and you have left two narrow alleyways, about 4 feet in width on each side of the midship bunks. These alleys are lined on each side with chests and trunks pushed partly under their respective owners' bunks, but projecting out on each side. So as to serve the double purpose of seats and tables to eat from and thus taking up all the passageways, with the exception of about a foot wide in the center, so that we cannot move about below deck.

If we want any exercise we must go on deck for it, and let us see what the chances are there. Arrived on deck we find it completely covered with rows of beef barrels. But the captain says we shall soon eat this up and then at least we shall have deck room -- but we did not have to wait for that. For one-night Old Boreas and Neptune eased us by, sweeping off nearly the whole deck-load, together with a long strip of the bulwarks, by a heavy sea that swept over us. And now as to the victualing department, we have two cooks and two little galleys to cook in, for about a hundred men all told. Of course, with such accommodations we cannot have much of a variety, nor many extra dishes. We have no tables and few dishes.

The way we manage to sustain life in this respect is as follows. As I said before there are 72 of us below decks, these are divided into 11 messes. Every man in the mess has to take his turn in rotation to act as Steward of his mess for a week. This Steward has to be on hand at the galley at mealtime, with his mess pans and coffee pot to receive his mess's rations. After securing his pan full of beef and pork and his pot of coffee, he starts with them for his mess, where the members are already seated. Each one upon his chest, tin plate and tin cup in hand, ready to devour (if he has an appetite) what is set before him. And if the weather and sea is as rough as it has been with us since we started, it is no easy matter to make out a meal.

For you have to look out for your plate upon your knees, your cup of coffee, handle your knife and fork as you can and keep all right side up, when the vessel is pitching about at all sorts of angles, every minute changing your position. After your meal is concluded, the Steward takes the plates and cleans them and stows all away for the next meal. But to a seasick man, as most of us have been, the very sight of such food is enough to turn one's stomach. And often whilst eating, or trying to force such stuff down, you will probably have a man vomiting on each side of you. In fact, the place smells as sour as a swill tub now. A well man would be sick here in less than 15 minutes. Such a sight as it is here below, I never expected to see.

About 70 men, all vomiting and groaning and grunting at once, the barque pitching about at a terrible rate. The wind howling and shrieking through the rigging, the sailors swearing at the Greenhorns. All is confusion.

Our Crew

Captain - Giles Spencer, of East Greenwich
1st Mate - Tom Sayce, of Providence
2nd Mate - Isaac Nickerson, of Pawtucket
President - William Roberts, of South Scituate, RI
Vice President - Laban Wade, of Woonsocket
Secretary - William Lune, of Pawtucket
Treasurer - Elisha Bucklin, of Pawtucket
Director - Horace Austin, of Central Falls
Director - Nelson Chace, of Providence
Director - Robert Taft, of East Greenwich
Director - Leonard Walker, of Sesconk

Cabin Mess
<u>Mess #1</u>
John Read, of Providence
William Chase, of Pawtucket
Lucius Nurse, of Lonsdale
Samuel Leonard, of Central Falls
Henry Williams, of Providence
Jeremiah Reynolds, of Providence
William Johnson, of Pawtucket
Abraham Sears, of Pawtucket
Henry Cleveland, of Pawtucket

<u>Mess #2</u>
Daniel A. Jenks, of Pawtucket
Elisha Brown, of Providence
Orrin Perrin, of Thompson, CT

Luther Fisher, of Thompson, CT
Tom Read, of Central Falls
John Atkinson, of Providence
Paul Dexter, of Providence

Mess #3
Harvey Bowen, of Pawtucket
Abraham Fletcher, of Providence
Herbert Ide, of Attleborough
William Shephard, of Providence
Freeman Winn, of Pawtucket
Levi Maxey, of Providence
Allen Reynolds, of Pawtucket

Mess No. 4
Nelson Jenks, of Smithfield
Allen Taylor, of Olneyville
William Kelly, of Blackstone
Nathaniel Shephardson, of Hopkinton, RI
John Young, of Pawtucket
John Horton, of Pawtucket
Shirley Ellsbree, of Valley Falls

Mess No. 5
Charles Richardson, of Pawtucket
Winsor Mowry, of Woonsocket
Cyrus Cooke, of Pawtucket
Leonard Read, of Pawtucket
Thomas Saunders, of Pawtucket
Francis Rett, of Blackstone

Mess No. 6
Thomas McCormick, of Pawtucket
John Templeton, of Pawtucket
James Page, of Providence
Jonathan Lambert, of Providence
Ezra Baker, of Pawtucket
Orrin Baker, of Pawtucket

Mess No. 7
Ebenezer Baker, of Pawtucket
Alfred Messinger, of Providence
Silas Pierce, of Pawtucket
Francis Pierce, of Rehobeth
George Sayles, of Blackstone
George Humes, of Blackstone

Mess No. 8
John Burgess, of Central Falls
Spencer Moury, of Pawtucket
James Smith, of Pawtucket
Welcome Whipple, of Cumberland
Hiram Perry, of Pawtucket
Davis Perry, of Pawtucket
George Murry, of Providence

Mess No. 9
Hiram Carter, of Pawtucket
Benjamin Smith, of Johnston
Louis Fales, of Blackstone

Nathaniel Baxter, of Pawtucket
William Hathaway, of Pawtucket
Asa Andrews, of Providence

<u>Mess No. 10</u>
Charles Randall, of Providence
Henry Arnold, of Woonsocket
Frederick Fish, of Providence
James Cady, of Gloucester, RI
Sanford Capron, of Lonsdale
Henry Cushman, of Pawtucket
Leander Burt, of Providence

<u>Mess No. 11</u>
Samuel Graham, of Pawtucket
James McCarty, of Central Falls
Christopher Skinner, of Attleborough
William Bonney, of Pawtucket
William Parsons, of Fairfax, VT
William Allen, of Central Falls
Obadiah Arnold, of Providence

<u>The Crew</u>
Starboard Watch:
Dyer
Manchester
Leister
Stetson
Hicks

Larboard Watch:
Bliss
Joyslin
Patt
Plunkett

1st Steward - James Gerrybine
2nd Steward - James Micklejohn
1st Cook - James Griffin
2nd Cook - Dwight Newport

99 souls all told.

2/28 Latitude 31° 8' Longitude 48° 4'
3/1 Latitude 30° 36' Longitude 45° 52'
3/2 Latitude 30° 48' Longitude 42° 44'
3/3 Latitude 30° 47' Longitude 41° 58'
3/4 Latitude 32° 10' Longitude 40° 15'
3/5 Latitude 33° 34' Longitude 38° 27'
3/6 Latitude 34° 32' Longitude 36° 45'
3/7 Latitude 35° 34' Longitude 34° 36'
3/8 Latitude 36° 38' Longitude 32° 16'
3/9 Latitude 37° 9' Longitude 30° 4'

Take A Balloon - 3/9

Well, here we are, nearly a month out and we are nearly as far north as when we started. I don't know much about these watercraft, but judging from appearances I should say that we might as well undertake to navigate a balloon, for we appear to have made but mighty little progress towards Cape Horn. Such weather and such a ship. Oh dear! We make Longitude but lose as much in our Latitude - make a mile leeway to every one ahead. Everything is upside down and wrong side out. Down below, boxes, chests, mess pans, old clothes and boots, stray shirts and pants are awfully mixed up. Whilst on deck, sea coal, mackerels, codfish and soft soap are pitching about in company, lovely to behold. As sick a state of affairs you never did see.

The wind has kicked up an awful sea and we are poor Greenhorns. Having thrown up everything but our boots, are about over our seasickness and able to begin to crawl about and grin at Old Neptune in derision, at his attempts to keep us down below. We intend now to run into the Azores, as we are about their Latitude.

Pico ~ Azores Islands - 3/11

"Land Ho!" Was the joyful cry that awakened me early this morning. And tumbling out of my bunk, I rushed up on deck to catch a glimpse of Old Mother Earth. And true enough there she lay, dead ahead. Looking like a dense blue cloud arising out of the sea, it was the peak of Pico, one of the Azores Islands. For a long time, I leaned over the rail gazing upon this (to me welcome sight) and at last when I was called away to breakfast, I did so with regret. But hurried down my rations of salt junk and stinking coffee, to again return and feast my eyes upon this welcome sight of terra firma.

As we gradually neared the land, the trees and rocks began to make their appearances and soon we could discern the snow-white cottages as they glistened in the morning sun. It was truly the most lovely sight, and well repaid me for all my past sufferings on the voyage. Oh, if someone that I knew of could but have been here to enjoy it with me, was the thought that was ever uppermost in my mind. Never was grass so green, or foliage so beautiful to me before. And as we glide along around this point, we behold still another island right ahead, for which we make and soon we come to anchor abreast the fort, on the island of Faial.

Faial ~ Azores Islands - 3/11

Last night about sundown liberty was given for one boat's crew to go ashore. And I — who had stowed myself away in the mizzen chains to be ready for a spring — dropped down into the boat, just as she swung clear of the ship. I was bound to get ashore as soon as possible. We reached the beach and got ashore without getting very wet and were met on the beach by an old Portuguese Tavern Keeper who conducted us to his house, where we got an excellent supper of eggs, fish etc. And there we remained until about 9 o'clock, endeavoring to make up as far as possible in the eating and drinking wine, for our short rations over the month past.

And now that I have got our company all seated at a regular table, with real earthen dishes to eat from, plenty of good palatable food, plenty of oranges and wines to drink, and fair dark eyed Señoritas to wait upon us and a steady floor beneath us, I will, whilst they are all so well occupied, attempt to describe this town and country. In the first place, it will be seen by my log of the voyage, that we have had contrary winds that have blown us much further to the north than we wished. We calculated to touch at the Cape de Verde Islands. But had no idea when we started off, of putting in here. But man proposes and God disposes. Fate decreed that we should stop here and I am glad of it. This group of islands belong to the Portuguese and of course most of the inhabitants are strong Catholics. Like all other Catholic countries, the inhabitants are mostly poor, dirty and ignorant beings. They have a large cathedral, one or two nunneries and several small chapels, as small as this city is.

The Padres are numerous, and of course insolent. They march about the city in their rich but homely dresses, the crowns of their heads shaved, feeling as big as so many turkey cocks amongst their brood. Whilst their supporters, the poor ignorant peasant, feels himself highly honored if he can but kiss his High Holiness's fingers. This city of Orto, I believe it is called, is the residence of all foreign Consuls and the principal town of the group. Winemaking and fruit growing appears to be the staple business of the country. The city is built on the side of the mountain, rising in terraces one above the other and from the sea presents a beautiful view. The streets are narrow, being in most cases mere alleyways and owing to the nature of the country are obliged to be well graved. As in the rainy season they look like so many small creeks, and were it not for the graving would soon be washed into the sea.

In fact, these islands are but mountain peaks that arise from the sea, having been thrown up by volcanic action in the early ages of the world. Looking across the bay (8 miles) the island of Pico is seen, with its cap of snow rising far above the vine clad hills below. The American Consul Mr. Dabney has a beautiful residence there. His house is situated in the center of a large garden of many acres, set out with orange, lemon and other tropical trees and is certainly the most lovely place I ever saw. He is a large wine raiser, and we visited his large wine vaults and sampled his wines. He has given our company permission to visit his grounds whenever we feel disposed to. But I have left our fellows at the public house long enough and will now return to them. During the evening we were joined by others of the company, and we altogether had a grand time of it. And I know not to what lengths we should have gone in our feastings, had it not been announced by someone who just entered that the streets were full of girls, anxious to get a sight of our crowd of fellows.

We broke up our carousal and went out into the street and sure enough, there were about 100 girls there, all jabbering in Portuguese and anxious to see the show. We sauntered around the town, visiting the shops and residences of the inhabitants and I must confess that some of the fellows got a little high on the wine that is sold at six cents per bottle. And before I retired for the night, they were making night musical, if not hideous, with their song of "I am bound to California, the Gold Mines for to see".

3/15 - Was awakened this morning by the report of our gun aboard ship. Upon going down to the pier, I saw that our barque had her colors at half-mast, and she was drifting into shore, having busted one of the cables in last night's gale. She was finally fetched up by the other cable and we have hired an anchor and cable of the American Consul, to hold by, until we can get our own up again.

The Consul's Garden ~ Orto, Faial

Yesterday visited the Consul's Garden in company with William Parsons. After passing through his Cooper's yard, we passed through a gate in the wall and found ourselves in a most beautiful flower garden, where we found flowers from all parts of the world. Passing on through paths lined with the box plant 12 and 15 feet in height and bordered with flowering shrubs and plants, we came to the house. Where we met Mrs. Dabney who, being a Boston woman, was of course glad to see any of her fellow countrymen and she had many questions to ask of us about home, as we walked through her grounds and eat of her fruit. She has two sons, the eldest is married to Prof. Webster's daughter of Boston and the youngest is engaged to another daughter who is on here now, spending winter with her sister.

We passed on through groves of orange, lemon and fig trees, through clusters of large rosebushes all in bloom and finally came to a summerhouse on a little eminence commanding a view far out to sea. And here on a windowsill I found written the following lines:

Tis calm out on the deep blue sea
The winds sleep on the waves
The banners sluggish listlessly
How hang about the stays
Awake ye winds, from this deep sleep
And o'er the dark sea roam
But in thy course across the sea
Oh, waft the Harbinger home
Away away why wait ye here
My only hope is there
This land to others may be dear
To me it brings despair
To me tis like a long, long night
A watching for the day
With straining eyes to catch the light

Of daybreak's glimmering ray
And oh the Harbinger would be
That light upon the soul
That day breaks glimmering to me
That to the watcher stole
For here I gaze with straining eyes
Far out upon the seas
For with her coming, oh there lies
All life can bring to me

(Singed) A Wanderer

No doubt this was written by young Dabney's wife (Webster's Daughter) as she sat here day after day watching for her husband's return from some of his trips to Boston, in his Father's Barque Harbinger. God bless you, young lady and may your life be one continual season of happiness, is the fervent prayer of one who has been the recipient of your kind feelings when in a strange land and one who knows the true value of such a wife as you must be.

We sat here in this old arbor a long time. Feasting our eyes with the fine view to be obtained here of the city around us, of the scene before us with the islands in the distance, snuffing the spiced odors that were wafted by us, by the light breeze as it swept through the groves of cinnamon, oranges, peach and lemon trees around us. But it would be useless for me to attempt to describe the thousand pleasant sensations I enjoyed whilst here on this beautiful island. To me, it seems a paradise. After leaving the garden we were shown the wine vaults and tasted the wines from old casks and hogsheads, covered with the same mold and rust of years.

Faial Crater

3/19 - Today we made up a party of six or eight to visit the crater on the island. It is at the top of the highest peak and about 9 miles they say from the city. After climbing up the rough paths and passing through many lovely little valleys, we at last came to this vast hole in the ground. I should think it was a mile across at the top and about three quarters of a mile across in the bottom and at least 900 feet deep. The top of the mountain is completely barren, not a shrub to be seen. The sides full of ravines and gullies exceedingly uneven and making traveling very bad. We descended to the bottom after a rough scramble and after collecting specimens for friends at home, climbed out again and returned to town, well satisfied with the trip.

3/20 - This is our last day ashore, as we sail at 2:00 PM today. Goodbye girls, goodbye all the good times we have had whilst here. Never shall I forget the many happy hours I have spent here, beautiful gem of the sea. Our stay here has been one long protracted gala day to most of us and never have I enjoyed myself better. Fruit of all kinds have we been feasted with, at about 9 pence a hatful. Wine has been our constant drink, at 6 cents a quart and pretty, lovely dark eyed Señoritas our constant companions. What more could man ask for? But our time has come to say farewell and at last we must again return to our miserable salt junk and pork rations.

3/21 Latitude 37° 56' Longitude 29° 4'
3/22 Latitude 35° 7' Longitude 28° 11'
3/23 Latitude 32° 3' Longitude 27° 51'

3/24 Latitude 29° 14' Longitude 27° 12'
3/25 Latitude 27° 10' Longitude 26° 56'
3/26 Latitude 24° 51' Longitude 26° 32'
3/27 Latitude 22° 35' Longitude 26° 14'
3/28 Latitude 19° 59' Longitude 26° 1'
Spoke barque Belvedere from NY for California 88 passengers all well
3/29 Latitude 18° 0' Longitude 25° 26'

Made Cape de Verde at noon. At dark, they are about 40 miles dead ahead, we will put in tomorrow I expect. Since we left Faial, we have had fine weather. Much better on ship than the first part of the voyage. There is such a sameness at sea that one can find but little to write about that would interest anyone.

Cape De Verdes Island ~ St. Vincent, Porta Granda - 3/30

We found ourselves this morning in the harbor. And a more desolate, barren, rocky place I never even read about. We came in here for wood and are getting it aboard today. But I do not see where it comes from, for there is not a tree to be seen. We found the Audley Clark from Newport for California with passengers here repairing, having sprung a leak out to sea. This island seems to be naught but a barren rocky mountain shooting up out of the sea and is inhabited by Africans who have a small village of mud huts near the beach, but what they can get there to support life is a mystery to me.

3/31 - Porta Granda. Went ashore this morning and took a cruise around amongst the Natives, visited their shanties and whatever else was worth seeing and found but mighty little at that. The town consists of a church without windows, made of mud and thatched with reeds. A hole in a rock with three cannons mounted on it, which they call a fort. About 40 mud huts inhabited by about 500 Natives, most of them clothed in Old Dame Nature's ready-made suit. There is no vegetation to be seen with the exception of here and there a sickly-looking evergreen shrub. There is an American cemetery here, where lie the remains of 12 seamen and two midshipmen, part of the crew of USS Preble who were buried here December 1844.

4/1 Left Porta Grand last night
4/1 Latitude 14° 49' Longitude 24° 40'
4/2 Latitude 12° 30' Longitude 23° 56'
4/3 Latitude 1° 58' Longitude 23° 17'
4/4 Latitude 7° 35' Longitude 22° 33'
4/5 Latitude 5° 25' Longitude 22° 10'
4/6 Latitude 3° 40' Longitude 21° 20' *Spoke Portuguese brig Audry bound for Brazil*
4/7 Latitude 2° 35' Longitude 20° 0'
4/8 Latitude 1° 18' Longitude 21° 36' *Four ships in sight today.*
4/9 Latitude 0° 42' North Longitude 21° 41'
Three ships in sight this morning. At noon spoke Alceste of Glasgow for Valparaiso, all well.
4/10 Latitude 0° 6' South Longitude 23° 9' West

Crossed The Equator - 4/11

Crossed the equator today. At dark we saw what we supposed to be Alceste, dead ahead. Lost sight of her in a black squall cloud. Early this morning passed a wreck supposed to be Alceste, hailed them and they needed no assistance as their ship was all right, having only lost their masts. They were just far enough ahead of us to catch the squall, which we escaped by our old tub being so poor a sailor. "The race is not always to the swift."

4/11 Latitude 1° 38' South Longitude 23° 9' West
4/12 Latitude 3° 17' South Longitude 24° 16' West
4/13 Latitude 4° 55' South Longitude 25° 45' West
4/14 Latitude 6° 35' South Longitude 26° 48' West
4/15 Latitude 8° 36' South Longitude 27° 37' West
4/16 Latitude 10° 26' South Longitude 28° 9' West
4/17 Latitude 12° 11' South Longitude 28° 40' West
4/18 Latitude 13° 41' South Longitude 28° 59' West
4/19 Latitude 16° 8' South Longitude 29° 3' West
4/20 Latitude 18° 44' South Longitude 29° 34' West
4/21 Latitude 19° 32' South Longitude 29° 25' West
4/22 Latitude 20° 6' South Longitude 31° 48' West
4/23 Latitude 21° 11' South Longitude 33° 27' West
4/24 Latitude 22° 15' South Longitude 34° 47' West

For the last few days we have had headwinds, but we are now steering our course. The monotony of sea life is very tedious, no change of the scene but the same view always presents itself. Naught but blue water around you and blue sky above you, with now and then a gale to stir you up. Many an hour have I whiled away, listening to the yarns as spun by our sailors. One was with Wilkes in his exploring expedition, was one of Drew Underhill's boat crew at the time he was killed by the Islanders in the Pacific. And points with pride to a scar on his cheek, the result of a wound received in trying to rescue his officer. Another was onboard the US Somers at the time of the mutiny, when young Spencer was hung.

4/25 Latitude 23° 49' South Longitude 35° 48' West

Fine weather today. Although time passes rather heavily here far out to sea, still we endeavor to make the best of it and use our best efforts to "drive dull care away". After our supper of salt beef and pork at eight bells, or 4:00 PM, we sometimes call up the violinist and all that wish to stir their legs "go in for a regular fore and aft breakdown". We sometimes try our hands at a Vaudeville, with bearded partners, but they are but a poor substitute for the Simon-pure article. Sometimes we try on the gloves and practice at hard knocks in self-defense. And best of all for exercise, we have the good old boyish game of tag. Fore and aft, above and below, we have it. And if in leaping over barrels and casks, one slips through into the slush tub, why all the better. Anything for a laugh.

4/26 Latitude 25° 38' South Longitude 37° 6' West
4/27 Latitude 27° 24' South Longitude 38° 31' West
4/28 Latitude 27° 51' South Longitude 37° 33' West
4/29 Latitude 28° 59' South Longitude 37° 40' West

Drinking Poisoned Water – 6/15

This morning it is dead calm again. Opened a cask of water this morning and found it, as usual, was as green and stunk worse than any stagnant food I ever saw. Still, we must drink it, for we have no other. When we left Boston, we thought we had good water, for we had paid for good and expected to get it. But it seems our Directors, to save money, instead of buying new casks bought a lot of oil casks and hired a company to burn them out and fill them for us. Now they say that old oil casks make as good water butts as anything else, if they are burned out clean before filling. But our rascally water men, knowing that we were bound for a long voyage and not fearing detection, only burned out about a dozen of them and the balance they filled up with water just as they were.

They then, in stowing the hold, put the good water near the hatch where we should use it first and consequently, we never discovered the imposition until far out to sea. Now we find that all our water is put up in casks with the settlings or sediment that arises from whale oil about a foot deep. So that when we open a cask, there is this loathsome mass of curry floating on top and our water tastes 10 times worse than it would to drink out of an oil can. I had expected to find hard fare, but this drinking whale oil and water mixed, is rather ahead of my time.

4/30 Latitude 30° 7' South Longitude 39° 18' West

A 10 knot breeze this morning and going along finely. As to that water business, we find upon examination that we have a few casks of sweet water and are to be allowed a pint a day for drinking to the man. As to the diluted whale oil, we can drink as much of that as we want. Our coffee and tea has to be made from this, and beautiful stuff it is. We have to hold our nose and gulp it down the best way we can, but tis awful.

Note: Text that was struck out -- "Smells like the contents of a chamber mug after it has stood about a week"

This kind of coffee, with our salt horse meat, sea crackers as hard as flints and oh occasionally a plum duff or pudding, boiled in salt water, forms our daily food and drink. Yesterday it rained quite hard. We took advantage of it to catch some 8 or 10 hogsheads of fresh water. By stopping up the scupper's holes, we caught all that fell on deck. And when it got deep enough to bail, we took our buckets and commenced filling up our empty hogs' heads - utterly regardless of tobacco quids etc. the deck was covered with. And now when we go to pump out of the barrels a drink, we have first to shove away the floating quids and goat pills before we can get at the water. But even this, as filthy as it is, is far better and much more palatable than our Boston oil-diluted stuff. A life on the ocean waves, indeed.

5/1 Latitude 32° 23' South Longitude 38° 55' West
5/2 Latitude 34° 5' South Longitude 37° 59' West
5/3 Latitude 36° 2' South Longitude 38° 1' West
5/4 Latitude 37° 29' South Longitude 37° 23' West
5/5 Latitude 38° 6' South Longitude 37° 27' West
5/6 Latitude 38° 43' South Longitude 39° 10' West

Sunday again and cold as blazes. For the past week we have had headwinds and blowing at times quite a gale from the Southwest. But today we have a little more favorable slant and are nearing our course. Two sails in sight this morning. One of our mass caught an albatross this morning with a hook and line that measured 9 feet across its wings from tip to tip. They, together with the haglet and other ocean birds, are quite numerous about here.

5/7 Latitude 39° 50' South Longitude 39° 36' West

The sail in sight yesterday it seems did not make any more headway than we did, as it is still in sight off abeam. The wind has hauled ahead again, and we are now headed Southeast by South. The weather begins to grow colder as we make progress southward and now on deck a pea jacket comes in play again. The squalls we experienced last week seem to be common in this Latitude and are called Pamperos, look for them at any season off the mouth of the Rio Platte. Today the men are all busy catching albatross by means of hook and lines thrown overboard and baited with pork. Rather a novel way of catching birds.

This is my cook week, or rather, I am Steward of the mess this week. I have already said that our company is divided into messes and these are like so many families. Every mess, by themselves, eat their regular two meals a day at 8:00 AM and 4:00 PM. My duty commenced by being called up this morning to get the mess's rations for the week from the store office. One quarter pound of sugar to the man, butter, pickles, according to the number of the mess. After procuring these rations comes breakfast, consisting of salt beef and pork and taros, a species of yam which we got at Faial, a poor substitute for potatoes. As we have no tables, we have to set the mess pans on a chest, take our plates on our knees and gather around the mess pan, to keep it from sliding away to leeward as the ship lurches and then gab and swallow our grub as we can.

After breakfast I wash dishes and stow them all snug in the mess chest for next meal. Then we pass away time as well as possible until eight bells afternoon, when we go through the same operations for supper, which consists of about the same articles of food as breakfast. The only variety we have is twice a week, beans boiled and plum duff - or pudding of the doughiest kind - as heavy as lead and about as palatable to me. Woe to the man that stumbles overboard with one of our duffs in his breadbasket, he could never swim with that load in him. Occasionally you will see a whole mess, dishes, pans and coffee pots slide to leeward in a lurch, sweeping all before them.

5/8 Latitude 40° 31' South Longitude 40° 7' West

Today there is a great number of birds around the ship, skimming about over the water's surface, picking up refuse thrown from the ship. Amongst the species are the albatross, measuring from 8 to 14 feet across their wings, the black and the speckled haglets, cape pigeons, cape gulls, sea hens, mother carey's chickens - mollymawks, etc. Today the wind is more favorable. Sent down main royal and fore top gallant mast and otherwise prepared for doubling Cape Horn.

5/9 Latitude 41° 6' Longitude 41° 11'
5/10 Latitude 42° 42' Longitude 42° 9'
5/11 Latitude 43° 20' Longitude 43° 19'
5/12 Latitude 45° 10' Longitude 42° 19'
5/13 Latitude 45° 4' Longitude 42° 8'
5/14 Latitude 44° 58' Longitude 42° 9'
5/15 Latitude 45° 37' Longitude 42° 30'
5/16 Latitude 46° 6' Longitude 41° 28'
5/17 Latitude 46° 20' Longitude 40° 48'
5/18 Latitude 46° 16' Longitude 41° 28'
5/19 Latitude 46° 30' Longitude 40° 45'
5/20 Latitude 45° 52' Longitude 42° 37'
5/21 Latitude 45° 11' Longitude 43° 27'
5/22 Latitude 46° 31' Longitude 46° 0'

Here is a specimen of Cape Horn, wind either dead ahead or else becalmed. Our chart looks like a spider's web, so crooked is our track. On the night of the 12th we encountered a very severe squall, with hail and snow. Since then, it has blown a perfect gale most of the time, from the Southwest and South, right square in our eyes. And this old tub cannot be brought within 16 points of the wind, and makes more leeway than headway.

5/23 Latitude 46° 4' Longitude 46° 23'
5/24 Latitude 46° 56' Longitude 45° 46'
5/25 Latitude 47° 51' Longitude 48° 40'
5/26 Latitude 49° 25' Longitude 47° 57'
5/27 Latitude 50° 39' Longitude 48° 42'
5/28 Latitude 50° 30' Longitude 50° 55'
5/29 Latitude 52° 9' Longitude 51° 4'
5/30 Latitude 53° 12' Longitude 52° 30'
5/31 Latitude 53° 57' Longitude 54° 0'
6/1 Latitude 53° 17' Longitude 55° 7'
6/2 Latitude 52° 5' Longitude 55° 42'
6/3 Latitude 51° 3' Longitude 56° 18'
6/4 Latitude 52° 2' Longitude 56° 42'

Made to Falkland Islands bearing south southwest from us. Such weather I never did see before, wind, hail, sleet and snow is the order of the day. Saw a sail at a distance yesterday. Cold, bitter cold is it here. I cannot write at present.

6/5 Latitude 52° 9' Longitude 57° 49'

The islands lay off to windward of us today and look terribly desolate and lonely. And causes one to almost shutter to look at them, so cold and frigid do they look encased in the snow. We would like to get to the windward of them, but it is impossible do so with this breeze from the southwest. It snows today quite hard, and our decks and the rigging are covered with ice.

6/6 Latitude 52° 27' Longitude 56° 49'

Spoke barque Black Warrior of New London, homeward bound from a whaling cruise. We have taken the opportunity to send home letters by her, as her captain kindly agreed to lay by us until we had time to write. This is the first homeward bound vessel we have seen since we left home. One who has never been to sea, can have no idea with what feelings we shook hands with the boat's crew of this ship who visited us. Theirs was the first new faces we had seen since we left port. It has been over two months since we left the last port. During that time, we have seen none but the same faces day after day. In addition to this, we have had headwinds day after day for weeks and take it all in all, we have had considerable fretting. But all our troubles were forgotten now, when we heard the cry forward of "Sail Ho dead ahead" and bearing down for us.

6/7 Latitude 52° 50' Longitude 55° 35'
6/8 Latitude 53° 35' Longitude 56° 34'
For the first time in over a month we heard the order to square the yards (fair wind).
6/9 Latitude 54° 10' Longitude 61° 29' - *Fair wind today again*
6/10 Latitude 55° 44' Longitude 64° 8' - *Made Staten Island today*
6/11 Latitude 57° 5' Longitude 64° 10'

The wind is dead ahead again. We are in a bad fix now respecting the affairs of this company. We organized at home as a joint stock company, intending to proceed to California and engage in mining operations as a company, and to be governed by our officers in our operations. But much dissatisfaction appears to exist in the company, and I have no doubt but we shall dissolve the partnership.

6/12 Latitude 56° 10' Longitude 66° 17'
6/13 Latitude 55° 43' Longitude 66° 34'
6/14 Latitude 57° 15' Longitude 69° 13'

Headwinds and sore heads make a ship's company anything but pleasant companions, and that is the case here. But according to observation we are now around Cape Horn, so goodbye to all ill feelings now, let us be cheerful whilst we may. Saw an English barque today, she signaled us and we understood as much of her signals as the Chinese would have been apt to. It is rather cold and disagreeable here, but not as severe as I imagined it would be within 23° of the South Pole in the dead of winter. The sun rises about 9 o'clock and sets about 3 PM, making rather long nights.

6/15 Latitude 56° 46' Longitude 68° 37'

Diego Ramirez Island – 6/17

Headwinds again and it seems we congratulated ourselves upon weathering the cape rather prematurely, as we find we are still too leeward of it, having been blown back by headwinds last night. Made the island of Diego Ramirez 3:00 PM about four points off our weather bow, so we were forced to about ship and steer for the south pole again. 2 sails off Starboard, 1 off Larboard quarter at noon. This morning, after the gale of last night, our ship presented a beautiful appearance. Barrels of slush, sea coal, soft soap and pickled mackerel, all stove in and their contents strewn about deck in admirable disorder. Whilst here and there might have been seen fragments of garments, hanging to the shrouds. All there was left of some poor fellow's last washing, who had carelessly left his clothes hanging overnight.

Down below, the scene was about the same. Men were hunting for stray boots, pants and other articles of clothing. Lost dishes, stray mess pans and numerous other articles too numerous to mention, which had rather unceremoniously taken their leave during the night. Bottles of the best New Orleans molasses lay lovingly mingling their sweets with the contents of an upset pickle jar in the mess chest and both were mixed with the butter, cheese and hard bread, all in a heap. But such is life on the ocean waves.

6/16 Latitude 57° 36' Longitude 68° 38'
6/17 Latitude 57° 2' Longitude 69° 57'

A Funeral At Sea - 6/18

Died last night during the gale, James Smith of Pawtucket. He has been sick all the voyage of consumption. We buried him at 12 o'clock a.m. At the appointed time the ship was hove to, the stars and stripes were raised half-mast and the body was brought up, sewed up in his blanket and weighted at the feet. Laid upon a plank resting on the rail, a prayer was read, the plank tipped, and the body was consigned to the deep and his spirit to its maker. A funeral at sea is a solemn site, it causes solemn thoughts to thus see one of our number launched over the side, to watch his body as it sinks down, down, beneath the blue waters until it disappears forever.

6/18 Latitude 57° 8' Longitude 70° 24'
6/19 Latitude 57° 15' Longitude 71° 49'
6/20 Latitude 56° 22' Longitude 74° 53'
6/21 Latitude 56° 14' Longitude 75° 22'
6/22 Latitude 54° 55' Longitude 76° 36'
6/23 Latitude 53° 6' Longitude 77° 5'
6/24 Latitude 52° 30' Longitude 77° 12'

"Sail Ho!" Is again the cry about dark. Today the Freemasons celebrate at Pawtucket and our friends at home are enjoying themselves in warm weather. May they not forget us poor mortals here in the depths of a Cape Horn winter, I could assure them that they are not forgotten. For oh how often in thought do I retrace my steps across the vast space that lies between me and home sweet home. And especially upon this day do I bring to mind…

Author's note: A copy of a poem by Clara, was inserted between these 2 pages of the journal. The poem sheet obscured some of the text on the page. This is the text that was visible:

…perhaps forever, but…memory will always…this one in particular…ing to mind today of a…the year, most sacred to…mory, because for years… …is was our anniversary…celebrated together, I… …she recalls it today…she thinks of the wan… …now. May she exercise a fa… disposition now, for I stand in need of it. No more shall… …meet

32

in childhood days,…pass, before we meet again… …Then be kind in memo…

6/25 Latitude 51° 24' Longitude 79° 6'
6/26 Latitude 49° 54' Longitude 79° 45'
6/27 Latitude 47° 6' Longitude 79° 16'
6/28 Latitude 45° 38' Longitude 78° 39'
6/29 Latitude 43° 30' Longitude 78° 6'
6/30 Latitude 41° 30' Longitude 77° 38'

Fine weather today. On the 26th there was a great commotion amongst the old dead-heads in the cabin on deck, owing to the sudden and very mysterious disappearance of a keg of port wine. And the ship was searched fore and aft to get, if possible, some trace of it. But without success.

Goodbye Cape Horn - 6/30

It seems pleasant to go on deck now every morning and feel the daily improvement in the temperature as we approach the warmer regions. A week ago, and oh how cold it was. But now we begin to have to peel off, one by one, our Cape Horn clothes and today it feels like summer again. We no longer run shivering below to try to gain warmth in our blankets but lie basking in the warmth of the sun's rays on deck. Our days begin to lengthen out to a more equal proportion and our nights are beginning to be reduced to a reasonable length. Goodbye Cape Horn, with your 18-hour nights and short, shivering days. Goodbye to your leaden-like skies, they are fast giving way to the more genial skies of the tropics. I have doubled the Cape. Never more do I wish to visit your inhospitable waters, your eternal head-winds and long dreary nights.

7/1 Latitude 39° 50' Longitude 75° 44'
7/2 Latitude 38° 48' Longitude 75° 22'
7/3 Latitude 37° 49' Longitude 75° 12'

Spoke a barque with the Belgian flag flying at her peak from Amsterdam for Valparaiso. She is a fast sailor, having come up and passed us and now at dark is hull down ahead. We expect to be in Talcahuana tomorrow to spend the fourth and the men are all busy in putting things to rights, after being knocked about off Cape Horn for a month or two. Some are washing their clothes, others are repairing their battered chests, which look rather the worse for wear after having been knocked about so long. Some are having their hair cut, all are shaved up again and we begin to present a decent appearance once more.

The gold news from California seems to have spread all over the world. When our Captain, in answer to the Belgian's hail this morning, replied bound for California, he laughed as though he understood all about it. Tomorrow is the glorious fourth and we hope to celebrate it on shore. And the prospect is fair for us to do so, if the wind don't shift in the night and drive us out to sea again. Oh, how I long to place my feet on shore once more. It is over three months now since we left the last port, and we are all in a fever to see other faces and to feast our eyes on something else than sky and water.

The Glorious Fourth - 7/4

Just as I expected, the wind shifted during the night and now in the morning we were in sight of the coast and about 30 miles to the south of the mouth of the Bay of Conception, our destination. What can't be cured must be endured and we must give it up, we can't spend this day ashore. 4:00 PM, light breeze all day from offshore. Porpoise, grampus and whale very plenty all around us and we have busied ourselves watching them and in casting longing eyes ashore. Feasting our eyes with the view thus once more afforded us of Old Mother Earth. We observed the day, by hoisting the stars and stripes, by an extra allowance of grub and by suspending all work.

7/4 Latitude 37° 19' Longitude 73° 44'
7/5 Latitude 37° 18' Longitude No Observation

During the night what little breeze there was, was off land and continues the same during the day. There was but little sleep aboard last night, for the younger portion of the men were bound to celebrate the day somehow and they succeeded in kicking up an awful noise at any rate. The evening's performance commenced by a small display of fireworks, that one of the men happened to have aboard. And after this had passed off, most of the older portion of the fellows turned in for the night. But had barely had time to drop off into the friendly embrace of Morpheus when they were awakened — by what — they hardly knew at first, but which proved to be a combination of most discordant sounds, produced by a band got up for the occasion. Consisting of about a dozen fellows who were doing their best to produce music from a cracked fife, a squeaking flageolet, a miserable apology for a flute.

And those that could not procure anything else had bars of steel, sheet iron, bells, tin pans, i.e. anything that would make a noise. And forward and back they trampled through the alleys in the steerage, banishing all idea of sleep and bent on having a time. But their wind gave out at last and quiet once more reined. The Old Fogys quit their growling and once more dropped off to sleep, when a cry was raised of "All Hands Ahoy to repel natives!" All were alive and awake in a moment and jumping out of their bunks were surprised to find that somehow the lanterns were all out and that darkness reined below. All was confusion in the hurry to dress, some swearing that their boots were stolen, some trying to force their legs through the arms of their jackets. Others, cursing their luck, run up on deck in their shirt flaps to see what the deuce was to pay — for an awful jabbering was heard away out forward, apparently on the sea ahead of us.

After a while though, the noise was found to proceed from the jib boom, where a few of the fellows had crawled and they were trying their hands at the native jargon. After this false alarm, the quiet of night was not again disturbed, and thus ended our fourth at sea.

Becalmed Off Talcahuana - 7/6

Still becalmed in sight of land, drifting to and fro as the currents will. There are a great number of birds in the water today and amongst them I notice two species I have not seen before. One is a bird that resembles in shape our seagull, but of a different color. It has a white body, the under part of the wing is also white, the upper park is tipped with black and the edges of the wings is tipped with white. It is the prettiest sea fowl I have seen. The other bird looks something like our duck, jet black with a white bill. Towards night some of the men lowered three of the boats and started for the shore to fish, about 10 miles distant I should judge. All night perfectly dead calm.

7/7 -Dead calm this morning and have drifted to the south. Much anxiety is occasioned on board by the non-appearance of one of our boat crews. Two of the boats returned last night and say that they pulled for the shore until nearly dark, when finding it so much further than they anticipated, they turned for the ship again which they succeeded in reaching. One about 8 o'clock, the other about 10:00 PM. We looked out anxiously all night for the return of the other. Fired pistols and burned lights at mast head, to direct them in the night, but they have not appeared as yet and we are now far out to sea. They may have kept on for shore and I hope they did. For they started without food, water or coats.

7/8 - Dead calm today and have drifted almost out of sight of land. If there is anything to try one's patience, it is to be right in sight of your port, after having been out to sea for three or four months, and to still be unable to run in. Our boat's crew have not made their appearance as yet. They must have hold for Talcahuana and I'll bet they had a hard time before they reached it, however we shall know all about it maybe someday. If we don't all die of old age, before we get a breeze. Dark — we have got it at last. A breeze sprung up since noon and we are now off abreast St. Mary's Island, mouth of Concepcion Bay.

7/9 - Last night lay off and on at the mouth of the bay, fearing to run in in the night. No one who has not been similarly situated, can conceive how cheerful a good smart breeze feels to us. In addition to our natural anxiety to get ashore once more, we feel an additional anxiety to do so now, on account of our missing comrades. We wish to know their fate. This morning we had drifted out of sight of land but at noon we had made the entrance of the bay. Here the wind died away and we got out two boats and commenced towing, but a little breeze springing up, we cast off the tow lines. And not stopping to pick up the boats, came on with the breeze and dropped anchor about 8:00 PM in Talcahuana.

Talcahuana, Chili ~ South America - 7/12

Well, well, here we are at last on 'tother side of the world. We have been here now for three days and I will endeavor to give a short description of things in general here. The scenery sailing up the bay is fine, presenting a shore of alternate hill and vale, woodland and farmland, dotted here and there with white cottages. The valleys are tolerably well wooded, the hills afford good grazing for the thousands of sheep that cover them. Immediately in front of the town, which is situated at the head of the bay, lies two islands which shelter the harbor from the heavy sea winds that otherwise would sweep through here.

Upon our arrival here we found our boat crew here, they having reached here the night after they left us. They say that they continued to pull for land until they lost sight of the ship and then it was decided upon to continue to pull on for shore. During the night they reached St. Mary's and found fresh water, which they begun to suffer from want of. In the morning they hailed a Chilean schooner and got passage to this port, where they were arrested as runaway seamen and would have been thrown into the calaboose if had not been for the American Consul who believed their story and became security for them.

We found here the Rising Sun of New York, bound to California and Gen. Taylor of Boston bound to California. The Obed Mitchell of New Bedford was also here bound to California. The Hopewell of Warren and Mary Wilder of Boston have been here and have left for California. Hurrah for California, all the world appears to be going that way. Here even they have the fever, and the girls say "You takee me California by gingo. Me love you velly much." Almost all of the foreign residents have left here for there and they are fitting up a condemned schooner here for the same port. But on the other hand, they say, tis very sickly there. The black vomit, yellow fever and so forth are slaying the adventurers by thousands. But no doubt exists of the quantity of gold to be found there, so never mind sickness and death where the prizes are so rich and plenty.

This town is like all other Spanish towns, built of mud, adobe and stone. And its inhabitants are the same that are to be found in all Spanish America. As I said before, it is at the head of Concepcion Bay and is the seaport town for the city of Concepcion, which lies 9 miles inland. There reside all the wealthy Chileans of this section and up there, society is much better than here. But here is the most miserable of all of them. As you land upon the beach in front of the Custom House (a two-story stone building) you are surrounded by a gang of the natives. All earnest to engage in your service as guides to some of the numerous fondas of the town.

Advancing up the main street, a stranger to these Latitudes will be surprised by the apparent fondness of the inhabitants for that truly Spanish amusement of fighting gamecocks. Here is one pegged down to the sidewalk in front of this fine-looking adobe house. A string is tied around his leg and a nail at the other end is driven into the ground to keep him from straying off the premises. And as we continue on up the street towards the plaza, we see them pegged out for an airing all along the streets. Let us go into this dry goods store and lo, upon the farther end of a counter we see the everlasting game bird there, and there goes a pretty looking Margarita with one under her arm. They are noble looking fowl and are the largest I ever saw. Go to the cock pit and you will find priests betting high upon their favorite bird and pretty-looking girls, all life and excitement in the game. This and bull fighting are their favorite amusements, and they will often stake their last dollar upon their favorites.

They are a nation of gamblers and if they cannot raise funds to gamble with, will gamble off their daily allowance of bread or clothing. Anything to gamble. The priests all gamble. Go to the barracks and you find the soldiers gambling. Peep into the calaboose and you see the prisoners gambling. Go to a shop to make a purchase and the storekeeper flings down his cards to wait upon you. But as I said before, I suppose one should not judge the whole race from the specimens he sees here. For the wealthy and educated live in the interior towns. Here the stranger will be surprised to see the numerous houses of ill fame which line the streets. The occupants of which are in their doors, extending earnest invitations to enter - and launching curses at your head as you pass them by. The rough-looking teams, with their wheels of solid wood, drawn by oxen yoked by the horns.

The horsemen seated in heavy, clumsy saddles with wooden stirrups of 2 pounds weight a piece and spurs of an inch in length prongs. The small, diminutive horses, with their riders encased in leather breeches, slouched hats and ponchos hanging loosely over their shoulders, always riding on the keen run, urging their poor beasts to the top of their speed. The numerous pretty black-eyed, black-haired girls who are eternally in the streets bareheaded. The shaven headed priests. All of these present themselves to your view at once, forming a gay and animated picture and bring forcibly to your mind that you are in a strange country and amongst strange people.

We push on through Jib Boom Street, as the foreigners all call it. And as we near the plaza we find the houses present a better appearance. And we find that there is a company of soldiers out in front of their barracks, drilling under a lieutenant of about 18 years of age. The city of Concepción formerly lay where this town now does. But it was destroyed by an earthquake years ago, which caused the water in the bay to recede in three large waves, leaving the bay dry for over 3 miles from the landing. And then, rushing back, it covered the city to a depth of about 70 feet. This town is surrounded by hills and just back of the town about 70 feet above it (I should judge) they have a cross erected and here is where they say the water came to at that time the city was destroyed.

After this, the wealthy ones went 9 miles into the interior, at the foot of a mountain and there built the present town of Concepcion and use this town merely as a landing place. I should think that there might be about 400 houses here all told, big and little, most all one story. Some of the best are good looking houses, but most are mere mud huts. Those that make any pretension to beauty are built in (or so as to form) a hollow square, with a large folding door in the center, sash-less but grated windows.

Concepcion City - 7/13

Today I started in company with seven others for a trip to this city, we go afoot to save money and to better enjoy the scenery. After crossing the hills back of Talcahuana we entered upon a sandy plain, dotted here and there with clumps of bushes, around and through which our road wound its way. We took it easy, being in no hurry, and as we met the peasants on their way to market with fruit, eggs, etc. we stopped them to examine their fruit to purchase if we liked. But most of all to converse with them as far as possible with our very limited knowledge of Spanish. Myself and one other dropped behind the party and let the rest go on ahead. Soon after we met two pleasant girls, with baskets of oranges on their heads, going to market. They offered us one apiece and laughed at us in our attempts to thank them in Spanish. And this hospitable feeling I find is characteristic of the country people, free and warm-hearted naturally, but suspicious and distrustful where they have had much intercourse with other nations at the seaport.

We arrived at this city about 11:00 AM and ordered dinner at a fonda kept by a Maine Yankee who lives here and has a Spanish wife. After dinner we took a walk around town and were much pleased with the appearance of the city. It is laid out in squares, every house forming a hollow square, streets on all sides, with a courtyard in the center. Houses all pretty much alike, one story and built of stone or adobe, all whitewashed, with blue door linings and windowsills. The streets in places are filled with the rubbish of fallen houses, where they lie as they fell in the great earthquake of "35, I believe it was. With the exception of these piles of bricks, the streets looked neat and all were well paved. But what strikes the Yankee as most singular, was that Sabbath-like stillness that prevailed.

The lack of noise and bustle that one always finds at home in towns of this size. The shops were filled with good assortments of goods, but all were packed away on shelves and in boxes, there was no display of goods. The storekeeper sat there smoking, and if you wished for an article he would wait upon you, but appeared perfectly indifferent whether you bought or not. In fact, this large city resembled some little country village at home, no life nor animation. As you pass through the streets you meet but few of the inhabitants and where they keep themselves, I do not see. Occasionally as you pass a house you see a bevy of damsels fair, who are curious to see the fair-haired Americans as they pass along. For from their somewhat isolated position, it is but seldom they see any strangers here. An occasional trading vessel stops at the port but few of their crew ever see the interior. And now in the rush to California, many are stopping here. Furnishing the inhabitants, many of them a chance to see Americans of the north for the first time.

All the Spanish are black headed and consequently the women think that white haired is a type of beauty and the scarcity of the article makes it valued by them. And I find that the height of Chilean womens' ambition is to get a towheaded American husband. Another thing, Americans treat their wives much better as a rule than the Spaniards do, are not so jealous and treat them more as equals. Therefore, they are most all anxious to marry foreigners. We had many invitations to walk into good-looking and no doubt respectable houses, and this hospitality on their part was as pleasant to us as it was unexpected. We left here at night with regret and I for one would have liked to have stopped here longer. But our, or my, purse would not admit of it. And so we left again for the ship, where we arrived about 9 o'clock.

7/25 - Talcahuana. Weighed anchor about noon today and are now on our way again for California. The Big Cameo of New York for California arrived at Talcahuana on the 14th, 150 days out. On the 15th barque Nautilus of same port for same, dropped anchor here. Rising Sun sailed from here on 15th. On the 17th steamer McKim dropped anchor here from New Orleans for California. All of these are passenger ships like our own, bound for the gold mines. I wonder if the whole civilized world has caught the gold fever, it would seem so.

We sold our barque here for $7500, to be delivered to the agent at San Francisco 30 days after our arrival. In addition to this, we take up about $3000 freight of flour and lumber at $27.50 per ton. Also, we take up eight Chilean sailors as passengers to take the vessel back to this port. These men gave $4000 bonds as security for their return with the vessel. They get $100 per month wages. Our Mate was offered $200 per month and 5% on the freight to take charge of the barque for five years but refused the offer, preferring to take his chances in the mines.

The firm that bought the vessel are estimated to be worth $700,000 and is the richest firm in the country, the senior partner being Vice President of the Republic at the present time. His son is agent of the firm for this port and is a smart young fellow, having been educated in Europe. We are at night out to sea, bowling along about 10 knots an hour on our course. Goodbye Chile, I shall long remember with pleasure my visit to this country, the Garden of South America as it is called.

7/26 Latitude Don't know Longitude 74° 16'
7/27 Latitude 34° 8' Longitude 74° 16'

We are sailing along nicely on our course. Our Chileans are all seasick and us Greenhorns of a few months ago can now laugh at them, as we were laughed at in our initiation. Our decks are badly lumbered up with freight, but for the sake of that $3000 freight money, we will put up with it. Today we harpooned two porpoises from the bow of the vessel and are to have fish for supper. Was reading a book today that brought to mind some of the fine and romantic scenes with a view of which I was favored whilst in Talcahuana. One day a party of us started from the ship for a trip over the hills to see what we could find in the way of game. We climbed the steep hills, crossed ravines, gulches and short plains. Until we at last were brought up all standing at a very deep ravine or canyon, as they call such precipitous chasms so frequent in this country.

This scene from the mouth of this canyon was one of the most wild and romantic I ever witnessed. The blue calm waters of the Pacific lay spread out before us, but at least 500 feet below where we stood. Whilst there, almost under our feet laid this deep canyon with its almost perpendicular banks of at least 500 feet in depth, full of lofty trees, filled with birds of brilliant plumage. Whilst far down, down at the bottom, you could just discern a little brook of clear cold water, winding its way along over and under the stones and rocks that impeded its course, which had been rolled down from the heights far above. From where we stood, looking beyond this you could catch glimpses of the deep and vast ocean, with its blue bosom as clear and calm as a mill pond, with not a wave or ripple to mar its surface.

Plunging down its steep but grass grown sides we, after much scrambling and a few scratches, reached the bottom of the chasm. And looking up from where we stood by the banks of the little rivulet, in a little grassy nook, we could catch only occasional glimpses of the blue sky above us through the heavy canopy of trees and vines that arched above. The trees running up as straight as arrows to the height of 40 or 50 feet without a limb, were overhead completely matted together with vines and long tassels of rattan drooping down from above, to within a few feet of the ground, forming a most lovely tower fit for fairy land. These running vines were, many of them, covered with beautiful flowers of the richest hues and filling the atmosphere with the most delicious fragrance. All the colors of the rainbow were shown in this gigantic tower of Mother Nature's. Flowers around, above and below us. Red, pink, blue and yellow, all were here. And to heighten the enchantment of the view, innumerable birds of most brilliant plumage flitted to and fro overhead, filling the air with their music. Here we partook of a collation, for which we had come prepared.

And after feasting to our hearts content and refreshing ourselves with a good cool draught from the brook, we reluctantly started to ascend the steep banks. From here we descended again to the beach, collected a few shells and started around another way for our ship. About dusk we arrived in the front of a Shepherd's hut at the foot of a small hill in a pleasant little valley. The sheep were grazing upon the side hill and upon the grass in front of the mud hut lay stretched an old man, surrounded by several children and two large dogs, whilst a horse and two jacks were feeding nearby. The children were frolicking with the dogs, whilst the old man was busily engaged in rolling up a cigarette. In the doorway sat a young woman, busy spinning wool.

As we came up, the lady asked us to enter the house and we did so, and were much pleased to see how neat and tidy everything appeared within. In one corner was the usual alter, a table covered with a very white cloth on which was placed a crucifix in a glass box, and by which the inmates seemed to set great store. The neat bed with its red pillow occupied another corner and this with a few stools and a small table comprised all the furniture. But everything looked neat and clean and happiness beamed from every feature of its inmates. I made up my mind that real pure domestic bliss and happiness is not enjoyed by the rich alone. For if ever I saw a picture of happiness, it was in this poor Chilean Shepherd's cottage.

7/28 Latitude 32° 56' South Longitude 74° 25' West
7/29 Latitude 30° 25' South Longitude 75° 14' West
7/30 Latitude 28° 21' South Longitude 76° 39' West
7/31 Latitude 27° 27' South Longitude 77° 22' West
8/1 Latitude 26° 0' South Longitude 78° 26' West
8/2 Latitude 24° 0' South Longitude 80° 14' West
8/3 Latitude 21° 48' South Longitude 82° 25' West
8/4 Latitude 19° 28' South Longitude 84° 49' West
8/5 Latitude 17° 5' South Longitude 86° 45' West
8/6 Latitude 14° 45' South Longitude 88° 29' West
8/7 Latitude 12° 51' South Longitude 89° 36' West
8/8 Latitude 10° 50' South Longitude 92° 19' West

"Blow gently sweet breezes." We are doing finely now, hardly a rope has had to be touched since we left port, but we are bounding along towards our destination. We are all in good spirits and are anxious to crowd along as fast as possible, so as to make our preparations for winter quarters before it overtakes us with its daily deluge of rain. Our Cape Horn companions, the haglets, have at last disappeared and our Captain says it is seldom you see them this far north. Well, a good riddance to everything from Cape Horn say I. We have now in their places the booby bird, marling spike and man of war bird who are always to be seen in our wake, picking up whatever the cook throws overboard.

On the 30th we passed a brig in the night. With this exception, we have not seen a sail since we left port. Flying fish, porpoise and occasionally a whale are the only sights to be seen here. On the night of the fourth, several flying fish were blown onboard.

8/10 Latitude 7° 18' South Longitude 93° 29' West
8/11 Latitude 5° 22' South Longitude 94° 30' West
8/12 Latitude 3° 56' South Longitude 95° 48' West
8/13 Latitude 2° 40' South Longitude 97° 4' West
8/14 Latitude 1° 30' South Longitude 98° 16' West
8/15 Latitude 0° 32' South Longitude 99° 12' West
8/16 Latitude 0° 41' North Longitude 100° 38' West

Crossed The Equator - 8/16

Crossed the line this morning and once more are on the right side of this ball of earth and water. It is something to know that the same stars shine upon you as shine upon the loved ones at home. And to think that you are now on the same side of the equator, even if a hemisphere does divide you. And there now is the north star again, looking like an old acquaintance upon its reappearance above the horizon. On the 12th a school of black fish, a species of whale, played around us for about an hour. But at last, upon the Captain's drawing blood from one with a harpoon, they all sunk from sight and we saw them no more. Yesterday a barque passed us off our Larboard quarter.

Today we have had some sport on board, catching porpoise from off our bows. Every day or two now we have a school of porpoise, skip jack or albacore around us. And when we catch one we think they relish very well here, but no doubt I'm sure we should consider them poor eating. But anything relishes out to sea, after being capped on salt junk and hard tack for a month or two.

8/17 Latitude 2° 43' North Longitude 102° 11' West
8/18 Latitude 4° 40' North Longitude 102° 45' West
8/19 Latitude 6° 9' North Longitude 103° 18' West
8/20 Latitude 6° 57' North Longitude 103° 37' West

Dead calm today. As a party were in bathing today a cry was raised of a shark, a shark astern. And such a rushing and squabbling, shouting and splashing as they made getting on board. But they all got aboard safe at last and upon looking out astern, true enough there lay his ugliness, wriggling his way along in our wake with his back fin high out of water. We rigged our hooks for him, but he carried off hook, bail, chain and all at one snap. Ug - Ug - how would a man's legs feel in that sort of a trap?

8/21 Latitude 7° 7' North Longitude 103° 44' West
8/22 Latitude 7° 52' North Longitude 104° 18' West
8/23 Latitude 9° 16' North Longitude 104° 46' West
8/24 Latitude 11° 54' North Longitude 105° 13' West
8/25 Latitude 14° 27' North Longitude 106° 57' West
8/26 Latitude 14° 53' North Longitude 107° 23' West

Very warm today indeed and has been for the past week, with the exception of the 22nd and 23rd when it was very squally - almost blowing a gale. But on the 24th we were becalmed, and since then it has been very warm. Men are all busy during the day at work upon tools, such as making pickaxes and handles, knives, pans and rockers for gold washing. At night most of us sleep on deck and give the thousands of rats and bed bugs a chance below. My hammock is slung between the main shrouds and there I roost for the night.

8/27 Latitude 15° 8' North Longitude 108° 14' West
8/28 Latitude 14° 58' North Longitude 109° 27' West
8/29 Latitude 14° 0' North Longitude 110° 23' West
8/30 Latitude 15° 2' North Longitude 110° 43' West
8/31 Latitude 15° 40' North Longitude 111° 9' West

Light and baffling breezes and dead calms are our portion at present and the sun pours down its hottest rays upon our devoted heads. Ugh, how durned hot it is here now. Pitch is frying out of the decks and the paint is blistering with heat, it is impossible to stand it below and we all hands sleep on deck. Hammocks are slung in every direction about deck and many is the laugh occasioned by the first, and generally unsuccessful, attempts of many to deposit their bones in these swinging beds.

9/1 Dead calm, no observation.
9/2 Latitude 15° 38' North Longitude 112° 18' West
9/3 Latitude 16° 6' North Longitude 112° 26' West

"Blow, blow, ye breezes blow and fan my fevered brow." Hot as ever today. Caught a shark yesterday and made out to get the bugger aboard. Had another grand gathering of the clans today, giving some of our embryo statesman an opportunity to practice in speechmaking. What a humbug this Velasco Company is - Nelse Jenks, Cape Cod Murray and a few others are dissatisfied because they cannot rule the roost, so they are trying to break up the company and I guess they will succeed. Well, let her rip.

9/4 - Last night, to crown the efforts of the day and to make all reparation possible, for the misery we had been enduring today, we were treated to a beautiful sunset scene. A most splendid scene indeed, painted in nature's brightest colors. The sun set behind a mass of heavy, dark purple clouds, tipped with gold on every edge. Above this bank of brilliant colors feted through the sea of green, light, floating clouds of pink, all edged with gold. The heavens above were, next to the horizon of a bright pea green, gradually growing darker as it arose, until it settled over in the east to a deep indigo blue. Brilliant indeed was the scene and we watched it until it faded from view.

9/5 Latitude 17° 14' North Longitude 114° 2' West
9/6 Latitude 18° 4' North Longitude 115° 29' West

Yesterday discovered a sail astern, which at dark was fast overhauling us, this morning the strange sail came up abeam and hailed us. She proved to be ship Mousam of New York bound to California with passengers. At dark she is hull down ahead. Well never say die, but I'll be blamed if I don't believe they will dig all the gold before we get there with this old ark. Vessels that had no idea of coming when we started have been fitted up since, got a cargo shipped and taking their passengers aboard, have started and overhauled us, passed by and laughing at us, want to know if we have any word to send on by them.

A No Confidence Vote - 9/7

A meeting was called today and it was voted that this company should dissolve upon our arrival at San Francisco. So, Mr. Nelse Jenks and a few other ambitious leaders have succeeded in accomplishing their object. Well so mote it be, we are all on our own hook now and can fight our own battles. The dull monotony of sea life is occasionally enlivened by a cry of "Sail Ho," or "there she blows" or "porpoise, porpoise" and whatever such a cry is raised. We are all on the alert and are as eager as boys in a country town to see a dogfight. Tonight, whilst eating our regular rations of beans at supper time, a cry was raised of porpoise, porpoise. A rush was made for deck and upon looking off the starboard beam, the ocean as far as you could see in that direction seemed to be alive with them. Springing 5 and 6 feet in the air, they rushed on towards us, thousands of them in the school.

Our best lance man was soon in the station on the martingale, with his iron poised already for a dart. Soon they are upon us and as they rush by the bows, he sends his iron chuck up to the hilt through a big lusty fellow. And by means of our tackle, we soon haul him flopping and floundering aboard. Our Chileans, not wishing to be outdone by the Yankees, had procured another iron and stationed one of their best men on the Bobstay. He, about the same time, made fast to one and such a yelling as his fellows made as they hauled him in never could be made by Yankee lungs. All were ripe for the fun now but we caught but these two, as they disappeared as soon as blood was drawn.

We had hardly recovered from this little excitement, when we heard another yelling out forward and rushing out that way we found it to proceed from our Cook. Who, having gone over the bows to do a small job, was lassoed by the sailors and drawn in onboard by the neck, in spite of his struggles to free himself. He finally convinced the sailors that he was no porpoise, although they swore they had lassoed him for one, and they let him go. He, swearing at the darn fools for "choking the breff outen him."

9/8 Latitude 19° 22' North Longitude 119° 47' West
9/9 Latitude 20° 3' North Longitude 119° 46' West
9/10 Latitude 20° 56' North Longitude 121° 8' West
9/11 Latitude 21° 55' North Longitude 122° 28' West

The property of James Smith, being in danger of becoming spoiled by damp and mold, was taken on deck and sold at auction for the benefit of his family at home. They sold well, fetched good prices. As the company is dissolved there is no one to take charge of such things, so it was considered best to turn his affects into ready cash. Spencer Mowry seemed to take the lead in selling these things and by the way I want to say a word or two about this Cape Cod gentleman. He was a Director elected at home and bought a portion of our cargo and was one of our business agents. After we left Boston we held a new election to elect officers for the year and he was unfortunate enough to lose his election. And consequently, had to mess below with the other working members of the association.

This did not suit the ambitious gentleman, for he was born to rule. He was not suited with his situation and was not at all backward in showing it. And upon the companies becoming dissatisfied with their officers and with one another he, instead of trying to heal the wounds, seemed to put himself to a great deal of unnecessary trouble to widen the breach. He finally got a party of the Cape Codites to declare for him and this was the first move towards a dissolution. He argued and plead with others and was continually stirring up the muddy waters, until the whole became riled alike. They have succeeded finely in getting the whole company by the ears and now we are as unsocial a lot of fellows as ever were cooped up in one ship.

This company is now dissolved, and the members are now all drawn off into small companies of from 6 to 10 in each. Leaving a few (about a dozen) who stand unaided and all alone upon their own respective bottoms to fight, sink or swim, as their fates decree. As for myself, having no trade and being light of weight and a mere boy, as they say, they the bone and sinew as they style themselves, do not want me and I am one of the single ones. Well damn them. I do not ask any favors of them, I am strong in faith and am conscious of my ability of taking tolerably good care of myself. But at the same time, I will admit that at times a dreadful consciousness of loneliness takes possession of me, as I think of being landed on the shores of a new country, alone and friendless.

I, a mere boy as yet, who has always lived at home surrounded by friends, to be thus situated, is not a very pleasant prospect. But to the devil with you dull care. If fate decrees that I shall sink, why so be it, it can't be helped. And if I swim, why all the better. For I will laugh at these selfish, hoggish, cod fish eaters in the days of my prosperity. John Young, John Templeton and John Horton go with me and we four will receive our shares together and have already secured a tent for four.

9/12 Latitude 23° 4' North Longitude 124° 18' West
9/13 Latitude 24° 29' North Longitude 125° 17' West
9/14 Latitude 25° 56' North Longitude 126° 46' West

9/15 Latitude 27° 15' North Longitude 128° 16' West

Today is a lonesome, dreary, rainy day and upon such a day there is no place but I would rather be in than this. The weather is such on deck that we are compelled to live below again. But oh, this steerage has become an awful place to put a civilized being. Our bunks have become hives for myriads of bedbugs and Spanish fleas perfectly ravenous by this time, owing to our long desertion of our bunks during the warm season. And in addition to these, large wolfish rats, roam fore and aft seeking whom they made devour. Hundreds of these great ravenous vermin swarm below. If we are much longer delayed, they will take possession of this ship.

9/16 - Head wind, rain and fog has been the order of the day for past several days. To break the dull monotony of the dreary day, we had a little excitement about noon, occasioned by seeing something out upon the sea that the Captain thought looked like a boat. The ship was hove to, a boat lowered and manned and pulled for the supposed wreck. It soon returned, towing a fragment of a spar, which proved to be the object we saw from deck. So no chance to save a shipwrecked crew this time. This spar was covered with barnacles and small crabs at one end, which weighed it down so that it rested in the water in almost an upright position.

The Doomed Velasco - 9/17

Head wind again, fog again, rain again and all hands have the doldrums of course again, as a natural consequence. Talk about doomed ships - flying Dutchman and such like. If this old tub "haint one of 'em,"

I'm mistaken. Head winds and calm are our daily portion — two points leeway to half a point headway, is our daily course. We started in a gale, got blowed away up into the regions of the North Pole for a starter, floated along, after a while we reached the South Pole or mighty near it. Whilst off Cape Horn where we were suffering from the intense cold, where it always was either raining, snowing or hailing, we were tossed about for weeks. Some days not holding our own, say nothing about gaining any on our course.

There we were kept by headwinds. For weeks at a time the wind being in the southwest with only occasionally a slant in our favor. And if we headed favorably it was sure to be very light and of short duration. Well, we consoled ourselves at that time with the idea that if we did ever get around that awful Horn (which was very doubtful) we should then have fair winds. But after at last succeeding in drifting around, we found on this side that our luck had not left us. Calms and headwinds still follow us, but nary fair breeze. With a few days' fair winds, we might be in port, but the Lord only knows when we shall get there. We are now some 700 miles from port and we may possibly reach there in the course of the year, if nothing happens.

Dos Amigos Hard Ship - 9/17

Tack ship. Are now beating up against the wind, heading northeast by east. Just before dark, spoke Mexican brigantine Dos Amigos from Mazatlán for California with passengers. She had her flag flying at half mast because they are out of provisions. We are to sell them a quantity in the morning and both ships are layed too for that purpose. I went on board in one of our boats and stayed an hour or two, and of all the crews

I ever saw, this was the hardest looking set, sure. The Captain is a Frenchman, the First Mate a German, the Second a Yankee and the crew is part Mexican, part Yankee. But the crowd of passengers took my eye. They were part and parcel of all nations, ragged, hairy and dirty and most starved at that.

They are mostly men who started from U.S.A. for California across through Mexico. A part are volunteers that enlisted in the late war and were left in Mexico after peace was declared. One party came all the way from Panama up the coast in an open boat to Mazatlán. Most of them had engaged passage on board brig Rowland of Havre, who was at Mazatlán taking passengers for California. She was to have sailed on 18th of August and all the passengers had their baggage onboard. But on the night previous to this date, she was blown onto a reef and became a total wreck, and 18 lives were lost. A portion of the passengers were served by the boats of an English Man of War and were landed again at Mazatlán - flat broke. Now their chances had become desperate indeed. But a New Orleans gambler stepped forward and advanced funds sufficient to procure them passage in this craft.

He is on board with the rest and all he has for security that he will ever see his money again is their notes. They are to pay $60 a piece for their passage and are very much crowded as to their quarters and are compelled to live upon short rations of miserable food. Jerk beef (moldy and full of maggots), garlic and wormy bread was their food, as long as it lasted. But this has given out now and they have been living on garlic for the past two days. Their sleeping apartment is down below, 4 feet from deck to ceiling. They say they have suffered a great deal from want of decent wholesome food on the voyage.

The men who came through from Vera Cruz say they also at times suffered much from hunger and thirst on the route. One party were 5 days without water and living upon wolves, snakes, etc. As to their looks, I could not tell a Yankee from a greaser. They all looked alike, sun burnt with long beards and mustaches and uncut hair. Their dress, a mixed-up mass. Part Yankee, part Mexican and part Indian. Some had ponchos, some serapas, some Navajo blankets or Mackinac blankets thrown over their shoulders. Some minus shoes or boots, some in moccasins, some minus hats, others wearing the ill looking Mexican sombrero. All more-or-less ragged and dirty, a sad looking and hungry lot. They brought us news of the death of ex-President Polk and General Worth. Also, of the spread of the cholera in the U.S.A. May it spare our friends at home. Anxiously I look forward to the time when I may receive letters from home.

9/30 - This morning the Mexican signaled for our boat and it was sent to them and returned with the little French Captain and a load of his passengers. We sold them 900 pounds of bread, one keg of pickles (a preventative of scurvy) and a barrel of mackerel. It did us good to see the poor devils pitch into our hard bread when we gave it to them. And were convinced from what we saw and heard that although we have had a long tedious voyage around the horn, still there are worse ways to get to California than this. It not only being much more comfortable but cheaper.

I spoke to several of them about their expenses and one told me he had been six months on the route, and it had cost him over $800 and all told similar stories. Well, after this I'll growl no more about our voyage if it takes a year to finish it. They say that some companies having experienced men as Captains got along finely and made quick trips across the country without trouble. But most of the companies after traveling for a while together would get to quarreling, get disheartened, split up and some would make back tracks for the States. Others would push on and sickness would overtake them, and the well ones would leave the sick to take care of themselves and push on ahead. Many died of want, thirst and cholera.

One boy of 18 from Matamoras started in a company of 18 men under Major Taylor (cousin of old Zack). Out of the 18, the Major and the boy are the only 2 that reached the Pacific, and the major was drowned at the time of the wreck of the Rowland. These are the accounts they give us of overland travel, and I would like if it were possible to relate some of their stories of trials on the route, but I have not time at present. But from what they say I should not like to take the trip myself, and I am much better satisfied with our old tub then I was two days ago. After getting his provision aboard, the Captain squared away, cheered us and soon left us far astern, as he has a craft that will sail 3 miles to our 2, certain.

4:00 PM the Dos Amigos is far ahead of us. Spoke the Johanna Quixota from Frisco for Sandwich Islands. Her Captain, in answer to our hail, replied he could not stop as "every minute's delay he was burning silver." Which we interpret as follows, that as he pays five dollars per day for seamen he cannot afford to stop to gossip.

9/21 Latitude 31° 28' North Longitude 132° 3' West
9/22 Latitude 32° 5' North Longitude 132° 3' West
9/23 Latitude 33° 50' North Longitude 131° 54' West
9/24 Latitude 35° 29' North Longitude 133° 1' West
9/25 Latitude 35° 45' North Longitude 133° 59' West

9/26 Latitude 35° 53' North Longitude 134° 35' West
9/27 Latitude 36° 26' North Longitude 133° 9' West
9/28 Latitude 37° 1' North Longitude 130° 53' West
9/29 Latitude 38° 24' North Longitude 128° 12' West
9/30 Latitude 38° 40' North Longitude 130° 19' West

Who cares whether we get to California this year or not? We have plenty to eat, drink and to wear and let her blow, who cares? Of course, it is as usual, headwind. Don't think we could have anything else aboard this craft. We think some of exploring this ocean for shoals and flats. Caught a porpoise today and saw two sail to the windward of us.

10/1 - Great progress. We make almost a dead calm and the atmosphere is so thick and hazy, one can scarcely see across the ship. Large quantities of driftwood and rock weed in the water around us indicate land "somewhere", so they say here. A heavy swell is setting us northward, or no, I am mistaken, the swell is from the north. Consequently, we are bound south. Some of these terribly weather-wise Sea Dogs say that they can smell land. I wouldn't be surprised if they did, for they "haint" washed themselves for months. But as to their smelling Old Mother Earth ~ it's all Bash ~ for The Old Man says we are 250 miles from land.

Square The Yards - 10/2

For the first time in over three weeks, we heard The Old Man give orders to square the yards. The wind, what little there is, having hauled to the west during the night. But Lord help us, t'would take 40 such breezes as this to push this ark through the water a knot an hour. Tis just wind enough to say "Haint a dead calm" and that's all you can say about it. Was quite unwell last night but took an emetic and played seasick a while and recovered, and today can see as far into the cloud that envelops us as any of them.

10/3 - Thick as mush and milk get, can't see across the ship. But little wind and that unfavorable. Porpoise meat is plenty on board this week, having harpooned five in the last day or two. Porpoise "haint bad to take" after living on salt junk for weeks and we think it quite a treat. A decent porpoise will weigh from 125 pounds to 150 and their meat looks like beef and is tender but rather too oily to be sought after much by epicures at home. But it takes a seahorse's appetite to appreciate such luxuries. Saw several sun fish today, first I have seen. At noon we had a little visitor from land, a small land bird alighted on deck and fed from the crumbs we offered it, it being too much fatigued to be afraid of us.

Long-Nosed Weather Dogs - 10/4

Some of our long-nosed Weather Dogs from Cape Cod smelled land again last night, after the little bird wasn't seen to alight on board and were terribly afraid of being cast onshore in this fog that has enveloped us for days. And nothing would do but we must heave too and throw the lead. And the Captain, to accommodate them did so, when our 150-fathom lead line run out like a shot but found no bottom. I suppose the little bird, together with a butterfly that flew on board today, were blown offshore and lost themselves in the fog.

Today we moved the Starboard Galley, hauled up the chain and got all ready to let go our anchors if we do run into land in this fog. We have not seen the sun for days and have to depend entirely upon our dead reckoning. This morning spoke with the ship Innes right from Francisco six days out. We lowered a boat and our Captain went on board. They say there is plenty of gold there, clothing and provision are cheap to what they have been and that hundreds are arriving there every day from all parts of the world. This Captain was also in a hurry to continue on his voyage. Says he; "short stories if you please, every minute is worth dollars to me, I'm bound out for lumber, which is worth now $250 per thousand at Francisco. My men all get $5 a day, so hurry up, no long yarns. Tis a fair wind for me and I mustn't lose it. Goodbye."

10/5 - Fair wind today. Last night the Captain, fearing to run too near land in this fog, shortened sail. This noon we made land looming up through the fog and at 6:00 PM we came to anchor in the mouth of Francisco Bay. We kept sail on the barque as long as she made any headway. But losing what little breeze there was, we begun to drift out to sea with the tide and current, which runs out here at about a 4-knot rate. So we came to anchor in the 40 fathom water. A large rock lays just ahead of us and high barren Mountains loom up through the fog on each side of us.

San Francisco Bay, California - 10/7

At last — at last. 234 days out and here we are safe and sound after a trip of (according to the ship's log) over 23,000 miles. A long, long road to travel but we have done it at last and our old tub true to the last, came into her port stern first. About 2:00 AM all hands were awakened by the gruff voice of the Mate, yelling; "All hands ahoy, the damned ship drags, hurry up here or we will go ashore amongst the breakers." I ran up with the rest, all was dark as pitch, but we could see breakers foam through the darkness on each side and ahead of us. Their booming roar was anything but agreeable music to us and all were more-or-less excited at the prospect of being wrecked upon these rocks.

And whether we were drifting in or out, or how long we had been drifting, no one seemed to know. "Come forward here the best Leadsman in the crowd and heave the lead," sung out The Old Man. And Luce Nurse, one of our fellows (an old Man of War man) jumped upon the rail and sung the soundings as we drifted along. Meanwhile the men were busy getting anchor and chain aboard. But we finally drifted by a ship at anchor, who in reply to the Captain's hail as to where he was replied, "in Francisco Harbor you darned fool, where did you suppose you was?" We dropped those mud hooks again and this morning we find ourselves off the North Beach, Francisco Harbor. I don't know how it is, but I will bet that of all the craft that ever came into this port, we are the only one that ever-backed in.

How the old tub ever managed to drift clear of all rocks and drift up without touching anywhere is strange to me ~ but here we are at last. As to how this country looks, I can't say. For all one can see from deck is fog-fog-fog, with occasional glimpses of hills around us and occasionally a boat shouts out from the fog bank ahead and steers across the bay to some unseen ship, I suppose. Our neighbors of the ship alongside proves to be a whaler from New Bedford, who was unfortunate enough to put in here and his crew has left him for the mines.

10/8 - Went ashore today. It is a difficult matter to describe this place. Imagine a town built of cloth, with here and there a wooden shanty, an adobe house or two. The streets filled with tents, the hills covered with tents, the valleys packed with tents, tents here, there and everywhere. 10,000 men of all nations and languages thrown helter-skelter into this town of tents. No system, no order but all the excitement, hurry and bustle. God's sun never shown upon another such a place. A few short months ago there was a small village of adobe houses, but now here is a town - or collection of tents and temporary houses - with a population of men from all parts of the world.

The streets are full of merchandise of every kind. Piles of flour in 50 and 100-pound sacks lie outdoors in large heaps. Beans in sacks. Preserved fruit of all kinds are laying around in piles, there not being storeroom for them. Most of the buildings are slight frames, covered with cloth, papered inside. A few are frame buildings, hastily put together without regard to beauty or durability. The future is never thought of. But with all men here, the great present - the present time - requires all their thought and energies to look after. Wages are high. Carpenters get $16 dollars a day, in fact all mechanics get that. Money is plenty, everyone has his pockets full. Charge a man all the way from $4 to $40 a day for board. Rents are the same. The Parker House – a two story frame - rents for $14,000 a month.

Land rents at about a dollar a foot, and in the business part of the city is worth as much as it is in Broadway New York. Provisions are cheap, markets glutted. Vessels of large draft are worth but a song, whilst small craft for navigating the rivers are worth small fortunes. There are about 900 craft here from all parts of the world. Freight up the river is $40 a ton and passage is $35 a head. Houses are built and disappear like magic, as they are torn down or removed by tenants whose short leases expire. Underpinning stuff is scarce, I should judge. As there are several two-story house buildings whose underpinning is boxes of tobacco.

At night the city is noisy, with the shouts of drunken boatmen and others who nightly squander their wages of the day in the gambling and drinking houses of the place. They can earn from two to $50 a day and at night it all goes on this way. Water is sold at $.10 a glass and liquor at 25, cigars $.25 a piece and everything in proportion. "Will you take my trunk to some Gamble House," says a gentleman the other day in my hearing to a rough-looking fellow on the landing. "Well, I reckon I will," says Rough, "how much will you give?" "A dollar," says stranger. "I'll give you five to carry it yourself," says Rough, tendering him a five-dollar piece. Such is life here at the present. Money is almost valueless.

San Francisco - 10/13

Murders, robberies and thefts are everyday affairs. Dead men are picked up in the streets nearly every morning. Bowie knives, revolvers and pistols of all kinds are part of a man's daily apparel. Men die in their tents unknown and uncared for, friendless and alone. Last night a boats crew from one of the U.S. Man of War in the harbor threw their midshipmen overboard and tried to drown him by striking him on the head with their oars and left him for dead, pulled for the shore and have not been seen since. The Middy was picked up alive. Death will be the portion of this crew if arrested.

This is truly a perfect Sodom.

Gamblers Paradise ought to be the name of this sink of iniquity, for they rule supreme here. Halls of gambling are on every corner; the public plaza is almost surrounded by them. "Make your bets gentlemen! Game made! Roll!" Is heard from every side. Thousands upon thousands change hands here daily. Piles of gold and silver coin, sacks of gold dust and big lumps of pure gold weigh down the tables in these saloons, which are crowded from morn till night and packed from night till morn with the eager worshipers of the Fickle Jade Fortune and the curious stranger, just arrived. Music is employed at $10 a night per man, to attract the eager, restless crowd that throng the streets.

It would be useless to attempt to convey anything of a correct picture of the state of affairs here and I must give it up. I confess that I am not capable of describing this most singular town and its inhabitants. Money is not worth much here in small quantities, but life is worth less. Murders are an everyday affair, so are robberies. It is certain death to be caught in the act. Hang a man here without the assistance of judge or jury. I would not like to look longingly at any of the numerous articles of merchandise that lay kicking around the streets, for fear of being hung on suspicion. So ready are the people to resort to this measure on the least suspicion of a rogue. And for all this, the city is full of rogues of the most desperate character, who daily commit acts that curdle the blood to think of.

Most of our men have already left here for the mines and I want to, as soon as possible. John Young has gone on ahead with the provisions and I am waiting behind to settle up our affairs and to get our share of the money due us. As soon as this can be arranged, I shall bid goodbye to this Sodom and see how I shall like the mines. We go to the southern mines, as we are told that this is the best place for the winter. John Horton stays behind with me and John Templeton has gone on with Young.

Her Great Bereavement - 10/25

There is a graveyard laid out here, which is fast filling up with the last remains of many of the eager crowd of adventurers that are dying off with the Scurvy and Dysentery that is very prevalent here. Visiting the cemetery today, I saw a young American lady weeping over a new made grave. I made bold to ask her if she had lost a friend, for the fair sight of a decent American woman in this country is enough to warm up one's heart and do away with all etiquette. For are we not all strangers in a strange land? She said that her husband had determined to go to California. She, last spring, gave up all the comforts of her home in New York and willingly separated from her friends and kindred, to accompany him and to be a partaker in all his woes, as well as his happiness, in his new home on the Pacific.

She was with him off Cape Horn, in the depths of a Cape Horn winter, caring little for the intense cold and as little for the danger, as long as he was by her side. At last, they arrived here, when he was taken sick and soon died of the Dysentery. And now she is here, left alone, almost penniless. Far from friends. A stranger in this, of all places in this world, a place inhabited by naught but wild adventurers with no female society and he, her husband, for whom she left all, lies buried at her feet. Hers was indeed a hard case. May God be to her a father indeed, for she needs his helping hand in this, her great bereavement.

Crowded Star - 10/30

We have at last received our money from the Treasurer and on the first of November we start for the mines. We have engaged passage in a small Mexican schooner called the Star, that runs from here to Stockton head of navigation on the San Joaquin. We pay $35 a head and I understand that 22 have engaged passage in her. If this be so, we shall be somewhat crowded for the craft is not over 20 feet in length. But the Captain says we are to consider ourselves in luck to get a passage at any rate. These boatmen, like everybody else here, are very independent creatures, have a perfect contempt for money apparently, but still are sure to charge enormously for every little favor. During the great rush for the mines, they know they can get all the freight and passengers they can carry and so they are perfectly independent and are not at all particular in their language.

But steamboats will soon make their appearance on these waters and then goodbye Mr. Boatman, you will have to lower your head a peg or two. The steamer Senator came into Francisco from New York whilst we lay off in the harbor and is now running up the Sacramento River. The old McKim is also running up that river but, as yet no boat has made its appearance on the San Joaquin. I am glad to leave this city of gamblers and am anxious to try my luck in the mines. The crew that attempted to murder the officer have been caught, tried and 2 have been hung at the yardarm.

Stockton, California - 11/4

We arrived here about dark tonight, from my notebook I copy the following. On the morning of the second we left the wharf at San Francisco, 22 of us packed on board the schooner Star. In addition to the passengers, we had a full cargo of potatoes in the hold. And worse than all, my blankets and pea jacket were rolled up in my hammock and stowed away below, where I could not get them and consequently, I made the trip in my shirtsleeves. We had no room to stir about aboard this miserable craft, so crowded were we.

As usual it was very foggy when we started from the wharf but after we had crossed the bay, it commenced raining and continued to all day and night. We had to sit and shiver it out. No protection from the cold rain pouring down upon us, soaking us through and through. Early in the evening we entered the mouth of the San Joaquin and came to anchor in front of a little collection of shanties called New York City. And here onboard the boat, we passed the first night and such a night as it was to me. With no covering to protect me from the cold rain and night air, I sat all night long shivering in my shirt sleeves. The rain pouring down upon my unprotected back, praying for the sun to rise, that we might hurry on and reach our journey's end. For at times, I suffered so from cold that I thought I should surely die before morning. But morning made its appearance at last and we rushed ashore to stretch our cramped-up legs and to endeavor to set the blood again in circulation through our chilled veins.

We found this town of New York to consist of three small shanties and one unfinished two-story frame house. One of the shanties fortunately was a blacksmith shop and I hovered around the forge until I got in a measure thawed out. The Audley Clark of Newport Rhode Island lay here, her men having succeeded in getting her up this far towards the mines. It was on board this craft that the mutineers of the bay were caught, last week. About an hour after landing we were summoned on board again and we continued on our voyage up the river. It continued to rain during the day and when night set in and found us still far from port, I shuttered to think that I should have to endure another night's misery like the last. But there was no help for it, and I could not even get on shore tonight. For this river is merely a drain for a large swamp of tules that extends for miles and miles. As far as the eye can reach on each side, the country here is perfectly level and the river winds in every direction through this vast swamp of weeds.

Ascend the mast to the cross trees and you can look above the tules (or reeds) and see similar craft to ours on all sides of you, in every direction as far as the eye can reach. Ahead, behind, to the right and left, in all directions. And all going up this same narrow river but following it in its crooks and turns as it winds its sluggish way to the bay. The swamp on each side is full of geese, duck and brant that make night hideous, with their quacking and splashing. Thousands upon thousands of these birds resort here for the winter. And on the night of the third, as I sat crouched up, shivering against the mast, trying in vain to catch a few moments sleep, these birds and other living creatures (what they all were I know not) kept up the most infernal din.

Seeming to be all around us in the water, splashing, screeching, yelling, grunting and making all sorts of most hideous noises. In my ignorance of the country, I knew not what they were. But imagined myself to be surrounded by alligators, crocodiles, big snakes and I don't know what I didn't think of that night. But at last daylight made its welcome appearance in the east and we up anchor, bent to the long sweeps and sped slowly on our way. The exercise at the sweeps soon started the blood to circulating through my veins again. And to cheer us up the sun shone out once more upon our wet and chilled backs. And we congratulated ourselves upon having a night's rest on shore tonight. As we glided along today, I could not help thinking of home and how much differently they were employed there than I was.

For today is Sunday you see. What would they think if they could but look from their cushioned pews at church and see us poor, wet and weary sinners? Pulling for dear life through this crookedest of all known rivers, to keep the blood from chilling in our very veins. We pulled along making but slow progress, but at night we made the landing at Stockton City.

Note: Words are scratched out at the bottom of this page.

Branch Hotel ~ Stockton City, California - 11/5

Last night immediately upon our arrival in this town, we started in search of a place to rest our weary frames. And after a short search, we found a place to spread our blankets undercover, on the deck of a ship that has been brought up here and has been converted into a hotel and store ship. The ship has been housed over and we finally got permission to spread our blankets on the floor by paying one dollar apiece for the privilege. We gladly paid this and very soon I was making up for lost time, by enjoying as sound a night's rest as I ever enjoyed in my life. This morning we awoke late, got our breakfast of fried beef, paid our dollar and much refreshed, started out to take a view of our present stopping place.

We found that this town was a miniature San Francisco. The houses were the same style, the inhabitants and business about the same. The city is laid out in squares, the streets cross each other at right angles. But as yet the inhabitants have not had time to construct anything but temporary shanties of cloth and a few frame buildings. There is but one toilet, a long, low, one-story building looking like a bowling alley. And in this we have taken up our quarters for the time being, paying four dollars a day for our board, with permission to sleep on the ground floor in the dining room.

The first object one sees upon landing is the gallows, under which is already three new made graves. Gambling appears to be one of the principal branches of business here. Mr. Weber's large storehouse is the best building in town, he is the original owner of the land where the town is built. This large one-story storehouse stands upon the levy and is surrounded by a large piazza, under which many of the strolling adventurers spread their blankets for their night's repose. The town is full of Packers, with their trains of mules and wagoners with their teams, loading for the mines about 80 miles distant. Freight from here to the mines is now $65 a hundred pounds. Owing to the late rains, the roads are almost impassable. Mud is from ankle to knee deep. Whilst innumerable streams, now perfect torrents, cross the road every few miles. In this place the mud in places is knee-deep in the principal streets and everywhere the walking is awful. Being built on a low plain only a few feet above the river there is no drainage, consequently mud is deep and plenty of it.

I bought a pair of blankets today and had to pay $16 for them. Our hotel is also one of the principal gambling houses of the town, all of the front part (a room about 20 by 40 feet in length) being used as a bar and gambling saloon. There are tender tables on each side of the room, that rent for $10 a night a piece, where the different gambling banks are in operation every night. Crowds jam the room full to over-flowing all day and night. And as we spread our blankets under the table in the back room for a night's rest, the cries of the gamblers at their games to "Pun' gala…Pun' gala", "Make your bets", "Roll on", "Game made", etc. serve to keep us alive to the knowledge that we are not yet out of Sodom. Amongst others engaged in this hellish occupation is one Judge Woods, an old man but a most desperate old sinner from Alabama. They say he lost over $100,000 at one sitting at a game of Monte last summer and has since then made another raise, by gambling off over $80,000 which he now has.

As I drop off to sleep the cries of "Pun' gala - Pun' gala" grow less and less, until in my dreams I am transferred across the continent to scenes far different, in the land of Roger Williams. Where all is quiet and hushed in the stillness of night. Whilst thus permitted to again revisit the loved scenes of childhood, I have a dreamy sort of knowledge that I am looking at these loved spots from a great distance. That although every loved object stands out in bold relief and all looks natural as life, still a vague consciousness exists that they are far beyond my reach. And as loved forms appear and disappear before my mental vision, I try to attract their attention. But all in vain. And in my efforts to obtain one kind look from them, they become suddenly alarmed and disappear. Friends take their places and rushing towards me, cry "Pun' gala - Pun' gala! Your game is made! Roll!" And I awake to find myself stretched on the floor in this Sodom. And my friends of dreamland have assumed human forms and still cry out from the bar room "Pun' gala - Pun' gala! Roll! The game is made!"

11/11 - Stockton California. Still here in this city waiting for a conveyance of some kind to Chinese Camp in the mines, where my partners have gone. It has rained most of the time this last week and what was perfectly awful a few days ago, in the way of mud and bad traveling, has become by this time second nature. And we now wade about, with the nasty sticky, mud knee deep and think but little of it. For we expect nothing else till spring.

The infernal din about our ears at the hotel no longer keeps us awake at night and we resign ourselves to our muddy beds, with thankfulness that it is no worse. And if some drunken fellow stumbles over our prostrate forms in his attempts to reach his nest further on, we roll over and request him to get up and pass on and quietly drop off to sleep again, regardless of the cries of "Pun' gala" from the outer room. During the week the little steamer Lawrence came puffing and blowing up the stream, looking like a large wheelbarrow, pushing its way along with its stern wheel and amidst cheers upon cheers it run up alongside the levee and discharged its load of gold seekers. This is the first steamboat that ever came up this river and its arrival was hailed with delight by the inhabitants of the place. I shall leave here very soon, if I have to go to the mines on foot. For I cannot stand this constant drain upon my pockets much longer.

Chinese Camp - 11/18

Arrived here about 3:00 PM and found John Young and Templeton in our tent, under an oak, all well and in good spirits. From my notebook I copy as follows; November 13 started in the company with Welcome Whipple to foot it up to the mines. Left John Horton to follow on with the team as soon as possible. Leaving Stockton with our blankets lashed to our backs, a haversack of provisions slung over our shoulders, we struck out through the mud for our tramp of 80 miles. At dark we had made about 6 miles and completely exhausted we stopped for the night under a big oak tree. Here we piled up wood, struck a fire, spread our blankets and turned in for the night. Such traveling was never seen before. The soil is clayey and as we stepped off every step brought up pounds weight of this putty-like substance which clung to our boots in large masses, making it very tiresome work. It rained all day and at night as we spread out our blankets on the mud it poured down in torrents.

But so exhausted were we that in spite of rain and mud we slept soundly all night, with the exception of being awakened occasionally by the near approach of some of the numerous head of coyotes (a small wolf) that roam these prairies in great numbers. They were barking and yelping around us all night. But we heeded them not, for they are cowardly. On the 14th we awoke early, it still raining in torrents. And replenishing our fire, we partook of our somewhat coarse but frugal meal and rolling up our blankets, we struck out again across the prairies on our road. After wading through the putty-like mud for about three hours, we reached the first tavern stand or roadhouse. A large tent with a smaller one attached, which answered for a kitchen. The rain still continuing to pour down, we concluded to stop here today and recruit. This being election day and this road stand being one of the polling stands, we three opened polls and voted for the constitution without slavery. No more votes were pulled at this station this day.

On the 13th we awoke much refreshed after our nights lodging in a dry place. And after breakfast we paid our bills (one dollar a meal and $.50 for lodging) and started on in good spirits, for it had ceased raining. The sun shone out and our road had become much better, not being so clayey. At noon we passed the Lone Tree Tent and at night about 8:00 PM arrived at the next house or tent on the Stanislaus River at Taylor's Ferry. Having crossed a plain today without a tree or shrub being seen on the route, and no running stream, or house, or tent, with but one exception about halfway (The Lone Tree). It is said to be 22 miles across this plain to the Twelve Mile Tent where we stopped last night. On the 16th I awoke from my sleep upon the ground floor of this house, so sore and stiff that I could hardly move. Great raw sores had made their appearance on my heels and toes where my boots had galled them - my joints were so stiff I could scarcely move and take it all-in-all, I was in great agony. But there was no help for it, I must push on.

So after breakfast we crossed the ferry and crawled along again. Our resting place last night was owned by Colonel Ker, a man who distinguished himself by his gallantry in the late war, where he was Colonel of Dragoons under General Taylor. Dark overtook us far from any house and we camped for the night in a clump of bushes by the roadside. Our progress during the day was slow, owing to my feet paining me so and my joints being so sore and lame from yesterday's over-exertions. Every step was an agony and I was forced to rest often during the day. At night as we lay by the bright campfire, we were startled by a loud yell near us. We knew not what it was, but thoughts of Indians, grizzly bears, wolves and panthers all rushed through our minds.

But we lay close and I said to myself; you may yell and be cussed but I won't stir from this bed of blankets and good warm, bright fire until I am obliged to. But these yells, together with the baying of a wolf at a distance, did not tend to make me sleep any the sounder, I'll warrant.

11/17 - We were up bright and early and soon ready to leave for more civilized regions, where your bedfellows were at least human. Who-who-who, ki-yi-yi were the noises we were treated to all last night. And there appeared to be a whole menagerie of wild beasts around us all night long.

At noon we dined at the Mountain End Tent for $1.50 a piece off of pickled salmon, sea bread and weak coffee. And at night we reached the Green Springs Tent and got supper and a chance to lay under the table for the night. As we were eating supper, about 20 Dutchmen arrived on their way down from the mines, and soon after an old gentleman and his daughter rode up and dismounted, so that we had quite a party of us all together. About dark it commenced raining again and our cloth tavern soon commenced to leak like a sieve and soon converted the ground floor into a rather damp couch for us. But it was the best there was to be had. And giving the young lady and her father the driest spot under the table, I spread my blankets next to hers and the Dutchmen had the rest to themselves.

All of this looks well enough in print, but just imagine a young lady, born and brought up in New York, having to camp out in this style. Glad to get the shelter of a table over her, to keep the big raindrops from the cloth roof from pouring upon her. And sleeping with her father on the ground, all in a row like so many pigs, with about 20 Dutchmen. "Tis a hard road to travel." The next morning, we arose bright and early. Young New York lady looked as bright as a morning glory as she arose from her muddy couch. Had breakfast and put out our best licks for Chinese Camp which we reached, as I said before, about 3:00 PM. Found the boys were well and hearty and liked the country first rate. There is plenty of game about here and they say there is lots of gold to be had for the digging. Dr. Austin and his company are here, also Cy Cook and partner Ned Reyser. Our tent is a first rate one and the boys have located it very pleasantly, on a little eminence commanding a view away down the valley towards the Stockton Road.

My Birthday ~ Chinese Camp
December 2, 1849

My birthday today and oh how lonely, how friendless, how homesick I have been all day. Oh God forbid that any friend of mine should ever suffer as I now do or feel so utterly bereft of friends. Here alone in a tent I sit, thousands of miles from home and friends, alone-alone-alone. No one to sympathize with me, not one kindly look to greet me as I return from my daily labor in the mines. John Young left me on the 24th of November to follow his brother Frank, who went below to San Francisco. He was the only one I cared for in our party and when he went, I was ready to give up, almost with despair. But go he would and stay I must.

And after he left us John Horton, the brute that he was, acted out his disposition and showed the cloven foot. He became so abusive that rather than stay with him longer, I left my tent - my claim - my little. All death itself would have been preferable to his society. And I would rather have starved than to tamely put up with his abuse. I am now under obligations to Captain Skinner of our company for shelter from the storms. I am at work with him in a little gulch below his tent, making about four dollars a day, whilst we have water. I shall call upon the Alcalde of this mining town, to enforce a settlement with Horton. I cannot afford to lose all my provisions in this way and I am bound to have my share.

Happy Hungry New Year - January 1, 1850

A happy new year to friends at home then I shall probably experience. Died last night at the Alcalde's tent; James Simmons of NJ, son of Senator James T. Simmons. On 4 December I went down onto the Tuolumne River about 6 miles from here to a mining town called Jacksonville and bought a tent for $32. Which I packed on my back, up the tallest and steepest kind of a mountain to this town, where I pitched it. The next thing was to get my share of the provisions from Horton and with the assistance of the Alcalde I made him disgorge, after a shower of abuse from the brute.

But he, or some other friend, entered my tent on the night of the 12th and stole every particle of it. Leaving me penniless and provisionless in this country, where provision cost from one dollar to $1.50 a pound. The provisions that were stolen from me were worth at least $250. Since then, I have grubbed along on what I could get. Sometimes living on a cake or two of hard bread, then again, as I was in luck, feasting on flapjacks and pork, with occasionally a taste of venison as some of my neighbors would kill one. Dr. Austin came kindly to my assistance and offered me credit at his company's store for any amount. But I have not called upon him as yet. I don't like to get into debt, if I can help it.

$1 Per Bite ~ Chinese Camp - February 1850

Another month has rolled along, and I am as poor as ever. My efforts do not seem to be crowned with that degree of success, that in my opinion they deserve. For whilst many around me are taking out gold at the rate of an ounce or two a day, I am glad to get a few dollars. Barely enough to sustain life. My food is all of the coarsest kind and stinted at that. At times I am glad to get enough of this, as poor as it is. Sea bread soaked in water and fried in pork fat, with occasionally a piece of salt pork fried. Coffee without sugar or milk, beans boiled with pork and as a luxury, occasionally a mess of flapjacks with molasses (at $1 per bite) and a haunch of venison. These have been my only articles of food.

Hadn't a man ought to make money who works hard and lives like this? But thus far I have not succeeded in doing so and it does seem hard to have such luck. And it makes me feel all the worse to hear how prosperous Horton and Templeton are in my old claim, that I was run out of by Hortons's abuse. It is said that they have taken out over $4000 since I was driven off.

I Must Succeed

Well, I will not despair. But Oh God thou knowest how much I stand in need of success. For with it I may return before it is too late. But without it, here must I remain. Drive me not to desperation by showering upon my head such long continued ill success. To work I am willing, from sunrise to sunset and I am willing to be kept on short allowance. But I must succeed, or I will never return to the home of my youth. During the past month we have had considerable rain and have as yet plenty of water for mining purposes. E. Skinner and his partner H. Barton of Troy NY and myself on the 19th, traded off our two tents for a large one valued at $80 and have since then all lived together.

During the month we have had three flurries of snow, which covered the ground at the time, but soon disappeared upon the sun making its appearance. Grizzly bears, deer and hare are very plenty here and most every day more or less of the two latter are killed and occasionally one of the former monsters. Was somewhat amused to hear a gang of western men talking about "hope killing a bar" the other day and for some time I knew not what they meant. But was at last informed that 'hope' in Western dialect meant "to help".

Varmint Companions

A "varmint" has bothered me considerably all the fore part of the past month and for a long time I knew not what it was. My tent was located in a little ravine, all alone by itself and between it and other tents was a thicket of underbrush. And many times, as I have set by the fire in front of my tent in the evening, I would be startled by an awful yell proceeding from this thicket. Again, at night I would often be awakened by this same horrible yell, close to my head, behind the tent. And once, as I was returning from a neighboring tent in the evening, I was startled nearly out of my boots, by this same "varmint" springing across my trail and disappearing in the darkness, yelling as it sprung by me.

I had heard so much of its screeching and yelling, that I had become a little uneasy about it, knowing that but a thin partition of cloth was all there was between me and the beast, whatever it was. But at last, one night I was awakened by its yell and soon after heard an awful splashing in a mining hole near my tent. And upon going out in the morning I found my enemy laying in the hole - drowned - it proved to be an enormous wildcat. Again, about a week before I sold my lonely tent in the ravine, I was awakened one morning early by something trampling along by my tent, grumbling and wheezing as it went. I started up and silently, cautiously, went to the door and peeped out. And the blood fairly curdled in my veins as I saw stalking along by an enormous Grizzly Bear. I watched the "varmint" till he passed on over the low hills beyond and then gave the alarm to some of my neighbors who sallied out in pursuit. And who during the forenoon succeeded in shooting him and upon dressing him he weighed 960 pounds. These are rather unpleasant companions for a fellow born in a civilized community, but "such is life" here.

For the past month we have been pestered with rogues in this camp, who have robbed tents of provisions, blankets and tools. On the night of the 30th there were no less than 15 tents and log cabins robbed. Our Cook Dwight Newport, who lives over the hill here, had his tent robbed of all its provision whilst he lay in it fast asleep.

Taint Thar ~ Chinese Camp - March 1850

The past month has been a dry one and now the water begins to fail us. And many of the miners are leaving for summer diggings on the rivers. I am now living in an India rubber tent that I bought for $20, having been forced to sell my share of the large one to pay a bill for provisions. C. Cook and E. Reyser are my neighbors now. Have had poor success as yet in the gold digging, "taint thar" when I dig for it. For the past month, boiled beans without pork and hard bread and water have been my constant diet.

Can't get the money to buy flour, pork etc. at $1.50 cents a pound. The roads from the mines are almost impassable and it takes a half dozen yoke of oxen to haul 1000 pounds up here from Stockton, through the mud. The road is lined with dead horses, mules and oxen that have died on the road. Animals sink in places clear up to their bellies in the sticky mud. Many of the Teamsters have brought in provisions by filling a good stout hog head with pork or bread, then drive an iron rod through it, affix shafts to this rod, hitch on their team and roll it up here in this way. Such roads were never seen before and a wagon is of no use, for it would sink in chuck-up to the body in the mud. This state of the roads has kept all kinds of provisions up to from $1 to $2 a pound. If that thief had not stolen mine last December, I should have been well supplied for this winter. But as it is, I have had hard work to keep body and soul together.

White Indians

They have had an Indian fight up above Sonora this past month, but it did not succeed in getting many scalps. They came upon them in a canyon about 15 miles from here. The Indians were headed by a white man, a renegade who was publicly cowhided here in January last. He this renegade (Old Grizzly is all the name we have for him) got drunk last January and his partner also, and during their spree got to quarreling about their ages. From words they passed to blows and had a regular backwoods rough and tumble, bite, kick and gouge fight. After their fight they agreed to toss up a dollar to see who should have the first shot at the other, with the only rifle they together possessed. Old Grizzly won the first chance and drawing up, blazed away and killed his partner first shot. Then laid down on his bunk and went to sleep, where he was found by the Alcalde who arrested him.

He was tried for this by the Alcalde who decided that in as much as it was a sort of a duel - both parties agreeing - it could not be considered a murder exactly - but still something ought to be done to the old fellow for Justice's sake. And so he compromised the matter, by having him cowhided and turned out of camp with the warning that if he ever came back, "he would hang him for sure". Old grizzly accordingly "made tracks" for parts unknown and now here he has turned up at the head of this band of Indians. He slapped his buckskinned thigh at the volunteers and cursing at the white-livered race, dared them to come on. But they could not catch him.

Swamped ~ Mouth of Sullivan's Creek - April 1850

The water having become so scarce at Chinese Camp that it was impossible to stay there. We (C. Cook, Keyser and myself) on 5 March hired two mules and packed our traps down onto this creek. After leaving our old camp we drove along across gulches and ravines until we arrived on the summit of the range of mountains that enclose Woods Creek. Descending this steep mountainside we reached Woods Creek which we forded and pitched our camp just above the junction of this creek and Woods. In the morning we awoke to find ourselves completely hemmed in by the waters around us. It having rained all night, the small creek had become a perfect torrent before morning. And now we found ourselves on an island.

For 11 days it continued to pour down in torrents and our small island barely afforded us room to keep dry and above water. Add to this our scant supply of provisions had about given out and for the last four days we lived on a few cakes of sea biscuit and water. But on the 16th the sun again made its appearance and the 17th we succeeded in reaching the mainland again and procured a new supply of grub.

Chilean Camp

We have spent all of this month prospecting for paying diggings but have met with but poor success as yet. On the 17th Cook and myself started out for grub and clothing. After reaching the "tother side of Jordan" or mainland, we commenced climbing the almost perpendicular mountains which hem in this creek. Arrived on the summit and we kept to its ridge until we reach the Chilean Camp, about 3 miles from our camp. This is a mining camp like the Chinese Camp and is situated on the high rolling lands above the creek and is what is called dry diggings. It takes its name from it being discovered by a party of Chileans, who still work here. Two brothers from Concepción named Antonio and Ambrosio seem to be the head ones amongst them and as we made their acquaintances last winter, they were glad to receive us now upon our visit to them.

Cook was not able to procure a pair of shoes here, a pair of which he stood much in need of. We pushed on to the next town of huts and tents called Yorktown - dry diggings 2 miles from Chilean camp. Here Cook met with no better success, and we next went to Woods Camp 2 miles further on. From here one mile further to Jamestown and still being unsuccessful in his search for leather, we concluded to push on to Sonora 6 miles further. For we had now got "our mad up and were bound to find a pair of shoes big enough for him or die trying". We reached Sonora about dark, found some of our Velasco boys here and stopped overnight with them. Sonora is the principal mining town of the south and is a busy stirring town. Cook found his shoes here and we returned to our camp the next day.

The 23rd we three started out to prospect a plain about 10 miles from here. It was a most lovely sight, acres upon acres of flowers of every hue lay spread out before us in this valley between two hills, but no gold could we discover. On this, the first of April, we hold our first county elections. We here at the mouth of this creek are constituted a township, or at least we are authorized to open polls here. Accordingly, we called a meeting and met at a big rock on Woods Creek at the junction. A big Scotchman took the votes in his hat and Cook and myself were Clerks of Election. A friend to one of the candidates was here, very active in securing votes for his friend, and as we did not know anything about either, of course he swept the board of every vote at this precinct. He even run around and gathered up Chinamen, Kanackas, South Americans, Mexicans and all other nations, it did not matter to him, he was bound to get the majority he said and I guess he did, if all his friends in other precincts worked as hard as this one did.

Humbug Creek, Tuolumne Co. - May 1850

Another move have I made within the past month as will be seen by the heading of this letter. On 2 April Cook and myself started from our old Camp on Sullivan's Creek for this newly discovered mining locality. Packing our tents, blankets, provisions, mining tools and cooking utensils onto a hired mule, we started off. One leading the way dragging the mule, the other behind whipping up. But at the very start, we came near being wrecked. For in climbing one of the mountains, our mule made a misstep and rolling over, away he went, pack and all, end over end down the mountainside, until he fetched up against a tree about 100 feet below. We succeeded in righting him and after getting him up again onto the narrow trail we found he limped considerably, but we crowded him on. At night we camped at Lewis Ferry on the Tuolumne River.

In the morning we crossed the river in a dugout canoe, swum the mule across the rapid stream and continued on our way up Moccasin Creek. About noon we reached the foot of an awful steep mountain which we had to cross, and when about half-way up, our mule fairly gave out and refused to proceed any further. We could not stop here for there was no water, so we were obliged to pack the things on our backs to the summit where we found a stream of water and encamped for the night, completely worn out by our tramp and other exertions of the day. The morning of the fourth we found our mule was too lame to proceed and to pass away time we took our rocker and prospected this little stream, then unknown, but since named Rattlesnake Creek.

We washed about 100 buckets of dirt and took out $31. I was anxious to stop here, and I tried to prevail upon Cook to do so. But no, he was bound to go on to our present place. For says he, we can get pounds there to where we can find ounces here. I had my doubts of this at the time, but as he had been there and prospected and I had not, I was forced to give in to him and we started on the next morning. But since then, men have located on this spot and are now taking it out by the pound - in the very spot that we prospected (so much for taking a fool's advice). On the morning of the fifth we packed up and started on following this little stream to its head. We came to a large flat surrounded by high quartz hills (since called Oak Flat). Crossing this flat we next came to a little stream running in the opposite direction (since called Savages Flat). Continuing on down this little valley we came to a creek that we named Big Creek. And after crossing this and ascending another mountain, we soon came to this spot (since named Humbug Creek) owing to its not proving so rich as was anticipated.

Soon after we located here, prospectors began to pour in and very soon we had a population of hundreds. The creek was tried and found wanting. And after giving it its present name, many left for other parts. On the 12th, after taking out about $100 from our claim, I hired a horse and Cook and I started for Jacksonville, for Keyser and our other tent, tools and provisions. On the 15th returned to our camp with a load of provisions and resumed operations. But after this we met with but poor success and now this creek is about deserted, there being but a few of us left of the crowd that was here a week ago. The places that we passed through on our way up here, then as silent as the grave, uninhabited by ought save the wild beasts of the forest, are now large mining camps of hundreds of tents. And the valleys resound with the chug-chug of hundreds of rockers.

Savage's Camp or Garrote - June 1850

I have been forced to take the back track and our pounds that Cook was so sure of never came to light. But this flat and Rattlesnake Creek which we passed by on our road up, has since then turned out to be very rich indeed - such is my luck - I took a fool's advice, when I listened to Cook on the morning of 4 April. They are taking it out by the pound where we worked and quit it. On the night of 8 May I slept alone on the Humbug Creek, not another soul within 6 miles me. All had left the creek but me and I could not stay alone and the next day I packed up and came to this place. I have prospected about considerably here but have not made much as yet. On the 12th of May, started for Jacksonville to see if

I could hear from home. As there are but few Post Offices in this country, we have to depend entirely upon the private Express Companies for our letters from home. The nearest Express Office is at Jacksonville, about 20 miles from here.

After a long and tiresome walk of 20 miles I reached the office, to be again disappointed by the harsh unwelcome news of "No letters for you sir." On the following morning I turned to retrace my steps to my solitary home in the mountains, but upon arriving at the ferry I found out that the rope had parted and the boat, with a load of passengers, had gone downstream. The passengers were clinging to treetops out in the stream when I arrived and I waited to see them rescued from their perilous situation before I retraced my steps to Jacksonville.

Meet Judge Lynch

The following day I returned to my camp, having crossed the river by the lower ferry. On the 15th a Mexican was caught stealing and was tried by Judge Lynch and sentenced to be whipped and branded. He accordingly received 30 lashes on the bare back and was branded with the T on the cheek. His ears were cropped and his head shaved, and he was then turned loose. On the 20th another Mexican was caught in the act of stealing $400 and before night he hung on a tree dead, having been executed by order of the same mob, Judge Lynch. Texan jurors have no mercy on a Mexican.

Big Oak Flat ~ Garrote - July 1850

The past month has been crowded with exciting events. On the seventh about noon a man came riding into camp, bareheaded, hallooing at the top of his voice; "Indians - Indians. The Indians have raised and are killing all the settlers at Big Oak Flat, about a mile from here!" In an instant all was confusion. Men quit their work, rushed to their camps for their firearms, hallooing as they went, "Look out for the Indians." Soon we mustered about 50 well-armed men and started for the scene of battle. When we arrived upon the ground the Indians had fled, leaving their Chief Lou Terior and 2 other Braves dead on the field and one other badly wounded. They had killed but one white man, a Texan by the name of Rose. He had five arrows in him, it was the first man I had ever seen shot.

And as I saw these four piled up on the ground, the blood flowing from their wounds, their faces distorted with pain, I felt a faintness come over me and I had to leave the spot. These Indians are a small tribe who have lived on this flat for I don't know how long. At any rate, they were here when the Whites first came. Well they and the Whites have lived peaceably together, until now. This morning Rose, who lives over with us, came over here to try to hire some of these Indians to pack dirt for him. He and the Chief got to quarreling about it and finally came to blows. The Chief's men instantly commenced shooting at Rose, when he out with his Bowie knife and killed the Chief. But before he struck the Chief he had been shot in several places by the Indians.

The Whites in the vicinity rushed to assist Rose but came too late to save his life. But soon enough to knock three of the red devils out of their saddles and the rest escaped, leaving their wigwams, blankets, etc.

and one sick squaw who was unable to run with the rest. After this battle, we lived in constant apprehension of a night attack and many of the more cowardly left the camp for more quiet regions. I will copy the following from my notebook, written down day by day during the month. On the eighth, news came in that last night the Indians sent into Big Oak Flat, asking if the Whites would give up to them the body of their Chief. And further wishing to know if the Whites would permit them to return to their village if they would promise to live peaceably for the future. The Whites told them to come back if they wished to and as long as they behaved, they would not molest them.

Accordingly, about 12 o'clock last night they returned and danced, groaned and yelled till morning around their dead, when they quietly vamoosed again for parts unknown. The conclusion is that they mean to try the fight some other time.

Chief Cyprianna

Today we organized a guard for our better protection. Six men are on guard at a time around the camp who stand half the night and are then relieved by six others who stand till morning. On the 11th the camp was taken by surprise as we saw Mr. Indians marching up the valley towards town. Now we thought they have come prepared to give us a trial and we gathered around our rendezvous ready to fight or not, as they saw fit. At the time of organizing the night guard, we had moved our tents and collected them altogether and had agreed upon a rendezvous in case of an attack. So now upon the alarm being given all rushed to this spot and all waited the approach of the tribe. They came along Indian file, their feathers fluttering, bows and arrows in hand and now we thought we are bound to have a fight, certain.

But we were disappointed in this for their Chief Cyprianna, who speaks Spanish, came forward and gave us to understand that his men wished for peace. After a long talk in Spanish between our Captain and the Chief, the Indians being told that if they wanted to come back to their village and live in peace with their white neighbors, they could do so. But if they ever drew bow on white men again, our Captain told them they would always find the Whites ready for them. After the Indians had agreed to everything, we let them come into camp. But I for one would not like to risk myself in their hands, if they had a chance to do me an injury. I felt the hair stiffened on my scalp as they went scowling by. I see they don't like us but fear us and I think that is about the only way to live on peaceable terms with them, is to make them fear you. They are to have a grand Pow Wow tonight as they burn their dead.

Prospecting Tuolumne and Merced

On the 12th a large party having been organized to start out on a prospecting tour up towards the head waters of the Tuolumne and Merced Rivers, I joined them and we started out this morning. The party is composed of 17 Americans and 14 Mexicans and we have 17 mules to pack our tools, provisions and blankets. At night we camped in a little but very fertile valley, where the grass and weeds were as high as your head. We camped near an old Indian village on a piece of rising ground that commanded a view of the whole valley. After stationing the guard for the night, we put out the campfires and turned in for the night.

Owing to the Indians being so hostile just at present, we have to be very careful to guard against surprise and we all take turns in standing guard two hours during the night. We have a Captain whose orders we are bound to obey during the trip. After supper, as we have no tents, we spread our blankets all in a row, picket our animals in front of us and station four men outside on each corner of the camp, who stay two hours when they are relieved by four others and so on during the night. The morning of the 13th I awoke shivering with cold, having but the one blanket between me and the ground and two over me and that too where ice was made during the night. After breakfast we started on through the wilderness and at night camped in a little valley on the highlands above the river near the Forks of the Tuolumne. During the day we have traveled for most of the time through forests of pine and cedar over a rolling country, with but few streams of water. And have been followed all day long by the red inhabitants of these parts, who doubtless are rather jealous of us and do not like the appearance of so large a body of men marching through their country.

As we were preparing supper tonight, a cry was raised of "Bars, Bars, Boys!" And as we started to our feet - three bears rushed from behind a thicket of underbrush and started off up the mountains at a 2-40 gait. Our fellows grabbed their rifles and started off in hot pursuit and such a yelling as we made. But our chase was all for naught, for the bears made 2 miles to our one and although many shots were fired, we did not succeed in stopping them. We returned to camp, finished our supper, got the animals up and picketed them out in front of our blankets, stationed the guard and turned in for the night. In the morning whilst a part of us prepared our breakfast, the others pack our animals and we were soon ready for a start. Saw fresh Indian signs all around the camp this morning, showing us that we are followed and watched in our daily progress through this new and hitherto unexplored region by the Indians of the country. We therefore have to be very careful to keep together and not give them any chance to pick off stragglers.

Soon after leaving camp we began to descend the steep mountain banks of the south fork of the Tuolumne, which here runs between two high and almost perpendicular mountains of at least 2000 feet in height. After tumbling and sliding down this bank, we reached the bottom of the canyon to find that it was impossible to ford it, as it was a perfect torrent of water. So, before we could proceed, we were obliged to build a bridge. We turned to and cutting down two trees that fortunately happened to grow side-by-side on the banks, we fell them across the stream and soon had a bridge over which we drove the mules and crossed ourselves. This work consumed the greater part of the day, but we pushed on.

And after crossing another large creek by fording, we encamped for the night on the opposite bank in a little valley of about 100 acres, completely surrounded on three sides by high mountains. The grass in this little open bottomland, or valley, was about waist deep and our animals feasted upon this excellent feed to them. Our camp for the night was in the center of this grass patch, the high mountains in the rear and on each side, with the creek in front.

Standing Guard

After supper, the fires were put out and the mules secured in front and the guard stationed as before. My turn to stand guard was from 12 to 2 AM and reluctantly I turned out of my blankets to go and sit two long hours on the bank of the creek and watch for Indians. It is no pleasant situation to be posted away off by yourself, in the dark cold night in a hostile Indian country. Every minute expecting to hear an arrow whiz by your ears from the bow of some concealed red skin, anxious for your scalp. And as I sat and watched this night I was more than ever on the alert, for I somehow had a mysterious consciousness of danger nearer me than usual. The mules were very restless and I knew that they saw danger. I knew there was either Indians very near us or some wild animal that the mules saw and we did not.

But my two hours passed by without my discovering any cause for alarm and as I aroused the new guard I cautioned them to look out, for there was Indians about "sure'. I soon after dropped off to sleep but had scarcely done so when the camp was aroused by the discharge of a rifle, followed in quick succession by three others. We were on our feet in an instant and ready for a fight. But after a few moments of confusion, we found that there was but little chance for a battle, as no foe made their appearance. And we saw no more of the Indians that night, although we could hear them hallooing on the mountain in our rear. In the morning we found that one or more Indians had crawled in the grass, inside of the guard and had succeeded in lancing two of our mules.

It seems that this red skin had crawled up in the tall grass, within 20 feet of where I sat on guard, and most probably was there when I called the guard. The mules saw him although I could not and soon after I was relieved by a man by the name of Swan. He, as he sat in my place, imagined he saw something moving in the grass. He hailed the Mexican who was on guard with him but had no sooner done so than the object jumped up and run - and he (Swan) fired at him and drew blood (as we found out in the morning) but did not succeed in stopping him. Of course, this alarm banished all ideas of sleep for the balance of the night. And in the morning we found that two of our mules were so badly wounded that they would probably die. This 15th day of June we lay by here in camp to see if our wounded animals are like to recover. About noon one of them died. And to spite the Indians - who are very fond of mule meat as an article of food - we built a large log fire about the carcass and burned it up.

Where White Men Never Tread

This day is Sunday, how much differently are we occupied today then our friends at home. We are here in a little pent-up canyon, surrounded by Indians, obliged to be constantly on our guard against an attack, in a country I suppose never visited by white men before. Whilst they are sitting in their cushioned pews at church, listening to the Word of God as preached by their Pastors, surrounded by friends and enjoying the many blessings of civilized life, God bless them all and be near to us today. On the morning of the 16th, we packed up our traps and proceeded on our uphill road. We passed on up the creek following a "blind trail", crossed one high mountain and came into a large but deserted Indian village.

Everything around here proved to us that the Indians had but just made a hasty retreat and we knew that they could not be a great way off. From here we found it almost impossible to proceed, being completely surrounded by high mountains covered to their summits with an almost impenetrable thicket of chimoselle. We were forced to come to a halt and a Texan by the name of Jim Clark and myself, after a hard scramble, pushed our way through to the summit of one of the mountains to see what the prospect was ahead. Arriving at the top we could look off for miles on each side of us. Away to the west 4 miles could be seen hill after hill covered with the dark pine forests, and afar off in the blue distance we could just see the San Joaquin Valley. Ahead of us for miles was naught but a succession of chimoselle hills, like the one we were on, rising one above the other, until afar off in the east. The further view was shut off by the lofty snowcapped peaks of the Sierra Nevadas.

And most lovely of all, away to our right could be seen a most wonderful waterfall. Appearing from this distance like a wide silver band, stretching from the top of the pine forest at its base, away up and over a lofty mountain top. It must be hundreds of feet in height, and I believe that we two were the first white men that ever saw this wonder of creation. From our position we could just hear way off in the distance its sullen roar, which upon a near approach must be almost deafening from its great rush of water from such a lofty altitude. We reluctantly returned to our party at the foot of the mountain, who upon hearing our report decided to return. Having been unsuccessful during our trip in prospecting for gold, we had come to the conclusion that we had penetrated beyond the gold bearing regions. At night we encamped at our old camping ground of June 13.

Back To Garrote, Poorer

On the morning of the 17th, we found that our other wounded animal had died during the night. And after burning him we started on our return and at night camped within 5 miles of Garrote. On the 18th reached Garrote again, somewhat poorer in pocket then when we started. But I was well satisfied with my trip. For the beauty of the wild and mountainous scenery, the daily excitement of the trip had well repaid me for all pecuniary losses. Upon my return to camp, I found that the water in this little creek, or rather rivulet, was fast drying up and many of the miners had left for the river diggings. Most of the Mexicans left here during the Indian troubles in the forepart of the month and now the camp presented a lonely appearance to what it did a month ago. I am at work at present just below town in the deep diggings but think I shall have to follow the crowd and seek for diggings on the river soon.

Jacksonville - August 1850

I left Garrote on the 5th of July and came to this place to try my fortunes on the banks of the Tuolumne River at the mouth of Woods Creek. It is a river mining town and at present looks quite lively and has a population of many hundreds. On the fourth I was at Garrote and celebrated the day by calling at a Mexican fonda and partaking of a regular Mexican dinner of chili colarow, frijoles, tortillas and chocolate. On the fifth started for this town and stopped for the night with a party of our fellows (Velasco Boys) at Stevens Bar about 6 miles above here on the river, where they are at work digging a raceway to turn the river.

On the 14th I returned to Savage's or Garrote. During my absence below, a party of Mexicans discovered gold on a creek about 2 miles from Garrote. And hearing of it on the 13th, I went over there and found about 300 miners working. Some are doing well, others nothing. One company of seven Mexicans have taken out in the week past 52 pounds of gold. Pretty good for them. On the 16th returned to Jacksonville and on the 27th went to work for Angela and Aldrich at their boarding house at six dollars a day and board. Burns, Angela and Aldrich are three

Providence men who keep a tavern here and run an express to Francisco. The Tavern is like all others, a cloth shanty and board is $16 dollars a week.

The Burns Affair

8/9 - A rumor has reached us that Burns has been murdered down below. He was the Express partner of this concern where I am at work. He had about $4000 with him when he went below, which he was carrying below for the miners, to send it home. His disappearance has caused quite a commotion here amongst the miners who have sent their dust by him. Some say he has run off with it and don't believe he has been murdered at all. It is as the Mexicans say a case of "Quien Sabe". At any rate it has played the deuce with this concern and will probably break them up.

8/13 - Angel returned from Francisco today and confirms the rumor of Burns disappearance and he thinks he has been murdered. Scarcely a day passes now but we hear of some horrible murder here in the mines. A few days since, two traders who kept a post or store on the Stockton Road a few miles from Chinese Camp were visited in the evening by five Mexicans who came in laughing and talking and bought some bread. Whilst the merchant had his back turned, one of them run him through with a knife or side sword that all Mexicans carry. And as the man fell dead, they robbed his store and left for parts unknown. No less than 30 murders have been committed in the southern mines this summer.

8/24 - No doubt now exists but what Burns has run away with the money he had in charge for others. This stand has been attached and it is to be sold at public auction. This morning Aldrich left here for Sonora to attend court, intending to return tonight without fail, as he has to be here early in the morning to meet his creditors. But as it became night, no Aldrich made his appearance, and we began to feel very uneasy on his account. At last, a great rough, redheaded villainous looking Sydneyite, rode up to the door and wanted to know if this was Aldrich's. We told him yes. "Has he got home yet?" Says he. "No. Have you seen him," we inquired.

He burst out into a horse laugh and replied that he had seen him and in fact had rode along from Curtisville with him, to within a short distance of town, when Aldrich he said suddenly disappeared. But says he wanted supper and will not wait for him, as he will be in soon. We waited until 9 o'clock and no Aldrich made his appearance and upon questioning the stranger pretty closely he acted so singular and contradicted himself so often, that I began to suspect foul play and had the fellow arrested. A party was soon raised to hunt for Aldrich's body, for we all thought that he too had been murdered. About 11 o'clock the party returned from the search and said they had been back on the road to a camp of Teamsters who had seen Aldrich and the Sydney duck pass by towards Jacksonville but had not seen him since.

8/25 - This morning a party consisting of about 130 Americans and Mexicans started out to scour the woods in search of the body and had not proceeded far before they found it. But it was alive, and homely as ever. After a while he had an opportunity to explain his mysterious sudden disappearance. He says as he left Curtisville old redhead overtook him, and they rode along easily together, chatting along the road. And in this way old Sydney warmed out of him that his name was Aldrich that he was in business here, but worse than all that, he had quite a quantity of money with him. They rode along thus until just after dusk when, as they passed a bunch of chimoselle, the stranger's mule jumped ahead and whirled around behind the club of bushes.

And at that instant a ball whistle by his ears, he saw a flash and heard the report of a pistol. His mule whirled and ran back up the road about 300 yards before he could fetch him up. When he did so he hailed the stranger and asked if he was hurt. He laughed and said no, said he had been shot at by someone and wanted to come on and help him hunt for the fellow. But his taking it so cool, began to smell a rat and spurs to his mule and retraced his steps to Curtisville where you stopped overnight. Of course, we could not prove that it was old Sydney that fired that shot so he was released from custody, but everyone believes that he was the man.

8/26 - Yesterday old Sydney, after his release from custody, stormed around a good deal about his treatment and finally got drunk on the strength of it. During his spree, he got to bragging about his shooting, what a dead shot he was etc. Finally, someone said "pishaw you can't shoot, if you could, you wouldn't have missed that fellow last night." "I'll be da__d if I would, if it hadn't been for my d__d mule skying just as I pulled trigger," says he. This was proof enough to me that he was the man. But these things are common nowadays, many a man disappears, and no one knows what ever becomes of them.

8/27 - Heard of President Taylor's death yesterday. Yesterday started for Garrote after my tent and fixings with a mule. Overtook old Sydney on the road. Did not like his company and having the fastest mule, I soon distanced him.

Letters From Home

Today returned to Jacksonville again and was happy to receive letters from home. This is the second letter or batch of letters I have received since I left home a year and a half ago, pretty regular in their correspondence I should say. It is hard - Oh how hard - to be thus disappointed. Time after time have I walked miles, over mountains and valleys in the hopes of getting letters from home and been obliged to return without.

Don't Insult The Lady

9/1 - Last night a man was shot at Hawkins Bar a few miles below us on the river for insulting another's wife. Served him right, the brute. A live woman arrived in this town today, the first I have seen since a long time ago, so long I have forgotten when. I am now boarding at Cook's Ranch, a large shanty made of brush on the bar opposite of Jacksonville and pay $16 a week board. We have here in this shanty about 50 boarders and as long as it holds dry, this shanty does as well as a better house.

River Company Setbacks

9/11 - It has rained all this afternoon. This is the first rain that has fallen since last April. This early rainstorm is likely to do an immense amount of damage to the river companies, who have been all summer digging raceways to turn the river and who as yet have not made a dollar. The Jacksonville Company have not yet finished their dam, but have it almost completed and in a short time would have had the river turned. But from present appearances I am afraid they will not do much, at least this summer, but Quien Sabe?

9/24 - Yesterday we had another shower of rain, the second of the season. And now today the water is pouring over the dam at this place and has already destroyed it for all practical purposes. This storm will sweep every dam in the country it is feared and thus ruin thousands who have invested all they were worth in such operations. On the 17th the Grizzly Company below town took $2400 out of their claim. This is a small river claim owned by 10 men and has paid well both this summer and last.

Meet Mrs. Bruin

On the 26th two men went out on the hill back of town to look for a jackass that belonged to them, when about half a mile from town they saw an old Grizzly Bear and two cubs. No sooner did Mrs. Bruin see them than she left her cubs and put out for the two men, who escaped her this time by climbing trees. Bruin, after growling around the foot of the trees for a while, seemed to think it labor lost and marched slowly off and disappeared in a clump of chimoselle. The men finally concluded that she had left for good and jumped down and started on the run for town. But they had barely got down when the bear darted out of the bush in hot pursuit. They had but one rifle between them and seeing that it was useless to run, as she gained upon them every jump, they turned upon her, the man with the rifle in advance.

He cocked his piece and awaited her approach. She rushed upon him as he fired, knocked his rifle from his hands and with one sweep of her tremendous claws knocked him senseless to the ground, taking a strip of flesh from the top of his head, down across the nose, half an inch broad and clear to the bone. She then laid down upon him and clawed and mouthed him, until her cubs called her off by their cries. The other man made his escape and run down into town and gave the alarm. A party started right out, but when they reached the spot the bear had left, but the victim of her maternal rage lay on the ground, a mass of blood and rags. We found that he was alive and carefully, tenderly brought him in. But he was beyond the doctor's reach. He died in the afternoon; he was terribly mangled. In addition to the wounds received at the first onset, he had a terrible hole cut under his arm, his thigh and right arm being also smashed all to jelly where she bit and tore him with her teeth.

A she bear with cubs is a terrible ugly beast to meet in a man's travels. They carry off too much lead for me to want to hunt for them.

A Miner's Sabbath

9/30 - Today is the Holy Sabbath and how differently is it observed here to what we have been accustomed at home. Indeed, almost all miners suspend their mining operations on this day, but this is their washing day. Today our clothes are patched if they need it and today we get up an extra dinner, if we can get the material for so doing. This is the auction day and there goes old Marshal now on horseback, the horse on the keen run, spurs a jingling as he goes, crying out as he rides along "How much am I offered for this fine, noble and spirited horse gentlemen, make me a bid, how much?" And every now and then you hear the "Pun' gala Pun' gala" of the gamblers, as they invite the suckers to risk their money on the cards.

The many grog shops, gambling saloons, bowling alleys etc. are on this day crowded. Full of long-bearded, dirty, ill-dressed men, many of them members at home of the first families. Judges, lawyers, doctors, broken merchants, all are alike here. Dirty and ill-looking miners who having worked hard all the week have come up from their various cabins and tents to hear the music at the saloons and to try to drive off, by the noise and confusion, all thoughts of those dear ones at home that most all of them are longing to see. This is Sunday in the mines, the noisiest day of the week. But today we had a new feature, a change from the ordinary course of events here - we've had preaching. Yes, tis a fact, we have had a sermon today by a Baptist Minister, a Mr. Woods I believe his name is.

The preaching came off in Angel and Company's old cloth house and was crowded full of miners. A more orderly congregation did not meet for the worship of God in any house of worship today than this was. All were listening attentively to what the Parson had to say, which is more than could be said of most other congregations in the east I'll bet. The hardened black leg, who had just quit his game of Monte, the rough old Arkan "saw" back woodsman whose every other word is an oath, all paid the strictest attention to the Preacher's words.

History Of The Mines ~ Jacksonville - October 1850

During this month I have been busy prospecting around this town in the banks of the river, with but very moderate success. Many of the miners have left the river, since the rainstorm of last month. Some to go below, others to seek for the diggings in the dry placers. The town begins to present a deserted appearance. River miners as a general thing have been very unsuccessful this past season. Having but little to write this month that would be interesting, I believe I will give a short history of the mining localities in this vicinity and how and by whom discovered and the origin of their names. This place was first settled early in the spring of "49. A party of prospectors following Woods Creek to its mouth, struck rich diggings just below its mouth on a bar on the east, or rather northern bank, of the river. Colonel Alden Jackson a wealthy merchant of Stockton hearing of it, sent a clerk with a stock of groceries up here to locate a store.

Dan Dykeman, this clerk, arrived here early in the season and established his trading post and thus laid the foundation of the present town. The town is built in a bend of the river at the mouth of Woods Creek on a high bar about 20 feet above the bed of the stream and is named after Colonel Jackson. Woods Creek, one of the richest streams in California, was first struck for gold in the fall of "48 by a company of prospectors under a Mr. Woods. They located first at what is now known as Woods Camp about 9 miles from here up the creek. Woods himself made money very fast and in the spring of "49 he and a man by the name of Jim Savage and another by the name of Foster, formed a partnership for the purpose of trading. And Woods started for Mexico to purchase a drove of mules. He succeeded in reaching the Mexican state of Sonora, bought a large herd of pack mules and started on (over land) for California.

But in trying to run them across the boundary without paying the export duties, he was caught in the act and all his train seized by the

Mexican authorities. He was a passenger on board the Dos Amigos that we spoke out to sea, on our way to this country. Where he now is I do not know. His partner Jim Savage, another pioneer, was a trader and discovered the rich diggings above here, now known as Garrote. He had great influence over the wild Indians of the country and ruled them as he pleased. He located amongst them in the fall of "48, and in the summer of "49 he had a large tribe of them all working for him, digging gold. He kept a trading post, and the Indians would work all day with their baskets and bowls, collecting the gold from the shallow ravines. And at night would spend it all at his trading post for red shirts, sugar etc. They knew nothing of the value of gold, and he piled up money fast.

It is said, how true I know not, that he urged the Indians to keep the Whites out of their country and was the cause of their hostility towards the Whites. But whether this be so or not, it is certain that the Indians did murder every white that attempted to penetrate into their country during the time that he was with them. In the fall of "49, Savage started down to Francisco with over $80,000 worth of gold. And meeting Woods there, who had just arrived from his disastrous trip to Mexico, Savage started on a spree and never quit it until he spent every dollar of his ill-gotten gains. Before his return in the spring, we had taken possession of his country and he moved with his tribe to the headwaters of the Merced River.

I was one of the first to penetrate this eureka of his and last April when I passed through his country, there was not a living soul to be seen. And the little gulches and ravines were just as his Indians had left them the fall before. But the crowd of prospectors that pushed out into the mountains in the spring soon settled down upon this spot and now there are large mining towns where a year ago Savage and his Indians held full sway. I have already told how Big Creek, Humbug Creek and Rattlesnake Creek got their names and by whom they were first discovered. Garrote was Savage's old camp and went by his name until the Mexicans gave it its present name. They gave it its present name after the Mexican was hung there by the miners on 20 May (an account of which will be found in this journal of that date). The name is that of the Spanish instrument of death, Garrote.

Big Oak Flat takes its name from the immense oak that stands about the center of the open and flat. And when I crossed it in April for the first time, was uninhabited. But it was soon settled by the crowd of prospectors that flooded that portion of the country, soon after I passed through it. Leaving Savage's region, we will return to the country about Woods Creek. Chinese Camp was first settled by a party of Mexicans, who discovered gold there in the summer of "49 and takes its name from a party of Chinese who located here in the fall. This was the first shipload of Chinese that were brought to the country, they were sent out by an English company to work the mines and were under the charge of two English clerks, who came out with them.

They arrived in Stockton with their Chinese vessel in the fall and proceeded to this spot where they built a good strong storehouse of logs and made other preparations to commence mining operations on a grand scale. But as wet weather sets in, Americans rushed to these diggings. And not liking such a monopoly of so much rich ground by a foreign company, they drove the Chinese off. Thus, fell to the ground Mr. John Bull's fancy speculation in mining. Next come the Chilean Camp and as I have already said, this takes its name from the fact that it was first discovered by and located by a party of Chilean prospectors, in the summer of "49. But I have drawn this article out to its allotted length at present with my descriptions of the settlement and origin of the mining localities here about.

As I arrived here so early in the day and was acquainted with all the pioneers of this section, I thought it would be best to make some minute of these things for future reference. For the early reminiscences of these places will at some future time be valuable. To myself, if not to others. I have only written of the things that I am personally knowing of and not from hearsay.

Rhode Island Bar ~ Jacksonville - November 1850

Have been hard at work for the past month on a claim down below town, on what we have named Rhode Island Bar. At last, I have found a claim that is paying me quite handsomely. I have washed out as high as $40 to the pan of dirt but have not made but about $200 over expenses as yet. During the month we have had but little rain, according to my notebook it was rainy on the:

2d of November - Rained all day
3d of November - Showers at intervals during the day
20th of November - Rained all night
21st of November - Rained all day and night
23d of November - Rained all night
24th of November - Rained all day and night
27th - 29th - 30th - Ditto, Ditto, Ditto

According to my notes we have had thus far 11 rainy days this season, the balance of the time it has been very pleasant weather. We have not had rain enough as yet to cause the river to rise enough to stop work on the bars, but all work in the beds of the stream has been suspended for the season. In the dry diggings at Chinese Camp, the miners have not been able to get water enough to commence operations as yet and I am rather doubtful of their doing much this winter. At any rate I shall stay here and take my chances. On the 20th the wind blew a perfect hurricane, prostrating tents, ripping the cloth roofs from the log cabins and raising the Old Harry generally.

Lucky Strike ~ Jacksonville - December 1850

Have worked on my claim all of this month, with the exception of an occasional stoppage on account of rain and high water. We have had but four rainy days this month, making but 15 days in all this season thus far. According to my notebook:

December 2d - Rained all day
December 13th - Rained all day
December 16th - Rained all day
December 17th - Rained all day

With the exception of these four days, we had for most of the time fair weather. On the 16th it blew a hurricane and in the night the ridge pole of our tent gave way and down come the tent, turning us out in the night to repair damages. The river has arisen so high that we have been compelled to stop washing dirt as our hole fills with water. On the third we washed out $150 from 25 buckets of dirt. Since 1 November myself and partner have taken out of our claim $1350 worth of gold. This has been the first lucky strike I have made in years mining but "better late than never". But now the water has arisen so that I expect we shall have to lay bye for some time before we can resume operations again. I wish we could but have a year's work like this and I would leave for home. How I long to once more see my friends at home. Hasten the time, I pray.

I'm Blessed ~ Jacksonville - January 1, 1851

Another Happy New Year's greeting send I to my friends at home. My prospects are far brighter now than they were a year ago. Life does not appear so dark and gloomy now as then. I hunger not, neither do I thirst today. I am blessed with good health, a plenty full store of provisions and fair prospects for the ensuing year. May God in his infinite mercy bless my parents, my sisters and that (other one) may he keep them in health and be near to me in the present year. May he keep us all, may our lives be spared to meet again before this new year runs its course.

1/31 - During the past month, according to my record of the weather, we have had but three rainy days. January 5th through the 7th it rained all day, making 18 rainy days this season thus far. It has been quite foggy at times during the month, but for most of the time we have had warm pleasant weather. Very different from our ideas of a California wet season, wet season indeed. Why more rain falls in New England every month of the year than falls here in the 12. As to the climate of this country, it cannot be surpassed and I don't believe it can be equaled by any. During the week ending the fourth we had beautiful warm, clear weather, not a cloud to be seen. The week ending the 11th was stormy for the first three days but then cleared off pleasant and continued so to its close. The week ending on the 18th was like a week in the month of June at home in old Rhode Island, not a cloud to be seen and has continued the same to the close of the month. Warm, beautiful, clear days and cool nights.

I'm Less Blessed

The river remains too high for us to work our claim as yet and I have spent the past month prospecting around in search of some other paying spot but have not met with very good success thus far. On the 12th Ned Le Favour and myself went up on to the flat between here and Curtisville prospecting and found just enough gold to induce us to move a tent and tools up there to give it a thorough trial. On the 13th we went to Chinese Camp for a tent that Ned had there. And on the 14th we hired a jack to pack it up the mountain and we pitched it at night on our prospecting flat. By the 16th we found that we had been the fool and could not make a dollar a day here. So we left the place in disgust, satisfied to let it alone. And since then, we have tried up and down the banks of the river up Woods Creek, in the gulches and in the flats, but unsuccessfully. And now at the end of the month I am not quite as rich as I was at its commencement.

Our Daily Murder Bread

During the month the Indians killed two Americans at Humboldt Creek and two at Maxwell's, so they say. Murders and robberies are an everyday occurrence, and it seems now if we do not hear of one or two murders a day that the day has passed by very quietly. In fact, it has become a sort of daily food to us. I haven't time nor space to chronicle 1/10 part of them. But as a sample I will copy from this week's paper the following account of an affair that came off at Curtisville 6 miles from here, on the night of the 25th and morning of the 26th of this month. "On the night of the 25th Tom, a miner, was bucking at a game of Monte dealt by Bill Bowen, known better by the name of Old Kentuck, Tom detected Kentuck in cheating and told him to quit that kind of fun. Bowen jumped up, drew his revolver and would have shot Tom on the spot if Aleck (a bystander) had not caught his arm. After this the party finally made up the matter, took a drink all round and went to bed.

On the following morning, Bowen met Aleck in the sink room of the tavern where they boarded and Aleck good-naturedly wishing him good morning, took off his coat to wash. Bowen says, "Ha ha, you want to fight?" And drew his pistol, aimed and fired at Aleck, who fell bleeding to the ground. As he attempted to rise, Bowen took deliberate aim and fired again and Aleck again fell over. And as Bowen was again taking aim at him, he was knocked down and "Hang Him" was the cry. A rope was soon around his neck and in a few moments, he was hanging on a meat rack and was dead before the life of Aleck was extinct. All this work was done in less than a quarter of an hour. A man was murdered in cold blood and his murderer hung and all inside of one short quarter of an hour. After this the breakfast bell rang and all hands sat down to a hearty breakfast after their mornings exercise."

Divine Deaths

Here is another specimen from the same weekly paper. This happened in Georgetown. A drunken Englishman named Divine killed his wife. During their residence in that town, she had supported the family by washing clothes. He, her husband, asked her for some money to gamble with and she told him to wait until he became sober. He rushed across the room for his pistol, but she anticipated him and threw it into a bucket of water. He then leapt into the street, snatched a rifle from a passerby, returned and shot her through the heart. It was Sunday and the town as usual on this day of the week was crowded with miners. They heard the report of the rifle and rushed to the house. In this country men do not talk, but act.

A neighboring "round tent", a gambling saloon, was immediately transformed into a courthouse. Divine the murderer was brought in and followed by a party bearing the warm corpse of his wife. She was gently laid on a large table near her husband. There stood the brute, side-by-side with his victim. The sight stung the people to madness, and no one thought of wasting words on a trial. Devine was seized and hurried to a tree, where a rope was soon swung over a limb. Just at this moment a man of great influence in the town attempted to prevail upon the mob to postpone their design, until a Coroner's inquest should be held and a summary trial, but still a trial had, after their verdict.

With much difficulty he succeeded in getting the crowd to consent, on conditions that the inquest and the trial should both be held on that day and as soon as the Coroner was at Coloma. 4 o'clock was given as the last moment they would wait for the Forms of Law. Whilst they waited, they were not idle. A jury had been impaneled, a coffin made, and a grave dug. As four o'clock approached the silence was broken by the deep whispers and hoarse murmurs of this court of Judge Lynch's. Rifles, pistols and Bowie knives were freely displayed. The sun at last began to settle in the west and the crowd could not wait any longer but tearing up the sides of the tent rushed in, just in time to see the last of the prisoner's guard rush out.

They seized Devine and at the head of a long procession, the murderer marched to his gallows and the body of his victim was borne in close behind him. Nailed to the fatal tree was a box marked "Help The Orphans" and many an ounce was poured into it from the purses of those who were about to hang the father. The body of the murdered wife and mother was lowered into a wider pit. And even while the wretched man gazed upon it and upon that empty but significant box by his side, the rope tightened around his neck and he swayed in the air. At the end of half an hour he was cut down and lowered into the grave by the side of his wife. And in less than 10 minutes Georgetown was as quiet as a grave. Not a man was to be seen in the streets and no one knew anything about the mob.

In the evening the Coroner made his appearance and summoned his jury. They met at sunrise around the unfilled grave while the end of a cut cord dangled above their heads. They whispered together for a few moments, then wrote upon a slip of paper their verdict. "Murdered by Devine her husband. The other died according to the will of God, by Justice of men." Here is but two cases, but they will suffice to give one an idea of life in the mines of California in 1850.

Duly Elected Desperados

In Francisco, the state of affairs are still worse. For the desperados have full swing there and do not fear Judge Lynch. Murderers fill all the offices. The Judges, Sheriffs and other offices of the law are the most desperate of all and the City Police is a gang of Highwayman and thieves. From the same paper, I copy a picture of Francisco. A man by the name of Bartley was killed in the Parker House by someone hungry for a man for breakfast, I suppose, and his funeral was held in the back part of the bar room. At the time the funeral service was being read over the corpse, two Monte tables were in full operation in the same room and crowds of men were betting their money on the cards. And as the Parson's solemn words, "I am the resurrection and the life" stroke your ears upon one side, from the other side came the "Pun' gala Pun' gala, Make your bets gentleman," of the gamblers.

But it will be impossible to convey anything like a correct idea of manners and things here, human life is but of little value. Men are murdered for the fun of the thing. And then (here in the mines) to carry out the joke, when we catch a fellow that is fond of such fun, why we instantly run him up a tree to keep the flies from blowing him. Just for the fun of it. But in Francisco they have still a funnier way of settling the thing, they call it letting the "Law take its course" and it is the most laughable of all to see what a course it takes. If the funny fellow that kills another - because he squinted at him maybe - is rich, why they say he did it in self-defense or it was an accident. He didn't mean to, didn't know his pistol would go off or some such thing and he comes out of the court room a hero. Judges are glad to drink with him and when "I John McDougal," comes to town, the judge introduces our hero to the jolly old Governor, and they all get drunk together and laugh over their many affairs "of honor". And "I John McDougal" laughingly wants to know of our hero, where he buries his dead etc.

Two men got to quarreling a short time since in Sonora. They were gambling and had a table between them, one jumps off and blazes away at the other across the table, misses his antagonist but kills a spectator in his rear. This antagonist follows suit and shoots at gambler number one but merely grazes him and kills a looker-on behind him. Thus, two spectators who happened to be looking on get killed. This being a law-and-order town, the Coroner is sent for, a jury impaneled, and a verdict of accidental death is rendered. Hurrah for California laws, say the gamblers. But will there not be a reckoning day some time? In the early settlement of the Mississippi Valley just such a gang had possession there, but at last there came a reckoning day and Natchez, Vicksburg and Memphis were cleaned out.

The same gang fled to Texas and took possession there but in due time came the days of the Regulators and Moderators and the Regulators swept out the vermin and now they have turned up here and rule this country with bloody hands. But a reckoning day is coming. Gamblers fill our courts. Our Judges are gamblers, our State Senators are gamblers, our Representatives, our Lawmakers, our Law Officers, Sheriffs, Deputies and Constables are all of the same class. And our trials by court are a perfect farce. A man is in prison for murder and he is allowed to escape, to murder all that testify against him. There is no safety save in Judge Lynch. Sodom or Gomorra never begun to be such sinks of iniquity as Sacramento, Stockton and Francisco have become. And if some of the many curses that fell upon those cities of old does not visit our towns, it will be because we live in a more merciful time.

But I have spun this subject out to as great a length as I intended to and shall not hereafter refer to any of the daily robberies and murders and lynchings, unless they happen in my immediate vicinity. This state of affairs cannot long continue. And when the tide turns, then California will be as desirable a place to make home as can be found on earth.

Societal Restraints

I believe that most of these evils arise from the utter absence of all society. We need the restraining influences of a woman's presence. We need homes. We want wives and children around us to give us some place of resort after our days of toil. And as we have no homes our only resort is to the many drinking and gambling saloons. Give to California the same family society that is to be found in all other parts of the world and these excesses would cease. Naturally, this country has every advantage. The best land in the world, thousands upon thousands of dollars worth of the richest mineral lands, farming land that the world can't beat, capable of producing abundantly all of the products of both the temperate and torrid zones. A climate unsurpassed for health and in fact it has all the good qualities necessary to make man happy and contented. All it lacks is society to restrain us and women to encourage us to pursue the paths of virtue in our search for wealth and happiness.

Elusive Ditch Piles - February 1851

During this short month I have been trying the banks and bars of creeks, gulches and the river to find if possible a paying claim but have not succeeded in making expenses. We have had during the month but two rainy days, or rather a feast of three.

February 18th - Rained an hour or two after noon
February 20th - Rained an hour or two after noon
February 21st - Rained an hour or two after noon

Making but 21 days this season that it has rained any at all and naught of these rainy days were but partially so. A mere shower or two during the day and then clearing off fine again towards night. Those that rushed to the dry diggings last fall after our September storm, expecting a long-wet season, have been again bitterly disappointed. For in most cases, they have not had water enough to make their living expenses. The last fall's early rain that swept away the river dams and the dry winter following, have all but ruined all the traders who trusted out their goods to miners, expecting to gather a bountiful harvest when the "river was turned on". Why last summer, a man was looked down upon as a poor coot if he had neglected to secure three or four shares in some of the many river damming companies.

They were all sanguine of making a pile, no doubt of it, at all. And they worked like heroes all summer long, digging long raceways across the bars. And after this, tugged and sweat, rolling rocks and logs to make their dams. And just before they did, they didn't. The rains fell, the river raised and away went dam and all downstream. Sweeping off hundreds of imaginary fortunes, at one fell swoop. Then was the river Damned…if not dammed. And with long faces, merchants and miners turned and fled to the dry diggings, to try and make good their losses of the summer by working the dry placers in the winter. But now they find the treacherous rain refuses to fall. Having succeeded in washing off their river works by an unusual early storm, it rested there and now refuses to make its appearance.

Savage On Savage

The Indians above here on the Merced, Agua Trio and the headwaters of this stream have been very troublesome for some time past. Having stolen many horses, mules and so forth, besides killing many unlucky traveling miners. Two or three volunteer parties have been organized to pursue the hounds and if possible, to whip them into terms. One party under Jim Savage it is said has had a fight off the Merced and it is also reported that he killed about 30 of them and lost three of his own men. Another party of volunteers who went up the Stanislaus it is reported have had an engagement with the red skins and the report says they killed about 40 of them. How true these reports are of course I cannot say, but at any rate we are having some fighting, that's sure.

And I think we are like to have trouble with these Indians for years to come. I have no doubt that most of the robberies laid to their account have been perpetrated by Whites, disguised as Indians. But the Indians are never backward to steal or murder for that matter, if they think they can do so with impunity. A red shirt or blanket is a very tempting sight to an Indian and if he can get possession, he is going to do so. I have looked in vain for a specimen of Fenimore Cooper's Indians.

The Two-Year Itch

Two years ago, this month we sailed from Boston for this place, intending to be gone on a two-year cruise gold hunting. But now the two years have rolled by and how much richer now are those that are left of us here alive than when we left home? And how much nearer are we prepared to return than we were a year ago? And where now are the members of that old Velasco Company? Many of the stoutest, most robust, have passed away forever. They will never more revisit the homes of their youth. Their parents, sisters, wives and sweethearts, have looked upon them for the last time. They have lain their bones where they were so sanguine of securing a fortune, peace to their ashes. But a few of the company of 100 will probably reach home, within the allotted time. Many now living, probably have left their homes in the east for good.

Disappointment is the common lot of all mankind but doubly severe does it fall upon the head of the ever-sanguine youth. It is hard, bitter, terribly hard to think that in all probability you have parted from all your friends forever, never to meet them again on earth. But such is to be the fate of many of us who are anxiously looking forward to the time when we may be enabled to bid farewell to this golden land and set our faces homeward bound. But whether we are to ever meet again on earth or not, let us ever cherish the affection, the loves of the olden time, may our friends at home not let "absence conquer love".

A Poet has said
Ah yes! We can bear the days burden and heat,
The dust and rude jostlings we find in the street,
And censoring whispers that float till they meet,
The ears they were never intended to greet,

If they love us sincerely at home
We can bear by the crowd to be hurried along,
Downtrodden, supplanted and oppressed by the strong;
We can bear even lashing and unprovoked wrong
If our hearts through it all can chant truly the song
Oh they love us most dearly at home
We can bear a wild storm, hail or rain
Heavy losses, instead of the long look for gain
Upbraidings and shadows that creep round our name
And threatened its brightness to hide or to stain
If they love us sincerely at home
Oh love us at home! For this treasure we plead,
With all else (this withheld) we are poor, indeed!
Take all, but leave this and with voices agreed
We will sing with glad hearts whatever our need,
They still love us, they love us at home.

Kanaka Creek - March 1851

Ned LeFavour and myself moved our round prospecting tent up on to this creek, for the purpose of working here for a month or two until the river falls sufficiently to admit of our working on our old river bar claims on the 23rd. This creek is about a mile from Jacksonville up the river. We have set a Long Tom in the creek and intend to give it a thorough trial at any rate. And if fortune does not smile upon us, let her frown and be d__d to her, for a fickle Old Jade as she is. For the last few days in this month, we have had dreadful cold and disagreeable weather with occasional flurries of snow, making it very uncomfortable in our new quarters. But we have built a fireplace and mud chimney to our tent now and we are quite comfortable. Quail and hare and large gray squirrel are very plenty here and we can have a stew of them at any time by hunting for an hour or so. I have a double-barreled shot gun and in the morning, whilst Ned is getting breakfast, I take the gun and start out and seldom return without a mess of one or the other for dinner.

The weather for the forepart of the month was very pleasant. But the last week has been awful, Snow, hail, rain and fog and winds have been our daily portion.

On the 19th - Rained at intervals during day & night
On the 20th - Snowed all night
On the 24th - Rained about an hour
On the 27th - Rained all the afternoon and night
On the 28th - Rained all day
On the 30th - Snowed all day and was the hardest I have ever seen in this country.

This makes 27 stormy days this season thus far. Not a very bad country for stormy weather this!

Bible Bowl

On Sunday the second day of this month, we had another preaching at Jacksonville. A Methodist missionary officiated on this occasion, his church for the location was an old bowling alley. At the time of his preaching there was an auction going on in the next tent, distant about 4 feet. On the other side was a gambling saloon full of noisy, drunken fellows. On the opposite side of the narrow street was two more in the full blast, whilst in the back part of the bowling alley, behind a thin screen of Lowell drillings, was a party playing cribbage. To those in the tent listening to the preacher, a curious medley of songs reached their ears. The speaker's loud sing-song discourse was heard above all others.

But at the same time, the cries of the auctioneer on the one side yells, curses and songs from the saloons on all sides, the music band of violins, accordions, flutes, banjos, flageolets and French horns. The loud cries of the gamblers, "Make your bets gentleman" and the busy gamblers in the back room as they counted their game, "fifteen two, fifteen four, double routine and his knob," all passed through your ears in one mass of sounds and forming a most singular accompaniment to the Preacher's words of advice. "How much am I offered for this fine... turn ye sinners...ere it be too late...from fifteen two...fifteen four and two are six with his nob which makes... your bets gentleman... Pun' gala down...we won't go home till morning...till morning does appear."

These were a few of the sounds that were constantly running into one another and forming an awful medley of songs, intermixed with rough oaths and sweet music, the clinking of glasses, the rattling of dice and toddy sticks, etc. During the discourse, an "hombre" who had been imbibing of something stronger than water, walked in. And seating himself on a narrow railing immediately in front of the Preacher, was soon so deeply engaged trying to profit by what he heard, that he lost all knowledge of earthly things. And losing his balance, over he went ker-flop to the ground, at the Preacher's feet. And there laid and snored like a brute (as he was) during the balance of the service.

Forgotten Victims

The Indians continue to kill and rob as usual and they, together with the organized bands of Mexican bandits that roam the country, make it anything but pleasant to travel. Dead men are as plenty on the roadsides and in the mountains as ever they were in the worst days of Italian robberies in Italy, that reputed home of highwaymen and bandits. To say nothing about the many, very many, highway murders and robberies on the roads leading below and in the different mining localities. The Indians are picking off all straggling parties of prospecting miners who attempt to penetrate the upper regions in search of gold.

In the vicinity of Humbug and Big Creeks they have murdered many that we knew and undoubtedly many a poor fellow has lost his life there that we never knew of. A friend of mine, who went on the exploring expedition of last June with me, Sam Day, was telling me a few days ago that about a month ago he was up in that country prospecting with a large party, when one morning they came across a dead body, with its lower limbs burned off, scalped and having five arrows still sticking into his body. Who he was, no one knows. Unknown and uncared for, he died a horrible death. And his friends at home will long look in vain for his return to again gladden their hearts by his presence. But he, with hundreds of others, will never be heard from more and his mysterious absence and silence will never be accounted for here on earth.

The Black Legs

In January last I gave an account of the murder and execution of the murderer at Curtisville. It will be recollected that the murderer Bowen was a gambler and was hung by the miners. I have already made the statement that our officers of the law are gamblers also, therefore it is easily accounted for why they took such active steps to arrest the miners who took a part in meting out justice to this black leg, who otherwise would have escaped all punishment at the hands of our County Officials. On the day Bowen was hung, the Sheriffs with a party of Deputies, all professional gamblers, started from the county seat Sonora, all armed and mounted to arrest the miners at Curtisville who had taken the most active part in the execution.

But the news of their approach was brought in ahead of them and when they arrived, they found the miners all ready for a fight, if necessary, determined that none of their number should be arrested for this offense. And the Black Legs had to return as they came, empty handed. This feeling of animosity between the miners and their Black Leg Officials is daily growing stronger and about the middle of this month this feeling occasioned a regular pitched battle at Sonora between the two parties. A keeper of a drinking and gambling shop, a great friend to all the Black Leg Fraternity, owned a garden on a flat a short distance from town. The miners in working up the creek had followed the lode into this garden, they continued to work on and soon the whole garden plot was staked off as a mining claims and men set into working them.

The garden owner ordered them off, but he might as well try to stop the wind from blowing as to stop gold hunters when on track of a rich lode. He went to his friends, the gamblers and they promised him assistance in driving off the dirty scalawags. With the Sheriff to back them, they sallied out well-armed. Determined to let the dirty, lousy, miners know who was boss, arrived upon the ground they found the miners ready for them. All armed with revolvers, rifles and knives and entrenched behind a bank of dirt. Mr. Gamblers were told thus far and no farther could they come. One of the "sports" drew a revolver and swore a mighty oath that they should leave the premises and fired at the spokesman of the miners. He fell dead almost instantly, having received several leaden pills that didn't digest, and now the battle commenced. And after a pretty hot fight the gamblers retreated back to town, leaving two of their number on the field and carrying off quite a quantity of lead about their bodies. That felt anything but comfortable, I'll warrant ye.

He's Just Foolin'

On the 19th we had a little excitement in Jacksonville. An Englishman whilst drunk drew his pistol on another bloat, who was playing cards with him and blazed away at him, putting a ball through the fellow's hat. A crowd rushed into the tent and arrested him, but he was soon liberated as he said he was only fooling - didn't mean to kill the fellow, only meant to scare him, etc. And when he found that some of the crowd was in earnest and did not like such fun, he got quite mad. To think he was such a poor shot and couldn't shoot a man 10 feet from him and offered to bet drinks all round that he could kill every time at 10 paces. And fairly swift to think he could not get anyone to fight him with the pistols at 10 paces, he was finally put under bond of $500 to keep the peace and left the Justices shanty swearing he would kill the fool that appeared against him, on sight. So, the fool that couldn't stand fooling like this, had to sneak away out of town to save his life.

Big Baby Business

Jacksonville begins to look old-fashioned again as the miners and traders flock in for summer diggings. Liquor and gambling saloons begin to multiply and increase and their bands of music are going night and day, making the town up here lively after its winter's rest. But best of all, a real live Yankee woman with her husband and babe have arrived here and intend to locate here for the summer. Hurrah, Hurrah for Jacksonville. They have opened a boarding house and are doing a big business, for all want to see the woman and kiss the baby.

By the way it is singular how much everyone thinks of this babe of the woods. It belongs to the town and we all brag of our smart baby and our good-looking woman. Last Sunday I saw it perched up on the Monte table on a big heap of dollars, kicking them about like so many pebbles, surrounded by a crowd of rough-looking miners who were bucking at Monte and caressing the child. It is in the streets all day long, in the care of some one of its many admirers (by the way it is but nine months old). It has over 2 pounds of gold lumps, which it has had presented to it from one and another.

How Do I Look?

This is a great subject to write about some at home might say, but ah but few know what it is to be for years shut out entirely from all female society, with naught to be seen for years but men. It takes a Californian to appreciate a woman's worth. God bless them all, what would man become if it was not for them? Why this one woman making her appearance here has done more already towards humanizing and civilizing this community than all the missionaries would have done in ages. We begin to pay more attention to dress and cleanliness already. What was considered alright a month ago is not quite the thing now. For instance, a month ago a man's flannel shirt might stick out a foot or two behind, but taint quite the thing now and tis so in everything.

We begin to ask how it looks etc. etc. Well, well I have spun a long yarn this month but have not said half that I would have liked to, but I haven't room for more. Here on our creek, we are trying our best to accumulate a sufficient of this yellow stuff to take us back again to the country of girls and homes. Ned says he wants to see Mary Drown very much. And I would like to see —no matter who—but oh I'd like to see her very much. And Ned and I sit night after night, smoking our pipes by the old campfire and build castles in the air of what we'll do when we see the gals again. Girls are sad flirts friend Ned, and you and I may both live to see its truth.

In a flurry of snow, I bid you adieu.

Kanaka Creek - April 1851

Still here at the close of this month of April, working hard for about $4 a day. The weather has been quite cool for this country all this month. Small game is very plenty here and we have lived on quail, squirrel and hare principally since we have been here.

During the month it has rained
On the 2d - Rained all night
On the 3d - Rained at intervals during day

On the 16th - Rained all day

On the 24th, it cleared up at last. Having rained more or less every day from the 16th to the above date, having been the wettest month of the year, we having had 11 days of rainy weather. Making in all 38 stormy, wet, days this season. As the rainy season is about over now, we shall have from this on but little, if any, rain again until next fall. Thus, can be seen that altogether this has been considered at home as a terrible rainy wet place during the winter, still it is far from the case. I have a faithful record of the weather this season and with the exception of these 38 stormy days in the last 12 months, the balance of the time we have had beautiful, clear and general warm days.

The terrible deluges of rain that we use to hear so much about have not been seen by your humble servant since his residence in this country. Our summers are hot and no mistake, but owing to the purity of the atmosphere we do not feel the heat so oppressively, as I have at times in New England.

Breakin' Bullies

We have a gang of Sydney ducks down below us on the creek who came up here to our claim on the seventh and ordered us off, claiming the ground as theirs. We hold them that they couldn't have it. We found the claim vacant, no one appeared to claim it and we took possession and now we meant to hold it. Fact is, I don't mean to be driven any more by men because they weigh a few pounds more than I do. I lost one claim by being bullied out of it by a hog (Horton I mean) and I mean to bring into requisition the assistance of art to supply the deficiencies of Nature, in all such cases for the future.

So, when Sydney commenced talking about whipping me off, I just told him I would give him one minute to leave the claim in. And if he was on the claim at the expiration of that time, I would shoot the top of his head off. I guess he thought I meant it, for he left in a hurry. I was thinking of Horton all the time I was talking with him and wished it had been him, Horton, that stood in the Sydneyite's shoes. On the 14th Old Marshal, the Deputy Sheriff of Jacksonville, came up and summoned us to appear before Squire Pike at Jacksonville on the 21st, to answer to a complaint of trespass entered against us by the Sydneyites. All right says I; we will be "thar" and the deputy laughingly told us that he would have the thing all arranged for us. "Only," says he, "call for a jury trial and have lots of your friends around the door of the Justices Tent to act as jurors when I get ready to summons them." All right again, thinks I now, I shall have a fine opportunity to judge what kind of a show a stranger would have here in a trial at law.

On the 21st Ned and I took our seats on two soap boxes in Squire Pike's grocery store, which upon such occasions was converted into a courtroom. Our counsel HB Hosmer, a half-lawyer half-miner of the town, was seated by my side on a cheese box. The Squire was perched up on a bread barrel in front of a rough table between our party and our opponents, who were seated liked ourselves, on soap boxes. Around the grocery tent, cocked up on the boxes, bales, kegs and barrels, were seated the crowd of friends and loafers who had to come to tend court. We, according to instruction, called for a jury trial and a bevy of friends, being conveniently near, were summonsed as jurors and the trial went on. The case was finally disposed of by the jury, bringing in that our humble selves were innocent of the charge of trespass, the claim was rightfully ours and that the Sydney Ducks should pay all costs, which footed up to $85. I got off by calling up all hands to the bar on the other side of the room and treating to blue rum all around. The Squire was very much pleased to think I beat the "dod rotted Sydney ducks," but was full as much pleased to see me treat the crowd at his bar, I guess.

Texian Renegades

On the night of the 21st a Texan got to quarreling with a Cherokee Indian about a game of cards down at Jacksonville and each one drew his Bowie, ready for a fight. But they were separated by mutual friends before any damage was done. The Cherokee lived on the opposite side of the river by himself and fearing the Texans would murder him during the night went over after his blankets and rifle, intending to sleep for the night on this side of the river. On his way back to town from his camp he had to pass through a thicket of willows by the riverside and as he came to this ticket he was shot at by the Texan, who lay on the ground like a snake, awaiting his approach. The ball whistled through his long hair, merely scratching his head as it passed by and he (always ready) raised his rifle and fired at the Texan in return, wounding him severely and instantly knocking all the desire to fight out of the half-civilized brute.

This happened about 2 o'clock in the morning and everyone says that Cherokee Bob ought to be hung for not killing the miserable Texian desperado, when he had so good a chance. These Texan renegades are a villainous gang and murder is a past time with them. I do not mean to be understood as saying that all Texians are of this stripe, not at all, quite the contrary. For some of my best friends hail from that state, but I speak of this gang of renegades that have been run out of Texas.

The Bar' Hunt

And now at the close of the month we are having fine weather again and a party are about starting out for a prospecting trip up the river on this side. But as I do not relish the idea of camping out so early in the season, I have declined going with them. Several of the party were at my tent last evening and as they were all Texians, of course they were all hunters, and I was much amused to hear them relate some of their hunting adventures. One of the most laughable was told by a hunter who has spent the winter at the Green Springs House, on the road to Stockton. It is a common practice for many of our best hunters to spend the wet season at some of the "Ranchos" in the valley or on the road, hunting for a living.

Our friend located at the Green Springs. There were several others, like himself, hunters that were stopping there and amongst others, an old Mountain-Man named Burke. A crack shot and according to his story, "great on bar huntin." Old Burke had a great "bar dog" too, that he bragged on a great deal. Well one fine morning the party, four in all, started out on the track of an old she grizzly that had made its appearance in the neighborhood the previous night. They tracked her to a chimoselle hill, where all signs of her whereabouts was lost. The party finally concluded to separate and Old Burke and his great "bar dog" and Dan, one of the hunters, were to go down through the canyon, whilst Hank and Jake Strong would keep along the ridge on each side of the canyon.

Old Burke and his dog started off down the steep almost perpendicular banks of the canyon, followed by Dan the Hunter. Old Burke made the best time and reached a bottom long way ahead of Dan, and was quietly wiping off the beads of sweat from his shining forehead when he was startled nearly out of his boots by an awful clatter up the canyon. And looking up to ascertain what it all meant, he saw Dan tearing away down the gulch - like all wrath - as he said, close behind Dan came the "bar dog making the loose stones fly in all directions." Old Burke says, "he just made up his mind when he saw this that that old she bar want far off sure," an he'd be "gaul-busted if he didn't gin her one shot fore he'd run."

And he hadn't long to wait, for he soon saw her ugly face as the party came out into open view, making a strange wake "for dat are bar dog's tail!" He braced himself up for the occasion and taking aim, blazed away at Mrs. Bruin. But the shot did not stop her locomotion one whit, on she came, like a young whirlwind. And old Burke says, "he stopped a minute to watch the affect of his shot," and he comed to the conclusion dat he'd follow suit and make he self scarce. For he didn't believe twas healthy to stop just thar any longer, and he dropped his rifle and made tracks down the gulch after Dan and the dog. And now commenced the race in earnest. And our hunters, from their position on the ridge far above, had a fine view of the track.

First came Dan, who had forgotten all about his "rheumatics" that he had been growling about all winter and was making 2-40 time in his course down the gulch. Next, with his nose close to Dan's heels came "dat ar bar dog" closely followed by Old Burke "he self" — only a few rods ahead of old ugliness — who, tongue-out-and-snortin' was fast gaining on the party and fairly making the old gulch smoke. On they flew, like good bottom nags as they were, until Dan luckily tripped and fell. The dog dodged by, but Old Burke was going too fast and couldn't gather quick enough and over he went, on top of Dan. And last of all Old Bruin herself. Being by this time close to old Burke's heels and going with such velocity, could not hold up nor turn out and over she went head, neck and heels over the party and continued to roll end over end down the steep gulch, until she fetched up way below against a rock, facing down the gulch.

And this either so jarred her memory, as to make her forget the chase, or she had got confused and thought the party was still ahead. At any rate, when she righted, she never turned to right or left but, giving a grunt as she rose, again she started off down the gulch as though the very devil was after her. Old Burke and Dan lay like logs, close to the ground, until Old Bruin had made tracks down the stream. And then they started up the canyon again and Jake says they never stopped running until they were within sight of Green Springs House. And old Burke says, "taint no use talkin, dem are old. The Grizzlies are awful fellers you shoot em and don't make nary difference, they pear to like lead. An the darned things run all the faster for ventilating."

"Taint nary use to talk," he says, to him bout running way. "Just might as well try to stop de wind from blowin by shooting at the cloud, as to stop one of dem Grizzlies with an ounce ball, ought to hunt em wid a cannon and nothing shorter." And Dan says he begs to be excused from going hunting bears anymore in this country. "Dot durned if it's pleasant to have a half ton of live bear meat rolled over a fellow."

Lovely Jacksonville - May 1851

Beautiful, warm, pleasant spring weather have we been blessed with all this month, scarcely a cloud to darken the sky for day after day. The hillsides, the valleys and the mountains upon all sides are covered with flowers of every hue. Small and simple taken singly, but collectively in the masses that carpet the earth upon all sides, presenting a most lovely view of varied hues and colors and filling the air with their sweet and spicy fragrance. Truly this country at this season of the year looks lovely indeed. On the 11th we moved back to Jacksonville and commenced work on Woods Creek - Ned and I could not make anything at Kanaka Creek and left it in disgust.

Dollar Buckets - June 1851

Fine warm weather during the month, the thermometer standing as high as 112° at noon in the shade and seldom running it below 90° at any time between 11:00 AM and a 4:00 PM. But still, we do not suffer so much here at this temperature as I have at home sometimes in the summer. Every night it is cool enough to make a pair of heavy woolen blankets comfortable. Have been very successful in my mining operations this month having made from $20 to $100 a day when washing. But our claim is now worked out and I am idle again. Our dirt paid us about one dollar to the bucket of dirt on an average.

The Boling Incident

On the 11th as Mr. Boling broke of the Masonic House of this town was on this way home from Knight's Ferry on the Stanislaus River, he was shot at twice. He stopped at the New York Tent for dinner, where he saw the Englishman that shot at another here last 19th of March, an account of which will be found in this journal of that date. This fellow had a quarrel with Mr. Boling about a month ago because he (Mr. B) refused to let him have a pistol to shoot a man he had a grudge against, and Boling put him out of his house at the time. The Englishman at the time swearing he would be revenged upon him for it.

Mr. Boling has never met him since, until this time at the dinner table. As soon as Boling took his seat, the Englishman and his two comrades left the house. Mr. Boling after dinner resumed his journey homeward but had not proceeded far on his road before he was shot at from behind a chimoselle bush by the roadside. The ball grazing his ear and partially stunning him, he fell from his saddle. But immediately recovering himself, he remounted and fired at the bush and heard a fall and grown. But whilst he stood listening, he was shot at again. The ball passing through his clothes, grazed his side. Upon this he concluded that he would not stop to fight it out and putting spurs to his horse, left the assassins to look out for themselves, glad to come out of the fight as well as he did. I suppose if he had succeeded in arresting the fellow and had him tried, he would have said he was only fooling and would have been liberated again.

Clerk Dick's Rage

On the 17th as I lay in my bunk at noon, I was aroused by the shrieks of a woman instantly followed by the report of a pistol. I rushed out of my tent and saw a man retreating before another, who was shooting as he ran. The street was full of men who seemed to be very anxious to leave a clean wake between the two men as they advanced up the street. The balls as they whistled by sounded rather unpleasant to a nervous man, but fortunately no one was shot or wounded but the combatants. After it was all over with and the quiet once more restored, I learned the particulars of the case. Frank Cook keeps a drinking and gambling saloon called The Mountain Brow. He got broke last winter at the Chinese Camp and a Stockton firm furnished him goods to start this shop on credit.

But to make all sure, they sent up a clerk of theirs to live with Cook until he paid his bill. Cook, although a married man at home, keeps a woman here and she and Dick the clerk do not agree at all. Some little time ago she insulted Dick at supper and upon his replying to her, she drew a pistol on him. He got it away from her and told her at the time if she ever undertook to play anymore of her pranks on him, he should, for the first offense shave her head. And if that did not satisfy her, he should crop her ears for her. They have got along peaceably until this noon, when she pitched into Dick again. And he, according to promise, seized her by the hair of the head and with one blow of his heavy Bowie knife chopped it all off close to her head.

She screamed for help and Cook who was in the back room rushed in, pistol in hand and shot Dick in the abdomen. But Dick's blood was up now, and he was like a grizzly - furious now he was shot - and dropping her, he rushed after Cook, drawing his pistol as he ran. Cook retreated up the street and Dick followed on, cocking and firing his six-shooter as he advanced, but he did not hit Cook, nor anybody else. And after he discharged the last barrel he returned to his tent and then, for the first time, did the exasperated crowd learn he wasn't shot in the commencement of the melee. The crowd were (before they knew the circumstances of the case) rather disposed to deal harshly with Dick for endangering the lives of the inhabitants. But upon learning the facts of the case, their sympathies were with him.

Killing Snow

Just for a specimen of the coolness of our bandits, I will copy from Sonora Herald of June 14 the following. A brutal murder in a secluded park of the Dragoon Gulch about one mile from Sonora on Tuesday last. The murdered man was Captain George W. Snow of North Frankfurt, Maine and the murderous villains were three Mexicans. It appears that the Mexicans had purchased a Long Tom from Capt. Snow the previous evening and directed him to call the next morning for his pay. This it appears was only a ruse to catch the victim as it was well-known that he carried a large amount of money about his person. Accordingly, Captain Snow called the next morning at their tent and was stabbed in two places as he entered the door. As he received their knives he shouted, and the Mexicans ran. Captain Snow ran to the gulch, where he fainted from loss of blood.

His friends soon arrived and conveyed him to his tent, where he soon died. It was discovered that the murderers had dug a grave in their tent, which they had covered with a rawhide and blankets and removed the dirt to avoid suspicion. The murderers had been at work for Captain Snow for some time previous and one of them had worked for a long time at the same Tom with him. Captain Snow had upon his person at the time 37 ounces of gold and $10 dollars in coin in his vest pocket and about $200 in his coat. The $200 was stolen afterwards from the man who had charge of it, whilst he was at the funeral of Captain Snow. The editor says this should be a warning to others, do not carry money about their persons.

Burglin' Mardis

The same paper says on Friday evening six men entered Mardis, Lippencott and Gleason's Store whilst Mr. Mardis was alone. Two of them held cocked pistols at his head, threatening that if he made the least alarm to blow his brains out. The other four carried off an iron safe containing $3000. The two villains soon left and Mardis gave the alarm. A party turned out in pursuit and compelled the villains to drop their booty and make their escape, this was at Camp Seco. These fellows are known but they have succeeded in getting off. Two of Captain Snow's murderers have since been caught and hung. The Marshal of Sonora who caught them in that city was shot at four times whilst in pursuit of them. This will do for a sample; every paper is full of like accounts from the mines.

Vigilante Justice

From San Francisco the same paper has the following. On Tuesday evening about 9 o'clock the office of Mr. Tirgin on Long Wharf was opened and a safe containing $1500 abstracted. Two men had been seen going down the wharf with a heavy package in a sack. And in a few moments one of them was seen to throw the sack into a boat and scull off into the harbor. Pursuit was given, the thief was caught, brought back and instead of being taken to the Station House was brought to the corner of Bush and Sansome Streets, to the house of Sam Brannan. A bell on the plaza was tolled twice, which proved to be the signal for the gathering of the Vigilance Committee, a secret society organized in Francisco for the purpose of bringing malefactors to speedy justice.

As soon as this Committee had assembled, the doors were closed, and the prisoner arraigned for trial. He gave his name as John Jenkins, but his real name is Symptom, and he is a Sydney duck. He was tried, found guilty and sentenced to be hung in an hour. The same bell then commenced tolling and by 1 o'clock a large crowd had collected. Sam Brannan addressed the multitude, spoke of the utter impossibility of getting justice done through the medium of the courts and asked the people if they had done right in thus combining to bring culprits to justice. They answered with a loud shout AYE - followed by cries to "Hang him! Hang him!" Mr. Brannan told them that the Vigilance Committee had allowed him an hour longer to live, and a Minister was then praying with him.

At 2 o'clock he was brought out, primed and handcuffed. A rope encircled him, inside of which walked two men holding his arms, while a third led him by a rope around his neck. The members of the Vigilance Committee surrounded him on all sides, revolvers in hand, eight deep, determined he should not be rescued by his friends the officials, or his friends out of office. By the time they reached the plaza it was one mass of human beings. An attempt was here made by the officers to rescue him and the cry of "Hang him" was more wildly shouted. A block and pulley were rigged to a beam from the piazza of the old adobe. And at a quarter past two at night the rope was manned. And with a jerk, the criminal was lifted from the ground and launched into eternity.

Thus, my prediction of January last is about to be fulfilled and the people themselves have taken the matter in hand, now that they find that the courts are so corrupt.

Don't Mess With Sonora's Marshal

On 18 June, I find the following in my notebook. This morning four men came riding into camp on the dead jump and making a few inquiries continued on up the river. They were in the pursuit of three Mexicans who murdered their host this morning at the Chinese Camp. Yesterday a Mexican was hung at Sonora for the murder of Captain Snow, today three more are to be hung for shooting at the Marshal. Yesterday, three Mexicans were shot and two more wounded for attacking the Marshal whilst he was trying to stop a fight.

I should want to be cased in cast steel before I took the Marshal of Sonora's berth. On the 26th from my notebook I make this extract - The party in the search or pursuit of the Chinese Camp murderers overtook them and killed two, the other escaped.

The Vigilance Committee

Francisco has again been burned to the ground by the gang of hounds that swarm there. All is excitement there. The Vigilance Committees are firmly organized and have become one of the institutions of the city. Suspected villains suddenly disappear from their accustomed haunts and their associates know not what becomes of them. But the fear begins to come over them, that they have fallen into the clutches of that dreaded secret tribunal, the inquisition of Francisco - the terrible Vigilance Committee.

Hardened rogues and well-known villains are suddenly surrounded in saloons, in the street, or at their homes, by a band of stern, well-armed men and are mysteriously marched off, to parts unknown. These secret mysterious visitors are the Police of the Vigilance Committee.

Life In San Francisco - July 1851

Here I am as yet not made a dollar this month but spent many a one. This town is lively with music at night from the many saloons. Everyone hires a band of music to attract the crowds of miners who, after a hard day's work, resort to them to drown dull care and to while away the few hours between sunset and bedtime. We have no happy homes to go to, no loving wives to receive us, no society. And our thoughts of home and its many pleasures, our recollections of those happy days spent there, would drive us to madness if we stayed in our miserable cabins. So, we all have to resort to the saloons to try and kill dull care.

I will close this journal by giving a copy from a paper laying before me of life in San Francisco in this present year of our Lord 1851. On one of the corners of Kearney and Washington streets stands an edifice in which the arch enemy of mankind lays his most cunning snares for the destruction of the unwary, the high-spirited and the unsuspecting. This, the famous El Dorado Saloon, is the most extensive gambling hall in the city. Next to this comes the Jenny Lind Theater - now building - then in the further corner another gambling saloon, the California Exchange. These front the plaza. On the west side of the plaza are the Bella Union and the other large gaming houses. These gambling saloons are patronized by everyone, because they are the only comfortable places in town to pass an evening.

They are the only substantial buildings erected and are crowded nightly by an excited crowd of all ages and pursuits, eager to try their luck at Roulette, Monte or Jaro. Gambling there is in fact so general that it has ceased to be a vice. And the fact that there are no churches to resort to on Sundays, helps the proprietors amazingly. These saloons are the principal attractions of the city. Several of them are spacious, roomy edifices extending from street to street and standing in a parallel line, so that the visitor may pass directly from one to the other, with only a narrow street to cross. They are open to the crowd, and it is very seldom of an evening especially that every available inch of standing room is not taken up, many being attracted thither from curiosity merely.

Paintings of considerable merit adorn the walls. The ceilings are handsomely frescoed and painted and the whole brilliantly lighted with hundreds of sperm candles. Each saloon has a fine orchestra which is kept going from early in the afternoon to the small hours of morning. Even female attractions are not wanting. To heighten the delusion, several of the dealers being bright-eyed French or Spanish girls "dressed to death in silks and satins." Liquors are dispensed with a liberal hand. There are a great many tables, devoted to as great a diversity of games and 9/10ths of the gamesters are Greenhorns, new arrivals, some just out from the States, others fresh from the mines, all forming groups, each a study in itself. A few of them were youths of from 16 to 21 years of age, but the majority were men in the full vigor of early life, whose means might be judged of in inverse proportion to the seediness of their attire.

The best dressed being usually the poorest of the assemblage, while the proprietors of the shocking-bad Chilean hats and red shirts seemed to be the possessors of any quantities of fortunatus & purses. The owners of which would take great pains to show the handle of a revolver or Bowie knife to convince strangers that they were not to be plundered without a struggle.

No Hope For Sinister Charlie

There is a remarkable personage at one of these places, a Faro Dealer whose awkward limping gait and furrowed features, indelibly marked with scars of some previous fight, awaken in the observer a desire to know something of his history. Night after night there he sits behind his Faro bank, dispensing the cards with that mechanical precision which characterizes the movements of the professional gambler. Not a trace of feeling visible on his lackluster countenance, whatever the fluctuations of the game. He is never seen to smile and very rarely driven from his equanimity by the curses or threats of those around him. I have been told the following story of him.

He arrived here in "49 from Missouri by the overland route. At home in Missouri, he had been a promising young merchant, fortune smiled upon him. He married an amiable young girl and for two short years he prospered and was happy. But then commenced his reverses, he was obliged to fail and was left in a destitute condition, with a wife and two children looking to him for support. He found a temporary home for his wife and children with a friend and started for California across the plains early in the spring of "49. After a long and tiresome journey of months he arrived in Sacramento Valley and turned his attention first to farming. He prospered and finally he opened a store, and in this he also prospered. He had erected for himself a rude but comfortable house and began to think of sending for his family to join him here in this country.

But at this time The Tempter crossed his path and he fell. During some of his occasional visits to Francisco he had met and made the acquaintance of a person some 10 years his senior whose frank address and easy, yet polished, manner prepossessed him in his favor, and they were soon on terms of intimacy. Charlie, our hero, had a weak and confiding disposition and he soon commenced to lend this newfound friend money, but which was invariably repaid. By degrees he was led to partake of his companion's enthusiasm for games of chance and soon was as much of a devotee as his instructor. His business went to the wall and at last he sold out, sent for his family and determined to never gamble — after one more trial to redeem his lost fortune. He finally came down to Francisco just before the steamer from the east was due, took rooms and awaited the arrival of his family.

He had never given that last trial yet and now he determined to make the last final struggle to regain what he had lost. He went, played all night and in the morning was penniless. That very day his wife arrived but he could not — would not — meet her. Conscience had rendered him a coward. He fled to Sacramento, telling his friends to tell his wife that he had been called back the day before by his business arrangements. They embarked onboard the Gold Hunter to follow him to Sacramento, but they never reached their destined port. For they were included amongst the victims of that dreaded catastrophe, by which that boat was lost.

As for the husband he is yet alive and his mutilated countenance and disfigured limbs tell their own story. Gambler, duelist and debauchee are written in every feature so strongly, as to remove all necessity of doubt. He believes that there is no relief for him on earth, nor hope in heaven and is possibly one of the most depraved and hardened and reckless of all the sinister characters in San Francisco.

Daniel Jenks Gold Rush Journal
Volume 2: 1852-1856

Marysville, California - January 1852

The new year found me in the good city of Marysville California, pursuing my new trade of Steward (I don't like the term Waiter) in Madame Wheeloch's Coffee House. I did not stay long at Mrs. Wheeloch's. We had an insurrection or mutiny amongst the waiters, and I quelled it by knocking one down with a soda bottle and the next day I left. I was then out of work again, but soon attained a job as cook at $75 a month at the Golden Gate Saloon and here I stopped a long time. During the short time I was at Mrs. Wheeloch's, I found that more was required of me than I was able to perform.

For instance, I was obliged to rise at 4 AM and see that the rooms were in order for the acceptance of customers at five. Breakfast was ready and from that time until 12 noon there was a constant throng to breakfast. At 12, the eating department was closed and then the rooms were to be prepared for supper (no dinner being given at this house). The floor was to be washed, the casters, cruelts, etc. to be filled and polished and everything put in apple pie order. This took until nearly 4 PM when supper was served and from that time until 12, and sometimes after 10 o'clock at night, it was a constant trot. Thus, leaving but 4 hours out of the 24 for sleep. This was too much for me and I was glad of an excuse to leave. But after leaving here what was I to do? I had no money and board was $14 per week. However, by chance and impudence, I managed to get along until I found another job. A little assurance is a useful commodity at times.

At the Golden Gate I had an easy time. This was one of the fashionable drinking houses where they provided a free lunch twice a day for the customers of the house. And my duty was to cook the three meals a day for the prospectors and bar keepers, five in all and cook the lunches. It is useless for me to say how often my pride was wounded at the idea of being obliged to perform at this servile duty. But I may say that it was often the case and my only consolation was that I was where no one knew me in my better days. Poverty gives us not only strange bedfellows, but also drives us at times into strange corners to seek wherewithal to supply the incessant demands of Dame Nature for food and nourishment. And fortunate is he that bends to the decrees of Fate and accepts of such fare as presents itself. A stranger, penniless, with the knowledge of no trade, I was forced to accept of any means to gain a livelihood.

Marysville, California - February 1852

Still at work cooking for a lot of whiskey guzzlers and gamblers and this includes the whole population of Marysville. Well, it is perfectly natural for men to love a change I suppose and after being confined all day to their business, all look for a little recreation in the evening. At home, men have hundreds of ways to amuse themselves. A man with a family returns to his home and enjoys himself there. A single man visits his female acquaintances, visits a concert, ball or some place of the kind but here are no such chances. And one must either stop at his place of business until bedtime or pass his time in such saloons as this.

And I must say most prefer passing an hour or two in one of the many saloons where they can always find plenty of the latest papers from all parts of the world to read, if they do not choose to injure their health and reputation (at home) by drinking and gambling.

Sacramento Valley Flood

This month I was enabled to see how a city looked overflowed. The Yuba and the Feather Rivers rose so high that the lower part of the city was completely covered. So that boats could row right into the second story windows of some of the stores and steamboats pass right up First Street onto the Plaza and come to anchor alongside some of the stores. Very much damage has been done to some of the merchants. Some of the brick houses have caved in and thousands of dollars' worth of goods have washed off and been destroyed by water. Sacramento Valley looks like a vast inland lake as far as you can see. Either way is naught but water, excepting an occasional piece of high land that is still above water, looking like so many islands.

The tribe of digger Indians at the mouth of the Yuba, about a mile from town, are driving a brisk trade at present during the flood. What with catching hares that have been driven out of their burrows by the water and catching up goods as they wash down stream, they are very busy for once. All drift goods are considered public property and the country is covered with boats picking up whatever they can lay their hands upon. Take it all in all, it is rather a singular looking spectacle this city presents at present. Merchants perched upon the roofs of their houses, where they have removed their goods. Streets are full of boats carrying passengers from one part of the city to another or carrying goods to some part still above water.

People eating their meals with (in some houses) the water on the floor over ankle deep. And in my kitchen, if the water raises 2 inches higher it will put the fire out in the stove, it's ankle deep now. All communication with the mines are cut off at present so long as the flood lasts. Sacramento of course, is in as bad a fix as our city. And the flood has done much more damage there than here, as the current is much stronger and sweeps right through the heart of the city. Here the current sweeps the opposite bank of the Yuba and were it not for a slough that crosses from Feather River, there would be no current here at all as it is. This current has done most of the damage here. This it was that caused the brick buildings to fall on First Street as it undermined them, they being California built and all know that is very slightly.

But enough of the flood, it run down in a few hours to its proper banks and was soon forgotten in the bustle of the spring trade. And soon the sites of the caved in houses were covered with the material and workmen for the building of far superior houses than those destroyed. The Plaza has been raised and all of the lower part of town has been filled up above high-water mark and not much danger is apprehended of, or from, another flood. And now in the latter part of February, here Spring has fairly set in and we are in the enjoyment of as fine pleasant weather as our friends will not see in the short of two months to come at home. Lettuce radishes in February, what think you Down Easters of that?

Marysville, California – Broken March 1852

Well, this month has been rather a broken one for me. In the fore part of it I came to the conclusion that I should never get my pay at the Golden Gate and after a short conversation on monetary affairs, I left. I next tried a hotel kept by a Texan named Armstrong. Stopped just 24 hours with him and left. Could not make up my mind to be governed by his wife, who looked upon her hands as no better than so many of her slaves at home. I very politely informed her that she had ought to have studied good manners at home before she ventured to leave for a country where such things as politeness and gentle manners were known and appreciated. And furthermore, that many in this country found themselves at times compelled to perform work that they could not help but despise. That, when at home, held as high a position probably in society as she did.

California Has Rats!!!

Of course, as I could not get my pay from the Golden Gate I was (to use a polite term) strapped. And what to do I did not know. But a butcher offered me lodgings and I boarded on credit at Charlie's Restaurant until I was offered a situation in the house as night cook, which of course I was under the circumstances, glad enough to accept. Here my duty was to commence my work at 10 o'clock in the evening and work until the same hour in the morning and get my sleep during the day. But this was easy work to what I had seen, and I was contented to work at this until I could better myself. My chief duty was to guard the house and provisions from the hosts of enormous rats that infest this and all other California cities.

A man can form no idea how plenty these vermin are here unless he has had the pleasure of residing in one of the cities here. I had an idea that I had seen a few rats at times in sundry places, previous to my arrival in this country. But there, well, I never did imagine that there were so many rats in the whole republic as I have seen in this city. I believe it to be impossible for a man to travel one quarter of a mile in these streets without squashing at least half a dozen rats in that time and driving droves ahead of him, sufficient to supply all Chinadom with rat pie for a month and a day. They are so plenty, it is impossible for them all to dodge you. And one of our boarders has a rat terrier dog that we keep at the house. Well, we let him out amongst them about 9 o'clock every night and he does well for a time, but the constant crunching of rats gives him the jaw ache. After about 15 minutes work and he then is done up for that night.

Between the rats and the women, I was kept tolerably busy this month. By the way there is a land lady at this house now and rest assured there is much difference in the conduct of Mrs. Stone of Charlie's restaurant, formerly of Boston and Mrs. Armstrong of the Southern and Western hotel, formerly from Texas. Mrs. Stone is a very amiable ladylike woman. They (Mr. and Mrs. Stone) are just out from Boston and hired this house about three weeks ago, as the former proprietor left for his home in Old Merry England. There has not been anything of importance as far as I can recollect transpired during this month.

The city is rapidly improving in appearances, many are preparing to build the coming summer and mostly large fireproof brick blocks. On the outskirts of the city many are building neat pretty cottages for their family residences, expecting their families out this summer to join them here.

Marysville, California - April 1852

I have changed around until I got to be Steward of this house. Babcock, who has filled the situation of head cook here all winter, hired the house for himself this month and employs me as Steward. We intend to leave this city next month for Shasta Butte Valley, about 300 miles north of this near Oregon, overland to the above-named country. We are both sick of this drudge's life and mean to try the mines for it.

Tanner's Gauntlet

There is a great excitement here respecting a man by the name of Tanner. This man has been teaming, hauling goods from here to the mines on the Feather River. In the fore part of the month, he was caught loading his team at one of the warehouses, on the outskirts of the town. He was taken, examined and bound over in the sum of $2000 to appear for trial, but that night endeavored to escape. Was caught by some men who were watching for him and brought to town in the morning, where after much excitement amongst the mob, was finally handed over to the tender mercies of the Vigilance Committee of Marysville. By this time the mob had increased to thousands and the universal cry was "Hang him! Hang him!"

The new mayor pled for hours for his delivery to the custody of the officers of the law, but for a long time his entreaties were met with scorn and derision by the wild mob. Meanwhile, the fellow's poor wife and two young children were running about the street, perfectly crazy with affright and their cries of terror could be heard above the excited cries and yells of the infuriate mob. About noon the Vigilants told the mayor that they had concluded to turn the prisoner out into the street. And if he could rescue him from the mob, he might. Accordingly, there was a rush for the door by the officers and mob, and the prisoner was turned out to run the gauntlet. And then what a sight.

The fellow started on the run for the jail, knowing that his only chance for life lay in his reaching it, the crowd pursued with whoop and yell. Sometimes the officers had him and then the mob. Such a running fight for about a half of a mile I never wish to see again. The prisoner's clothes were all torn off in the melee and many heads were bloody. But the officer finally won the day and got him secured in the jail. This is a sample of the proceedings under Judge Lynch's government, a disgrace to any civilized country. God knows that where such proceedings are allowed, I do not wish to make it my home. Tanner will, in all probability, be executed by the Officers of Law. But this bloodthirsty mob were not satisfied with this, they must torture the poor fellow their own way.

His wife and family have always had a good name and she is worth some money, made by taking in washing. They are Sydney people and this accounts in a measure for the strong prejudice against them. But it wouldn't matter but little to the mob where their victim came from, so they could get to enjoy the spectacle of a hanging scrape. They have a perfect mania for this species of amusement in this country.

Off To Oregon – Glorious May 1852

A glorious month of May, my favorite month in this country is the month of flowers. The fields are far as the eye can reach, covered with flowers of every hue and form. And of all times in the year, I like to travel in such a time as this. On the 10th of May, Babcock and myself, having purchased us an Oregon pony and mule, bid farewell to Marysville and started off up the valley on the road to Oregon. We promised ourselves much pleasure in the trip and we were not disappointed. We stopped for dinner at Charlie's Ranch on the Feather River, 18 miles from Marysville.

Here the road crosses the river by a ford and ferry and keeping on up the road in a few miles you reach Hamilton, a California city of three or four houses besides the public house. We made but a short stay here and continued on up the river, passing a large Indian town on the road and finally about dusk reached a public house built of cloth and stopped for the night. We found we had missed our road and were now on the road to the Feather River mines. But our host informed us that it was but a few miles across the country to the right road and we could soon find it in the morning. After picketing our horses for the night in the grass knee-high, we turned in and slept soundly until morning.

Sacramento Valley - 5/11

We started early in the morning to resume our journey. Passing on up the Sacramento Valley through alternate groves of oaks and fields of wild oats, occasionally fording some small stream, we at night stopped at a ranch about 15 miles from Tehama on the Sacramento River.

5/12 - This morning we were up with the lark. And before we could distinguish objects plainly, were on our flight from the rest of the bedbugs, lice, fleas and cockroaches where we had endeavored in vain to sleep the night before.

Old Settler's Ranch - 5/12

About sunrise we arrived at an old Settler's ranch, where we had an excellent breakfast of salmon, venison etc. and were waited upon by two smart looking Indian girls, who this old fellow has raised. I was perfectly envious of this old fellow in his possession of such a lovely spot as this. A fine clear stream of water rushes on close by his house, the banks of which are lined with stately oaks and wild flowering shrubs that filled the air with their sweet perfume. His house is built of adobe or sun-dried brick and a large projecting roof, after the Mexican style and all whitewashed inside and out and is built in a grove of large, noble old oaks.

In fact, it is just the place for a man that loves solitude and would like to live an independent, free and easy life. Such spots as this will in time be valuable and were it not for friends at home, I would set me down for life in such a place and bid the world defiance. Let it wag on its own way but let me enjoy my own snug and quiet home with a partner to share my lot in such a place and I would be content. But as beautiful as it was, we could not stop here and after a ride of about two hours we reached the Sacramento River opposite of Tehama, which town consists of one large public house with the stables and other outhouses. Not wishing to cross here, we kept on the east bank. We now begun to find a change in the general appearance of the countryside. It now became more hilly, for previous to this we have had almost a level road.

Private Sanctum

After riding until about 10 o'clock we finally came upon a farm and riding up to the house (which was surrounded by swarms of Indian children capering about under the fine old oaks) we inquired of a man who appeared to be the owner if we could get dinner with him. "Well, I reckon," was his answer. And we accordingly dismounted, saw our animals had plenty of barley before them and then, upon a horn being blown, we went in to dinner. The fare was homely but substantial and plenty of it and here, as in the morning, we were waited upon by two smart, tidy-looking, Indian girls. Everything showed plainly that the prospector was a wealthy man.

Although his was a log house, everything appeared to go on like a well-regulated farmhouse at home, although it was in charge of these Indian girls alone. After dinner we accompanied the old man to what he called his private sanctum, for the purpose of having a smoke. We found this was a sort of a summerhouse and storeroom combined, built of hewn logs, weather boarded outside, lined with a sheeting inside. Situated on a knoll in a grove of majestic oaks, it commanded a view of his whole cultivated land which lay immediately in front of us. A point enclosed on three sides by water of the creek that came rushing down from the mountains by his house and emptied itself into the Sacramento, which formed the other enclosure on the left. This building was full of casks, barrels and boxes of goods and provisions for the use of his Indians that work for him and his hired white hands. Going to a cask, he drew us a glass of whiskey apiece and then sat down to enjoy his pipe and had a short conversation with us.

He has been in this country a great while and made a fortune in the first two or three years after gold was discovered by trading between Sacramento City and Redding Springs, as Shasta City was then called. And now has retired to his farm to spend the balance of his days in as pretty a place as mortal need wish to find. He reckoned we might do well at Yreka (as Shasta Butte Valley is now called) said there was a right smart chance of miners there and as we looked like right pert young men, would probably make a right smart chance of money up there. Said he did not go much on the blue-bellied Yankees as a general thing, as they were too picayunish. Finally told us he did not keep a public house, nor entertain strangers, but as it was a long ride to the next house, he could not send us away hungry. And finally concluded by charging us $6 for our fare and bid us good day.

We felt highly edified with his lecture on the difference between Eastern and Western men, as to their picayunish, but could not for the life of us see where the difference was.

Miserable Hovel – 5/12

After riding until nearly sunset we came again upon the noble Sacramento River, which here runs along rather more rapidly and is hemmed in by perfectly perpendicular banks of about from 50 to 100 feet in height. Crossing by ferry, we found our road lay through a very broken country of low hills and ravines. About an hour after dark, we stopped at a miserable hovel in a bleak, barren valley where we finally succeeded in procuring feed, such as it was, for ourselves and animals.

5/13 -After a miserable night's rest on the bare ground, we made an early start for better accommodations. And about sun an hour high, reached an inn where we made up for last night's fast. After breakfast we traveled on and by noon reached a creek where there was a public house kept by an old Trapper and made a dinner off of venison and roast beaver. Here I by accident came near losing a finger, having got caught in a beaver trap that lay on a settee. About an hour of sundown, we started on our winding way for Shasta City 12 miles distant. And after three hours hard riding over a very mountainous country arrived at Shasta.

5/16 - We found the next morning after our arrival that we should have some pretty hard days tramp after leaving here, and through a hostile Indian country. And we concluded to lay over a day or two. For you may depend upon it, I was pretty stiff and our animals felt a little used up.

Shasta City

Shasta City is built in a narrow ravine with not level ground enough to have a level street. There is but one main street running parallel with the ravine, one side of which is about 6 feet higher than the other. The stranger arriving here from any other country would say the principal business must be gambling, but this is a feature of very many towns of (this) size in California. Of course, the town is supported by its trade with the smaller mining towns to the north and west of here, it is the depot for northern traders. The section of mining country laying between and on the Sacramento, Trinity, Klamath, Scott and Shasta rivers come here for their merchandise.

It is a poor place for a town, but probably will for a long time continue a good business place. Being entirely surrounded by lofty mountains I found it to be excessively warm, although I could see snow on the peaks within a few miles of us in great plenty.

The Road To Yreka - 5/16

This morning we started out on our course upwards, towards Yreka. We found it to be a tiresome road before we had gone far, for almost immediately after leaving we began climbing a very steep mountain. After winding around through ravines and steep canyons and passing over one high ridge, we descended into Clear Creek Valley. And keeping on up the creek, all of the time ascending, we came about noon to the first mountain house where we took dinner. Leaving this we continued ascending until about 4:00 PM we came to the Upper Mountain House, halted to get a good drink of Mountain Dew. And found the proprietor dressing a wound in his arm, where he had been shot with an arrow 15 minutes before, about 500 yards above his house at his spring. This somewhat alarmed us, but go on we would. And after examining our pistols, we started on for the summit now in view just ahead.

The mountain is covered to the summit with large pines and firs. An incident occurred here which delayed us a little. Two men afoot had joined us at the Mountain House, one of whom was just out from the States. As we made the summit and looked back, we could not see our traveling companions and we hallooed for them. The old miner replied that his friend had completely given out and could not stir another foot but had lain down. In vain we told them to make one more exertion and get up to us and we would let him ride down to the river. It was perfectly useless, he could not move and I went back for him, got him onto my horse and started up again. All of the time expecting to hear an arrow whiz by my ear, but we got on without trouble and about dark arrived at the Bridge House on Trinity River.

Here we found we had missed the trail again and were on the way to Weaverville. But by taking a cut across the low mountains, keeping a blind trail up the river, we would come out in about 8 miles to where the Yreka Trail crossed the river. And then it was 30 miles from there to the next house. The Indians were very bad on this road and had killed a great many Whites in the past three or four months. Pleasant news this, was it not?

Gary's Ranch - 5/17

Early in the morning we started out in the quest of our blind trail, which our host told us (pointing to a tree) passed right close by that. We found a sort of a deer trail which we followed over hill and dale for about 10 miles when we came upon our road at the old ferry. There was formerly a house here but all that stood there at present was the blackened walls of the old log inn, which had been burnt by the Indians and its inmates murdered a short time before. Hurrying on we rode until just at dark we came in sight of Gary's Ranch, where we were soon cutting and carving and filling ourselves off on an immense haunch of venison. The old log tavern was full of customers, travelers going below in the company with the Express. All was well. Life, fun and frolic until bedtime. When they began to drop off one or two at a time, roll themselves in their blankets on the ground floor and soon all was hushed but the deep grunt of some old porcupine of a snoring miner.

5/18 - Before light we were all up and eating breakfast and before sunrise we were in our saddles and away. We now had a 16 mile stretch before we came to another house, where we dined and then 16 miles over Scott's Mountain before we could find another house. We had a party of about a dozen miners on foot for company today and jogged along up the Trinity River, crossing gulches and ravines innumerable until we came to the halfway house.

We made a most miserable dinner of boiled beans and coffee without bread and was glad to leave and take the road again. From here you commence climbing this mountain. About sunset we reached the divide and putting spurs to our animals we descended as rapidly as the character of the trail would admit.

Martin's Ranch - 5/18

And about an hour after dark, we came stumbling along and fetched up at Martin's Ranch (on the other side of Jordan) or in other words, in the head of Scott's Valley. We found our host was a dirty, slovenly, good-natured, old Frontiersman who gave us a hearty reception and set before us plenty of bacon, venison, coffee and bread and give us the softest place on the ground floor to lie on.

5/19 - Early in the morning we started out for Yreka. After fording several branches of Scott's River, we came upon the main fork, which we swam. And continuing down the stream we soon came out into a wide beautiful and fertile valley. We took it easy here, as our last day or two's trip had been pretty severe. And as we had passed through the worst of the Indian country, we felt safe. Night overtook us some 12 miles from the town and we stopped at a roadhouse for the night. This valley is already settling up very fast and no doubt in a few years will be all taken up and improved.

5/20 - After taking breakfast, our animals were saddled, and we mounted and put off for Yreka. After a pleasant ride of about three hours were in sight of the town, which is built in a valley about a quarter mile in width and is much more of a town than I expected to see. We put up at Leonard's Hotel, where we were received kindly by Mrs. Leonard. Although she informed us she had closed her house for the present, but if we felt disposed to share the same as she did, we could board with her until we could better ourselves. We concluded to stop with her in preference to going to the other houses.

Yreka - June 1852

We stopped in Yreka, prospecting for diggings about ten days when not being successful in finding anything and our cash getting low, we took to the saddle again, on the hunt for diggings. Strapping our blankets, a ham, 25 pounds of flour, a little coffee and sugar, pickaxe, shovel, pan, coffee pot and fry pan onto the animals behind us. We recrossed the bridge between Scott's and Yreka valleys again by another pass and came down into Cherry Creek, here we encamped. That night Babcock found an old acquaintance here, a Dutchman who joined with us as he was also on the hunt for diggings. This creek appeared to offer no chance to us as it was all claimed up and I turned in to my bunk on the ground with a heavy heart that night, for I was broke and the prospect ahead far from bright.

Prospecting Salmon River Mountains

The next day we crossed a ridge, then a creek which we never stopped to prospect, but kept on over another high ridge and came upon a little creek where there were four men at work, and here we encamped. We stopped about a week at this place prospecting but could find nothing. Finally, we packed up and started on our rolling way and that night encamped on another creek in the same valley. Next morning, we started across the valley to prospect some creeks running down out of the Salmon River Mountains. And after wading and swimming innumerable small streams we encamped at night on a rapid creek which emptied into Scott's River from the right. Here we stopped nearly a month, encamped under an immense arborvitae tree. We tried this creek in various places but never succeeded in finding a good prospect.

We were joined here by three other prospectors: Pat Ford, Wormer and Ben Rogers. Ford came out to this country with Stevenson's Regiment from New York. After trying here until we were satisfied, we split up our party and Babcock returned to Yreka. Leaving me and Ben Rogers and a party of Dutchman who had joined us the night before. By this time the whole country was up in arms fighting Indians and we were apprehensive of an attack as the red skins knew we were up in the mountains. The farmers were fortifying their houses and one Johnson's Ranch, about 3 miles from us, was attacked by a band but were finally driven off, leaving two of their numbers laying on the ground.

Leonard's House ~ Yreka - July 1852

I remained here on this creek until about the 10th of this month, when Babcock came after me to go with him to Yreka. Leonard wanted us to take charge of a restaurant he was about to open. And you may believe we gladly accepted of his offer, as it began to look squally for us. For we had spent all of our cash by this time. In fact, mine had all gone long ago. We started early in the morning and traveling through the Scott's Valley found the settlers were getting together an expedition to fight the Indians. We arrived in Yreka by night in company with the volunteers. As soon as I arrived, we went to work for Leonard and on the 16th, we opened house. Poor Ben Rogers was shot the night we left the creek by one of the Dutchmen who mistook him for an Indian.

Rogue River Valley War ~ Yreka - August 1852

We still hold forth at Leonard's Restaurant, which we now keep in our names. This past month, little has been heard of but the Indian murders. It is not safe to go 5 miles from town in any direction. On the emigrant trail, whole tribes have attacked trains and killed all of the party. There has been a volunteer company raised and sent out from here to protect the emigrants. In the Rogue River Valley they are at war, in between here and Shasta many have been killed. But for all this, men still travel as usual. But generally go in parties, well-armed, to protect themselves in case of an attack. They come down into the valley nights and drive off stock from the farms and, in fact, no man can say when he is safe if he stirs 5 miles from town.

The Destitute & Sick - September 1852

My life in this business has not much worthy of recording, all days are about alike. The only variety we have is an occasional row and shooting of pistols in which no one is ever hurt. Plenty of loud talk, which amounts to nothing more nor less then talk. These frontier men are rather a rough set, but I manage to keep along and make money out of them. The Indians in Rogue River Valley have agreed to a treaty of peace and all is quiet there now. Our volunteers have had several fights on the emigrant trail and killed some of 30 or 40 red skins they say. Many families have arrived here, all pretty destitute and many quite sick.

The Yreka Fire - October 1852

We have had the misfortune of having all of our part of the town burned down this month, which has injured my business very much. As the town now stands I am away, outside of everything and everybody. The fire burned up to my house and there stopped. I shall have to change my place of business and open a new house in the other section of the town. This will take all I have made this summer. But if times are good this winter, I shall soon make it up.

Callahan's Ranch - 10/28

Started this morning in company with the Express for Shasta City to purchase goods for my new house and at night stopped at a new house at the head of the valley called Callahan's Ranch, where we found an excellent table spread for us of good things of which we did ample justice.

Shasta - November 1852

We arrived in Shasta this morning and I proceeded to make inquiries amongst the merchants to see if I could get my outfit here. But found that I should be obliged to go to Marysville for them and the next morning at 4 o'clock I jumped aboard the stage for a ride of 24 hours to Marysville.

Marysville - 11/3

We arrived in Marysville this morning about 4 o'clock and you may depend I was tired enough to go to bed as soon as possible. In the morning after breakfast, I took a walk around town and was surprised to see how the city has improved in appearances since I left here not six months since. The whole appearance of it has altered and one would hardly know it was the same place. Whole rows of stately fireproof brick buildings have sprung up, as if by magic.

11/4 - Having purchased those articles which I could not find at Shasta and anxious to get back into the mountains before the roads become impassable, I must say with some regret I bid my Marysville friends adieu and at 12 o'clock noon I got aboard the stage for another long tiresome journey of 150 miles to Shasta.

Take The Stage

A word or two respecting this line of stages may not be uninteresting in days to come. It was established this past summer by Hall and Crandal and makes the trip of over 200 miles from Sacramento City by the way of Marysville, Hamilton and Tehama to Shasta city in about 36 hours constant travel. Changes horses about every 10 miles and has, I have been told, over 300 horses on the route, most of which are the half wild horses of California. I don't believe there is a route in the world that is like it. Sometimes it takes a man to both lead horses and to hold them, when they are brought out of the station stables. We had 22 passengers this trip at $20 apiece and I was obliged to take a deck passage.

And to improve the prospect, it commenced raining as we started out. Truly a pleasant prospect was ahead of us for the next 24 hours, at least. But what can't be helped, must be endured. Just fancy a ride of 36 hours duration (for thus long it took us) on the roof of a common Concorde coach. So crowded that I was obliged to ride the whole distance with my legs hanging over the iron rail around the top of the coach and no chance to alter my position, and it raining. And the cold bleak winds, seeming to cut to the very bone and to have the prospect before you of having to endure it for 36 hours. However, as I said before, off we started at 12 o'clock and we finally reached Hamilton just after dusk where we found a miserable supper waiting us, which we partook of however, for we by this time needed some nourishment.

And after supper we fortified ourselves by a strong glass of Mountain Dew (and who would not drink a little ardent in such a time) and off we started again. The night was twice as dark as a stack of black cats and miserably cold, but we worried along through the mud, fording streams 3 and 4 feet deep. Sometimes all hands tumbling out and off to foot it up some steep slough bank, stopping at every house to warm up the inner-man and to relight our pipes. And finally reached Neil's Ranch about midnight where they had (anticipating a hungry crowd) prepared a splendid supper for us. For a half hour we forgot our misery and all was fun and frolic. So highly did we relish the change.

But again, the horn was blown and away we started on the full run as usual, being impossible to hold these wild animals in. But they soon got the metal drawn out of them and relapsed again into the old jog trot. Finally, about daybreak we reached the Sacramento River opposite Tehama. And waking the Ferryman, who lay in his boat since midnight waiting for us, we crossed over and sat down to breakfast at the Tehama

House, which had been waiting for us all night as the usual time of arrival here is midnight. But owing to the muddy roads and overladen coach, we were six hours later than usual. This is the best roadhouse I have seen in this country and reminds one of the descriptions of old-fashioned stage houses in the olden times in the eastern states. After partaking of a most splendid breakfast of salmon, white trout, venison etc. we started on again. And after a right smart chance of fooling up mountains, fording streams and getting stuck in the mud several times, we at last reached Shasta City after dark. And swallowing supper as quick as possible, put off to bed.

As for myself, I went to bed with the fever and ague fastened to me as my share of the consequences of this night's work.

Shasta - 11/11

I have been obliged to wait here at Shasta until today to find a pack train go up to Yreka, as most of the Packers dare not start up at this time for fear of being caught in the mountains after it commences snowing. But I have at last succeeded in getting it (my goods) started on the road and tomorrow I follow after. I was happy to meet an old acquaintance here, Mr. Frank Young formerly of Pawtucket, who is down from Weaverville (where he is stopping at present) after goods. We boarded together whilst here and parted today as he started this morning for Weaverville.

11/12 - Started on mule back this morning in company with E. Raynes of Crown Rogers Company Express to return. Took it easy today as we travel but 12 miles this heat and about noon stopped at the Tower House on Clear Creek.

Gary's Ranch - 11/13

By the time it was fairly light we were on the road. Our party is increased to eight and we had a very pleasant ride through a very mountainous country and at night found ourselves at Gary's Ranch, having traveled over 30 miles and not a house on the road. We found a large party here on the road down and there was hardly room to stow us all inside. But by laying 'heads and points', sort of dovetailing, we managed to all find room on the ground floor. Well we all lived through the night but it was nip and tuck, and a smart chance more nip than tuck. For of all the lousy bed buggy, flea begotten, vermin of all sort, overridden places that I have found yet (and I've seen some) this Gary's Ranch beats the hull billing that I ever did see. Such tossing, tumbling, grunting, cursing, scratching and growling I never did see.

Until one individual swore, he couldn't - nor he wouldn't - stand it any longer and jumping up swore that every man must turn out and take an inward draught of mild poison, to counteract so many external applications of it. And hauling Gary out of his blankets, made him get up and liquor. Then concluding that would not be sufficient, took another and another etc. And when they finally rolled themselves up again, I reckon that no common array of vermin could awaken them. In the morning we eat breakfast by candlelight and put out. And after another hard day's ride, arrived at Callahan's Ranch in Scott's Valley after dark with a glorious appetite. Which we soon satisfied at his table.

Fouch's Hacienda ~ Long Gulch - 11/14

Arrived home by dark and found that Bob had closed up and had a new building nearly fitted up for us on Miner Street. The new location is an excellent one and if any business is done here this winter, we can't help but do well. All of our old patrons live in this vicinity, it is in the business part of the town and a very commodious house.

The Grand Opening – November 25, 1852

We opened our new house tonight with a ball supper and had more than we could accommodate and about 30 ladies (Western), newly arrived emigrants mostly. Provisions are expensive at present, but we can live and make money at present prices if they don't get much higher. Flour is $37.50 per hundred. Our goods all arrived in good shape about a week ago, just in time for us. Everyone anticipates a prosperous winter as it looks very favorable for rain now. There are not many provisions in town, but many trains are on the road in here from Oregon, if they arrive in time before the winter fairly sets in.

The Grand Closing - December 25, 1852

It is a month now since I opened and tonight, I was obliged to close again. As there is not a pound of flour, coffee, tea, sugar, bacon, beans, vegetables or anything close to be had, for love or money, in this country. We are reduced to straight beef. The last flour was sold at $3 a pound and salt at $16 dollars a pound. I kept my house open 10 days after all the others had to close, but I have to cave now. It has snowed for the past three weeks almost incessantly, and it is impossible to either get in or out of here. All the roads are blocked up. The volunteers came in from the emigrant road about a fortnight ago, bringing in two wounded men on litters and about 50 scalps, which lay out in my woodhouse now.

Trapped, Sick & Starving - January 1853

I must confess that this is squeezing a man into a mighty tight corner to be cornered up here in the mountains, about 2000 of us without a morsel of eatables, butter, beef and no salt at that and no possible way of escape. It takes the women down the worst and many have died through want of proper food. Some have made desperate attempts to escape and get over the mountains. If they have succeeded, they must have endured great hardships before they got over. Many have gone out into the lower mountains and killed venison to live on and those that are left here depend entirely upon the butchers who are driving in beef from the head of the valley (where they live on what they can browse).

And they are killing and cutting up beef night and day. There is a constant throng around the two stalls all day. They (the Butchers) are obliged to trust everyone, or it would be taken from them anyhow. But sometimes they get out of beef for a day and then we have to fast until they get more in. Or if we are in luck and can find a pig or sheep, we knock it over and eat it. As to myself, I have the ague all of the time since that night's ride from Marysville. And of this and starvation together, has made me look and feel rather ghostish.

Feeding On Air

One day we (there are seven of us) got up rather late and could get no beef for breakfast, it was all gone. So we fed on air that day. At night there had none arrived and we made a supper of the same. Next day the beef had not arrived and we went out on a hunt, seeking what we might devour. Bob found a pig and shot him and brought him up and we broiled and ate every last bit, at one meal. Hogs stand no-show now. All is made common stock, it is slay and eat wherever you can find anything eatable. Good many live on trout which begin to make their appearance in the creek and if it don't dry up before long, we shall have to top off on mules and dog meat. I have a good fat dog I have had my eye on for some time, if the worst comes to worse.

One hombre found a sack of barley a short time ago and we had a grand blowout on that. Ground it in a coffee mill and made it into cakes. To be sure the straw or chaff rather scratched a fellow's throat, but it was a great luxury as long as it lasted. But of all things we miss, salt is missed the most. I had no idea of its value before. If we had that we could do very well. But straight beef, a man can eat eternally of it and never satisfy his hunger. They say that the report has gone abroad that if a Packer should get over the mountains and get in here, they would take his flour from him and not pay for it but distribute it around. Therefore, they don't try to get further than Jacksonville. Well, I don't know how that would be, but I know that if they would not trust those that had not money, they would not starve but would take it by force. They have made the Butchers shell out, money or no money and I believe it to be right. I don't mean to starve, so long as there is anyone else that lives.

I wonder what some of our mighty fine young men at home would think of this kind of fare. If it was not for this blasted ague and fever I would not care so much. But that of itself is enough to kill a man, without the assistance of short commons. I am so all fired thin, don't make any shadow now worth speaking about. Kind of a misty, vaporizing shadow is all.

The Dying - February 1853

Well, I am alive yet and that's all thanks to the powers above. It has dried up at last and now, if it don't take a new hold again, we may eventually get something to eat. Many of the emigrants that arrived in the fall have died. It is hard getting use to live without eating, but in a few more weeks we could learn to do it I think, or die trying. We have the seriner reduced to a fraction now. Beef holds out well. I think the stock must find it rather tight grubbing as well as ourselves. Meat looks like blue lightning, taint as much grease in one as would oil a watch tallow, and sells at one dollar a pound. That and beef is all there is for sale now. No, there is some rot gut liquor yet at fifty cents a mouth full. I don't know who has got all the money, unless it is the Butcher, haven't seen a dollar in a month. I am flat broke. Lost $2000 dollars by this scrape and in debt at that. Can't be helped. Suppose some would say it was all for the best, but I can't look at it in that light. No how I can twist about.

I shall go home in the spring (in a Horn) I reckon. Have to break my promise this time sure. Seven eighths starved and the balance shaking with the ague. Fine prospect this glorious country, make five dollars a day and it costs ten to live. Making money fast? I wonder if all the fools have left the States yet, there is a good big swad of us out here.

Blue Flour Train - 2/28

At last, it has come. 50 mules laden with flour which has been soaking in sacks on the road all winter, arrived a few days since. It is all sold at $150 per hundred and as blue as indigo at that.

Unfit For Duty - March 1853

Well, it is useless to hold out any longer with this kind of luck. When flour got down to $50 a sack, I opened my house again and struggled on making a desperate effort to keep above water, but I had to sink. There is no money, everyone is broke. And after a little storm this month flour rose to one dollar a pound again and we had to cave, shut up shop, give up every cents worth we had to our creditors and left the concern flat broke. With upwards of $2000 worth of accounts which we probably never will get $500 for.

I am totally unfit for work, having the ague every few days. I tried mining but was forced to give up, could not stand it. Bob has left and here am I, flat broke, flat on my back, unable to work and all alone in a miserable shanty, brooding over my hard luck. Is this all for the best?

Broke, Sick & Alone - April 1853

Well, I will keep up my logbook until I get through with this world. Some folks nod and shake their heads and say poor fellow he is going in, but I never believe it, to be sure. I suppose I look miserable bad, but I don't believe the ague will be victorious. I think I shall worry through it yet. But it is horrible to be as sick as I am alone, not a cent of money, not bedclothes enough to keep me warm when the ague is on me. Not money to buy food after the fever has left me. To have no one to care for me when the crazy fit is upon me, for they say I rave like a madman when I have the fever. And I know that I am senseless and there I lay out in a shanty back of town all alone, by myself.

Note: Text is written in another hand at the bottom of this page, presumably by Daniel's sister Maria; "My poor brother why was you to suffer thus. God only knows and He is a just and wise God too."

I'm Cursed - May 1853

I do not know but I suppose it is all right, but I cannot see why I should be cursed in this manner. Oh my God, did I ever think that I should be reduced so low as this, by poverty and sickness. Give me health and I will ask favors of no man. But what can a sick man do in a strange land, amongst strangers. My pride will not allow me to beg, and I go hungry. I have been 30 and 40 hours at a time without a mouth full, my bowels fairly working and gnawing for food. I have been sat down by sacks of barley and chawed barley an hour at a stretch to appease my hunger. And laughing and talking all the time with the storekeeper, to prevent him from mistrusting how miserable I actually was.

No, I must keep it to myself if I starve, for I know that I have no means to pay and I will not give them an opportunity to give me alms. I cannot, will not beg.

Saved By An Englishman - June 1853

Being unable to work I was obliged to accept an offer from an Englishman, however much it cut across grain with my pride. Probably mistrusting my poverty-stricken situation, he offered me a living with him. On the condition that I should assist him when I felt able to about his house. He kept a bowling saloon and bar and cooked his own food.

It was all the chance I saw to stave off actual starvation and I went and lived with him. Sometimes cooking our meals, sometimes tending bar and making myself as useful as possible under the circumstances.

7/4 - I could not stand this sort of business any longer. And come what might, I was determined I would not fill this servile situation any longer and I left last night. Today I assisted all day and night at the Yreka House, out of friendship to the proprietor.

Rogue River Valley Indians

I have forgotten to mention that the Indians have broken out again in the Rogue River Valley and are now at war there. They have murdered many men, burned down farmhouses, destroyed farms and are 10 times worse than ever. The settlers have all their families moved into a blockhouse and they are formed into volunteer companies, mustered into US service for the time of the war. They have had several engagements with the Indians and thus far I think the Indians have had the best of it. Many have been killed on both sides, but I think there has been more Whites than Indians. This is a fine country for Indian fights and if they were a little smarter, they could do an immense amount of damage to the Whites and always keep themselves out of harm's way.

By retreating to the mountains where the Whites could not follow, at least could not follow as they usually travel with a large band of pack horses and riding animals. If after burning some ranch or murdering some poor Packer they are pursued by the mounted volunteers, they put out for the mountains. And they, being afoot, can travel over country where it would be impossible to follow with animals. And if the Whites pursue them on foot, they soon get out of provisions and have to turn back. Whereas the red skins can live on roots and pine bark for weeks at a time. Especially if they can occasionally kill a hare, gross, bear or deer. And then again, they have stowed away in the mountains dried salmon and venison and with those supplies, they are always prepared.

And as this whole country is naught but a continual strain of mountain peaks, ridges and deep canyons and ravines they, by keeping guard on the peaks around their camp, can always see an army full half a day before they could reach them. And are by this means always able to avoid an engagement if they choose and are like Paddy's flea. You can put your finger on where they ought to be, but when you get there the nest may still be warm, but the bird will be away. Probably right in sight on the next peak beyond, where they will insult their foes by daring them on to fight, always knowing themselves to be at a safe distance. And if they are followed, they disappear over the ridge and the next you know they are committing some depredations in your rear. Several times the companies have been divided when in the pursuit of some small band, in order to endeavor to cut off their retreat.

But it is useless, they know every pass, trail and cut off in the country. Sometimes these divided parties have been attacked by the Indians and in every instance have got the worst of the fight. Our Yreka company got caught in that way and lost every horse, blanket and five killed before they got clear of it. In fact, the devils have every advantage over the Whites in such a country. You never see an Indian in one of these fights, all you have to guide you is the direction the smoke of their rifles arises.

Ravaging Rogue River

If some of our good eastern friends could take a peek into this part of the world just now and see the roads strewn with dead mules, horses, oxen and broken wagons. And knew that each one of these was a putrefying monument or trace left by these red devils, to mark the spot where the most inhuman butcheries had been committed on the riders and drivers of these animals. Then look to the right and left, wherever you will as you travel through Rogue River Valley and naught meets the eye but the blackened remains of some Settler's log cabin home. This, probably the scene of some midnight butchery; the farms all going to ruin, fences are destroyed, grain fields burned up. And what families are left cooped up in a blockhouse where, owing to their crowded state, sickness has appeared amongst them.

And further if he could see the poor and widowed mother, weeping and groaning over the loss of her only son, her only stay. The wife and children mourning the loss of a husband and father killed by these red skins. I say if all of this, which is a daily sight here, could be seen by them in all of its horrors, we would not hear so much said about the poor red men of the forest. Lo the poor Indian.

Hiram Woods' Ranch - August 1853

Well, I have managed to keep above ground thus far, in spite of want, poverty and the ague. The major part of the time this month I have spent on a farm belonging to a friend of mine from Ohio, by the name of the Woods, Mr. Hiram Woods (I must record his name in full, for I do not want to ever forget it). His farm is about 3 miles from town on the Shasta Road. He thought, I suppose, that I must be tolerability hard up and asked me to come out and stay with him and live on vegetables a while to see if they would not benefit to me. Of a certainty I never use to go out there, but I felt better immediately. Whether it was a change of scene or grub, I don't know. But I use to get so tired of Yreka, that I have many times thought if I could only get away from this blasted town I would get better immediately.

Whilst out there, I enjoyed good health and it seemed to cheer me up and the only few happy hours I have seen in this miserable year (to me) have been at friend Woods' Ranch. May he never again know what it is to suffer by sickness away from friends. He has known the miseries of such a situation before this and knows how a poor devil feels. He is the son of a Farmer (well of in this world's goods) who lives somewhere in Ohio. Hiram, being of rather a romantic or adventurous cast, enlisted under Cassius Clay and went to fight the Mexicans in the last war, after many miner troubles and hardships. He, with his companions in arms, were taken prisoners by an overwhelming force of Mexicans and were sent to the city of Perote as prisoners of war. What he suffered on his foot march of over 1000 miles as a prisoner, we can hardly imagine.

But it was enough for me that the recollection of his own sufferings opened his heart to make him sympathize with others in somewhat similar circumstances. And his adventures served to pass away the time very pleasantly as he used to relate them evenings, as we lay out in the front of his cabin under the fine old forest trees, after his day's work was over. I have learned already that such adventures are much more pleasant to hear of whilst sitting around a comfortable fire at home, then to experience in actual life.

Shasta Indian Medicine

One night whilst out here, three squaws and a young buck about 16 years old came along over the mountain from Scott's Valley and encamped in front of the ranch for the night. One of the squaws was sick and looked very bad, she was about 20 I should judge. The others were one, an old hag of a thing, the other was the medicine squaw of the tribe. They are Shastas. I saw them doctoring her all night but with what success I don't know. They built a fire under one of the big pines and lay the sick squaw down near it on her blanket. Then taking one of the baskets off of one of their heads, they commenced heating some water and boiling roots in it by throwing into this hot stones.

These head coverings are made to fit the head like a skull cap and are woven so close they hold water and serve the double purpose of stew pan, camp kettle and bonnet. After the roots had simmered pretty well, the Medicine Woman, or Doctor as we would call her, took a mouthful and pressing her lips to the affected part, appeared to blow it into the flesh. As it were at any rate, after keeping her mouth glued to the spot for two or three minutes she would turn and get another mouth full and keep repeating this operation until we left. All the time the other two squaws were chanting or singing a sort of a song or hymn which, although not very musical to our ears, did sound very mournful as it echoed through the old forest.

They, keeping time with the music as it would swell and die away by constantly rocking their bodies to and fro and occasionally throwing up their hands, as though appealing to the Great Spirit to answer their prayer or chanting supplication, whatever it was. The young buck took no part in the business but sat scowling at us for intruding, I suppose. We finally left them and turned into our blankets and in the morning about an hour before daybreak I was awakened by the same mournful sound of (I don't know what to call it, whether singing or praying) I suppose it was intended for a sort of a prayer for the sick one. At any rate I don't know, as I never heard anything so touchingly mournful in my life as this sounded to me this morning. I lay and listened awhile and then got up and went out and sat down by them around their fire.

They paid no attention to me but continued on as before. And certainly, I would as soon have interrupted a funeral sermon as to have interrupted these wild savages at their devotions, or whatever they may be called. Here we sat until the sun rose. And the moment it made its appearance, the chant died away instantly. I ought to say that the sucking and blowing operation was going on all this time as the night before.

The White Wolves

The Shasta Indians have not taken any part (as a tribe at least) in the Indian wars this summer and they profess to be great friends to the Whites. And have several times gone out with the Whites to fight other tribes that were hostile. They live in this valley. This month though they were attacked by a party of Whites and most shamefully misused, in my humble opinion. And the worst of it is that in all probability some poor fellow will have to suffer for the cruelty of these White Wolves, that fight so well when there is no danger to their own precious scalps.

The circumstances of this case are as follows.

The Shastas have been encamped all summer on Shasta River, but finding that salmon (their principal dependence for winter's food) was scarce this year (owing to the fish dam below) they started out on a visit to the Scott's Valley Indians to help splice out their winter's stock. They went over and procured what fish they could and were returning, when I met the whole tribe in the woods about a mile above the ranch. I stopped and talked some five minutes with them in their jargon and finally told them that they had better not go through Yreka but keep right across the valley to their old camping ground. For I knew that all was excitement in town and the sight of a red skin was certain death with some. It appears they met others afterwards that advised them the same as myself and they followed it.

Upon getting over into the valley they saw Indian smoke on the Shasta Butte. And knowing of old what this meant (that it was the usual defiance thrown out to them by the Pit River Indians whenever they invaded their territory), they were anxious to learn from some white man what these Pit River Indians had done. Accordingly seeing a white man, they rode to overtake him. He became alarmed, thought a whole tribe of red skins were after his scalp and tore out for the nearest house and got in a short distance ahead. The farmer had two digger Indian boys that he had brought up from Sacramento Valley. And he made out to smuggle one of these off for Yreka, where he raised the alarm that his master's house was surrounded by Indians etc. There was a big crowd of the valiant numbskulls raised immediately and off they started in pursuit.

The Shastas meanwhile, after being so unsuccessful in their pursuit of knowledge, had drawn off at a distance from the house and were consulting about what they were to do under the circumstances. When they spied the digger boy on his road for town, they put after him to find out what the devil was to pay. But the digger had the best horse, and they didn't overtake him. Things begun to look rather squally with them now and they didn't know how to solve all this. So, they sent a buck up onto the hill in the front of town to see what was going on in Yreka. He saw the valiant band of heroes start and knew enough of the Whites by this time, to know they were after blood. And from the course they were steering, saw that they were out for them.

He gave the alarm and they fled up the valley, but being hampered with the women, children and their dried salmon, they could not reach the mountains before the heroes were close at their heels. They dove into a swampy bank of willows and by this means managed to escape with little loss, to live to pay the Whites off in their own coin some future day. There was but one Indian shot and what do you suppose it was? A young woman that could talk English tolerably well, was sent out of the brush by her friends to ask the Whites what they were after them for. And she, in order to show them that they had no cause to fear, stripped off the upper part of her dress to show them she was a female. But she had no sooner made her appearance outside of the willows then she was shot in the breast.

And this, not being glory enough for one man to bear, he the brave fellow, caught her by the hair and took her scalp. His name ought to be immortalized, it was William Hathaway of Missouri, that state of brave fellows. Immediately as she was shot, one of the Whites toppled over, with an ounce ball through his lungs. And this ended the battle. The result of all this, thus far, is that we are in a fine mess right at home now. And in all probability, many a man will bite the dust for this. Ever since then, signal fires have been seen all around us on the peaks of the mountains. Kindled by the Indians to inform other tribes at a distance that they have at last taking up the hatchet of war against the Whites. Having always assisted the Whites against other surrounding warlike tribes, this small band is now, by no willing act of theirs, placed in a rather uncomfortable situation, and all through their former friendship for the Whites.

This summer a band of Modoc Indians visited Yreka and upon their leaving town were followed by the Shastas and badly whipped. And their horses taken from them. The Whites made the Shastas give up the horses again to the Modoc. But singular to relate, every horse died that night.

Modoc Indians

These Modocs are a hostile tribe that live out on the emigrant road and are the ones that murdered so many emigrants last fall, and the ones that the Shastas helped the Whites to whip. It is singular what a difference there is between the Indians above and below Trinity Mountains. All below are digger Indians. Flat nose, short thick set, with heads of hair 2 inches thick, sprouting out about an inch above the eyes. All above are a superior class altogether, being light made, tall, athletic, nobly built men with light complexions. Thin heads of hair and a smart intelligent looking countenance, far superior to any other Indians I have ever seen.

'Attack' On Woods' Ranch

In the latter part of this month, I was out at Woods' Ranch, which now is ready for an attack which is expected every night. For no man can consider himself as safe anywhere out of town. One night we were terribly alarmed in the night by what we were ready to swear were Indians. The house is made of light split boards and of course would offer about as much protection from a rifle ball as so much cloth. This night we were all awakened by something outdoors charging along the road at a terrible rate. They come down through the pines and right for the house, where they appeared to halt under cover of the heavy timber.

Woods whispers us to gather our arms and lay down on the ground, for if they fired at the house, they would not hit us there. Accordingly, we lay low, whilst Woods was trying to find out the position of the enemy through a knot hole. "By heavens the woods are full of them," says he, "now boys keep quiet and don't one of you stir until I give you the word and lay low." He need not have told me. For you can bet there was not much of my body above ground. And here we lay I don't know how long and occasionally we could hear the enemy stirring about carefully outside. "It's all fired curious the blasted varmint didn't make a move," says Woods. "I reckon they'll wait till about daybreak," says Bob. Blast this eternal country, where a man has to sleep with one eye open for Indians.

I'd a right smart chance rather be in Holt's Bottom fighting gallinippers as big as a four-year-old, than to be tucked up in this style by a dad-rotted lot of bloodsucking, red skinned devils. I say, "Woods they have got one of the yearlings haven't they, didn't you hear it bloat?" Here we were took all aback by Woods bursting out into a horse laugh. And finally when he got his breath, exclaiming "well we are a pretty set of dod blasted fools to lay here skeered half out of what few wits we have, by a darned lot of calves." And sure enough, it was a herd of young stock that belonged to the ranch that had got startled by something in the woods and had ran to the house, and there stopped under the big pines.

2-Cent Diggin's - September 1853

As the weather begins to become cooler, it reminds me that I must find some place where I can lay my head. I cannot live this hand-to-mouth style in the winter, however I might do in the summer. It seems rather hard that I should be obliged to go without the actual necessities of life, when I have over $1500 owing me in this town. And by men, every one of them able to pay me what they owe me. But if they don't feel disposed to pay, it is useless trying to make them. Knowing my situation and that, sick or well, I must find diggings somewhere or starve, I started out prospecting and was gone a month out in the ravines and mountains, myself and another. By ourselves packing from 50 to 75 pounds on our backs over the hills, mountains and gulches, expecting to run into a nest of Indians every day and for my part not caring much if I did.

For I begin to think it don't make much difference whether I waste away by want of proper food and at regular intervals and the ague, or am knocked down by a rifle ball from some red skin's gun. After trying every place that there was any probability of finding the blasted ore and many places that there was no probability of ever getting water, we returned to Yreka again without finding, put it all together, two cents.

3/4 Froze In Yreka

So, you see it is not all gold here, but occasionally a little soil and rocks. Well, where to go to when we get back, we didn't know. We must find someplace to spread our miserable bed, for the nights are bitter cold this time of the year. We finally got permission to sleep in a deserted butcher shop and here I passed five or six of the most uncomfortable nights I ever experienced. We had but three single blankets between us and there was no chance to build a fire. And here we lay three quarter froze, praying for daylight when people would get up and open their shops. This was fine for the ague. Shake all day with the ague and all night with the cold, but this was only part.

I am writing this now from recollection. As at the time you may depend, I had plenty to do to find wherewith to fill my stomach, without bothering my head with my journal. But now I got food sufficient to keep body and soul in partnership at this time. I could not say I got a meal here, another there, a piece of pie at one place, a few sardines at another, sometimes one meal a day, sometimes two and sometimes two days to one meal. Finally, the butcher shop was rented and we moved to a pine log back of town. And we were foolish we didn't do it sooner. For here we had a rousing fire all night at one end of the log and we lay down by it. Being careful to put it out in the morning to save it for the next night.

We next get the use of a cabin for a short time and short enough it was. For we moved our three blankets in the morning and then each one started out for a hunt for grub. And at night when we returned, there was a family of emigrants in it. We all occupied it in common that night. Our tribe consisted of an old grass widow, a very hypocritical Methodist, her two daughters, one of about 18 the other 14, her son about 16 and two boys about 18 and ourselves. All in one room. The next day I resolved that kill or cure, live or die, I would live this ground hog life no more.

Mule Train To Crescent City - October 1853

It was about the last of this month that I got permission to go out with an acquaintance who owned a pack train on a trip to Crescent City, where he was a going after a load of goods. This Crescent City is nearly west of here on the coast, a place settled this spring. Accordingly, I mounted a pack saddle on the bell mare (the lead animal of a train) and with rope, stirrups and rope bridal and a big cow bell around the mare's neck, I rolled out of Yreka. Glad to get away from a place where, within a few months, I had suffered so much. This place being far beyond wagon navigation, except by way of Oregon, all goods are brought up on mule's backs by pack trains. These mules carry from 250 to as high as sometimes 400 pounds on their backs.

Their loads, being divided into two side packs and a top pack, are lashed onto a pack saddle or aparaho and girted on as tight as two strong men can draw the girt. And then the pack is constantly getting loose and has to be drawn tighter every few miles. They always have a bell horse or mare who goes ahead and the others follow after without driving, sometimes 200 mules in a train. Again at night they are turned loose to graze the road and a good train of mules never stray from the bell mare, but are always found near her in the morning. We had 30 animals in our train and myself, John McGill, the owner of part of the train, Charles Edes, Boss Packer George Clay and Francisco, a Mexican Packer.

The first day we traveled across Shasta Valley, crossed the Klamath River and encamped for the night opposite Cottonwood on the Klamath. It rained all night and this morning as I endeavored to build a fire, I found it was somewhat difficult to make it burn. But I finally succeeded in getting bread, beef and tea cooked and sat down to breakfast just at sunrise. We are up by the time day first begins to break in the east. And whilst I build a fire and get breakfast, the balance hunt up the mules and drive them up to camp, where they arrange themselves along as close as they can stand in a line in front of the packs.

There they are haltered and made fast by knotting the halters through, from one to the other. Making a continual string so that no one mule can start without the whole band starting. We there sit down around the fry pan and dip in, for plates, knives and forks are unknown amongst Packers. After this the animals are saddled, the grub basket and cooking utensils are lashed on and off we start for another day's tramp, for Packers don't get but two meals a day. Today has been a fine pleasant day. And following the road of Cottonwood Creek, we crossed a few rolling hills and finally about 3 o'clock were on the summit of the Siskiyou Mountains, the present boundary line between California and Oregon.

Descending on the other side through a damp, dark forest of firs, arborvitaes and pines we, after many twists and turns, reached the valley of a tributary of Rogue River. Called by some Bear Creek, by others Golden Valley. Where we encamped for the night on the banks of the creek, under some magnificent balm of gilead trees. After a hearty supper of bread, beef and tea we can lay down for a good night's rest.

Waggoner's Ranch - 10/27

This morning we were up by break of day and I busied myself in getting breakfast whilst the balance were out hunting up the mules. The mules were not all found until nearly noon, about this time we got started. And passing down the valley, we encamped at night about 10 miles from Jacksonville and near Waggoner's Ranch, where the settlers of this valley fortified themselves the past season against the Indians. We passed several burnt cabins today, the scene of some of the past season's fighting. The farmers are just returning to their farms and are harvesting what remains of their crops. After supper I went across the valley to a farmhouse to get a bowl of bread and milk and was very much interested by the lady's account of her trial during the past season.

Jacksonville, Oregon - 10/28

This is the prettiest valley I ever saw. It is nearly all taken up by settlers and looks more like the old country than any place I have ever seen. We reached Jacksonville about noon and stopped about an hour to make some few purchases for the trip, such as beef, as we will be unable to procure them after leaving here. This is the County seat and is a right smart chance of a town for Oregon. There are very good mines in this vicinity and are paying very well, when they can get water. Leaving the town we kept up a gulch to its head and crossing a low mountain to Applegate Creek we encamped for the night. We are now in that part of the country where the war was carried on the fiercest. And there is any amount of burned houses on every side of us.

Ambush Swamp - 10/29

We kept down Applegate Creek today until afternoon, when we crossed a steep mountain and encamped in Illinois River Valley near the ruins of Mooney's Ranch. As usual today our road was lined with ruins of cabins, barns and fences half burned. Applegate Creek runs through a deep ravine, the mountains rising some 1500 feet on each side and heavily wooded with pine and fir. They afford an excellent retreat for the red skins. We have passed through one place where the trail, about 4 feet wide, had been cut through a dense swamp of balsam trees for about a mile. Here was a great place for Indians last summer and well it might be. For it might have been full of them and the traveler never could have seen one until it was too late.

Smith's River Mountain - 10/30

Crossing Illinois River we kept on up the valley, crossing several small streams and at night encamped at the foot of the Long or Smith's River Mountain near Gates' Ranch. This valley is not a very interesting looking place, as far as I have seen. But very little arable land and no mines, although Althouse, Rough and Ready and Sailor Diggings are near here, but not on the road. It is very cold tonight and as we sleep on the ground in the open air, we are obliged to build large fires to keep warm. But we have plenty of blankets under the packs and with 10 or 12 of these for a bed, we sleep very comfortable. This at home would be considered a poor way of trying to cure a fever, but I have not felt so well in the past year as I now do.

Cold Springs House - 10/31

This morning I had to pull right hard to get out from under my heap of saddle blankets and mats, as they were frozen down to the ground. The place was a little muddy when I made my bed last night and during the night it froze quite hard. This morning we made an early start to enable us to get over the mountain before night, as there is no feed until you reach Smith's River on the other side. After riding over a rough country for four miles, we crossed a little creek and began to ascend the mountain. The trail is about 4 feet wide and winds around in a zigzag course up a barren, rocky ridge to the summit. About 11 o'clock we reached the top and winding around the ridge the road soon brought us to the first mountain house, which was built in a swag or little sink.

Stopping to get a taste of Mountain Dew and to light our pipes, we started on again to overtake the train. For a band of mules never stop until night when once they are started. We soon caught up and from the peak where we were, we could see our road for 12 miles before us. This road follows a ridge of mountains (or backbone as they call it here) which runs in a half circle. Keeping to the road we shortly came to Elk Camp, the halfway house where we left our feed for the return trip. This is the only comfortable looking place on today's road and is about halfway in the circle of the mountain. And is in a measure protected from the cold winds by a grove of pines and by the position of the mountains on each side.

After leaving here we came to the Cold Springs House. A miserable shanty and in a miserable bleak place, surrounded by a forest of dead pines. From here we could look back 12 miles and as far as you can see it was one continual string of mules. We soon began to descend and about an hour after dark we crossed Smith's River and encamped.

Mule Road To Hardscrabble Creek - 11/3

This morning we took our time as we were near the end of the journey and did not get started until about 10 o'clock. Many of the trains got in ahead of us and we put out after them. Crossing Smith's River again, we rode down about a mile where we had to take to the side of the mountain. The road here is cut in a zigzag course up the side of a very steep mountain and it, to a person unaccustomed to California mule roads, would look dangerous. The trains ahead of us are almost over our heads at times as they wind around up the steep and crooked road. And a misstep would tumble them down upon us.

I don't know much about angles and could not say whether the face of the mountain had a pitch of 45° or not. But it was as steep as any gothic roof ever made. And as the road was only about 4 feet wide, if a mule had made a false step to one side he could never have stopped until he had reached the bottom, about 1000 feet below. The train immediately ahead of us was driven by two men, about 20 animals. And as one rode ahead and the other behind, they were strung out for about a quarter of a mile. About midway there was a gray mule that would occasionally stop, of course this stopped all travel behind her. The owner who was just ahead of me hallooed, cursed and endeavored to hit her by throwing stones, but it was useless. She was out of reach high above us, almost over our heads, looking down upon us.

Finding that he could not get at her, he drew his pistol in his rage and shot at her. The ball must have come very near her, for she shook her head and started on and did not bother us anymore. About 3/4 way up we came across a footman, clinging to a tree on the side of the trail. He asked us if there were many more coming, we told him there were about 200 more to come yet. He gives a groan and swore he had been hanging there then about half an hour, to let the trains pass. But he had to hang an hour or longer before the trail would be open for him to go down.

We finally got over this mountain to Hardscrabble Creek (rightly named), where we were obliged to wait for the up trains to get down from the mountain before us, which is worse than the one we just crossed. We could see the trains way up the mountain, coming down with their loads of goods for the mines. And about noon they had all got down, leaving the trail clear for us to begin the ascent. We hurried on and after a toilsome tramp of about an hour we gained the summit and had a fine view of the Pacific before us. The dull heavy boom of the surf sounded rather singular to me, as I had not heard it for some time and the view from this place was splendid. Before us lay the great ocean and Crescent City. All around were lofty mountains and far away below us lay Smith's River. So far below, that we could scarcely hear its roar of waters as it dashed on over its rapid rocky bed.

Unbelievable Redwoods

We again descended by an easier road and soon reached the river again, which we swam. And landing on the southern bank again, we followed the road into a swamp of redwood trees and here I must attempt to describe the sight which lay before me. These redwoods, or firs of the arborvitae species, were all of mammoth proportions. There were trees from 15 to 30 feet in diameter and from 150 to upwards of 300 feet in height. Many of them have been burned out in the center by fires. And it can scarcely be credited by those who have never seen this forest, but it is an absolute fact that I rode into the heart of a tree on my mule and turned him around inside of the tree and rode out again. And the tree was all alive and thick with foliage.

One we measured and it was 22 feet inside where it had been burned out and it was also alive and growing. Most of the trees are free of limbs for 100 feet or more. The ground is covered with fallen trees and, it being impossible to get a road through them or to move them, it winds around them. And when the foremost mules had to go around a fallen tree, those behind could not see the riders on the other side. In some instances, seed has fallen and lodged in the bark of a fallen tree, taking root there. And the trees have grown from these seeds 2 and 3 feet through the roots running down both sides of the old trunk into the ground and there they are growing, perched up 15 feet in the air.

But it is useless attempting to describe this forest, it must be seen before a person can begin to believe it. I saw a man at Crescent City who had recently returned from the States, who said that his friends at home believed all the gold stories that they had ever heard. But when he told them of some of the wonders to be seen in this forest, they sat him down at once as one of the biggest liars out and never would believe anything he said afterwards. "And boys," says he, "whatever you do when you get home, never open your heads about these redwoods." Well, well I don't blame them much if when they hear that there are trees big enough out here that out of one tree, if you could work it up, you could build a two-story frame house, or fence in a quarter section of land with a seven-rail fence. If they don't believe it, one cannot be much surprised.

But for all that, it's a fact. Friend Clark told me of an Indian retrial that he found near this ranch (near this forest). There is one of these trees that have been burned out in the heart and has falling with the burned part down. The Indians have dug the earth from under it as it lays and have made a depot for provisions in it, in case of war. There is but one entrance through the roots, just big enough for a person to pass-through on his hands and knees. But after you once get in, there is a room or cave inside of the tree from 12 to 15 feet in height, about 12 feet wide and 50 feet in length. Quite a spacious hall and big enough to secret a whole tribe of red skins.

Crescent City

After leaving this forest we came out into Crescent Valley and riding down the valley about 12 miles we reached the city just before dark and encamped on the beach below the town. We found this to be a miserable harbor, having no protection against gales or heavy seas. Two brigs lay ashore here now. One a perfect wreck, the other they are trying to get off again. Crescent City was settled by Yreka speculators last fall and it is a small town as yet and I think always will be. The houses are built facing the beach, all in a line, just above the high-water mark. All back of the town is swampland. There are about 60 houses I should judge, all good frame houses and fitted up in very good style.

But it is such a miserable apology for a harbor, that I don't believe the town will ever be much larger. It depends upon the mines for its support. But Yreka will not trade here much, in my opinion, if they ever succeed in getting a wagon road from there to Sacramento Valley, as they now talk of. Sailor Diggings, Althouse, Applegate, Klamath River and Jacksonville may trade here, as they are much nearer. We have to stop here for several days to get our load, as the rush from the traders in the mines has drained them all here and we wait for a new supply by the next steamer from Francisco.

Back To The Mines - 11/7

The steamer having arrived we got our load ready and this morning started out on our return for the mines. It has rained for several days past and I expect we will find it a hard road to travel. This morning it cleared up and about noon we got underway. But by the time we got started it commenced a drizzly rain and owing to the muddy state of the roads, we got along very slowly. Our mules were constantly miring and the loads had to be taken off and repacked time and again. After dusk had fairly set in, we encamped about halfway up the valley and about 6 miles from the town. It was no easy job to start a fire out in the rain, with wet wood, but we finally succeeded and after getting our supper of beef and bread, made preparations for the night's rest.

11/8 - We made a sort of a shanty with our blankets to protect us from the rain and made out very comfortably for the night. This morning it rains quite hard and the boss says it is too wet to travel today and would be liable to damage the freight, which is principally clothing. We lay here all day, working hard to keep comfortable in our blanket shed. By keeping up a rousing fire in front we made out to keep warm, although wet to the skin. This is a very pretty valley, and I should judge it to be excellent soil for farming purposes. It is protected from the sea gales by a dense redwood swamp on the west and on the north and east by the low mountains, covered with large pines. Here I found (in the valley) a species of the crab apple, plum and cherry trees in their wild state and the many excellent berries, some of which I had never seen before.

Redwood Swamp - 11/9

This morning we found to be as rainy as the day before and consequently we layover today. The mules were drove up, counted and after breakfast turned loose again to graze. Two hunters came into camp this forenoon, to get us to assist them in bringing an elk they had shot up to the road. Two of us saddled a mule and put off into the swamp with them and soon found the carcass and packed it out of the swamp, receiving a quarter of it for our trouble. This swamp was like the one on Smith's River, full of the mammoth redwood trees. Even the weeds and bunches of swamp tuft grass grew to immense height and length here. The bogs, or bunches of bug grass, were 4 and 5 feet high and weeds - common swamp weeds - 10 and 12 feet in height. The trees a hundred feet without a limb and so thick overhead that the sun's rays never penetrate through them.

Fording The Mule Train

11/10 - This morning it being clear weather we struck our blanket shed, packed up and started on for another day's tramp. The roads are muddy from the effects of the recent rains and before we had gone many miles we found that they were growing no better very fast. We tramped along up the valley a few miles when we took over a little hill and commenced to descend on the other side into the swamp on Smith's River. Here the soil is clayey and the hill being quite steep, our mules slipped badly. Sometimes in making a short turn in the crooked zigzag road, they would come down with such force that they were unable to turn. And away they would go end over end down the hill, until they fetched up against a log and there they would lay until released.

Sometimes three or four would slide off, all in a heap. I saw some of them slide down a declivity in this way 20 or 30 feet and never lift a hoof. How the deuce they stand so much knocking about I can't see. Well we finally reached the river after a slippery fashion. Just as you come upon the river there is a steep bank to come down and four of the mules slid down at this. And not being quick enough to take the short crook in the road, they keeled over and rolled to the bottom. Whilst the men were setting them on their pins, I was ordered to ford the river and gain the opposite side and encamp. Obeying orders, I urged my pony in. The bell mare and balance of the train following on. About midway in the stream, we struck the current. I saw it was too deep to ford, and that the animals could not stem it, but it was too late to turn back.

In vain I urged my pony to breast it, but downstream he would go and soon we were swimming. My horse struggled hard and I plunged off of him and struck out for the bank to endeavor to head the mules upstream. For by this time, they were all in deep water. I ran to a point below and caught the first one by the head gear and held it up against the bank. By this time the whole train were floundering about in the channel, drifting downstream. Sometimes their heads, and then their heels, above water. I thought the whole pack were going to the devil, sure. But by my stopping the head one as I did, the balance made an effort and drifted, kicked and swam until they reached the bank above us. All strung along, clawing to raise themselves out of the water but the bank was too steep.

The men finally swam across and unpacked them where they were, in the water. One mule however was unable to make the point and the last I saw of her she went by over the rapids, her heels up and head under. We expected she was gone, sure enough. And after we had got the balance of them out onto the bank, we were surprised to hear a mule braying below us. We looked below and about a quarter of a mile below on a high rocky bank stood our lost mule, minus the load, braying loud enough to assure us she was worth many a dead mule yet. I waded and swam down to her and when I arrived there, found in an eddy a 10-gallon keg of brandy, part of her load which had probably got knocked loose when she went over the rapids and let her come right side up again.

Taking a wide circuit, I finally reached camp with her before dark. Of course, we were as wet as men generally get to be and we built a rousing fire. And it commencing to rain again, we made a shanty by the fire and soon were quite comfortable again. We have damaged many a dollar's worth of goods by this day's work and all to save paying ferry-age, but it's no business of mine. I nearly ruined sister Eliza's miniature by this scrape, it was in my breast pocket.

Clark Ranch - 11/12

We have been laying up here the past two days, endeavoring to dry our load again. But it's rather uphill work, as it has rained most of the time. I have not been dry since we left Crescent City. Some would say this was not a good treatment to cure a man of a fever of 17 months standing, but I feel better than ever under this cold-water treatment. I found an old acquaintance living near here on a ranch, Dan Clark formerly of Pawtucket I mean. He has selected a clear spot of about 100 acres of the river below here and has a crop of barley sewn. He has a very pretty but lonely spot, it being bounded on one side by the river and on all others by the big tree forest or swamp.

It is perfectly safe from stray cattle and all the fence he has is a set of bars from one big tree to another, on the opposite side of his road to the ferry. The balance, being enclosed by the swamp, needs no fence. Here Dan lives as happily as a Lord, has his pet mule, dog, cat, a few hens and a cow. His ground will raise 10 times as much as he needs. When he wants meat he can, by going out an hour into the forest, kill a bear, elk or dear anytime. If he wants fish, what better fish swims than he can catch at any time in Smith's River? Whoever saw any better fish then the salmon, salmon trout or speckled trout, with which this river abounds? Then if he wants fowl, down on the lagoon nearby he can get as many duck, geese and brant as he can pack. If he wants money to spend, he goes and kills a load of game, saddles his mule, packs it to town and sells it. In fact, he says he is suited to a dot. Don't care a continental darn whether the 10-hour system is adopted or not, no bell calls him to work now.

Slippery Hardscrabble Mountain - 11/13

This morning it being fair, we packed up and started again on our road. But not being able to get a very early start, we only reached the bench on the top of Hardscrabble Mountain about 4 miles and in plain sight of the bar below, where we started in the morning. The road up this mountain was very slippery and steep and our mules were constantly slipping off the road, rolling down the mountain until fetching up against a stop. There they would lay and flounce about until they were set up again. We had so much of this kind of work to do that we were unable to get further than the bench above mentioned, where are we encamped for the night. Two other trains were in camp here waiting for morning to go down, as it is impossible for two trains to pass one another on the road down. All down trains group in the afternoon, up trains in the morning.

11/14 - We got an early start this morning and by 10 o'clock we started down the mountain. This is certainly the worst mountain I ever saw a road on. It is as near perpendicular as mountains generally get to be. Almost beneath your feet, 1500 feet below lies the river. The road is cut out of the side of the mountain, just wide enough for a mule with load to pass. And a false step to the one side would send it crashing to the bottom 1500 feet below. And the only way to cut a road was in a zigzag course, like the shape of the Z. In making the angles of the road a mule has to be cautious, or away he goes over the sides.

And when a person is below, it don't look pleasant to look up almost overhead and see the mules far away up above him, picking their way along. By noon we arrived at the bottom and found several trains waiting for the road to clear so they could begin to climb up. At night we encamped again on Smith's River, near the forks.

Bar Fight

Today it rains and we are to lay here for the day. Last night George Clay and the Mexican got drunk and we had an awful time of it for a while. We three had made a shanty of pack blankets and slept together. They have been rather mutinous for some time past and last night they tapped one of the kegs of whiskey and got drunk. Soon after we lay down Clay begun to talk Spanish to the Mexican, trying to lead him into a rupture with the Boss Packer. They soon get to quarreling and Clay struck the greaser. Out flew a knife in an instant and had I not laid between them; Clay would have never seen another day. But as it was, he sprung up and run out and Frank after him with his knife, they chased one another all over the bar. But we finally got them separated and shifted bedfellows and got through the night without a murder. Misfortune gives us strange bedfellows sometimes in this glorious country.

11/16 - Last night we were awakened by the water running over us and jumping up found that the lower part of the bar, where we were, was all covered with water, the river (owing to the rains) having risen this high. We were all up and commenced moving the goods to a higher part of the bar. And after about two hours hard work, we had them secure again and we took possession of a deserted cabin at the upper end of the bar for a while. Here we passed the remainder of the night very comfortably. In hunting the mules this morning we found that two were missing and the men have been hunting all day unsuccessfully for them.

It continues to pour down rain as hard as ever and we are obliged to stop here until it lights up, and no one can tell when that may be.

Big Bar on Smith's River - 11/29

Here we are as yet and here have we been since the 15th and it has rained every day since. We are very comfortable here in the old cabin but are getting mighty tired of the fried bacon. We tried to hunt but could not find a thing to kill, the elk and deer have disappeared. The river has risen so high that the ferry boat above us has been washed off and now we have to remain here until they can fit up a canoe to ferry ourselves and goods across. This will be ready in a day or two and then, if it ever lights up raining, we shall push ahead. There are several trains stopping here with us, all weather bound. This sort of life is worse than mining. I have been wet through every day since we left the town and I am expecting to see blue mold appear all over me soon, if I don't get a peep at the sun. And then the living fried rusty bacon and bread for breakfast, and again bread and bacon for supper.

Here Comes The Sun - 11/30

Hurrah for us, here is the sun at last. We packed up and left Big Bar this morning and after a hard day's work we reached the ferry and got our freight across by dark. Traveled about 2 miles today. All is hurry and bustle here, for as I said before, the large ferry has gone downstream and all of the travel has to cross in a dugout canoe. We packed our freight on a high bank, covered it and then took supper at the ferry house. Ye powers, what have I made in the eatables this night? Talk of Codfish.

Well, I didn't use to ever be fond of this in Yankeedom, but I made it suffer this night. We stopped in the house this night and for once on this trip I slept warm and comfortable, if my bed was a pine plank. The house is full of travelers bound for the mines and of course it was lively enough.

Camp Foot Rock - 12/4

It has rained every day since we arrived at the ferry, and of course this put a stop to our travel. We have had plenty of company at the house and the time passed off very pleasantly. This morning as it has cleared up, we packed the mules and rolled out on our journey. We soon began to climb the Smith's River Mountain. And after a weary, toilsome day's work, night overtook us on a bench or rather a ridge of the mountain, near the summit. We were obliged to stop for the night where we were. After a fruitless search for water, we went supperless to bed on the side of the mountain. For in addition to our other troubles, our mule with the grub and cooking utensils has got lost and left behind.

Frank has returned to hunt it up but did not get back until after midnight. After we had turned in for a sleep, a Dutchman stopped at our camp and wanted to stop with us for the night. We let him do so, but we emptied his wallet of provisions for him, before he got to sleep. This is a great place for an encampment, not a spear of grass for our mules nor a drink of water, not a place level enough to make your bed on, without being in danger of rolling to the foot of the canyon on either side of the ridge before morning. Had to build a big pile of rock and lay with your feet embraced against them to keep from sliding downhill in your sleep.

Packers generally start from the ferry in the morning and reach Elk Camp the first night, where they feed their mules and the next day go down the mountain on the other side to Gates' Ranch in Illinois Valley. But our worn-out train could not do it, as they have been in government service in the Rogue River war all summer and are now not fit to pack. Two are left behind tonight and they will have to lay out with their packs of 250-pound weight on all night. Mules had not ought to be driven after dark. For if they are, they are most sure to skulk out, hide and lay down by the road. And of course, it does not improve them much to lay all night with their load lashed to them. After all, I believe packing mules over these mountains is just the hardest, most aggravating, dirty and meanest trade I know of.

Packers are proverbially lousy and 'as lousy as a Packer' is a common expression. But previous to this trip I never knew how many of these interesting little insects a man could carry about with him and live through it. But I know to a fraction now. And when I get over the regular allowance (40 to the square inch of shirt) I haul off shirt and hold it over the fire, until I reduce the quantity to the right number and then go on again and increase.

Elk Camp House - 12/5

This morning we were up by daybreak and after hunting the mules up, we found two were missing. We tracked them up the road apiece and I was sent out ahead to overtake them and bring them back. Saddling my pony, I started off in pursuit. About 10 o'clock I overtook them and started back, overtook (or rather) met the train at the Cold Springs House. We worried along as fast as possible over the rocky ridges, but night again overtook us at least 4 miles from the next landing place. But on we must go. And by dint of constant hallooing, beating and pushing, we arrived at the Elk Camp House about 10 o'clock on as dark a night as I ever saw. Two mules were lost and left behind, somewhere since dark and the Mexican is also missing. It being so wet and cold up here, the boss concluded to stop in the house tonight. And after making the mules fast, we turned in for the night undercover.

Gates' Ranch - 12/6

This morning the Mexican, Frank, arrived in camp, half froze and as black as a Negro. He got lost after dark, could not find his way in and was obliged to crawl into a hollow burned-out log, to protect himself from the severe storm. The other two mules were found this morning. And in spite of the severe rain and snowstorm we were obliged to travel, for there is no feed for animals up here. We traveled along quite briskly today, as the mules appeared as anxious to leave this cold place as we were. And after a long day's tramp we reached the creek at the foot of the mountain at dark. But here was no feed and we pushed on through the rain, sometimes traveling for a half a mile at a time in water knee deep and pitch dark, endeavoring to urge on the weary mules by halloos and about 10 o'clock we saw a light ahead. We soon after reached Gates' Ranch where, after securing the cargo and turning the mules loose, we partook of an excellent supper and turned in to sleep.

12/7 - We took possession of an old log house today to camp in and as it bids fair to be a warm day, have concluded to lay by and dry our cargo as much as possible, as the clothing begins to look rather moldy. There is no doubt that the owners of the train will have to pay a pretty good bill of damages as many of the goods are badly injured by water. After noon we have been busy all day unpacking and spreading out our goods to dry. The whole of the dry goods are badly damaged. The flour is wet and everything but the liquors are about ruined. $500 will not pay the damage done. This will not be a very profitable trip to the owners, but this is no fish of mine. And I believe the hard fare and constant soaking I have had for the past month and better, has cured me of the ague. So, I am well satisfied.

12/8 - This morning we packed up and started on again. A Jew asked for permission to join us today as he was afraid to go through alone on account of the Indians. We, of course, were willing he should, and we jogged along down the valley together. We found all of the creeks very high and at night when we encamped near Illinois River, we were as usual wet through about waist high. But we have got well used to this by this time and to have dry feet of a night would be a rarity. At dark we encamped under a grove of pines on the river and we soon had a rousing campfire and prepared our supper of bacon and beans. Whilst I cooked supper, one of the band erected a blanket hut and we soon had the grub stowed away and turned in to our blanket bed, tired enough to sleep sound until morning comes again.

Deer Creek - 12/9

This morning is very foggy, but we were up by daybreak and we soon had the mules up and breakfast prepared. After breakfast had been eaten and I had stowed the grub and cooking fixings into the Cook's basket, ready for packing, I assisted McGill to catch his pony, a half wild Cayuse horse and a fine time we had of it. Chasing him over hill and dale, through tickets of chaparral, over rocks and ravines until about 10 o'clock before we got him corralled. We then started off and soon reached the ford on the river. It was quite high, but we made out to get over without accident. And keeping on down the valley to Mooney Ranch, we turned to the left from the old trail and struck out up a ravine and crossing a low ridge came onto Deer Creek.

We are obliged to go a different road back from the one we took down, owing to Applegate Creek being too high to ford and there is no ferry. As we came onto Deer Creek we had to go through a thick swampy grove of underbrush on its bank. And as this is out of the way of travelers and in the heart of the (later hostile) Indian country, I was on the lookout for red skins all the time. I rode on, and as I entered the swamp I had my suspicions there were Indians about, by seeing a fire by the roadside. I went on however and following the old trail I soon reached the ford and plunged in but found it too deep to ford. As I turned back, there were six big buck Indians, all armed, standing on the bank. They were friendly however and led me higher up the stream where there was a good crossing.

I crossed and encamped on the other side in a grove of oaks. We built a big fire, got supper and just at dark the Indians left us and returned to the swamp close by. These are the devils that murdered so many Whites this summer. And I did not feel exactly as safe as I might be having to camp so near them, no house within 20 miles and no telling how many of them there are in the swamp.

The Hornets' Nest - 12/10

I believe the Jew was awake all night through fear of the red skins. For as I got up at break of day, there he sat by the fire with his pistol in his lap. We were all anxious to get away from this hornets' nest and made an early start and crossed several hills and valleys before we struck Slate Creek. During the day we passed several deserted farms; the house burned down, fences the same and crops going to ruin. Each one the scene of a hellish murder by these same red devils we camped near last night. At present there is not a house in this country between the Rogue River and Illinois River. All the farms are deserted and the country is given up to the Indians again.

We help ourselves to a lot of turnips and potatoes at one of the deserted ranches. Keeping down Slate Creek to its mouth, we came on to Applegate and soon after dark we encamped on its banks. After much trouble we succeeded in getting a fire started in the rain, and tired and wet we turned in under our shed of blankets.

Our Indian Chief - 12/11

This morning we were aroused by an awful hallooing and yelling of Indians on the opposite side of the creek. And two of us went down to the side of the creek to see what it was all about, as well as we could for the fog. But the moment we made our appearance it was all hushed up in a moment and we heard no more from them. As we were eating breakfast, the Chief and his squaw came riding into camp and sat down by the fire and had a long chat with me, whilst the men were packing the animals. He said he had had a "hias close warwar" or peace talk with the

Boston, or white captain, and he had come down to keep us company through his country, to see that no bad Indians troubled us whilst within his territory. He said he could not control all of his young men; some would do bad in spite of him. And in fact, he talked and looked like a smart intelligent man.

About 10 o'clock we got underway and started down the creek and soon came to Rogue River. Our Chief showed us the ford and we crossed over. The Chief bid us goodbye here and said we were now out of his grounds and consequently must look out for ourselves, as whatever happened to us from this on, he was not to blame for. We told him we intended to always be able to defend ourselves and moved on up Rogue River and encamped opposite a ferry house. Whilst on Applegate this morning we passed the first Indian burial place I have ever seen in this country.

The graves were covered with little white quartz stone and freshwater clam and snails' shells at the heads of the grave. A large basket was stuck bottom up on a stake and the whole was enclosed in a square of large white boulders, arranged along in lines, so as to form a square. The digger Indians burn their dead and bury the ashes, some hang the ashes up in trees in the baskets, close woven for the purpose. But these northern Indians are a far superior race of beings to the lower California Indian. They are more intelligent looking and much larger.

Table Rock Mountain - 12/13

Layed too yesterday as it rained and busied ourselves by killing off our surplus livestock in the shape of peaches. This morning we started on again and keeping up the river valley for most of the day stopped at night, about 8 miles below Jacksonville. Our road today has been lined with ruined farms, burnt houses and barns, the fruits of last summer's war. Table Mountain, the scene of so many Indian fights, is close by here. It is a singular looking mountain, being perfectly level on top and on three sides it presents a perpendicular wall of rock. This has always been a favorite resort of the Indians in time of war. During the last summer's war, they were in the habit of sending out the youngsters from their camp near here to burn the farmhouses.

Whilst the Whites were in pursuit of these incendiaries, the Warriors would put out in an opposite direction and commit some depredation. It was in the range of mountains back of Table Rock where a party from Captain Goodell's Yreka Volunteers were surprised and four men killed. They were out on a scout, about a dozen of them, when at noon as they were encamped in a little open glade in the forest they were surrounded and fired upon. They retreated to the timber, fighting their way through until they got to cover, where they kept up a fight from behind the trees until assistance came. As the balance of the scouts came up the Indians retreated, carrying off all of the horses and blankets of the company.

I expect the Whites were not very anxious to follow them with their small force, as they got off with their plunder. This war has ruined many of the farmers here and has discouraged many a one from settling here.

Jacksonville - 12/14

We reached Jacksonville about 11 o'clock. Passed through and encamped a little after noon about 3 miles beyond, in an oak grove near the road. After unpacking our mules and fixing up our camp, all but one of us returned to the town to procure beef and to get a straight meal, as they say here. Or in other words, to get a good dinner at some public house. For I began to feel that I would like a change from bacon and beans, our principal food for the past two months nearly. After a good hearty dinner, we took a stroll about this one-horse town until night when we returned to camp. Jacksonville is like all other mining towns, built of split boards and canvas. And the principal part of the business being gambling, rum shops, eating houses and a few clothing stores. I found it to be a dull place to me.

12/15 - This morning as usual we were up before day and the men were out in search of the mules. After a while they returned with a part of them, but the others could not be found. We lay here until nearly night before we found the others, when the boss swore we should pack up if we didn't get over a mile before dark. Accordingly, the mules were packed and about sundown we got started on the road and made about 4 miles before we encamped. It was plumb dark before we halted and we encamped for the night on a ridge, or rather a low grassy mound by the side of the road, without water and but very little wood. However, after about two hours work, we got our supper and turned in to our blankets and passed a very disagreeable night. As from the position of the camp, the cold night wind had a fair rake at us.

Worse Than A Dog's Life

12/16 - After a long search in the fog, we found our animals and packed up. We worked our way along through the mud up the valley and at night encamped by the side of a little rivulet in an oak grove. And although the night was tolerably cold, we fared much better than we did last night when exposed to the cold, bleak night's air on the summit of the grass mound.

12/17 - This morning we rolled out on our road and crossed the Siskiyou and camped in a little valley just over the summit. Whilst on the mountain we were in snow about a foot deep and in an hour, we were in a grassy little valley at its foot. A party of US Dragoons are encamped near us, on their way to Rogue River where they have established a fort called Fort Lane.

12/18 - We reached the Klamath about sundown, were ferried across and camped near the river. As we begin to near Yreka, I cannot help asking myself what am I to do when I get in? I have recovered my health, but I have no place to rest my head. I have no money to buy me food but shall have to trust to chance to provide both. And as Madam Fortune has eternally scowled upon me here before, I have not much faith in her pursuing any different course toward me for the time to come. Hang this sort of a life, it is worse than a dog's. Aye, many a time have I envied them their lot. I am willing to work as hard as I can and will do anything I can to get out of the accursed land of disappointment and misery. I have had enough of gold seeking, hard knocks, no pay and all I will ask for now is enough to carry me home in decent shape.

No Show Yreka - 12/19

Having got an early start this morning, we passed through Shasta River Valley and reached Yreka at dark, having been out on the trip nearly 2 months. After unloading our animals, I went with the balance of the Packers and took possession of an old cabin back of town, where we stopped for the night. Yreka is the same old hole as ever, no work to be had, no show as far as I can see for a poor man. Although it has rained all the time we were on the road, there has been none here of any consequence, there is not enough to enable men to work to any advantage in the mines. I believe this land is too high to have much rain and it will be very seldom that they will have a wet winter here. Tomorrow I must sally out in search of work of some kind, as I cannot live here long without it.

Long Gulch - December 25, 1853

Last night I moved down to Long Gulch, about 2 miles below town. And in company with two others took possession of a cabin there, intending to find a place to mine. Two of us started a ground sluice in a bank of Yreka Creek near here, the other went to work on a claim in the gulch. By putting a revolver that I had given me at Crescent City up at poker, I made a raise of $60. Which furnished me with provisions for a start. And if my sluice pays, I will be alright again. A ground sluice is a ditch about a foot wide, with a fall of about 4 inches to the foot. Into this the water is turned and then the dirt is thrown in. By loosening it up with a fork about twice a day and throwing out the stone, the dirt washes off and leaves the gold on the bottom. At the end of the week, they are washed down and the bottom cleaned up with a cradle.

Unhappy New Year - January 1, 1854

Another year is past and gone, and I am poorer than ever. This is encouraging. To work like a slave, live like a hog, deprived of every comfort known to civilized beings. To suffer from hunger, to shiver with the cold, to be exposed to all sorts of weather, to run a constant eternal race between want and misery. To be exposed to death every day of your life, either through Indians, robbers or from being crushed to death in the mines. And after all, to be worse off every year in every sense of the word. I am not working for a fortune now, but for enough to sustain life and possibly I may get enough to carry me back again to the civilized world.

If I could do this, I would be satisfied. For it is all folly to ever expect to make anything more than this. 9/10 of the people here would return home tomorrow if they could get there. A man with money to come here and settle for 10 years at least, can make money here yet. But for a man to come out expecting to make a fortune mining is all folly, there is about one in 5000 that make a raise of a thousand or fifteen hundred dollars. And the balance of them never have over a hundred or two dollars. If people at home only could learn from the experience of others, there would not be such a rush out here every spring. The chances are worse than any lottery that I ever heard of.

The Mines Owe Us $39

The weather here is not very favorable for miners, it is dry all summer and not much better thus far this winter. And at present, the thermometer is below zero. This is not very comfortable weather to live in tents or split board house. The ground is froze so hard, it cannot be washed and consequently all mining operations are suspended until it thaws again.

1/5 - We washed up our sleeves today and wonderful to relate, took an ounce from it. Yes, one whole ounce of gold dust. Well let's see, now as this is a fair specimen of thousands of days' work in this fortune making country, how it has paid us on an average. Two of us credit by five days hard work and our food for that time, although nothing but beef and bread with coffee, has cost us a dollar apiece at least, that is $10 for grub. We had to hire water to wash with, at the rate of $3 per day, which makes $15. Our work ought to be worth at least $3 a day which makes $30, and we received for all $16.

So, you see the mines owed us $39 to square accounts on this job. And to call our work nothing, our actual expenses for water and food was $9 more than we received. And this is the way we make money in this country.

Brass Bed

1/10 - Well after this sluicing job was over, I did not feel like pitching in again right of at any rate. And as I have one pair of blankets, I have not been very comfortable in this miserable cabin, with the thermometer below zero. I rolled out of this therefore and went back to town to stop, until it gets to be decent weather again. One consolation we have is that our severe winter weather seldom lasts over a fortnight, or three weeks. Arrived at town I went to a boarding house and boarded there as though I was made of money. And I had not a cent to bless myself with. But who is going to freeze to death when a little brass will ensure him a warm bed? Not I, if I can help myself.

Dirty Long John

1/20 - As it has moderated a little, I returned to the Gulch today and went to work on a claim in the bed of the gulch. But as usual, I could not make over four bits a day by hard work. This would nearly support myself, but not quite, but I could see no other show to better my condition and kept on. I do not like the men I am at work with and as soon as I can, shall leave them. At present I have no other alternative than to keep in with them. They are a couple of yellow breeched Missourians and think a great deal more of themselves than anyone else appears to, but this is perfectly natural for birds of this specie. The only bump on their whole head is that of self-conceit. One has already got the name of Dirty Long John, owing to his slovenly appearance.

My Long Gulch Claim - 1/22

We bought a claim today in the gulch that has paid very well this summer past. And I am of the opinion that it will continue to pay tolerably well for some time to come, if we can get water to wash with. It has paid over $6000 this summer to its old workers, if it will give me one sixth as much, I will be willing to leave it and go home. We bought it on time to pay when we took it out, as we had no money. My old friend McGill wants to get into a claim, and I think I can manage to get the others out and get him in their place. If I can, I shall do it sure. There is but very little water in the gulch at present and if it does not rain before long, we shall have to dry up mining soon. I am sick and tired of mining but there is no other show to get along now, it is with me. To use a Western phrase, root pig or die…work or starve.

And when I think that I am ruining my health and wasting away my time in the prime of life out here in this infernal country, I am mad with myself to think what a fool I have been to bring myself to this straight. There is no society, no amusements nothing but hard work, coarse fare and miserable grub at exorbitant prices. A miner is better off than a Packer, but his life is a most miserable one.

A Miner's Life

At daybreak he crawls from his nest of blankets on the ground, builds a fire, fries his beef, boils his coffee and gets breakfast by sunrise. He then starts out, pipe in mouth, to work in the mud and water until noon. When he goes to his cabin, cooks his dinner of beef, bread and coffee, lights his pipe and puts out again to work. At night he returns to his miserable shanty, wet to the skin, half dead with fatigue and as hungry as a wolf. But he has several things to do yet, his day's work is not finished. But arming himself with his axe, he starts out for his night's wood. Cuts it down and packs it to his cabin, builds a fire, goes after his bucket of water and when this is all done, he then can commence getting his supper. He mixes his dough and sets the bread to baking for tomorrow's and tonight's use, this will cook in about a half hour.

Meanwhile he fries his beef, makes his coffee, which he has ground by pounding in a bag, for want of a mill. And after all this he sets down, sick and weary, half-famished, to devour his meal. About an hour after dark, supper finished, he lights his old pipe and can sit smoking in a fit of doldrums at home all evening, or try to stave off all his miseries by spending the evening at town in the gambling halls or rum shops. And he need not go far to find one or both, for they are very conveniently close by in the mines. Here all is noise and confusion. Drunken men quarreling, others bucking their hard-earned money at some of the gambling banks. Others playing poker, seven up euchre or some other game for money, liquors or pies. And the sameness of the night's work is occasionally broken by someone being shot or stabbed in a quarrel and drunken fit of anger. This is a miner's life.

You in the east that are so anxious to reach this country would not be so very anxious if you could but realize the predations and hardships attending one here. And not only this, but 9 out of 10 just making a living and no more. Many say now; "oh if I had only been here in "49, I would have been alright." Yes, yes but I say as it is now, so was it then. Many a one did not make over expenses.

1/24 - Today we commenced work on our new claim. McGill bought in and we got rid of our Long John partner. Most of the time today we were fitting up our cloth house, as I have lived a hog's life with my old partners as long as I'd like to. Mac and myself live together alone. The other one lives in the old cabin with John as they two agree very well, birds of a feather mate together is an old saying that applies very well to them. The weather still holds dry as ever, no sign of rain. I'm rather inclined to think that the gateway gave out last winter and let down two- or three-years allowance at once.

Waterless Claims - February 1854

Mac and myself are at work in the claim having got rid of the other scally bird about a week after we commenced work. The ground has not paid us at all so far, but we live and work on in hopes of it improving soon. No rain as yet and times are very dull in town on this account. There are but few that are able to work. In this gulch we have about one sluice head of water, or rather mud, as it runs through about 50 Toms before it reaches us. And if it does not rain soon, even this small allowance must fail us soon.

A miner's life is so much one thing, day after day, that I can find but little interest in keeping up my journal. All days are alike to him. It's work, work, work, day after day, six days in the week and on the seventh, wash clothes and patch them. Or go to town for your week's provisions, get your picks sharpened and then back again to work another week and so on, as long as you continue to mine.

An Eternal Fool

And then what a business it is to give a man the blue devils, especially evenings after a hard day's work and no pay. Whilst at work during the day one has enough to think of to keep his work going ahead. But in the evenings after supper when the pipe is lit, we have no amusements to pass away the time. And to sit moping over the embers is a mighty fine way of conjuring up these indigo-colored imps. Then it is, when a man's thoughts wander back over life's track and dwells upon other places, other forms, far away at home. He contrasts his present manner of living with that at home, he thinks of his friends far away, opens his old letters from these friends and peruses them, again and again. Longs to see his good old parents, his brothers and sisters and can but think, what an eternal fool he was to leave such a home, such true friends, to come to this fortune hunting country for the sake of the few dollars he may get by wearing out his constitution in the often times fruitless search of it.

"A contented mind is better than riches," writes my father. And I say he is a fortunate man that can be contented. It is not all that can enjoy the blessings of a contented mind, riches or not. And I don't believe I could be contented anywhere long at a time. I was not at home, where I had every comfort. And I am just as positive I am not here, where I have none. But let the world wag on as it may, I shall always try to keep on top and never go under - until I can hold no longer. So mote it be, say I.

All Work And No Pay - March 1854

Another month has rolled around, another full moon has made its appearance and lastly another big strip has been taken on our claim and 'halo chick erman' or in other words no pay for it, good again. For me, I am doing a right smart chance of business in making enough to get food. And of course, I am very thankful to be enabled to do that, as much as some might turn up their noses at it. To be sure we have to work harder, live 10 times worse and address a d__d__d (well there I came that near swearing, but I take it all back). What I meant to say was, we fare and dress and work harder than any set of Paddys ever did on any railroad or canal. But what of all that? We are gold miners, it's worth something to be able to look after the precious stuff.

The Innards Win - April 1854

Just as I told you, haint made nary red cent ahead of grub yet. Tight race between my hands and innards to see which would come out ahead and old innards won it by some considerable amount. What a pity that this devouring, eating institution called the abdominal parts, could not be dispensed with. It's a mighty costly one in this one-horse country, where coarse grub costs so much. If some ingenious Yankee could only invent some way of living independent of it, I would take out a patent right immediately and make my eternal fortune in a little less than no time at all. At the present rate I am anxious to know how long it will take for a man to make a fortune, it's a problem that is a little ahead of me. I can't solve it to my satisfaction, although tolerably good at figures.

Job Never Mined For Gold

This is one glorious country surely. Hurrah for golden California, long may she wave. Everyone can make their fortunes here, if they only live long enough. And if there is anyone who doubts it, let him come and try it for himself. Now here am I, have not tried over five years and have nearly made as much as would keep me in this short time and no one knows how rich I may be at the end of the year 1900, if I only persevere and don't use myself up in that time. Nothing like perseverance, all the newspapers say that. Only have patience, you are bound to strike it. Be Job like. But between you and me, old father Job never mined for gold.

"If he had, he must have gin in talk about him," says a Missourian. "What did he know about patience? He never drove an ox team across the plains."

Now this who-haw navigator had a heap of horse sense, was a pert youth, right smart chance of a feller and all this, but he never had mined a poor claim as yet. He thought driving the horned horses across the plains was some on patience, but he knew more about the virtues of it after he had got to mining, I will venture to say. Now I have given myself credit for being a pretty persevering sort of a chap as a general thing, but this kind of work rather tries even my patience at times, as persevering as I am. And if old Madam Fortune don't look more favorably upon me before long and drive off that ugly misshapen daughter of hers, Miss Fortune, I shall be obliged to lose my good opinion of myself and cast aside all acquaintance with patience, take to the blue devils for companionship, as poor society as they are to a miserable old batch of a miner and come out at last a confirmed old growl. Ye fates and graces forbid it. Selah.

Unworthy Claims - May 1854

Well, here is another month passed by and no richer today than I was a month ago. Most assuredly our claim is not worth working, but it is as good as any hereabouts, for as near as I can figure it up there is not more than one in a hundred making over expenses. Our water has mostly gone and soon we shall have to quit work again and lay off six or eight months until it rains again, sometime next winter. Already it begins to be very warm and in about a month from now it will be about 120 degrees. Very pretty sort of weather to work picking and shoveling. Talk of railroad Paddys, they are nowhere.

Old Channels Pay - June 1854

This month we struck a lead, or old channel, running through our claim. Which pays very well and has somewhat encouraged us to hold on to the claim. As it is now, the water is nearly gone and we shall not be able to do much at it until next winter. Meanwhile we have a drain and tail race to cut, which will take a long time to finish and we shall not commence upon that until it gets a little cooler weather. At present it is very hot, dry weather. Too bad for any white man to work out in it, but us poor devils have to stand it. Whether we like it or not is immaterial to our old task master, Bad Luck. It is no pleasant job to keep up a journal and nothing to note down but my constant bad luck in mining. It is a dull life at the best. But when it don't pay, it is superlatively dull.

The Glorious Fourth - July 1854

Yreka begins to recover from the effects of the fire that (I forgot to mention) swept over it last month. And now they are laying the foundation for solid brick blocks, instead of the old split board houses that were destroyed by the fire. The glorious fourth was celebrated here by everyone drinking just as much whiskey as they saw fit, at two bits a glass. And by an oration delivered by some big-head, I don't know who, by a great deal of drunken shouting and a few free fights.

In fact, there was no attempt made to get up a regular fourth celebration. But all the miners knocked off work and went to town to see what they could find there to amuse them. The day passed off without any more than the usual amount of drunkenness and fighting, and by dark most of the miners had returned to their homes. More than ever disgusted with the country where, even on the great day of the nation, they found it to be impossible to amuse themselves any other way than by making brutes of themselves and swilling down poisoned liquors.

Yreka's Aristocrats

Some of the chosen few got up a ball and supper as usual at night, but of course the dirty miners were not expected to attend. For strange as it may appear, they have even here, an aristocratic set. Composed of the lawyers, physicians, merchants and loafing community in general. These few have nothing but their good clothes, for which they are in debt a little money and a right smart chance of assurance and self-conceit, set themselves up for a superior class of beings. And as far as their knowledge extends, endeavor to ape the higher circles in our large cities of the Atlantic states. Having never associated with this class at home and having gained what little knowledge they have of the manners and ways of nabobs from novels and such like sources, they make themselves perfectly ridiculous by trying to assume these French airs.

But if the men appear ridiculous, what can I say of the women? Why the ass in the lion's skin was wisdom itself, compared to these web-footed, round-shouldered, ill found and was favored, homely, backward, diffident, ignorant gawky-looking women. Why as for my part, I think the native squaws are better looking. Aye more intelligent looking and certainly better formed and much more graceful in their carriage and general demeanor. And for all their homeliness (in every sense of the word) they assume all the airs of a court belle. And you may judge how well it sets upon them. These things are what compose the society of Yreka City Siskiyou County, the would-be capital of a new state.

I've never had much of a chance by acquaintance to find out of what material this aristocracy was composed of in the east, but I know enough to see what asses these muggings are making of themselves here. Well, these Western Lords and Ladies look down upon a miner as to one far beneath them in the scale of society and I need not say there is many a miner that returns this feeling of contempt tenfold. I do not think it anything to brag of, but still, to show that there are men in the mines that have an idea above a shovel and pick, I would say that on this gulch there is one Polish Count and two German Barons. Besides many an American sovereign that in all probability have seen at home nearly as good society as these frontier women that are here and who cannot imagine that there is any city can outshine this dog's hole Yreka. It is the biggest they ever saw, and they cannot believe in any one surpassing it.

Jack Barker Was From Holt's Bottom

I was somewhat amused at the remarks of a long gander-shanked Missouri boy by the name of Jack Barker. He came to this country last fall, followed an ox team across the plains and was from Platte County, Holt's Bottom. We were talking about the army and Jack asked if there was going to be another war. Yes, says I, Uncle Sam has declared war against Missouri. "What fur," says Jack. Oh, something about the Iowa boundary. "Well," says Jack, "I know one thing, if the troops ever go for to take Holt's Bottom, they are gone in. For you just bet there is a heap of men in that thar bottom and Uncle Sam never could begin to take that place.

And if he did, what in thunder would he do when he got to Jefferson? Why that thar place is darned near as big as Yreka and he naught as well try to whip this ar town as to take that. For they are right peert shot and you bet there's a smart chance on em." This was enough, and we all sided in with Jack that Uncle Sam was bound to get the derndest thrashing out if he ventured into Holt's Bottom. Jack knew about as much of how the world was made as an emigrant that came in last fall. He had been emigrating all his life, had spent most of his time running after an ox team. After his arrival here he heard for the first time of Australia and he found also that it was still to the westward of this country. This was enough for him and after he had a talk with the old woman about keeping on, he hitched up and rode out with his ox team for Australia, going the land route.

But woe to him, he reached the Pacific in about three weeks and there was obliged to stop, for he could neither ford nor swim this stream.

Rebuilding Yreka - August 1854

This month I have lived at Yreka, as the water has entirely dried-up on Long Gulch. At first, I tried cooking and went to work at a French restaurant, but this did not suit me. And I quit it after four days trial and went out to McBeth's Ranch and stopped a few days with him. Then came into town and clerked it for about 3 weeks, whilst his old clerk was absent on business out of town. After the old clerk's return, I had nothing more to do and was obliged to lay idle. Yreka is quite lively at the present, owing to there being so much building being done. All the burnt district is being rapidly rebuilt and with strong fireproof brick houses in place of the old shells that were destroyed.

Gulch Claim Business - September 1854

I have bought my old partners interest (on time) and sold two thirds to Messers Potter and Tifft at an advance of $200. We set in this latter part of the month to drain the claim and I expect we have a big job before us. There has been quite a rush of Pawtucket men up here this past month or two. I think they will all get disappointed in their expectations of making their piles this winter. I can just tell them it is no fool of a job to make a sufficient to board one's self sometimes in this land of golden. And if they don't find out the secret of men being poor here before the winter is out and they are through, I will give up prospecting for the future. Let them try mining a while and see if there is not something besides gold to be found here.

Diggin' The Gulch - October 1854

We have been at work all of this month on our raceway and drain, it is a slow job and a hard one. When completed it will be about 150 feet long, two wide and from 10 to 23 feet deep, cut through the bedrock from 1 to 4 feet the whole distance. The weather thus far has been very dry but very little rain has fallen thus far, and the water has not made its appearance in the gulch as yet. All are making preparations to wash as soon as it does appear. Times are quite lively in town as there is a host of prospectors (men in search for diggings) arrived here from below and from Oregon. If we have a wet winter, all will be well. But if it does not pour down rain in abundance, of course we cannot wash and business will be 10 times worse than ever. Everything in this country depends upon the state of the weather.

Still No Water - November 1854

Another of the winter, or wet months, has passed by and still no sign of water. By this time the businessmen as well as the miners are watching the signs in the heavens very closely for symptoms of rain. But thus far all have been disappointed, no rain has fell, no water has made its appearance and many of the traveling miners have already left for other parts lower down in the world, where rain clouds occasionally make their appearance. And bless the hard-working miner with plenty of water to wash his dirt. We are still at work on our race and have commenced a large strip for washing, if we ever get water enough. I would like, if it were possible, to get out money enough to take me home next spring and if we could get to wash all winter, I have no doubt I could do it. I am very well satisfied I could.

What A Charming Life - December 1854

No rain as yet, but frost enough to freeze up all creation. Everything is covered an inch deep with frost, it looks as though it had been snowing. It is pretty cold weather to work out in, but we still keep at it, stripping off top dirt. Our race is finished and we are all ready to wash if we had water, but that we cannot get. I believe it grows colder up here every year. The thermometer runs as low as 10 and 12 degrees below zero most every night now and we are up at all times of the night throwing wood to the fire, to keep from freezing. I have taken possession of the hearth and stretch out right by the fire and then it is just as much as I can do to keep comfortable then. Oh, this is a charming life to lead, very romantic and all that. But I have worn all of the romance out of me, long ago, by the rough knocks received here.

A Long Gulch New Year - January 1855

I wish all friends a much happier new year than I expect to find. It has commenced well. For last night (New Year's Eve) I walked the hills and trails all night, being unable to either sit down or lay down on account of a severe pain in the kidneys, with which I have been troubled more or less all winter. It commenced snowing about 12 o'clock last night and this morning it is about 2 feet deep. If this should go off by rain, we shall have plenty of water. But if it acts as it did last winter and melts gradually by the sun, it will do us no good.

Everyone is in good spirits now, in anticipation of having plenty of water. I hope it may be so. But I have lost very near all hope of having any such luck now. The merchants have taken advantage of this little storm to run provisions up to almost famine prices again. Flour is $25 a hundred.

Don't Make It Worse - 1/31

The snow has almost all disappeared and no rain, and but very little water. We have managed to wash a little but have not water sufficient to work to advantage. Potter and Tifft have got discouraged and want to leave here. I shall hang on and see it out now, if I don't make a farthing. And it is no use to do otherwise, for I cannot go home and I never will leave here now to hunt up other mines. It is very discouraging to be thus eternally hedged off by such bad luck, but it is no use to give in and fret one's self to death on this account. If I could better my condition by leaving I would do so, but I cannot see how it is to be done and I am afraid to stir, for fear of making a bad matter worse.

No More Townsmen - February 1855

At last I am alone again, having bought my partners out and they have left. Well joy go with them for I am not sorry that they have left, and I can do better with any other man than a town's man. They think they have a perfect right to ride a countryman rough shod. But I gave them to understand that as for myself, I stood on my own bottom and asked no favors from anyone and was responsible to no one but myself for my actions. If there was ought about me they did not like, to them I would say I asked not for your company and wished it not but it was forced upon me. And they could leave as readily as they came.

As to Mr. Potter, he is a gentleman. But the other is a low-lived backbiting, slandering, snake in the grass and no-good friend to anyone but himself.

Yreka's Weather

I have not been able to wash much thus far and of course have but little money. It has not rained any to speak of thus far and I don't think it will this winter. The weather has been moderated and now we are having pleasant spring weather, the sun shines out warm and everything indicates that our short but severe winter has passed away. Well, well if we are to have no rain, I am glad of it, for I do dread cold weather. The heat I can stand, but these cold frosty days and nights kill me for all work. I am of no account in cold weather, that is sure. Our winters here are very short, seldom lasting over a month of right cold weather and often not over weeks.

All the balance of the year it is pleasant and warm weather. True, in the summer months it is pretty hot, sometimes as high as 120 and over, but still take it all in all, I believe I'd like it much better than the climate in the east, where the winters are nearly 5 months of right cold weather. Bah, it makes me shiver to think of it and I dread trying it again.

Rockin' The Gulch - March 1855

Having looked in vain for sufficient water to sluice wash my claim, I commenced washing my big cut by rocker power today. It is now warm and as pleasant as it generally is in May at home. I wish we could have some of those old-fashioned rainstorms that we used to have way down east in the spring of the year out here now. How many thousands of dollars would they be worth here, but it can't be so. There is something out of order with the watering pot up here, all the holes stopped up somehow. Or else it got drained in the spring of 53 and it never has filled up since. Don't know which, but I'm sure something is out of kilter. We shall all have to go back to the "49 method of washing and keep the Chinese company, with their cradles and buckets for carrying dust to the water. If the water will not come to us, we must go to the water I suppose.

Chinaman Game

The Chinese are flocking in here pretty fast, having been driven from the mines below by the tax gatherers. There is a great deal of prejudice against them throughout the country and I cannot see why it is. For they are a peaceable, industrious set of harmless beings, but I expect it is just that account that they alone are singled out for persecution. Why not tax the John Bulls, the French crabeaus, the Spanish greasers and in fact all other foreigners as well as these poor devils? Why? Just because other foreigners would not submit to it, and for no other reason in the world John Chinaman is game for all the villains in the state.

From John Bigler down to Joaquin, and they all rob him alike. Bigler robs him by a legal tax and all the balance of the villains by an illegal one, whenever they catch him with money. And the beauty of the thing is that he can never appear in a court to testify against a man that has robbed him. So that all they have to do is to be sure no white man is a witness of the robbery and they are sure of getting off without trouble. A pretty equality this and one that I cannot see the justness of, through the effects of my Yankee education, I presume. These Chinese must have strange ideas of a republican government. When the government, after robbing them of six dollars a month as long as they live here, turns them over to the tender mercies of all the villains in the state, to plunder them still further.

And they are not allowed to testify against the villain who thus goes Scott-free. And then if, after running this gauntlet between the Whites, they escaped the Indians, who are all down on them, they are in big luck. It is singular what a hatred every Indian in the country has towards them.

What Are They?

I was on the top of Scott's Mountain one day about a year ago when the first band of Chinese that had ever been up here came along on their way to these mines. Packing their tools, clothing and provisions on bamboo poles across their shoulders and strung out along the road down the mountain for half a mile. Before they hove in sight, I had sat down on a fallen tree by the roadside talking to a small band of Indian squaws and children, who had stopped to rest here. We were busy jabbering on in their jargon when the Chinese drove in sight, toiling on up the mountain. The squaws noticed them in a minute and began to scowl upon them a look of intense scorn and hatred.

They passed on up the road when the squaws looked at me and asked who, or what, they were. "Wake Boston, wake siwash?" Says they. That is, they are neither white men nor Indians, what are they? I told them they were Indians from a long way off. "Wake, wake siwash," says they and they would not have it, that they were Indians and finally asked me if they were friends of the Whites. I told them they were, but I could see that it would not be very safe for the Chinese to fall into their clutches.

Strippin' The Gulch - April 1855

Have been all of the latter part of this month stripping off the top dirt from another big cut. From the 26th of March to the 15th of this month I washed out of my first cut, $391. But a good part of this had to go towards paying up back debts contracted during the winter. Thus, it goes, making money fast at times - but spending it always. Of course, all hope of rain this season is passed and now we have a long spell of dry weather ahead, seven months at least, before we can expect any more rain. Seven months to come, scarcely a cloud to be seen, day after day a clear hot and dry burning sky and not a drop of rain. The little water there was in the gulch is fast disappearing. But we have enough spring water on the bedrock to wash with rockers all summer long. And I think I shall drift, or tunnel underground, this summer and wash enough with a rocker to support myself, if nothing better can be done.

The Yreka Ditch - May 1855

The water has entirely dried-up, and I have to wait a week or two now for the bank to dry sufficiently to enable me to tunnel under it. I have washed out about $150 this month and my expenses have nearly eaten it up. So that as the winter's work is about over now, I can see how I stand on this job. As usual I have not made anything. If I could have had water to work with, I should have done tolerably well. But there it is. There was no water. The merchants, despairing of ever seeing any more rain up here, are making every effort to bring in water from the Shasta River. If they succeed in this, it will make Yreka a brisk business place for years to come.

If they do not succeed in doing it, they might as well close-up shop and leave here whilst they can. For as it is now, they can never hope to do anything whilst they depend solely upon the rainstorms. For two years past there has not been one good storm and it is all chance whether it ever rains here again enough to fill the ravines and gulches, so that men can work their claims to any advantage. This depending entirely upon the heavens for support of such a town as this, is leaning upon rather a slender staff. And they begin to find it out now, as they look over their books and see long accounts of two years of standing against miners who have good claims but who cannot work them, for want of water.

This ditch is a large undertaking for a little town like Yreka, being over 80 miles in length by the course the ditch would have to take. They contemplate cutting it 4 feet deep, 4 feet wide at the bottom and six at the top. To cut such a ditch 80 miles where wages are $3 a day and board, is a going to take some money, sure.

Get A Mess - June 1855

Loafing again this month, water has dried up and the bank is too wet to drift. By traveling from here to town and back and occasionally hunting for quails and hares on the mountains back of the house, I have managed to pass away the time. The quail are very plenty here this summer and I can have a mess of them anytime by going out an hour or two in the morning. Sometimes I take my gun and start for the river about 2 miles from here after a mess of wild duck. If neither duck nor quail hungry, I try for a mess of rabbit which are very plenty here. But hunting over these mountains is a great deal like hard work and I had rather work all day any time.

The Nation's Sabbath - July 4, 1855

I have commenced drifting the first of this month. This morning we must all lay aside our implements of labor to keep sacred the Nation's Sabbath. The Sons of Temperance celebrated the day here by a procession and big dinner of course. An oration is to be delivered and an address to the Sons. I went up to Yreka about 9 o'clock and I found the streets were tolerably full of miners from the surrounding mines, all bent up on seeing all these sports the day would afford up here in the mountains. As a substitute for a cannon, the blacksmiths had contrived to make two anvils produce the desired amount of noise, by filling up one of the holes in one of them with powder and then putting the other anvil over it, they would touch it off. This would make a very loud report and answered its purpose very well.

Soon after I arrived in town a party of men in masks, dressed in costume, made their appearance in the streets. Mounted and in line of procession, they call themselves The Earthquakes and are a sort of an offset to the Sons of Temperance. These last being the Sons of Bacchus. The captain is mounted on a knock-kneed mule and amongst his followers are Scotts in short breeches and plaids, Yankees in nankeen pants and bell-crowned hats and many costumes that it would trouble a theatrical costumer to tell what nation they belonged to. And at the tail end rides the Pope of Rome. A very good idea, and in the right place.

This is rather a burlesque on the Temperance procession, but this is a free country and I suppose the Sons of Bacchus have just as much right to celebrate the day as the Sons of Temperance. All passed off very pleasantly, both societies had their parade and dinner and at night there was no more drunkenness than there would have been in an eastern town of this size. Not as much I think, although most every other house has a liquor bar. At night there was the usual ball party and to accommodate friend Brown of the Lafayette House, I assisted him about his supper table at night. I worked all night for him as the supper did not come off until about 10 o'clock.

How any young man can enjoy himself much at such parties as they get up here, gets me. All of the women are married and most of them 30 or 40 years old, with young ones old enough to take their place in the ballroom. But it is Hobson's choice here, take this or none. I went to bed about daybreak just as well satisfied as though I had spent $10 instead of making that amount, as I did.

Driftin' The Gulch - August 1855

I have been at work drifting for the past two months, windlassing up the dirt onto the surface to wash as soon we can get water to wash it. We wash the bedrock with a rocker in the tunnel and have washed out about $300 of it. And if the dirt only pays as well as all think it will, I am all right for a trip to the east next spring. Tunneling in such a wet bank as this is very expensive, as every foot of it has to be timbered and floored overhead. Besides, as it caves badly, I have to pay big wages to get anyone to work in it. Sometimes it will cave in a cart load at a time and it is no pleasant job to be at work 30 feet underground and have it caving in on you, nearly burying you up at times. But what will men not do for money? And especially in this country do men get perfectly reckless, after so many years of disappointment.

Beware, The Poor Indian - September 1855

Still at work drifting and with the usual success, small pay. The Indians have broken out again in Oregon and this time it bids fair to be a general war throughout the whole territory. A short time since, they attacked a party of miners on the Klamath and killed nearly all of them and then fled across the Siskiyou Mountains into Oregon. They were pursued by a party of Whites and tracked to the Indian reservation in Rogue River Valley. The Whites demanded that they should be delivered up to them, but the agent refused to do it, denying the right of the Whites to demand them. Since then, they have murdered a party of Oregon Teamsters on the road to this place and killed their team of oxen, which lay by the side of the road, a warning to others to beware the poor Indian the eastern writers have so much sympathy for.

The Indians Prepare For War - October 1855

I am at work drifting out my claim as fast as possible in anticipation of having an early and wet winter. The Indians in Rogue River Valley have nearly all left the reservation and taken to the mountains, preparing for war. They have killed several travelers already and it is very dangerous to be on the road now. In fact, most all travel has ceased between here and Oregon. The settlers have called for assistance again but few care about going over this year, as they were not thanked for their assistance last time they were called upon. Our Uncle Sam, in his settlement with the volunteers of the last war, brought them all in debt to Government for clothing and other necessaries furnished them at the time. And of course, they are not anxious to increase the debt.

War In Oregon! - November 1855

I have been obliged to stop my drifting as the bank is rather too damp to be safe to work in. The war in Oregon is under full headway now and our government will have a pretty big bill to foot before the poor Indians can be induced to put a stop to their pleasant recreation of cutting throats, shooting and burning the cruel Whites. Over 50 Whites have lost their lives already, but I presume it would be considered the height of cruelty to kill the poor ignorant savages, to save further destruction of life and property. To be sure the first ones that are apt to suffer are the very ones that have been friends to these red devils.

Where Are Cooper's Indians?

As long as I have lived in Indian country, I have never yet met with a living specimen of one of Cooper's Indian heroes. And if some of the eastern writers, who are eternally prating about the poor Indian, would just emigrate out here and live a short time amongst them, he would form a different idea of them than they have of them from reading of romantic heroes and Indian heroines in the novels of Cooper and company. Let them settle here and lose a brother or two. Let them work hard for a year or two to build up a home here to be destroyed by them in a night.

Let them, like Mr. Wagoner, always treat them kindly, feed them when hungry, clothe them when naked and then return after a day's absence to find his house burned down, his wife murdered, and his daughter carried off. A captive to satisfy the lust of one of these snakes he has nourished and kept alive through his generosity. Or as in the case of Mr. Harris, a band of Indians approached the house, headed and led on by one that had lived upon him for nearly a year. Harris was shot down in his door by the very Indian he had been so kind to. Mrs. Harris kept the whole tribe off of her until dark, by loading and firing of her husband's revolver at them. Here is a sample or two of the fine and noble Indian characters from real life, not much romance about this. Lo the poor Indian has but few friends in an Indian country. But away off yonder, in the old thick-settled States, where people are not obliged to sleep with one eye open to watch whilst the other sleeps, there he has friends. And they can afford to be so there, they are out of danger.

It Never Rains In California - December 1855

There is no water in the gulch as yet and I think there is but a poor prospect of there being any great quantity this winter. This is a singular part of the world, it never rains here. Unless by accident a solitary cloud gets strayed away from the lower country and it gets blown over the Trinity Mountain. I have been building a reservoir and ditch this month in order to catch what little may come. About the 24th the wind got round in the northwest and it has been very cold ever since, so that it kept us pretty busy cutting wood and hauling it to keep warm in our cloth house. The snow is about 8 inches deep now and if it were possible for it to rain now, we might have plenty of water.

But I begin to believe it to be almost impossible for it to rain here anymore. The only salvation for this town is in the big ditch they are cutting from Shasta River. Until that is completed, this place is bound to be a dull one for business. For miners cannot work without water and if they are not at work, all business is stopped. The war in Oregon still rages as furiously as ever and the Indians are killing about three Whites for every one they lose. Over 120 Whites are known to have been killed by the poor Indians in Rogue River Valley this season. Thus far we have not been molested by them, although it is but 60 miles from here to the heart of the Indian country, where all this fighting is going on.

Deadly Business: Squaws For Guns

I begin to believe that the red skins are a heap smarter than the Oregonians. In 1850 the Indians rose against the Whites and murdered several of the farmers. But were finally surrounded on Table Rock, where they might've been all killed out, but they agreed to make a treaty of peace and they were let off. At this time, they were armed with bow and arrow only. They found they could not stand their hand with these, against the rifles of the Whites. They accordingly sent their squaws out to gather up all the arms and ammunition they could, in any way, get hold of. The squaws managed the thing very well and sold themselves to procure arms and powder. Every tea caddy was picked up and converted into balls.

And finally, in 1853 when they had completed all their preparations and were all ready, they commenced the war again by murdering all who had been friendly to them. They fought the Whites a much better, harder fight this time, for most of them were armed with rifles. 10 Whites were killed to where there was one the year before, 10 for every Indian that was scalped. They fought as long as their powder, lead and caps held out, and towards winter when these began to grow scarce and their supply of provision began to fail them, then they complied with the earnest request of the Whites and made another treaty. Experience taught them that they must lay in larger supplies and for two years they busied themselves in picking up all the ammunition they could, and the bucks have been constantly practicing with their rifles to improve their aim and skill.

This fall, everything being ready, war has been declared again and for the past two months they have shown the Oregonians how well they have improved this time. They never lacked bravery and now they do not lack in skill in the use of firearms. For they are better armed and are better shots with the rifle than the Whites, and can and have, whipped an equal number of Whites in a fair fight. Every man, horse, mule, ox that they have killed have been shot in the head. If they don't give the Oregonians all they can do for a long time to come, I am badly mistaken.

It used to be fun for them to fight, but it is getting to be rather serious work now. For they understand a rifle too well.

My Folly - January 1856

Another year is past and gone and still am I a wanderer here in this land of bright hopes and bitter disappointments. How much nearer am I to the goal of my ambition? How much richer than last year at this time? Answer says none. And I must conclude that it is all folly to waste my time in longer search. Up to the present time we have been confined for most of the time to our cabins, owing to the excessive coldness of the weather. Not being the owner of a thermometer, I cannot say how low the mercury has run, but I can say that it just lay over anything for coldness that I have seen since I left home. We commenced washing today. There is no news of importance this month thus far. The Indian war in Oregon still rages and probably will for a long time to come.

Experience Is A Stern Teacher - 2/16

Well at last, the problem is solved. I have washed up all of my dirt and have not cleared enough to carry me home. Well so be it, my good old parents used to say - it's all for the best. They can now have a chance of practicing this virtue of patient resignation to the will of the ruler of the fates of miners, as well as the balance of the universe. Tomorrow I must commence drifting again. And if God spares my life, I will toil on until I can pay my debts and return home. It is a dangerous place to work and nothing but my greatest desire to return this spring would induce me to work it. The owners of the Yreka ditch are making every exertion to bring the water in soon. They have had about 500 hands at work the past two weeks at $5 per day to the man.

As to the war 40 miles from us over in Rogue River Country, it appears the picayune settlers are about to bend the knee to the red skins again and beg of them to lay down their arms and make (what they call) a treaty. Poor fools are they, so shortsighted as not to see that such conduct emboldens these red devils to commit further depredations as soon as they can lay in another stock of provisions and ammunition. They (the settlers) want to cultivate their ground they say, to put in another crop. Have they any assurance that they will ever harvest it? I say no, but fools will not learn even by experience and I know that he is a stern teacher. In other parts of Oregon, the volunteers are doing good execution and are pursuing the red skins and giving them their just desserts, whipping them in every engagement thus far. Unassisted by General Wool too.

My Only Friend - March 1856

Another month has passed by and we are now about to commence a new one. It is night and I am, as usual, alone in my cloth shanty. The log fire blazes cheerfully in the old mud fireplace. My dog Nigel, my only true friend here at least, lays stretched before the fire, his large intelligent eyes fastened upon me, seeming as though he would like to read my thoughts. I was thinking of home, of home as it used to be, years ago. Of the many pleasant hours spent there. Of my old friends and companions and finally of the many oh how many changes that must have taken place there. Would that I had been content when there, but I could not be. It never was intended for me, it was my fate to lead a different life. And were I to return, I know that the change would be so…

Note: Pages appear to be torn out of the journal after this page.

Blackfeet Attack Seattle

…mother and another woman were taken prisoners by the Indians in the commencement of this war, the two women died soon after in the Indian camp and now the other has been burned. A Mrs. Benedict had a narrow escape from them whilst on the road, but her escort succeeded in getting her off unharmed, although she had two balls shot through her rail and lost her dresses. On 20 January in Northern Oregon, they made a grand attack on a town called Seattle. There were about 900 Indians of the Blackfeet tribe surrounded the town but were finally, after three days fighting, driven off by the US Cutter Decatur. Opening her batteries and showering upon them broadsides of shells and grape shot. I am mistaken about it being Mrs. Wagoner that was taken prisoner by the Rogue River tribe, the prisoners were Mrs. Haines and daughter and Miss Wagoner - Mrs. Wagoner was killed by them at the time the others were taken prisoner.

California Justice

I was sued for a small debt and my claim was attached on 25 February. It was done out of malice to make me a bill of expense. I was obliged to go to town to attend to it and whilst there was summoned as a juror in a petit larceny case. The justice was an old leather head from some border state. And the jurors were men that follow it for a living, always lounging around the courts for the purpose being summoned as jurors. There was no evidence to convict the prisoners and after the jury went out, I gave it as my opinion. After considerable talking, in which some proposed to play a game of seven up to say whether they should be sent up or let go, we came to the conclusion to not agree much. To the chagrin of the loafer jurors, who thus lost their fee.

In vain they agreed to side with either party. They were willing to send them in as guilty, or not, only let's agree says they. But it was no use, they lost that half days work. Now according to my humble opinion this is rather a poor way of obtaining justice, where jurors are made out of this sort of material.

Rogue River Massacre - 3/9

This week we have received news from Crescent City and were pained to hear of another horrible massacre of Whites by the Indians at the mouth of Rogue River. Report says that every settler of the south side have been killed, some 20 in all and Ben Wright amongst the rest. A call has been made for assistance but the Government troops at Port Orford, a military station up the coast, were unable to comply. And it depends upon the citizens whether they receive any assistance or not. The settlers and miners of Gold Beach have all moved into a blockhouse and have about 20 days of provisions on hand. They are hemmed in on all sides and unless they get assistance from some quarter soon, they must either die of starvation or attempt to fight their way through to Crescent City. There are about 600 Indians surrounding them, waiting for a chance to finish them.

Throughout Oregon the red devils are murdering the Whites wherever they catch one, and thus far it appears they have the best of it. They are confident of success and begin to have a feeling of contempt towards our Uncle Sam, having whipped his soldiers at every battle and sometimes with an inferior number. This appears to be disbelieved by the eastern papers, but it is a fact that last fall in Rogue River Valley the US troops under Captain Smith retreated before an inferior number of Indians.

Broken Promises & Lies

No other country in the world, I will venture to say, ever could begin to be so slack in its water arrangements as this. We have not had one good rainstorm since the spring of 1853. It's a fact. I am sure that there has not been half an inch of water fell in the past winter, the ground is as hard and dry as it ever is in summer. I don't know what is to become of us here if we do not get some rain soon and it is too late to look for much now. Well, well I promised to return home this spring, but I cannot do it. Whoever thought there was such an infernal dry hole as this. It has always been told to me the mountains are the place to find rainy wet weather, but I know better than that now.

If I ever do get out of this infernal hole, I hope I may die of thirst if I ever go up this high to settle again. I have told lies enough this past month, whilst trying to sell out, to blast me for all time to come.

Yreka's Grand Highway Robbery - 3/16

We have received no news of importance from the Indian war in Oregon this week, as usual the people are growling about US troops not fighting them as they ought see. We in Yreka have had a grand highway robbery excitement. The Express of Rhodes and Company with Messrs. Hickman, Sommercamp and three others were stopped on the Trinity Mountain by five robbers and were obliged to shell out all they had (about $3000). And then they were tied up to trees, where they were found by the stage passengers when they came on soon after.

As for myself I have been all the past week stripping off top dirt preparatory to washing. I tried as hard as ever I could to sell out so as I could go home, but the fates willed it otherwise. And there is no other alternative but to work on until I may possibly get enough ahead to take me home.

Note: A page appears to be torn out of the journal after this page.

War In Oregon Rages On

The Indian war in Oregon is still going on as usual, a few more Whites have been waylaid, murdered and scalped. Several skirmishes have come off between the red skins and volunteers. And the great Wool has returned from San Francisco with 1000 or so more troops to guard him from danger at Vancouver, where he lays with his brave soldiers whilst the volunteers are out fighting. I cannot see of what earthly account these dirty, lousy, ill-looking, ill-begotten and worse-looking regulars are. They are marched about the frontiers, from fort to fort, but are never in the way of the Indians. The volunteers must always do all the fighting.

My Disappointing Results – 3/26

On the next page I have copied from my daybook an account of the years' work. A year ago, I commenced keeping an account of my receipts and expenses with the following result.

	Received	Expenses
March	$397.00	$367.00
April	$125.50	$153.00
May	$7.50	$10.00
June	$0	$71.00
July	$292.50	$76.00
Aug	$159.75	$178.00
Sept	$187.00	$194.00
Oct	$0	$75.00
Nov	$0	$40.00
Dec	$31.00	$85.00
Jan	$266.00	$389.00
Feb	$235.50	$75.00

	Received	Expenses
March	$0	$0
TOTAL	**$1701.75**	**$1652.00**

This is making money with a vengeance? Look on the next page and see how it was spent. With the exception of the money spent for meals, lodgings and a few luxuries at Yreka, all the balance I was obliged to pay out for tools, food, clothes, hired hands etc. And this will show how it was spent.

Beef	$248.75	Tools	$106.00
Flour	$82.50	Clothes	$81.00
Vegetables	$71.25	Candles	$48.75
Beans	$12.00	Nails	$4.87 1/2
Sugar & Molasses	$55.75	Tobacco	$17.00
Butter	$41.00	Medicine	$10.62 1/2
Fruit	$38.50	Pies	$12.37 1/2
Coffee & Tea	$15.00	Wood	$10.00
Pepper & Salt	$0	Books	$28.00
Soap Saleratus	$20.75	Old Accounts	$126.50
Mustard	$0	Lawsuit	$20.00
TOTAL	**$585.50**		**$465.12 1/2**

RECAPITULATION

For Provisions	$585.50
For Hired Hands	$465.12 1/2
For Actual Necessities	$465.12 1/2
For Expenses At Yreka	$136.25
	$1652.00

And now in conclusion, I would say that any man that can lay up money here can do more than I can. For out of the whole amount, I can see but one item that I could do well without, that is tobacco. Some would think this was rather discouraging and I am almost of that opinion myself, but of what use is it to be discouraged? I must keep on at work and if it possibly ever could be so, I may after a while get money enough to carry me back. And as soon as I do, I shall make the dust to fly for a while sure. I would not be so anxious to return were it not for my parents continually worrying and fretting about it and in truth they are growing old, and I ought to return to them and God knows I would now if I could.

I promised to return, but how am I to do it without money? Yes, I promised to return this spring as soon as I washed my dirt, well spring came, my dirt was washed, but instead of the $2000 or $3000 I was confident of having, I had not enough to pay my debts. All for the best I expect.

It Rained! - April 1856

Today we have had the first good rainstorm we have had in a year. Tolerably dry, this fine place to mine in. We have made out to get water enough to drink thus far. When that gives out, I shall take to brandy, as we have a large supply on hand in the market. The Butchers say we should be lucky to get beef enough this summer, for there is no appearance of any grass yet and the beef now looks like blue lightening and is tougher than sole leather. When the beef gives out, I am going to emigrate. Can't stand another starvation. The one of "53 liked to have killed me and one now would, I am afraid. The prospect of a fortune grows most beautifully less every day. Grub claims are in great demand just now. Mine comes very near being one, but don't quite come up to the scratch.

4/5 - During the past week we have had several light rainstorms and occasionally a flurry of hail. This may be of service to the farmers, but it does us miners no good, there is not enough of it. In the farming countries below, there is a great want of rain. According to the accounts received from there by the newspapers, thousands of beef have died for want of grass. This is the driest winter we have had since the gold discovery.

There's Fighting Everywhere

In Oregon the Indians are as usual committing all sorts of depredations. Rogue River Valley on 23 March they attacked six men of Captain O'Neil's company, killing two and wounding two more. The two wounded with the other two reached Hayes' Ranch, where one of the wounded soon died. Soon after, they attacked the ranch but were eventually driven off. On the 25th they attacked a pack train on the road near Slate Creek, killed one man and wounded another and captured 28 mules with their cargoes, in which was 25 pounds of powder. A charge was made after them, upon the receipt of the news at Hayes' Ranch, by several companies of volunteers that were stationed there.

The number of Indians was supposed to be about 300 who occupied the road on both sides, concealed in the bushes. Captain George's company from Yreka advanced, keeping the road until near the summit of the ridge between Deer Creek and Illinois River, when a deadly fire was poured in from the hillsides, killing four men. It was impossible to get a shot at them in return and the volunteers had to retreat, losing 40 of their horses, saddles and bridles in their retreat. Thus it goes, the Indians invariably get the best of it. On Cow Creek they have had another fight in which the Whites lost two men and six Indians were shot. That is a little better.

A Lieutenant of this company, having by some means got in the rear of his company when an attack was made, jumped off his mule to get a shot at an Indian. When lo and behold what should he see in a few minutes, but an Indian mounted on it and riding up the hill. He became enraged at the sight, assumed the command and charged on after him, killed three Indians, took his mule and three Indian horses. It would be a good thing if the same success should attend the recapturing of all the animals these red devils have taken.

It Sure Smells Like War

At the north fork of the Coquille, Captain Buoy had a fight last week and killed eight red skins. By the Military Express, the news of the week is that Captain Hayes' company had a fight at Connell's Prairie on the 10th, four Whites were wounded and 20 red devils lost their scalps. This is the news of the week past, and for the last three or four months it has been about the same. And still General Wool says there is no war in Oregon. I am not a military man but if this is not war, it smells most decidedly like it. Mounted companies of volunteers are traveling in all directions throughout the territory, every day there is a fight somewhere, all travel is stopped, or nearly so, and no man can foretell when the end of all this may be. We have to fight it out ourselves, unassisted by our Uncle Sam's present agents.

This has been a good week for the devils in Rogue River, they having lost but six men (at the attack at Hayes) and have killed seven Whites and captured about 70 mules and horses and about 10,000 pounds of groceries and clothing from the pack train. We begin to get a few touches of the same kind now, for last week a band of these poor Indians came over the mountain and drove off eight horses from a ranch about 10 miles from Yreka in Shasta Valley. I expect we shall have to fight down here yet and it is singular that they have not been over here before this. A mounted guard has been posted on the mountain to escort travelers between here and Oregon. All of this military duty in Oregon has to be done by the volunteers, as the Government says there is no war here.

Blockhouse Last Stands

About 100 men are surrounded in their blockhouse at the mouth of Rogue River by the Indians 400 strong. The last accounts from them March 12, they had but four days provisions. An express arrived at Portland from Port Orford, bringing this news. Also, that a whale boat left there to communicate with these Whites but was swamped in trying to land and all were killed as they landed. At Port Orford, there are about 80 men (including 30 US troops) caged up in a blockhouse. They are prepared to stand a siege but are daily expecting to see the town burned. A rumor says that the Coquille and Coos Bay bands have left to join the bands in the mountains.

If this be true, all the property along the coast as far as the mouth of the Umpqua River will be destroyed. It appears as though the red devils are about to retake Oregon. Most of the farmers have lost nearly all of their stock and many have lost their all. Lo, the poor Indian.

More Indian Troubles - 4/13

We have had several light showers of rain and hail the past week. The news from Oregon this week is worse than ever. In Rogue River Valley, or rather on one of its tributaries the Illinois, near Gates' Ranch a party of Indians about 300 strong attacked a pack train, killed all the Packers (5) and took 36 mules with their cargoes of ammunition, groceries etc. In these last two affairs the Indians have taken 140 mules and their cargoes, 25 pounds of powder, 50 pounds of lead and 300 boxes of percussion caps. Most of the miners have left Sailor Diggings, about 25 only stopping there and these are living in a fort. The Indians have located themselves off the road from here to Crescent City, their main object being to waylay pack trains and travelers.

In respect to the battle fought by Captain George's company a week ago, we have learned the following. It appears that when they attacked the Indians, they were charging up the hill to meet the savages who were rushing down upon them. The red skins reserved their fire until the Whites got very close upon them. And no sooner did the firing commence on the part of the Indians, then nearly the whole of the volunteers beat a retreat. A very few only stood their ground, Kennedy, Collins, Olney, McCarten were four of these, they were killed. They fought with perfect desperateness until they were relieved by a party of horsemen who induced the runaways to rally and again charged up the hill a mile and a half to the top, driving the red devils before them and killing six of them. Here they escaped.

Torching Cascades

In Northern Oregon on 25 March, the Indians attacked the town at Cascades on the Columbia, took it, burned every house, killed three men, two women and three girls before they could reach the blockhouse. On the 26th the steamer Belle on her way up met Captain Kilcorn in a bateau coming down from the Cascades, with a load of women who brought the news that on the previous night the town was attacked by about 800 Indians. It was burned to the ground and when he left, they had surrounded the fort or blockhouse and were fighting to get possession of it. Upon the receipt of this news at Portland, a volunteer company was immediately raised and just started up the river on board a steamer.

Another steamer (Belle) started from Vancouver with 40 regulars (what an army).

She arrived at the Cascades next morning and succeeded in landing her men, undercover of howitzers. The Indians in large numbers resisted them but they succeeded in making a landing. The Indians were finally driven off and the people in the fort rescued. How many were killed is not known, Governor Curry says 14, others say over 20. The number of Indians killed is not known, 16 were taken prisoner, 15 of which were condemned to be instantly shot. There are now 250 US troops there. A letter from Vancouver says that the Indians were within 6 miles of that place and were laying waste to the country over which they travelled, murdering all ages, sexes and condition of people.

Alarm & Confusion

The whole country is in a state of alarm and confusion. God only knows where or when will be the end of this. On White River on the 10th, a party of volunteers were attacked by about 150 Indians. Two volleys were fired before the troops could return fire. The battle lasted nearly all day, when the Indians made good their retreat. Four Whites were wounded, about 20 poor Indians killed. This is the news of the week, summed up in a few words and in all probability, this will be the character of the news for many weeks to come.

Indian Bill

In our own valley the Indians paid a visit to Captain Martin's Ranch and drove off 10 horses. They were pursued by the Captain and a few others, but nothing was seen by them of either stock or Indians. We are all expecting a rush upon us this summer by these red skins, but are prepared to give them a warm welcome. Last week a Negro by the name of Bill endeavored to entice the Scott's Valley Indians to commence a war here. These Indians are a small band who have been living at the fort in Scott's Valley for two or three years passed. Bill made them agree to join him at Sheep Rock in this valley and from here they were to start out, under him as their leader, on a foray against the White settlers in the valley. Bill started out ahead for the place and upon his leaving, the Indians informed the commanding officer at the fort of his proceedings. They are now out on his track; I hope they may catch him.

Dry Ditches & Highwaymen

Business is dull here as yet and all are complaining, we want water. Miners, traders, all want water to enable them to prosper. The heavens have dried up and the Yreka Ditch Company have not succeeded as yet in getting any in here. The ditch is finished but it takes a long time for water to run 80 miles through a new ditch, as dry as the country now is. In the mines but very few are at work, all are waiting for the water. The citizens of Shasta have found about $15,000 of the money taken from the express by the Highwayman on Trinity Mountain. They captured the leader sometime since near Marysville and he led them to where he had to secret his part. And they soon found the other, after a search of two or three days. As for myself I have been for the past two weeks stripping off top dirt preparatory to washing in case we ever get water sufficient.

4/27 - For the past two weeks we have had many light snow, hail and rainstorms with occasionally a fair day, but not enough water has fallen to do us miners any good. The Yreka Ditch is finished, but the water has not reached us yet. We have not heard much news lately from the Indian war in Oregon. A party of US soldiers released the settlers at the mouth of Rogue River from their long confinement and afterwards attacked the red skins, killing about 20. This is about all the news; times are dull and no prospects of a very speedy improvement. Even the poor miserable Chinese, who live off two bits a day, complained that they cannot make a living. I have been for a month past digging a big strip, uncovering wash dirt preparatory to washing, in case we ever get water enough.

What A Miserable Life

4/28 - Home sweet, sweet home. Oh, would that I could but look upon it once more. What a miserable life is this we miners lead. Here in my miserable cabin have I sat for the whole of this long Sabbath evening alone. Not a sound outside to break the awful death-like stillness, save the hooting of the owls and the occasional deep bay of the stealthy wolf on the mountains in the rear of my cabin. All else is hushed in the stillness of death and my thoughts have wandered far away o'er mountain and plain to my home in the east. I cannot describe the feelings that come over me as I think of other days and contrast my present situation and manner of living with my situation there. But oh how dreary, how lonely does it seem to know you are alone, without a kind friend near you. Far away from all that man holds dear, secluded from the balance of the world, shut up and hemmed in, in this miserable mountain gulch.

4/30 - Today we have had quite a rainstorm, more rain has fallen in fact then at any one storm this season. Sunday night there was a horrible murder committed near here on the Blue Gulch. A poor old Scotchman, who lived alone in his cabin was found Monday morning lying dead upon the floor, stabbed in a horrible manner. As yet no clue can be obtained of who the murderers can be. I see by the papers from below that the police of Marysville have caught the balance of the gang of highway robbers that robbed the Express on Trinity Mountain a short time since. One of the robbers resisted and was shot dead, the balance are now in jail at Shasta.

The water in the Yreka ditch is making its way slowly along and tonight it has reached the flats above town and crossed the flume at Humbug Gulch. If nothing happens to prevent it, we may get water here to work with this summer. The weather the past month has had more of the appearance of winter then at any previous time. In March it was very dry and warm, the thermometer running as high as 90° during the month. And we all predicted a hot dry summer, but this month we have had a snow, hail or rainstorm nearly every day with cold, raw winds from the northwest and southeast. The storms however have been light, not much water falling. But making a heap of bluster and preparations for very little rain, so that although we have had a great deal of stormy weather, it has not done us miners any good.

Not enough water having fallen to have any effect upon the streams here. But if it does us no good it must be a fine thing for the farmers and will make many a dollar for them. The fields of wheat and barley look very promising, the grass has started up anew and the whole country looks 8000 times better than it did a month ago.

Golden Era Poetry - May 1856

Sad memory with my spirit now, is busy with the past,
And deep within my heart alcove I listen to the last,
The whisperings of other days come shadowing o'er my soul,
Like fleecy clouds athwart the sky beyond my kins control.
Such thoughts as these are crowding fast upon my troubled brain,
Like daydreams ye are gone for aye and n'er will come again,
But memory with an iron rule holds o'er my spirit sway,
For ye are never absent from my weary heart a day.

Golden Era - April 20, 1855 Mrs. E. L. Mull

Tonight, as I sat by my cabin fire, my eyes fell upon the above piece of poetry in the Golden Era which suited me so well and expressed my own feelings so much better than I could myself. I took the liberty of copying them into this journal.

D A Jenckes – Yreka

Sick And Alone In The Wilderness - 5/5

It is now past midnight and as I sit here by the fire in my cabin, the rain pours down upon the cloth roof in all the fury of a spring storm. I am sick, and the pain caused by a blister on my back has driven me from my hard bed and compels me to pass a part of the night at least in a rough chair by the fire. My partner is a bed, and I am alone in my misery. To be sick at home surrounded by friends and all the comforts of life is thought to be a severe trial, but oh what a difference between sickness there and here. For the past two years I have suffered at intervals from a complaint of the kidneys, this is the trouble at the present time. Although suffering much from the acute pain I was obliged to work all the morning, but at noon I gave up, could not stand it.

A neighbor, a large, rough, big whiskered friend of a miner, recommended a blister plaster. And as he had one that had been used but once for a singular purpose, he kindly offered to give it to me and attend to it as he understood how. Accordingly, he applied it to the affected part and waited upon me in addressing it after the blister was drawn. But what man ever could fill a woman's place at a sickbed? As I tossed and rolled with pain on my hard bed, my head aching as though it would burst, how you long for those thousand little nothings that a woman always finds to alleviate pain. A camphor bottle or vial of aromatic salts or, above all else, a woman's hand to press my aching head and soothe the pain.

How I've longed for a cup of tea and toast, but there was naught in the house but coffee, beef and bread. The fire went out, my partner was off somewhere and I must lay shivering with cold or get up and cut wood and build a fire. I was feverish, wanted a cup of water, got up and none in the cabin, had to go to the spring after it. All of these little things are thought of only when sick, but then a person thinks of home. Then again when the rough miner had jerked the blister off and reapplied the oil to the raw flesh, a soft piece of cloth was wanted to bind around the sore to keep the rough flannel shirt from irritating yet. But an old flour sack was all that could be found, and this caused me so much pain I was obliged to get up and pass the night by the fire.

To while away the time I, having nothing to read, took my journal and have attempted to describe the situation of a sick miner, but it is useless for me to attempt it. For one must be placed in a similar situation before you can have any idea how much misery a man can endure and live through it, before he can begin to appreciate a woman's worth, or to enjoy the blessings of a home.

Long Gulch
Midnight
May 5th AD 1856

Note: Text is written at the bottom of this page, presumably by sister Maria, it reads: "My dear bro, would that it could have been otherwise but God's will be done."

Two Totally Different Wars - 5/7

The mail arrived last night from the States and I received a letter from home, all well there. The New York Tribune has a long article concerning the Rogue River War and the Oregon war in general. It derives its information from a General Wool's dispatches to the government, I believe. He says he does not believe all Indians are saints any more than white men. Very singular that. However, if he has any doubts on the subject, let him look back and take a review of their saintly proceedings in this section since the first Whites set foot in this part of terra firma. About the first murders that were committed here were upon a company of men who were looking out for a wagon road trail between Oregon and California, this I believe was in 51.

From that time until the summer of 52, it was unsafe for a small party to travel anywhere through this section of the country. In 52 they broke out into open hostilities. Volunteers were raised and after a short time they succeeded in corralling them on Table Rock. Here the Whites might have saved themselves all further trouble, and some two or 300 lives that have since been cut short by these devils, had they massacred them on the spot. But no, the treacherous fiends sued for mercy and it was granted them and a treaty made. From this time until the following summer all was quiet, with the exception of an occasional murder of some poor white traveler.

Meanwhile the Indians, profiting by the lesson taught them of the superiority of the rifle over the bow and arrow, endeavored to procure arm. But how were they to do it? They had neither money or property to exchange for firearms. But at last an idea struck them that they knew would, if carried out, procure both arms and ammunition. They could sell their squaws to some of the Whites and procure these much-coveted death dealers. It was accordingly done and quite a trade was carried on between these unprincipled Whites and the Indians. A squaw would fetch about $100. The trade being mostly a barter trade, generally a horse for a squaw and sometimes a little ammunition thrown in. Some exchanged rifles and pistols for squaws and soon they were all well-armed with knife, pistol, rifle and ammunition in exchange for their squaws. In vain, the more prudent Whites protested against this sort of trade and pointed out the danger of arming these Indians, but it was of no use, it was done secretly by these amorous swains.

And now whatever may be said of the foolishness of the Whites, the Indians have no right to complain of the loss of their women, since they were the only ones who benefited by this transfer.

The Poor Indians' Plan

Much has been said concerning the maltreatment of the poor Indians and this (so called) robbery of the squaw etc. But I know that from the first it has been a plan of their own concocting and the means they made use of to procure firearms. They, thinking that after they had procured arms, could easily kill off the Whites and recover their squaws again. It is a mistaken idea of Mr. Greeley's that the red skins know and acknowledge the superiority of the Whites, quite the contrary. They still believe that they will eventually drive the Whites from the country. Well now that they had procured arms, what is the next step taken by these Indians?

In the summer of 53 they had completed all of their arrangements and made one more endeavor to rid the country of the Whites. And who were the first victims, think you? Why the first man killed was at the Mountain House, the proprietor of which was murdered by an Indian he had kept for nearly a year and who had always professed a great attachment for him. From this time on, murder after murder was committed, houses were burned, stock killed, farms destroyed, and it seemed as though they would succeed in carrying out their threat of extermination. But finally, as winter approached and they saw they would suffer from want, they agreed to make another treaty. At this time Fort Lane was established and the Indians were brought in and fed at Government expense. They could not possibly ask for more.

And many a poor sick and unfortunate miner would have gladly exchanged places with these poor devils. When asked why they did not burn all of the farmhouses in the valley, they said they wanted them for their own use after the Whites have been driven off. No idea of inferiority here, Greeley to the contrary notwithstanding. From this time on, he had but little trouble with them. Government supplied all their wants and they had naught to do but laugh and grow fat. To be sure, stragglers from the reservation would occasionally sally out and joining Typsee (a renegade chief), attack a train and murder a man or two for the fun of the thing. But no serious disturbance occurred until last fall. A party came on to California ground on the Klamath River and killed some eight or 10 miners without any provocation whatever. For the Klamath River is some 60 miles from this Rogue River Reservation and the lofty Siskiyou Mountains lies between them.

Who Has The Rights?

Well, I hope and know that there is no body of Americans that are going to see their countrymen butchered in the night and not resent it. And then who could say it would not be his turn next? A party of volunteers were immediately raised and started on the trail of these murderers and traced them (they say) to the Indian reservation area Fort Lane. They had proof sufficient that they had lived there before, they traced them near to there and they demanded them from the Chief. They were not given up however and finally a party of them being found, they were attacked, and some say 20 were killed. No, I don't say these were the identical Indians that committed the murders, but we all believe such a massacre could not have been committed without the tribe knowing it.

Of course, the ball now was open for the season and has not closed yet. And I for one hope it may never close until the last buck Indian old enough to fight may be removed from this world of temptations to a better or worse. Their only object in warring with the Whites is to drive them from the country. If we have no right here - and Greeley and all his sort mean to say this - why we can then understand them. But, if we have a right to till this soil, to make homes here, we must subdue these Indians before we can be safe for a moment.

James Beaufort - Eye Witness

To return to his letter in the Tribune of April 5, he has an extract from one of General Wool's reports, wherein he says…"Upwards of a hundred Indians, chiefly women and children, have collected at Fort Jones for protection. And that Captain Judah, the commanding officer, informs him that there are constant threats of a night attack upon his fort, for the purpose of killing these inoffensive people." Now it is singular that almost all of my acquaintants here within 10 miles of Fort Jones, I cannot hear of one who ever heard of this talk before. It's all moonshine.

Again, here is another extract with a few facts annexed. "… at a Council held by the superintendent 30 miles from Port Orford, an Indian shot a white man. As usual he was demanded that he might be hung. He was protected by the troops and whilst in their charge they were crossing the river in a boat, he was killed by a party of Whites who shot him. The soldiers returned the fire killing three Whites." Here is a very pretty little affair. So it seems that the foreign-born, low-lived regulars, are sent out here to protect the Indians, against the Whites? But what are the facts of this case? I will tell you. James Beaufort (an old friend of mine) and his partner followed otter hunting for a living. Whilst out last fall on a hunt in what they supposed was a friendly country, Jim's partner was shot dead before his eyes by an Indian.

Jim marked him. And the next time he saw him he was with a party of soldiers and as he had sworn to be the avenger of his partner's death, he kept his oath and shot him in his tracks. But no sooner had he fired then these Dutch, Irish, American soldiers fired and killed him and two others. Thus, four white men were killed for one Indian. Well, this is just about the proportion. And when the Indians can't make out the compliment, Uncle Sam's troops do it for them. As to this letter from Captain Smith considering the attack upon the two camps of friendly Indians on the reservation at Fort Lane, I have shown what a friendly feeling they had towards the Whites and the causes of this attack. And who blames the settlers of Willamette Valley for not wanting such friendly neighbors?

War Doesn't Pay

As to its moneymaking features I don't know anything about the justness of the war in upper Oregon, nor what the chances are to make a fortune out of it there. But if the volunteers don't make more this campaign than they did in "53, it would hardly pay a man to go for the purpose of moneymaking. In "53, Government brought the volunteers all in debt to it in its settlement with them. Although I have not heard of anyone being patriotic enough to pay the balance due Government for the privilege of having such a grand Indian hunt. There are several young men of my acquaintance here crippled for life in that war. Some of whom are disabled for work and who owe large doctors' bills contracted at that time. They did not make much out of the war.

One who, previously to the war, was worth about $2000 volunteered, was shot in the arm and in the hand, spent all his money getting cured and came out in the end with a stiff arm and crooked hand. Totally unfit for hard work for life. He did not make his pile in the war.

Wise Media Solomons

The fact is the papers, so far removed from the seat of all these troubles, should not judge us and our motives. For they cannot be as well-informed as those who live and suffer in the heart of all these Indian troubles. All their ideas of Indians and Indian affairs come to them second handed. And all of this romantic nobleness of character and disposition that they always give to Indian character cannot be found in real life, but only has an existence in the brain of some romance writer. How many of these wise Solomons ever lived in or near an Indian country? Very few indeed, or there would not be so much said about the poor Indian. And then again, they derive much of their information from newspapers printed hundreds of miles from the scene of all these troubles.

What do Francisco people know of these troubles? They get their news all secondhand. And why is it all papers located in the interior never have a word to say in favor of the poor Indian? In fact, judge not of that you cannot possibly have knowledge of, but through interested and unfair sources.

Yreka's Dry Ditch

5/21 - For the past two days it has been very cold and stormy, having more of the appearance of winter then spring weather. But in spite of all the rain we have had, the water in the Gulch has dried up to less than a Tom head and we are unable to work. But the Yreka Ditch promises to furnish us with this precious article soon, as the water in it increases quite fast considering the distance it runs over new ground, which has to be soaked by the seepage water. The Chinese are flocking in here by droves, but they generally pass on through to either Klamath or Rogue River. They preferring poor diggings and plenty of water, to a little better diggings and no water to work them. And they are right in that.

The Vigilance Committee Reorganizes

6/24 - I have been at work this month past and have neglected thus far to write any and it has not been on account of scarcity of news either, for the past month has been big with events. About 18 May James King of Francisco was shot in the most public street of the city, in broad daylight, by one Casey. Upon the report of the pistol a large crowd gathered and soon there was a cry raised of "Hang him! Hang the murderer!" And a rush upon the jail was talked of when another cry was raised that the Vigilant Committees were forming again, after an adjournment of four years and over. And the mob were assured that they would see that justice was done the murderer. The crowd seemed disposed to trust the business in their hands and gradually dispersed.

Meanwhile the Vigilants had reorganized and were taking in new members as fast as proof was given of the applicants' good standing in society. Thus matters stood until the following Sunday when the Vigilants turned out an army of 20 companies of one hundred men, each all armed. They marched in two battalions in regular soldier fashion off to the jail, surrounded it, placed a cannon before the door and demanded of the Sheriff the two murderers Casey and Cora (who shot the US Marshal Richardson last fall). After some parlay, they were delivered up to them and were carried off to their quarters for confinement and trial. During the week they were found guilty of murder and hung from the roof of the committee building. Having now got the power in their own hands, they determined to rid the city of some of its rogues.

Several arrests were made by them as Casey had confessed that the killing of King was a pre-concerted piece of business and it had fallen to his lot to do the deed. King, as editor of the Bulletin, had become a dangerous man to them, as he was constantly exposing their wholesale swindles in and out of office. Accordingly, King was murdered the first opportunity.

Election Fraud Exposed

Among the arrests made by the Vigilants was Yankee Sullivan the prairie fighter. He wrote out a confession of his misdeeds and afterwards became so feared of being hung, he committed suicide. In his confession he brought to light the whole operation of ballot box stuffing and fraudulent elections. It would be too much of a task for me to describe all the villains brought to light by confessions of these villains. Suffice it to say that from the middle of May up to the present time the Vigilants have had full power below, have sent off from 4 to 6 by every steamer and continue to make arrests as fast as they procure proof of a man's guilt. They now number about 6000 men, all well-armed, have about 25 cannons at their fortified building on Sacramento Street and are prepared for the devil, Tom Walker or Governor Johnson.

The governor of the state has declared Francisco in a state of revolt and called upon them to surrender their prisoners off to the authorities, but the Vigilants swear they will not do it. As the officers of the city are nothing but a pack of thieves who have been stuffed into office by their brother thieves outside, and who they are bound to protect from all harm whenever arrested as part payment for service at election day. The governor has called for volunteers and can't get any, while the Vigilants are increasing their number daily.

Captain Smith Sees The Light?

In the north, the war with the Indians is still prosecuted but not with as much vigor as formally. The volunteers appearing to have made up their minds to let US do his own fighting hereafter, as they are not likely to get even thanks for their services. The latest report from there is that Colonel Wright and some dozen or two of his Shanghai soldiers, had been killed away up in the Walla Walla nation somewhere. In Rogue River the volunteers have mostly all left. Captain Smith who has had command of Fort Lane for a long time, and who first published such awful accounts of cruelties to the poor Indians near his command, following his course of friendship for the poor Indian, called upon them to come into his camp at the Meadows and make a treaty.

They came in and pitched into him, killing a dozen or two of his men and wounding him. They do say now that he has been heard to slightly insinuate that these poor Indians were a little ungrateful. But don't you believe it, they are the same poor Indians you extolled to the skies last fall. Fact is Captain the Whites are sorry, to that is, are quite sorry they wounded you, rather it had been something worse. Captain Buchanan afterword came upon this band of treaty-loving savages and pitched in and killed over 40 of them. Lo, the poor Indian. Four men have been found dead in Shasta Valley, murdered by the red skins. Another has been found dead in Scott's Valley, murdered by some white Indian I think, who thought now was a good killing time and the blame would all rest on Mr. Indian's shoulders.

So, you see, between the contending parties above, and of those below, the Vigilants of Francisco and the Indians in Oregon, we have plenty of exciting news.

You No Payee - 6/26

Whew, how awful cold it is today. Yesterday the thermometer stood way up in the 90° top and today down, I should judge, mighty near freezing. Upon returning from town today I found my cabinet door covered with certain loosely made, crooked, ill-shapen characters drawn in charcoal. I studied them sometime to try to conjure up some reasonable meaning for it, but it was no use. I thought it must be some John Chinaman's work, before I noticed every moon-struck one of them that passed my door that day gazed at the characters on the door and looked at me as savagely as it is possible for them to look, with such fisogs as they wear.

What could it all mean? Was I singled out for some purpose by these long-tailed animals to try their jugglery upon? Had they spotted me to rob my house, knowing I lived alone? In vain I tried to solve the mystery. Finally, I recollected I had seen several houses spotted this way before and I never heard of anything serious happening to them afterwards and I was gradually regaining my usual tone of mind when along came a Chinaman that talked a little English. I hailed him and besieged him if he had any friendship for anything (aside from his long tail) that he would translate this handwriting on the wall.

He looked and smiled and said, "he ver good John, one Chinaman washee you shirt..ha...you no pay him...ha...ver good...spose you no pay he, he write you no payee on you door. Sarbe John." Yes, yes I know it all then. I owed a Chinaman six bits for washing three shirts and he had made my own door his account book, so that his countrymen could all see at a glance how much I was indebted to Chinadom.

The Vigilants Take Control - 6/26

News was received here tonight that the Vigilants had surrounded Palmer, Cook and Company banking house to search for a suspected character who they believed to be secreted there. Judge Terry resisted them and stabbed a man, upon which he was arrested and carried off to the committee rooms by the Vigilants. San Francisco looks like a city in time of war. The Vigilants are fortified on Sacramento Street and are constantly drilling their army by sections. The 6000 are divided into companies of a hundred men, regularly officered and formed into regiments. The whole governed by an executive committee of about 40 men.

Guards and sentinels are on duty constantly, whilst mounted companies are on guard about the city day and night. They say they have been governed by robbers, murderers and thieves long enough and are bound to rid the country of them or die trying. Thus far the people are with them.

Yreka's Ditch Is Wet - 6/27

Shasta Butte is the highest peak in California, I believe. Its peak is covered with snow the year round. The Yreka water ditch, which brings water from a stream at its base, is now in complete order. And the water is now running past my cabin down the ditch to the lower flats. Thus far but little water has been sold, but we are in hopes of soon receiving a supply from it. A great quantity of water soaks away through the dry ground but the head increases slowly in the ditch and all agree that from this time on there will be no scarcity of water here.

Vigilance Committee: The Rest Of The Story

The Vigilants and the course they are pursuing is the only topic of the day. The people - that is the merchants, the artisans and miners - throughout the country appear to take sides with them. Whilst the loafers, gamblers, office holders and seekers and politicians are opposed to them. Now what has caused this sudden outbreak, certainly not the murder of King alone, for such murders are too common an occurrence to create such a sensation. No, it was not that, but this event was the last drop that filled the cup to overflowing. For years, Francisco has been in the hands of a party of political robbers. Gamblers and robbers have, through the assistance of gambling judges of elections, been elected to fill all the offices of importance.

Herbert, a Monte Dealer, robber and murderer and Denver, another known murderer, are our representatives at Washington. How are such men elected? Yankee Sullivan in his confession has given us an idea how all this has been done. The County judge (I believe it is) appoints the inspectors and judges of elections. Now he, being one of the right stripe himself, appoints his own tools for the purpose. For instance, Yankee Sullivan was appointed judge and two others of the same tribe inspectors at one of the districts below. Election day came, two men ran for the office of supervisor of that district. The voters polled their votes and deposited them in the ballot box. But the party in power wish to reward Casey with this office but knew he could never be elected by the people.

So they had a patent ballot box, with false bottoms, in which were stowed votes enough to outnumber all the voters in the district. So that when the votes were counted, lo and behold James Casey was found to be elected to the office, when in fact, not a man voted for him and he had not run for it. All wonder how it could be, but in a day or two it ceases to be a wonder and is forgotten. In this way have these rascals been elected time after time. And it is a well-known fact that the officers of this state are the most desperate men in it. Well bye-and-bye one of their tools murders a man, he is arrested and smiles at the idea of being punished. He goes through a mock trial before his partners-in-guilt who occupy the bench, is conveyed to jail by his friend, the Sheriff, is fed on the delicacies of the market at jail by his partner the jailer, at the people's expense, and finally pardoned by the governor. His grateful patron.

And the only object obtained by this farce is an additional amount of tax to come out of the people. In this way have all the elections been frauds, and all the ends of Law and Justice defeated. Taxes have accumulated so fast that although last year Francisco paid at the average rate of $40 on every head of its population, she still run behind her expenses. Her merchants and laborers and the mechanics could not stand it any longer and as it was impossible to get a hearing through the ballot box, they must some other way. The Bulletin, Mr. King's paper, was the only paper independent enough to raise its voice against these shameless rascals. He alone waged a war against them and for this he was killed. The knowledge of this caused the outburst of public feeling, long pent up. Casey and Cora were hung. So far the authorities did not interfere, but this was only the beginning.

The Committee began to look below the surface for the causes of all this rascality and began to arrest the ballot box stuffers; Yankee Sullivan, Mulligan, Duane etc. Now, the authorities began to nestle their tricks were about to be discovered and all of their machinery for making officeholders exposed to public gaze. They call upon the Governor for help, he sends it in the shape of a proclamation; commanding the Vigilants to disperse, to deliver their prisoners up to the authorities etc. His proclamation was laughed at. He then declared the city to be in a state of revolt and appointed a lot of his gambling friend Generals, Colonels, Mayors and Captains and ordered them to enroll the militia of the state and hold themselves in readiness to be called upon at short notice.

Enrolling offices were opened, but naught but gamblers enrolled. All others having joined the Vigilants who had proceeded to fortify their building to stand an assault. Thus, matters stood the last news from there. Vigilant Fort, as it is called, has about 25 cannon in and around it and a breastwork of sandbags in front. All of their prisoners are sent off out of the country as fast as arrested. They are all desperados of the worst class. Last night we received a fuller account of the last great act in the revolutionary drama now being enacted at Francisco. The Marshal of the Vigilants proceeded to hunt up one Maloney, a ballot box stuffer and found him in company with Judge Terry, at Dr. Aches office. The Marshall proceeded to arrest the man, who resisted.

A scuffle ensued and they finally got into the street. When there, Judge Terry drew a pistol and shot a man. Upon which the Marshal took his pistol from him. When Terry drew a knife and plunged it into him giving, it is thought, a mortal wound. Judge Terry then retreated to the armory of the Francisco Blues, followed by about 20 friends, where they endeavored to make themselves secure. But in less than 15 minutes, 1500 armed Vigilants surrounded the building. And to avoid further bloodshed, the judge gave himself up and was conveyed to the Vigilant's Fort, where he was confined to await his trial by the committee. The Vigilants then proceeded to take possession of all the arms of the state that were found in the armories. And took about 75 prisoners, men known to be enrolled against them in Governor Johnson's army.

They next took two barque loads of arms, sent down from Sacramento for the use of the state party. They have disarmed all men known to be opposed to them and made them take an oath to not take up arms against them. General Wool was called upon to interfere on behalf of the state, but refused. And the Vigilants threaten if the US interfere, that they will declare themselves an independent state. But this last is all hearsay and cannot be relied upon. Thus matters stood at last accounts. All is in excitement; all are anxiously looking forward to the probable result of all this and what action our US Government will take in the premises.

Another Glorious Fourth has passed away and I am as poor as ever, still obliged to toil on in these everlasting mines of disappointment. Well so mote it be, there is nothing like it to try one's patience. The news from below is that the Vigilants have possession of Francisco yet and are like to keep it. Nothing further has been done as yet with Judge Terry, he is still in the hands of the Committee. Hopkins, his victim, was still alive when last heard from.

Fireworks: Millhouse & Blunt - July 4, 1856

From Oregon we have nothing of importance, save that the story of Colonel Wright's death is reported to be false. As the last news reports him in good health and active in pursuit of the enemy. In Rogue River country it appears to be very quiet now. The fourth was celebrated here by the order of E. Clampus Vitus, who marched through the streets with music, had an oration delivered before them and afterwards partook of the dinner at the Yreka House. About noon the stage arrived from below and we received the States papers of June 5.

Whilst reading an account of the attack on Lawrence in Kansas by a mob of Missourians and others, I heard a cry in the street of "Shoot him! Shoot the rascal!" And others swearing no man should arrest a friend of theirs. And going to the door I saw a man running down the opposite side of the street followed by Deputy Sheriff Millhouse, pistol in hand, followed by a crowd of drunken miners, whooping and yelling. Swearing all sorts of vengeance on anyone who attempted to arrest a friend of theirs. They turned a corner and I followed to see what would be the result. The officer pursued him down this street about 200 yards, got in front of him and called upon him to surrender, he refused and struck the officer, who returned it with a blow over the head with his revolver.

They finally clinched and fell. When they were separated and Blunt, the prisoner, started back up the street in charge of his friends, the officer following him, intent upon making the arrest. I met them about halfway up the street, the prisoner and three or four of his friends ahead, the officer, pistol in hand, with a torn coat and bloody head immediately behind, and followed by a mob of about 200. Just as I met them Blunt turned his head, saw the officer and exclaiming "There he is", struck him a blow between the eyes and sent him reeling past me, across the street. Blunt followed him up, caught him by the throat and struck him again, when Millhouse fired at him and I think must have missed him.

However, they separated and Millhouse fired again. He then retreated towards the Sheriff's office, Blunt following him, when Millhouse turned again, fired and shot the man through the neck, severing the jugular vein. Blunt fell dead a few yards from the spot and Millhouse made his escape to the Sheriff's office. The mob was now furious, with cries of "Hang him! Hang him!" But a large posse of men rallied to the support of the Sheriff and as the building is a two-story fireproof, they found it to be impossible to gain an entrance through its iron doors. The Sheriff addressed the crowd from his window, but his promises to keep the prisoner or fugitive safe was all of no avail. Have him and hang him, they would.

Meanwhile, the more sober part of the citizens were gathering to sustain the Sheriff. An immense lot of pistols, rifles and muskets with ammunition were passed up to the besieged party, by ropes let down from above. The excited mob yelling, cursing and shouting a vengeance on all that opposed them, but not daring to make a break upon the besieged party, now well prepared for an attack. At dark the bars were all closed and many of the shops, and a strong guard posted in a building opposite of the Sheriff's office to protect the door of his office. At midnight the mob had mostly dispersed, threatening to return on the morrow. The Sheriff's office looks like a fort. Thus, ended 4 July 1856.

Miner Street Mob - 7/5

This morning the crowd began to gather again, although they are not as many as yesterday. The liquor bars are all closed, and they can't get their Dutch courage up to fighting heat. All sorts of rumors are afloat respecting the forces that are expected from the mines and the causes for the shooting affair. The Sheriff's office is well guarded, to resist an attack. It appears that the cause of Blunt's arrest was that he and several of his friends were up in the upper part of Miner Street, creating a disturbance amongst the Chinese prostitutes, who have taken possession of that portion of the town. Millhouse attempted to arrest Blunt for it and he resisted him and broke and run, followed by his friends and backed by all the rowdies in town.

About 2:00 PM several of the low lived ringleaders of yesterday's mob got a crowd together and started up Miner Street, to clean out the Chinese. And as they dared not attempt to take the Sheriff's office, they would wreak their vengeance on these poor, cowardly Chinese. Accordingly, about 200 or more started up and sacked every house in that section, turning the poor miserable prostitutes into the streets and then, running them out of town. With not only hoots and yells, but also kicks and blows chasing them along until they fell down, exhausted through fear. Truly a more shameful, cowardly and barbaric a scene I never witnessed.

Shame upon us Americans, that we allow such proceedings in our republican government. I will bet my life there was not a man in that crowd from New England. Talk of the red savages, I would rather risk myself amongst any known tribe of red skins than these half-civilized border Americans. They are perfect brutes. And like most of the brute creation, will not fight unless in a crowd of vastly superior numbers, or opposed to some known cowardly foe. Bah, I am sick and disgusted with all such things. They are not men.

I'd Like A Shot At Taylor

After having their fill of this kind of fun they've returned to the business part of town, making threats of burning the town if Millhouse was not given up. But pushaw, such things as these are not dangerous foes. Midnight. I stopped in town tonight as one of the guards but apprehend no danger, unless it may be from a fire, for this we are prepared as well as circumstances will admit of.

7/6 - Today all shops as well as liquor bars are closed, by request of the Sheriff Mr. Fair. The mob have mostly dispersed and as they robbed the Chinese of some $1000 or upwards yesterday in their row with them, they're probably satisfied with their day's work and willing to quit for a time. They threatened if the law does not hang Millhouse, they will take him then, in spite of law or order. Let the cowards try it, I would like a shot at Taylor their ringleader. He is a miserable, low-lived, riot-loving, mischief-maker, as I too well know from private experience. Aye, and a coward to boot.

Subpoenaed As A Witness

7/8 - Have just returned from Yreka where I have been to attend court having been subpoenaed as a witness in Millhouse's trial. Did not testify today and shall have to attend tomorrow. The excitement has about died away, but Sheriff Fair still keeps the guard on duty to prevent trouble. The prisoner is escorted to and from the courthouse by a guard armed with rifles and sidearms who also are stationed in the courthouse during the trial. I think there is no doubt but Millhouse will be released by the court. And then we shall see whether the mob will make good their threats of hanging him. I don't think they will, for it is not composed of the right materials to do much execution. They are all gas.

The End Of War In Oregon

News was received tonight that a party of Packers, three in number with 25 pack mules, were attacked on Siskiyou Mountain by a party of Modoc Indians and one man killed. The other two fled to the valley, raised a party of men, returned and found a dead body and three dead mules, they also found nine of their mules alive. 13 of them were driven off by the red skins. 20 volunteers started on their trail, but we have not heard from them since. This occurred on Sunday morning last, about 40 miles from here, near the scene of the wagon massacre last fall. So, it seems that now the war in Oregon has about dried up, and that we are to have a touch of it here.

The Modocs have been at peace with us during the Oregon war. Extracts from a letter written by General L. of the Oregon volunteers dated June 30: "The governor has ordered the disbanding of all the troops now in service in Southern Oregon. I have just returned from the coast, having made the campaign of the entire length of the rivers and drove all the Indians into the camp of the regulars. Besides killing a great many, capturing about 100 and delivering them to the Indian agent. All have now come in and delivered up their arms and are to be removed to the reserve in Yamhill County. 600 have gone and about 800 are at Port Orford.

Tyhee John's band have not yet delivered up their arms but had promised to do so in the two days after my leaving Port Orford, on the 26th. I am sure he will do so, as some of his warriors have come in, amongst them is one of the old John's sons and one of his best warriors. The trip up the big Meadows to the mouth of Rogue River was very successful, my command driving the Indians and whipping them at every place we met them. Just before my command met the regulars under Colonel Buchanan, a part of the troops 103 strong under Captain Smith were defeated by the Indians under old John. Smith having 11 killed and 21 wounded." So, it seems at last we are going to have peace again on the border, that is if we can keep the Modocs down on our side of the boundary line.

Tyhee John has been the great terror of the settlers ever since the war broke out and has been principally instrumental in prolonging it to the present time. His tribe are the bravest of the brave.

My Best Friend Is Gone - 7/9

Poor Nigel, my only true friend in this miserable country, is dead. It is singular how a man separated from all friends, in a far distant land, away from all female society, separated from all that makes life dear, with no one near him that he can place that degree of confidence in to make of him a bosom friend. It is singular how in the absence of these, a man becomes attached to a pet brute, a dog for instance, but so it is. Poor Nigel, I miss you. You have been my sole companion for months, you at least were always ready to receive me, with every demonstration of joy. You were no hypocrite, no base motives influenced you. You were never happier than in my society, grieved at my departure and welcomed me upon my return. But it is passed away, not even this poor dumb friend could be spared to me. And I am all alone, again.

7/15 - Officer Millhouse, who has been having his trial for the past week, was acquitted last night. The judge having decided that he was justified in pursuing the course he did.

A Perfect Slave

For the two past days I have been getting out timber for drifting, having sold half of my claim. Would to God I could raise money enough to leave this infernal hole. I am a perfect slave here for the merchants.

Work, work, work and no pay, barely enough to support me. If pride did not forbid it, I would send home for money to get out of this miserable place. I have lost all hope. Never felt so desperate as now, God knows what I would not do for money enough to get away from here. God help me to keep from the paths of sin. But oh, this life is awful.

Sunday July 27
Life's springtime is a world of dreams,
Of pleasing hopes and fantasies,
Where many a brilliant thought gem gleams,
And o'er our pathway glances.
No cares or press the hearts may time,
No shadow deepen o'er it,
No clouds to it's glad day time,
No fears to rise before it.

BUT

Life's autumn comes and o'er the heart,
It's fond ties rudely crushing,
Bidding its brightest hopes depart,
Reality is rushing.
And memory through the dim lit past,
Looks back to youths sweet dreamings,
And it dwells bid joys too bright to last,
In Summers passion gleaming.

JSG

California Riots - 8/7

I have for the past month been very busy on my claim, striving earnestly to get enough money to enable me to join my friends at home by next Thanksgiving Day, that glorious day of family reunions, in old New England. Since our Yreka riot, we have had news of several in different parts of the state. At Los Angeles on the 19th of July, a Constable shot a native Californian by the name of Ruis whilst levying an attachment on some of his property. He was arrested and admitted to bail. The Mexicans took offense at this and gathered in large numbers, for the purpose of making an attack upon the town.

They had with them a small brass cannon which they took from a priest. They were finally dispersed, but not until they had shot the City Marshal. At San Francisco, one Hetherington shot a Dr. Randall in a public bar. The Vigilant Committee arrested him and on 29 July they hung him, together with one Brace, another murderer. At 2 o'clock the military companies of the committee commenced issuing from their fort and marched and counter-marched, all around the neighboring blocks. At 4 o'clock there were five companies stationed opposite the fort. Three at the corner of Sacramento and Davis streets and the cross streets leading to the locality were occupied by companies of the Dragoons. When all was ready, prisoners were brought out and hung.

Judge Terry is still confined in their fort and probably will stay there until he is banished from the country.

More Modoc Mischief

The cities of Nevada and Placerville have both been destroyed by fire the past month. About 200 men have been raised here to go out into the Modoc country, to punish them for the many murders and robberies committed by them recently. They are enlisted for three months and the last company left here about a week ago. Last evening a detachment arrived in town from the lakes (in the Modoc country) bringing the official reports of four battles with the Indians. On the 29th Captain Martin's company made a descent upon a large rancheria, or town, burned it and killed one Indian. A body of mounted warriors came down into the valley and Captain Martin, with 29 men, gave chase.

The Indians were pursued about 14 miles when they took refuge on a rocky hill and the chase was abandoned. One Indian was killed. On the return to camp, it was found that John Albin was missing. His body was found three days afterwards near the hill where the Indians were left. He had, after finding himself mortally wounded, broken his pistol and rifle to prevent them from falling into the hands of the enemy. On the 31st Lieutenant Warman attacked a large body of warriors near Tule Lake. After four hours hard fighting in which one man was killed and two of his men wounded, the volunteers were compelled to retire, leaving the Indians master of the field.

The Indians were first seen at Bloody Point (so called on account of it being a point where several families were massacred in 1852). They fled from here into Tule Lake, where it was impossible to dislodge them. Eight Indians were killed in this fight. In the evening General Cosby discovered a band of Indians who had not got off the mountain at the time of the fight. Returning to the lake he gave chase with 10 men, killed three and captured eight stolen horses. Poor Warman was an intimate friend of mine, as noble-hearted man as ever lived. He was with me in June 52 as you can see by referring to my journal of that date. John Alban is another good man as ever lived. He was wounded in the Rogue River War of "53.

From Oregon we have nothing new of any importance. The bloodthirsty volunteers at the Dallas (who according to General Wool's account, indiscriminately slaughter them) have just brought in a band of 110 Deschute Indians and turned them over to Captain Jordan USA. The war is about closed there, and many of the Indians have been brought in to the reservations. One SR Lewis was killed at Scott's Bar on Sunday morning last by a Cherokee. All owing to whiskey, that curse to all who use it.

My Log Cabin Home - 8/10

Who is there that can better appreciate the pleasures of a home than a California miner? God willing, I will use my best exertions to find a different home than this country affords, and that shortly. For how truly can I say in the language of the poet:

Home is not merely four square walls,
Though with pictures hung and gilded,
Home is where affection calls,
Filled with shrines the heart hath builded.
Home! Go watch the faithful dove,
Sailing 'neath the heavens above us,
Home is where there's one to love,

Home is where there's one to love us!
~~~~~~~~~~~~~~~~~~~~~~~~~~~

Home's not merely roof and room,
It needs something to endear it,
Home is where the heart can bloom,
Where there's some kind lip to cheer it.
What is home with none to meet?
None to welcome none to greet us?
Home is sweet and only sweet,
Where there's one to love us!

My Log Cabin Home - Long Gulch

My Desperate Hope - 8/17

Still at work drifting out wash dirt and although the thermometer stands at 110° in the shade, I am willing to work on in the hopes of soon being able to see the time when I may lay down the shovel and pick for good. My parents think it hard that I do not come home, but God knows how willingly I would do so were I able to. We hear by the papers from below that the Vigilants have liberated Judge Terry.

8/25 - Was obliged to quit work this morning to doctor my back, as I have completely given out. The doctors say it is a bilious complaint I have. Well, well so it goes, eternally some drawback. The Vigilants have disbanded after having a grand turn out at Francisco.

Highwaymen, Politicians & Indians - September 25, 1856

Another month has passed away and still am I delving away in old Mother Earth, in the desperate hope of soon being enabled to join my friends in my old New England, home sweet home. No water as yet and I am still drifting out dirt on my claim in Long Gulch. Politics seems to be all the rage here now, although we have plenty of exciting news in our own state. Highwaymen are as thick on the different roads in the state as politicians at a convention and just about as grasping in their demands. The Indians are as bad as ever, both here and in Oregon. Our volunteer army seems to be very quiet, as aside from the reports of their marching and counter-marchings around the lakes, we have no news from them. Meanwhile the red skins are prowling about and killing every stray traveler they lay their eyes upon.

Daniel Jenks Gold Rush Journal
Volume 3: 1857-1859

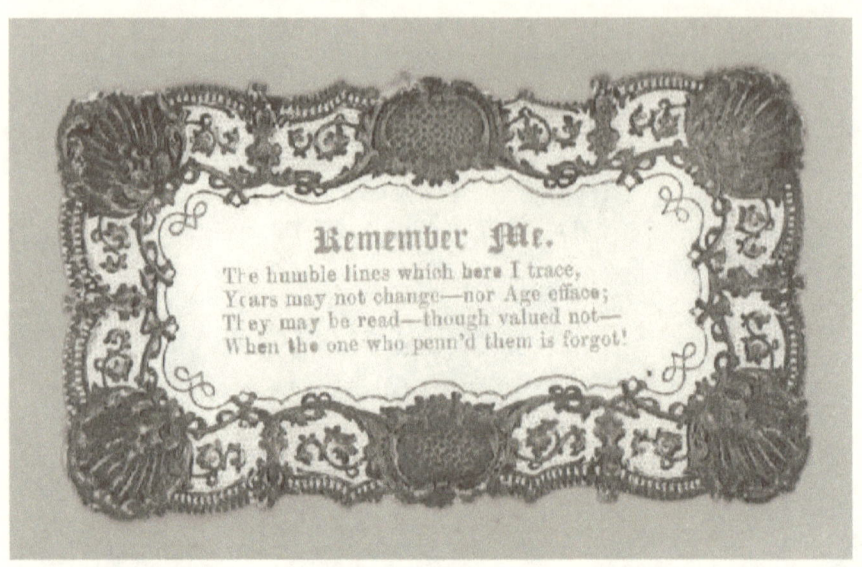

Remember Me

The humble lines which here I trace,
Years may not change—nor age efface;
They may be read—though valued not—
When the one who penn'd them is forgot.

Happy Holidays? - January 1, 1857

A Happy New Year to you say my friends, and I say I hope it may prove so. This is the eighth one I have seen here and may it be the last to find me on the Pacific Coast. Today we have had fine weather for a rarity, for since the middle of November it has snowed most of the time and at present there is about three feet of snow on the hill back of the cabin. Although we have had very disagreeable weather, all are glad to see it. For it is favorable weather for a wet spring and plenty of water. Of course, all work is suspended for the present, but all are looking forward for spring to open. As to the good time coming, we have looked so long for in vain; water, water, water is the great and universal cry.

During the month of October, I worked at my drift. About November 1st I finished that job and since then have been unable to do any work, on account of the weather. As to news, with the exception of the election in November, all has been quiet. Our troops returned from Modoc Country in October and the Indians have been quiet ever since.

Slavery Schemes

In the absence of anything to excite us, a party have tried to organize an expedition to Mexico. One of the filibuster species and a company talk of going from Yreka. Joy go with them. Fact is, we have so many poor gentlemen here from the south who consider it beneath a Gentleman's dignity to work, who have not sense enough to get a living without. That in the absence of a sufficiency of offices for them all to feed at the public expense, have to get up something of this sort. And as one crowd under the immortal Walker have succeeded so well thus far, they are anxious to follow in his illustrious footsteps and try their fortunes at it. And again they are sustained and encouraged in it by such men as Jeff Davis and others of his slavery extension stripe, who rule at Washington City. Well may their friend and master, Diablo, sustain them and God speed them from our shores.

For we have an over abundant stock on hand here now. They fill all our offices and swindle us by high taxes, which they manage to pocket and still are not satisfied. But forsooth, would make this a slave state too. Oh but they are a beautiful set, with all their gentlemanly dignity and pride of birth, looking down with utter contempt upon us of northern origin, with our northern ideas of thrift and manly labor. Away with this self-conceited aristocracy, better live under a monarchial government at once than be ruled by these asses in lions' skins, whose every bray shows their utter insignificance to all eyes but their own. All I can do is vote against them at every election - and getting beat as often as I vote.

For I never (with one exception) voted on the winning side. And more, I never expect to until time pries open the eyes of the stupidly blind who vote for them. But hold, enough, I am running into politics ~ when I meant to have written on other subjects nearer my heart.

Merry With Who?

The Merry Christmas and New Year's holidays are past, and with them all the merry festivals we are apt to celebrate these occasions with. But the memory of other days, which on these occasions are awakened in a man's mind, have not as yet passed by. Wednesday close brought Christmas eve and with it the papers, wishing their readers a Merry Christmas. Today's papers wish us a happy New Year with articles intended to call to memory the happy days of youth of home. They succeeded in my case for a while. But like champagne, which when its first effects pass by is sure to leave one a headache, so their Christmas and New Year articles. While they did for a while recall the memories of Merry Christmas in the past, eventually made me more gloomy and sad then I would have been had I not read them.

At home, in years long gone, the salutation Merry Christmas meant something. For those who used it were sure to endeavor to make it so. But here it sounded too much like mockery. Merry! Merry with whom? Where are my friends that I might be merry with? There are none here and though the eighth year of my sojourn here in this golden land draws to a close, the absence of all pleasurable anticipations for the morrow made me feel like a stranger in a strange land. As I sat in my cabin thus musing on Christmas Day Night, with naught to disturb my thoughts from Auld Lang Syne, I recalled to mind the Merry Christmas eves of my childhood days. How I anticipated the pleasures and presents of the morrow, endeavoring to guess what were the toys or play things good Santa Claus had in store for us. I have no occasion to guess now.

I anticipated no pleasures or presents now. No little tokens of regard or affection and as the chilly air came stealthily through the chinks and cracks of my cabin and the stillness of night would occasionally be broken by the yelping of coyotes, or occasionally the deep howl of a wolf, or hooting of the owl, the gloom of loneliness, of melancholy, became almost insupportable. I felt that I was lonely and almost friendless. A happy New Year say you? What is there in this miner's life of ours that promises happiness in the forthcoming year? Is it happiness to look forward to another year of toil unrequited? Of disappointments? Another year of separation from friends near and dear? Another year of deprivations, of longing for home and kindred? If this is happiness, I expect it. But go to, reserve such mockeries for other ears than mine.

The Longest Day - January 2, 1857

Laid in bed this morning, as usual of late, until I couldn't stand it any longer. In vain I turned and twisted; it was no use. Couldn't get another wink of sleep, so was obliged to get up about 10:00 AM. Opened the door, looked out and found it as usual, snowing like all wrath. Built a fire, put on the coffee pot, fried my beef and got breakfast. Was as long as possible doing all this, in order to get rid of as much of today as possible. But all of this being done at last, and my dishes are washed (i.e. plate), my pipe filled and alight, how was I to get rid of the balance of the day?

Well, I ventured out and waded through the snow, up to another cabin of miserable miners, helped them torment their cat about an hour, talked a little upon all sorts of subjects, wondered how much more snow was stored up aloft etc., and finally left them for the next cabin. Arrived safe after a severe struggle, walked in and found the Norwegian gentleman Mr. Byzer very busy with his own thoughts and, as usual, not very talkative. Sat awhile and helped him look the fire out of countenance and left him still in a deep study. Under some apprehensions that I should be unable to pass away all of my spare time unless I made longer calls, as there was but two more cabins to visit on this side of the Gulch, therefore determined to make longer visits.

With this intention, I opened the door of the Kentucky Representative and was met by a frozen potato, striking me between the two eyes, which had been aimed at the dog. But as the Gentleman's skill at throwing was not equal to his rifle shooting, had missed the dog and hit the Yankee. Kentuck apologized, cursed the dog, the weather, and bid me to enter, all in one breath. The gentleman talked some time of the ingratitude of dogs in general, and his in particular, who had just stolen the last bit of meat in the house. Left here with the intention of calling on my other neighbor. Arrived there at last, walked in and found the Texan gentleman earnestly engaged in a contest with the Blue Devils, who appeared to have taken possession of his cabin. Helped him all I could for about an hour, but they finally got the best of us and we give in.

First salutation from Texas was, "mighty white country this Yank, haint it?" I couldn't deny it sort a looked that way. "Heap wusern Yankeedom I reckon aint it?" Says he. A trifle, I replied. After this we looked at the fire about an hour, when I made a desperate effort and proposed a game of cribbage. We played from this time on, and I don't know as any of us got a game or not. But finally, after going round the board the Lord only knows how many times, we concluded to quit, and I started for home. On the way, I saw a man sinking a shaft through the snow and asked him what he was about. Said he had a cabin some whar thar about and he allowed me to sink a shaft and drift about a while, and see if he could strike it.

Wished him luck in his undertaking and pushed on in the dark for home. Thinking by the way of Siberia, Iceland, the Arctic seas and Symmes Hole, and came very near walking slap down friend Fairchild's chimney. Looked down and saw he had slap jacks for supper and dropped a flake of snow as big as my hat into his frypan. Heard him mutter to himself something about big snowflakes, never saw the light before, a heavy storm, etc. But I passed on my way and finally reached home. Built a fire, boiled my coffee, fried my beef, boiled a few frozen potatoes and made an excellent supper. Then lit my pipe and prepared for another contest with the immortal blues. Fought about an hour and finally concluded to write this, for a weapon to use against mine adversary and have succeeded very well thus far.

And now you see how we pass away the long winter days and nights in the mines. For today is a fair sample of the past month and will be, for no one knows how long to come. Beautiful is it not? But never say die. The longest day has an end and I reckon that will be the case with this long winter season. Good night. I'm off to my blankets.

The Beauties Of Solitude

Snow, snow, snow and no end to it. Pile it up mountains high. Well, well what's the use in growling, it's just what we want. But it's awful to think of this, being cooped up and hemmed in, in a cabin 10 x 8 feet square for a month or two. All alone with one's thoughts and no way to dissipate the blues, which in spite of one's best efforts to the contrary, will force themselves in upon a man. There is about 5 feet of snow upon the ground and it's still a snowing. That venerable old chap — the oldest inhabitant — never saw this life before Siberia, Da Kanes, Arctic Sea nor Dan Jenks' Cape Horn, were no whar in comparison to this Old Dame Nature.

Looks as though she were dead and laid out froze to death. It's an old saying; it never rains but it pours. And it applies very well to our winters, for we have had more snow this winter than we have had since 53, put it altogether. No one ever saw a set of fellows so hard pushed for means to pass away time as are to be found right here at present. Can't go anywhere for snow, read all the books that were to be found, aye have read everything but the Bible. Couldn't find a copy of that in this section. Found nearly everything else, some that might as well not have been found. Andrew Jackson Davis', Works On Spiritualism for instance. By the way, wonder what's the reason he don't analyze those spirits commonly called Blue Devils.

They can't be good spirits, don't think I would like to know his opinion on the subject. Think it very singular he never mentions them at all in his very scientific works. A treaties on this subject would interest me very much just now. Anything would interest me now, except it might be a treaties on the beauties of solitude. That would make me furious. T'would have the same effect upon me as singing ~ A life on the ocean wave ~ generally has on a seasick man. Solitude - Bah - no more of it, an ye love me. Why I came very near laying myself liable to prosecution for assault and battery, just by hearing an Irishman singing ~ oh I am a mountaineer ~ etc. Just as though it was the most glorious kind of a life to lead. Hang the mountains say I. Or if that's impossible, banish them from my sight.

And just see the difference now, on the same day another fellow (and a sensible fellow was he) came along singing ~ oh give me a cot in the valley I love ~ etc. And I took him in and feasted him on the jerk beef and slap jack, with a dessert of pork and beans, out of joy to find at least one man who has an ear for music of the right sort. I went to bed that night and dreamt all about the cot in the vale, with the little wife etc. The only drawback was I couldn't see her face and woke up in the morning singing a medley of Home Sweet Home, Give Me A Cot. True love ne'er forgets and be gone dull care. Oh, the pleasures of that nice dream amply repaid me for the somewhat lavish expenditure of grub fixings the night before.

Since then, I have been very sensitive on solitude, single blessedness etc. and all such romantic fol de rols. And am like an old Trapper of my acquaintance who says; "You see Dan these yer fellers what write these yer books and things are derned fools. They just sit their lazy pisin carcasses down before a good warm fire, in a good warm cabin in some sick place as York or Frisco and go to congerin up all these ar fine doings on the prairies in ther timber and mountains gassin about fine buck ingins and squaws and all this ar.

Dat rot ther pisin picture, they never wor chased nigh to death by a red devil just hungry for ther hey'ar, nor had a bead drawn on them by a durned tar head squaw just hungry for thur blood. Never were froze up in the mountains, nor melted down to a grease spot on the prairies and all this sort of thing looks mighty romantic as ye call it and all that sort of stuff. But let em try it on once an you hearn my horn toot if they don't get all this yer fol de rol rubbed out on em an begin to think thers a right smart chance more hey'ar than wool to be got, you can just set me down for a Muggins."

A city life would be very romantic to me just now. I think about one third of my life has been spent in the mountains and the wilds of California, amongst the emigrating pioneer Frontiersmen, Trappers, Wolverines, Hoosiers, Hawkeyes, Buckeyes, Missouri pukes, Grizzlies,

Wildcats and Digger Indians and I have at times been nearly froze, with the mercury down to 20° below zero. Again, have stewed and simmered with it at 120° above. Have also ascertained, to a dead certainty, how long a man can live on faith and an empty stomach. Have learnt how to sleep in a hostile Indian country, with both eyes open and on guard. All of these accomplishments have I acquired, besides many more too numerous to mention. And as my education in this branch is finished, I would like to step out and try my powers at some other.

Cut Off From All Creation

Since the fourth we have had an awful cold spell, don't know exactly how cold, but heard one fellow say the mercury rundown clean through the thermometer, broke a hole through, went out the bottom, down through the snow, at least 5 feet below zero. That beats Dr. Kane. By chance, I lived through it. Lay on the hearth with one mattress under me, one over and four pair of Mackinac blankets and a rousing fire by my side and then like to have froze. Bread, beans and beef all like so much pig iron, froze hard as a brick. Oh, but twas awful to think of but now it has moderated and we are having fine weather, with a prospect of warm rain soon. I think winter is about over and we have seen the worst of it.

1/12 - It commenced raining last night and has rained all this day, with a prospect of a long continuance. So mote it be. A man froze to death on the mountain last week. All communication with the balance of creation is cut off and has been for about three weeks.

1/14 - Since the 12th the weather has been very foggy and warm, so that the snow begins to melt away slowly. Today the sun shines out warm and the fog has disappeared altogether. My partner and myself have been at work today making our sluice boxes for washing our dirt.

1/15 - No mail as yet, as the road over the mountains is impassable. Wonder what the balance of the world is about? The outsiders I mean. At present we are hemmed in and cut off from all the balance of creation and have been for over a month, and are thrown upon our own resources for amusements, gossip, etc. We are fortunate in having plenty of provisions of all kinds. For were it otherwise, we should suffer as bad as in the winter of 52 and 53. Today has been a warm and pleasant one, but oh me ~ we miners had much rather see it rain so as to give us one good flood of rain for once.

What an awful dry place is this. Is it impossible for it to rain here? It certainly appears so. No wonder this place looks volcanic. Faith, I believe it's about time for another general burst up of this part of the world. It's dry enough sure for the purpose, for we have had no rain now of any account for four years. Snow enough but no rain. The snow is going off gradually doing no one any good, as usual. But I am setting my sluices today in the hopes of soon getting water enough to wash my drift dirt at least. And if we do not get water enough to sluice wash my claim, why all I have to say is (in the words of some immortal writer, I don't know who), Let Her Rip. I will not wait any longer for Dame Fortune's smiles, but will 'vamoose gel rancho chingarho' - aye, that I will.

Workin' The Gulch - 1/16

It froze hard last night and was cold all the fore part of the day and at night was warm and foggy. Worked all day cleaning out my ditch for conveying water on to the claim, when we get it. The Express arrived last night from below, bringing papers from San Francisco to the 6th. He crossed Scott's Mountain on snowshoes, the snow is over 20 feet deep on the trail.

1/17 - Mail arrived today, nothing for me. Quite pleasant in fore part of today, in the evening it rained. As I write this (about 11:00 PM) it is raining quite hard, may it so continue for 40 days and nights.

1/25 - Commenced washing my drift dirt on Wednesday last. During the past week the weather has been warm and very foggy. My dirt does not pay as well as I expected. But by practicing economy this spring, I am in hopes of realizing enough from it to enable me to return home in May next. Although in mining it is uncertainty, still my prospects are fair to do so. It is useless for me to stop here mining any longer, for I do believe I might work until I was gray-headed and not make more than a living. I have tried it eight years, or nearly that long and that's long enough to follow a losing business.

2/1 - The weather still continues as last week, very foggy. We had two showers of rain during the week. It increased the head of water in the gulch to a tolerably fair sluice head so that we stopped work on our drift dirt, to sluice out our gulch claim. Our dirt has yielded thus far 30 ounces (no great shakes that). On Friday I commenced sluicing off the top dirt and have done very well at that, thus far. Having moved more dirt since then, than I could with a wheelbarrow in six months' time.

It is quite sickly here just at present, owing to having so much damn foggy weather, I presume. The sickness appears to be a slow fever and has in many cases terminated fatally.

A Miner's Funeral – 2/3

Was aroused from my bed this morning by a call for assistance to help dig out a man from under a slide of dirt. I arose, dressed myself and rushed out to the bank and found that my old friend Peter Megan was buried up by a slide or avalanche from the bank under which he was at work. We soon dug him out and carried him to his cabin nearby, where he soon breathed his last. Poor fellow. A few nights since, we were talking of returning to the Atlantic States together in a few months and now he has taken his departure on a far different journey from that he anticipated then. By using great economy, he had saved about $1500 with which he was going to leave. He had it buried somewhere but no one knows where and now it is lost to all.

2/4 - I watched the corpse last night whilst his mess mates slept, as they were about used up by yesterday's work. This morning we got the hearse, and the miners collected together from the cabins in this vicinity. And following the hearse we started for the Yreka graveyard. There were about 50 of us following on foot the remains of our friend to the grave, where his remains were deposited without either prayer or funeral sermon. As the Methodist Preacher in the town was too busy with a protracted meeting and revival to say a prayer for us benighted heathen, unless we paid him for coming down. We had no objection to buying and paying for anything that was needed at the funeral, but we did not like to buy prayers. So we went without.

Scarce Wood ~ Massacres A Plenty - 2/5

Since Sunday last, we have had another cold spell with occasionally flurries of snow and frosty nights, so that the water in the gulch has dried up to one or two sluice heads. Of course my work is stopped again for the present. Today the sun shines out clear, but it looks cold and cheerless, and the air seems full of frost. Wood is scarce and worth $16 a cord and hard work to get any at that price. So, I have to stump it i.e., cut stumps for firewood.

Lockhart's Ferry Massacre

2/6 - News was received here today of another massacre by the red devils. Lockhart's two ferries on Pit River have been burned and five men at least murdered, namely Harry Lockhart, Z. Rogers, Mr. Boles and two others.

2/8 - During the past few days we had very cold, clear frosty weather. The U.S. Mail arrived today and the letters being distributed I received one from sister Eliza, which I have answered this evening. A man arrived in Yreka Friday morning who states that he and another started it from here on the 25th for Lockhart's Ferry, packing food sufficient as he thought to last him there, but which gave out some distance this side and he was obliged to kill his dog for food.

Next day they arrived at the ferry and found it had been burned by the Indians. Traveled on to the next and found it had met the same fate and that in all probability all the Whites had been massacred, five in number. They fought their way across the river and traveling all night reached the remains of their dog, breakfasted off of him and finally reached this valley Thursday night. One of the party is now at a ranch at the head of the valley, sick from exposure and the hardships he has been through. They say that after they arrived at the first ferry, most famished for want of food and found it burned, they built a raft and crossed the river and went on to the next, found it destroyed and plenty of evidence of murder committed. They started back but found they were headed off by Indians.

They kept them at a distance and finally escaped in the night, traveled 20 miles through the snow to the remains of the dog, eat the balance of him and finally reached here completely exhausted. A party are organizing to go out to Pit River in search of these savages. If they meet them, woe betide them.

Chief Lalakes

2/10 - Whilst in Yreka today, a tribe of Indians came into town from Klamath Lake. They are generally known as Lalakes Indians, he (Lalakes) being their Chief. They came in for the purpose of satisfying a treaty made with them last summer. This is but a small tribe of peaceable Indians, they are noble looking fellows every one. Lalakes is a very large and very intelligent looking Indian. They brought their squaws and papooses along and are encamped just outside of the town. They were supplied with beef and flour by the citizens and made in every way as comfortable as they could wish. They say this has been an awful hard winter for them, "halo muckanue halo marvich" etc. And the snow was 5 feet deep in their valley when they left there five days ago.

So, you see, we are feeding one band of half-famished Indians and are supplying provisions and arms to a party of our townsmen, who are now out in the mountains in pursuit of another band. Talk about our thirsting for the blood of these red skins, Mr. New York Tribune Greeley. I doubt very much whether you would like the poor Indians so well if you could only live out here a short time. Here, whilst I stood looking at these ferocious looking fellows as they passed on the street, Frank Rogers came up to me and asked who and what they were. I told him they were Lalakes tribe.

He said no more. But there was murder in his eyes. His father was killed in the last massacre at Pit River. The news of which only reached here two days ago. If Frank keeps sober, there will be no difficulty. But if he does not, there is a big chance for some trouble yet.

A Night At The Yreka Theatre - 2/12

We had the hardest rainstorm today I have seen in a year. Tonight, I went up to Yreka to see a local play written by Sniktaw, performed at the Yreka Theatre by amateur players. It was a description of a justice court in this town, and in examining witnesses and jurors many of our prominent citizens received some pretty severe hits. Our County Officers, District Judge and some of the merchants were somewhat irritated to have their old sores chaffed in this way. But the miners who were present, and there was about 800 there, gave cheer after cheer as they recognized the different characters personated.

Our Sheriffs $17,000 wife, lawyer Robinson's Virginia Pocahontas blood, Senator Cosby's Kentucky blood, Parson Stratton's usury and horse jockeying, George Peters trunks of law books etc. All these and many others were touched up in style. But in order to give some insight into the merits of the piece, I must explain some of the characters. First and foremost then, there is Dave Colton, the richest Man in Yreka now. Made his fortune out of the Sheriff's office in two years. After his election he wanted a wife and went to the States for one. Got her, brought her here, then made out a bill against the State calling for $1700 for services rendered in pursuing a runaway thief to the States.

He caught no thief, but he caught a wife and made the state pay for her. He's a good Democrat and the Democratic legislature paid the bill. Judge Robinson is from Virginia and for fear we might forget it, he always reminds us of that and his Pocahontas blood every time he makes a speech. Senator Cosby does the same, respecting his noble Kentucky origin. The Reverend Mr. Stratton came up here as poor as a church mouse about three years ago. Was a shining lamp in the church, until he made a fortune somehow. Then he left preaching and turned Shylock and is the most exacting and hardest-hearted, old usurer and horse-jockey in the whole country. Judge Peters District Judge, being a single man in this country, keeps a Mexican woman.

A short time since, a trunk was brought from below by the Express, directed to the District Judge and sent at the State's expense. The Judge, expecting it was a package of law books, opened it in the Express Office and it was full of women's apparel. He swore it was not for him. But that night the trunk disappeared. In the play they detected two thieves with this trunk and tried them before a Justice. When they brought these little affairs to light, it was capital fun for us outsiders to see these fellows touched up.

Lantern Thin

Water aplenty today and have been at work sluicing off top dirt. Think I must take Sniktaw's advice and give the merchants the top (or refuse) dirt and keep the bottom or wash dirt all to myself. If I don't do something of the kind, I never shall make enough to carry me home, unless I manage to work steadier. As it has been, for the past three months I have not been able to work on average over one day in a week. Such another frosty winter I never have seen on this coast and never want to see again. Oh but awful, where wood's scarce and coal unknown. If I had about 2 inches of fat on my ribs, I might stand it. But as it is, I am likely to choke up with anchor frost, am thin enough now to make a good magic lantern.

February 14th
Ah! why in flowers arrayed?
Those festive wreaths less quickly fade,
Then briefly blooming joy!
Those high-priced friends who share your mirth,
Are counterfeits of brittle earth,
Faults coin in death's alloy.

~~~~~~~~~~~~~~~~~

The bliss your notes could once inspire,
When lightly o'er the God like lyre,
Your nimble fingers passed;
Shall spring the same from others skill,
When you're forgot, the music still,
The player shall outlast!

Antonia of Rome

~~~~~~~~~~~~~~~~~~~~~~~~

The sun touched clouds that mount the sky,
That briefly glows to warm the eye,
That fades we know not where;
Is image of the little breath,
Of life. And then, the doom of death,
That you and I must share!

Daniel A. Jenks - Yreka Cal.

Sickly Again – 2/16

Very unpleasant weather today as it has snowed for the greater part of last night and today. The water has increased enough in the gulch to allow me to sluice again and I have been at work at it today.

2/17 - Fine pleasant weather today and am at work sluicing.

2/18 - Snowing again today. It freezes hard every night for the past week. Worked on the claim today sluicing.

2/19 - Fair weather, today am at work sluicing,

3/1 - Have been sick for about a week past, the old complaint (i.e.) kidney disease, pain in the back bilious and costive. Oh, the misery of a sick miner, it is horrible, we have none of the comforts usually found in a sickroom. The past week we have had very disagreeable weather. First it blowed, then it snowed, then it mixed in a little rain and froze, then thawed and finally, as it had tried everything else, it moderated. And today the sun has made its appearance. During this mixed-up sort of weather, I was suffering almost martyrdom with my back. And the weather being so cold, I had to keep up the good fire. Now this is no small job when a man is well, but now it seemed as though it would kill me to go up on the mountain and pack it down to my cabin.

3/5 - Moved my cabin last Sunday and have been ever since fitting it up.

My Upside-Down Chimney - 3/6

Fine weather today. Have been hard at work today sluicing my claim. Intended to write some tonight but oh me, the smoke. My chimney has a beautiful, strong draft - but it is wrong-side-up. The draft is down, instead of up the chimney. Well, well storm away. I insist upon my right to do as I please in my own cabin, smoke or no smoke. You will smoke though, in spite of my impotent wrath. May the man who invented smoky chimneys be obliged to occupy the smoky side of the fireplace in that region where, according to popular belief, they burn brimstone.

A Miner's Spring – 5/5

Well, well, two whole months have passed by since my last entry in this journal. Then we were suffering with the cold frosty weather, now all is changed. The weather clear and warm, the fields and hillsides clothed in green and decked with flowers of every hue, whose fragrance fill the air. Lovely Spring, how I love thee. Emblematic of youth, full of promises of a bright and pleasant future. In these two months past I have been very, very busy. Actually working night and day and sometimes seven days to the week, improving the only chance I have ever had to wash off the top dirt from my claim.

But now at last we have finished this job and are now ready to commence cleaning up the bedrock. We have sluiced off about 20 feet deep of dirt, having got about 800 feet of sluice boxes set, have just finished our drain and as I said before, are now ready to commence washing up the bedrock. This is the first season we have had sufficient water to do anything at mining since I have been here. We are all ready now to wash up, how it may pay us for this hard work remains to be seen, the future will tell. Today we had a good soaking rainstorm, the first for over a month.

5/10 - Commenced washing on the eighth and divided $50 tonight.

5/17 - Washed all the past week and took out $100. The water is fast running down and I am afraid we shall run short soon.

Massacre Of The Filibusters - 5/24

Took out $145 this week. The Yreka Canal is dry at present (undergoing repairs) but we are in hopes of receiving water from it in a few days. The weather is beginning to feel summer-like again. Thus far we have had very cool nights and cloudy, windy days. Sad news has been received here from Sonora Mexico. The filibusters I spoke of in January last, under the command of the Honorable Mr. H. Crabb have nearly all been massacred by the greasers. Full accounts of which are to be seen in all the papers of the day. Thus ends another expedition of the friends of manifest destiny. Walker's Nicaragua scheme will be the next to fizzle out and I hope it may be the last.

Yreka Canal Script - 5/31

Took out $120 from the claim this week. Very pleasant weather this week. No news of importance to record. Water is getting scarce but by the assistance of our reservoir, we made out to wash some every day. Oh, if us miners could but work-steady the year around and have a plenty of water, we could manage to enjoy life tolerably well. For if a man is making money to lay up for old age, or to enable himself to pass away his latter days comfortably, he can well forego present pleasures and live on pleasant anticipations of a future happiness. And surely it seems that we are to succeed. For we, as a general thing, are both prudent and economical.

6/7 - Took out $96 this week. Now although this is tolerable fair wages, still it is not paying as I expected it would and does not pay as it will higher up on the claim, of this I am a very well satisfied. And I am in the hopes water will hold out, so as to enable me to work on all summer. And if it does I am not at all alarmed, but I will make a good thing out of this yet. The weather as usual at this time of the year is fine, rather cooler than usual if anything.

The Yreka Canal Company talk of repudiating their water script. I think it is very unjust, to say the least. This script was issued to the miners hereabouts for work done on the ditch at the time when the company was bankrupt. And when, if it had not been for this, the ditch would have never been completed.

Ready To Vamoose – 6/14

Received $130 from our claim this week. Edgar Potter, returning from Francisco, sent for me. Went up to Yreka, saw him and he gave me such news from home I am anxious to return, money or no money. Resolved to sell out at any price, rather than occasion my family anymore uneasiness on my account. This resolve may be for my personal interest, but I do not believe it. However, let the result be as it may, I am determined to comply with my parents' wishes and leave the results to time and fortune to decide. I believe that there is money in this claim that will amply repay me for all the time spent on it, but I shall not get it. I do the work for someone else to reap the benefit.

6/21 - Took out $50 this week. Have not found a purchaser as yet for my claim. No one has any money, all are broke and want to buy on credit, I can't stand this kind of a trade. Am in hopes of soon finding someone who can raise me $350 dollars cash. Am very anxious to vamoose these diggings but have not the means. Walker's Nicaragua party have gone in, had to leave the country, too bad there is another slavery extension scheme collapsed. Never mind Mr. Walker you have friends high in command who are determined to acquire more slave territory, who will yet find an occupation for you and your peculiar avocation, and who may in the end accomplish their objective. Though they've ruined this country in the attempt.

6/28 - The water has about dried up in the gulch, but we are in hopes of receiving a supply from the Yreka Canal soon. As it is now, we cannot work one half of the time and have not made but $52 this week.

6/30 - No water this week and have been busy setting four new sluices.

Sellin' The Gulch

Yesterday I had an offer for my claim and although I did not think I was getting more than half enough for it, I concluded to sell and return home, at least for a visit. Although if I can find anything to do there I shall stop for good. Having squared all up, I started this morning for home. Left Yreka at 4:00 AM in William Sullivan's coach, en route for Shasta city. After all, it was with some regret that I bid adieu to Yreka, probably for good. It seemed much like leaving home, for it has been my home for years. It was a beautiful morning. I could but contrast the present appearance of the country with what it was years ago when I first arrived here. Then it was a wilderness, inhabited by the native tribes of Indians. And herds of deer and antelope grazed on the green slopes of the surrounding mountains. But now, how changed. Dotted here and there with farmhouses, the prairie of former days covered now with fields of waving green and herds of cattle, have taken the place of the wild game of other days.

Homeward Bound – July 6, 1857

After a ride of 20 miles, we stopped to breakfast at Steven's Ranch and did ample justice to the good wife's fried eggs and cornbread. About 10 o'clock we entered the forest at the head of the valley near Burn's Sawmill and at the foot of Shasta Butte. Our drive from this on was through the heavy pine timber, over hill and dale until noon, when we reached the Soda Springs on the Sacramento River, 40 miles from Yreka and the termination of the present wagon road. Here we partook of an excellent dinner, helped ourselves to a drink of soda, pure from Old Nature's fountain and mounting our mules started on down the river canyon at a 2-40 gait.

Dog Creek House – 7/7

Arrived at the halfway house Dog Creek last night about an hour after dark. Sore and weary after a mule ride over as bad a trail as I ever saw, we partook of a miserable supper and retired early to rest. This morning started before sunrise and after a long disagreeable ride of 30 miles stopped to get a miserable dinner, at a miserable cabin, kept by a miserable specimen of humanity. After a short halt we started again and by 4 o'clock were at Shasta City, glad enough to have got through with mule riding and very well pleased to find ourselves pretty well out of the mountains and once more in a civilized community, and in a country of wagon roads and stages.

Shasta City - 7/8

After reposing all night in a lousy bed, it was with but little regret I left it at 3:00 AM to take the stage for Sacramento. We had a full load, but I was fortunate enough to secure an inside seat. We had a rather dusty time of it, but I enjoyed the ride down the valley very much. Took dinner at Tehama, crossed the river and by sundown were at Oroville where we took supper. Leaving Oroville we kept on down the valley and about midnight arrived at Marysville, where we soon found beds and put them to immediate use. I was surprised to see how this city has grown and improved since I lived here.

Marysville - 7/9

After breakfast took the stage again for Sacramento City. Crossed the Yuba River and pushed on down the valley, perfectly enveloped in clouds of dust. I do not see, as the country along the road looks much different from what it did years ago, but I suppose that this portion of the valley is not very well adapted to farming, in all probability it is too dry.

Sacramento City - 7/10

About noon arrived at Sacramento City the capital of the state, and the finest looking city on the Pacific Coast. Although I arrived in time to take the steamboat for the bay, I concluded to stop here for the day. As

I am in no particular hurry to crowd ahead and then again, I am pretty well worn down with the last day or two's work. Awoke this morning considerably refreshed after a good bath and a thorough change of clothing. At 2 o'clock took the boat for San Francisco and arrived there at about 10:00 PM and put up at the What Cheer House kept by R. Woodward, formerly of Providence Rhode Island. We had a beautiful sail down the Sacramento River and I found much to admire in the scenery along the banks as we glided along. About dark we entered the head of the bay and in a short time hauled up at the wharf at Benicia to take on and discharge a few passengers, after which we up stream and steered direct for Old Frisco.

San Francisco - 7/11

The What Cheer House of this city where I am stopping, depends mostly upon mountain men for its support, although there are many mechanics that board here. At present there are about 400 stopping here, one-half of whom (at least) are miners waiting for the Atlantic steamers to sail. It is conducted on the European style. That is, borders can get their meals here or elsewhere as it suits them. Their rooms are kept neat and clean, the house is open all night, there is a large library in the house, a bathing house, barbershop and everything handy and convenient for their customers. Water is forced into every room in the house by means of a small engine in the kitchen, worked by steam, which is made by the fire in the cooking range. The house is lighted by gas made on the premises. In fact, it is a town of itself, within itself.

Time And Fortune – 7/13

Today went in search of an old friend of my youth, who I have not seen for nearly 10 years. I found him doing business on Sacramento Street. James R. Richards looked natural as life, although time has left his mark upon him as well as myself. How it brought to mind other days as I looked upon him. Who would have believed it years ago when I saw him last, had it been told us then that when we next met again it would be on the Pacific Coast, in a city that then we had no knowledge of. That then, in fact, had no existence. How little we know the changes, trials and hardships Time and Fortune has in store for us. Well it is, we have no fore knowledge of it.

Note: Text at the bottom of this page reads: "afterwards drowned while on his way to San Francisco."

The City Life ~ San Francisco – 7/14

Sauntered around this phoenix-like city today, in search of novelties and truly I found a plenty. No other city in the world I will venture to say presents just such a variety of nations as this. Here are streets of Chinese stores, warehouses and dwellings where a man might well imagine himself in Canton or Shanghai, judging from appearances. In other places are German lager beer saloons, all after the old fatherland style and here are the Mexican fandangos, the French cafés, the English Porter shops etc. All nations and tongues are here. Tonight, went to see the Negro Opera at McGuries. The singing suited me very well, but I suppose I am no judge of music and therefore I'll not say any more about that.

7/16 - This morning started out with Sam Hamilton for a ride up to the San Jose Road. Went out by the Old Mission and called upon a Pawtucket man who keeps a milk rancho. Left him and rode on to the San Bruno House, about 15 miles from San Francisco. After a short stay here returned to the city, much pleased with my ride but not very much in favor of the country. It undoubtedly is a great farming country, but a more desolate looking place I never saw. At night went to see Miss Ince at the Metropolitan Theater. It was crowded full, as it was a benefit night.

Neptune's Tribute ~ Onboard John L. Stevens

7/20 - Having secured a ticket for New York via the John L. Stevens I came onboard, carpetbag in hand, secured my birth, bid farewell to my friends ashore and at 9:00 AM we drew out from the wharf and were soon on our way for Panama. We have about 600 passengers on board. All strangers to me. Noon, we are now outside the heads and fairly at sea again. Old Don Neptune is claiming his tribute from many of the passengers, obliging them to cast up their accounts and to discharge all shore ballast, preparatory to laying in a supply of sea store. Evening, the day has passed off quite pleasantly to all but the seasick ones. They look rather blue.

7/27 - Thus far on our voyage all has gone on smoothly. There has been some growling about the grub, but that is always expected at sea. Arrived at Manzanilla about noon today where we are to take in a lot of silver in bars from the mines in this vicinity. We lay here until about dark when we got underway again. Of course, we were not allowed to go ashore here, but the natives came out in their boats and supplied us with fruit. Judging from what I could see of the town from onboard ship, I should say it was not much of a place.

Acapulco, Mexico – 7/30

Arrived here about 10:00 PM and whilst the ship was getting aboard her supplies of coal, water, beef, many of the passengers availed themselves of the opportunity offered to stretch their legs onshore, myself included. We were rowed ashore by a crew of Mexicans and enjoyed ourselves very much for an hour or two in running over the city. But as it was in the middle of the night, we of course could not see much of the town. Returning aboard found the crew busy hauling up, by the horns, a lot of beef from out of the water alongside. I thought it a singular sight to me, a new way of getting stock aboard ship. Left here about 4:00 AM.

Panama – 8/3

Arrived here last night about 12 o'clock and came to anchor at the usual anchorage, about 3 or 4 miles from the city landing on the opposite side of the bay. This morning there is a beautiful view from the deck of the city of Panama and the surrounding country of the bay and its numerous islands. The ship at an early hour was surrounded by the natives with their boats and as many of us were anxious to get ashore we did not wait for the company's small steamboat but went in the natives' boats. As for myself I had better have stopped onboard a while, for although we bargained to be set ashore for $.50 each, it cost me $3 before I got there.

Aspinall – 8/3

After we left the ship in the thief's boat, we were carried across the bay toward Panama and landed on a reef of rocks, or rather the boat grounded within about 10 feet of the reef. We were immediately surrounded by the miserable thieves who infest this hole of a place, all jabbering in Spanish for a job. Here we were hard and fast, and unless we hired the thieves to carry us ashore must swim for it. So we were compelled to hire them to set us ashore by paying them a dollar a piece to carry us about 10 feet. And then another dollar to get our baggage and another half to help us with it up to the depot. This entrance into the city disgusted me so with the place, that I am very much afraid I should not do it justice were I to attempt to describe it. The town is like all other Spanish towns on the continent, apparently going to ruin.

The buildings have an ancient moss-covered look, peculiar to the species. Streets narrow and filthy, the inhabitants the same and even the atmosphere has a nasty, sticky, feeling. I was glad to leave the miserable hole and after a short and pleasant ride of about 47 miles across the Isthmus, passing several villages of mud huts on our way, we arrived at the American town of Aspinall. Here we stopped until about 9:00 PM, when we left on board the Central America Steamer for New York. In addition to our number of passengers, we took on over a hundred Man of War's men from a US frigate at Panama on their way home.

Steamer Central America – 8/10

"Man overboard, man overboard," is the cry fore and aft. Soon the ship is stopped, the boats lowered and away in search of the poor unfortunate. An hour is past, rockets have been fired for the boats return and here they come. "Have you got him? Did you see him?" "No, no," is the answer. Take the boats aboard again and get underway, he is in Davy Jones Locker long before this. The poor fellow (one of the discharged seamen from the frigate Independence on his way home after a three-year absence) lay stretched out on the seat around by the rail forward and rolled over in his sleep overboard, right forward of the wheel, probably the wheel struck him killing him instantly.

New York – August 12, 1857

Arrived here 12:00 PM and soon left the steamer for French Hotel A: 1 Chatham Street.

8/13 – Stopped in this city today to recruit a little after a long voyage.

8/14 – Took the steamer for Fall River tonight. The old Empire State looks perfectly natural and as good as ever. No one who has not been placed in a similar situation can imagine what my feelings are as I approach home after an absence of over eight years. How I watch for the old landmarks, even the passengers on the boat seem like old friends, although I look in vain for a familiar face.

Home Again - August 15, 1857

At about 11 o'clock I arrived in Pawtucket; my heart was in my mouth. I never was so excited in my life. I was soon to see my friends again. How would they look? Would they know me etc. were questions that rushed through my mind. But I will not attempt to describe my feelings, nor my reception by my father, mother and sisters upon whom I came all unexpectedly, as they were not aware of my being on the way home. The old town has changed some in eight years and over, but not for the worse. The greatest change however is in the people. I, to be sure, found many of my old friends here. But oh, what a hoot of strangers. I shall have to commence anew again and form a new set of acquaintances.

Pawtucket - September 1st

Although home again, still I am not as well contented as I ought to be. I find I have nothing to do here and as idleness breeds discontent, so am I now suffering the natural consequences of a life of this kind. My parents, God bless them, do everything that lays in their power to make my stay with them pass off agreeably and pleasantly, but for all their best endeavors I find that time drags heavily. I must find something to employ myself about, some active business that will require all my time. Then I should probably enjoy myself here. For certainly I have everything here but this, to make life pleasant.

The U.S. Economy Collapses

10/1 - No business as yet and a very dull prospect ahead. In fact, all business is suspended at present. Never was the like seen before by anyone in this country. The banks have suspended and all business is prostrated. The cotton factories, the life of this section of the country, have most all stopped. And those that have not stopped entirely have commenced running half time and will stop altogether as soon as they run out their stock in hand. Thousands who depend entirely upon their wages to keep body and soul together, are thrown out of employment and have no other prospect ahead to avoid starvation, then assistance from the town authorities. Hard times come again is the song in everyone's mouth.

The financial panic has spread all over the country and nothing else is talked of. Most of the banks of the country have suspended. Thousands of the first business houses have failed and all the others have had to have extensions granted, to enable them to keep their heads above water. Business of all kinds is dead from north to south. From Boston to St. Louis, it is all the same. All the operatives of the different trades and manufacturys are thrown out of employment. Want and misery stalk boldly through the land. The Alms Houses are full and the towns cannot provide for 1/16 of their poor who need assistance.

11/8 - Another week has passed by and no better prospects ahead. All is doubt and uncertainty concerning the future. A singular state of affairs truly. The country is full of provisions, never had better crops in the world. But for lack of money, many are actually starving. Western and Southern men will not sell their produce at the present market prices. Therefore, they injure the North and East in two ways if they do not sell.

They cannot pay their indebtedness to us and at the same time are keeping our food from us. "No," they say, "do you suppose I am going to sell my produce at present low prices to pay my debts? No, no, not I." But what do they expect? Do they think to get the old high prices for produce when they, by their vote, are endeavoring to bring the consumers to a free trade level with Great Britain?

11/9 - The West and South have for a long time been in favor of free trade. They can now see how beautiful it has commenced working. We send out of the country about $5 for manufactured goods, where we receive $1 back for grain and the cottons. This of course keeps the country drained of specie and our money is employed there to make the goods for us which we could just as well make ourselves, if we paid laborers no more than they do. But the labor has always commanded good wages here and it is in the interest of government to keep it up, but they say no. Well now they have shut up the manufacturys, the great consumers and where is their market? White flour, corn and cotton prices have fell. It is no use, what ruins one section of the country is bound to affect all other sections.

11/17 - All business is suspended as yet, no improvement in the times as yet and but poor encouragement ahead, at least for some time. All businessmen agree in saying that there never was seen such times before in this country. The Mormons in Utah Territory have broken out in open hostilities towards the US government, having taken 78 government wagons and burnt them. Walker of Nicaragua notoriety has sailed again with about 500 men. Joy go with him, but he has a hard road to travel if he expects to succeed in conquering that country. Our president made a grand flourish of trumpets in his inaugural address, respecting his treatment and opinion of filibusters and now we can see what it all amounts to ~ Bosh ~ Buncombe ~ Nothing Else.

Long Gulch Is Payin'?

12/17 - Received two letters yesterday from California, one from Edgar W. Potter and one from Isaiah G. Douthitt of Yreka. It seems from these that my old claim has been paying from 24-26 ounces per week since I left. Such is my luck. I answered them today. Since my last entry, business has remained as then. Perfectly dead. The New York banks resumed specie payment last Monday. Massachusetts followed suit, but Rhode Island remains as before. The weather remains fine. We have had no snow as yet and thus far have had quite warm weather.

First Baptist Sewing Circle

12/18 - After a storm comes a calm thought I this morning, as I came down from my room and found all the family laying around endeavoring to recover from the effects of yesterday's excitement. Said excitement being occasioned by the grand gathering of the First Baptist Sewing Circle at the house of Deacon G.J. Jenks, my respected sire. As to the weather, it continues warm and pleasant as of yet. Which is very favorable for the many poor who are thrown out of employment this winter by the stoppage of all business here. To look at Pawtucket now, one would think it was about time to lay it out for sure enough, it is as dead as Hamlet's ghost. Hoorah for free trade, you fools. For lo and behold, its fruits are before ye.

A Pawtucket Sunday – 12/20

We have had a very warm and pleasant day and in the afternoon I attended church. The Reverend Mr. Bernard, Pastor of First Baptist Church in this town, is quite an interesting speaker and appears to be quite a popular man here. He is brother to the artist of that name of New York who has acquired quite a name by his panoramic views of the Mississippi and of Palestine. In the evening I called with my sister upon Cousin Ellen Benedict and had a very pleasant time. She is a splendid looking girl and fine company. Her brother Curtis is quite an artist and in my humble opinion, with the proper training, would make an excellent landscape painter.

The Unemployment Crisis

12/23 - Business affairs begin to look very little better, as yet there is but very slight improvement. Some of the factories have started up on short time, more to give their hands employment then from any expectation of making anything. According to a statement in the Providence Journal, there are now over 10,000 factory hands out of employment in this state. This is about the number that are out of employment altogether, to say nothing of those who are working halftime or three days in the week and of these are operatives in the cotton business alone. How many more are thrown out of employment who are or have been engaged in other kinds of manufacturys is not known. What an awful amount of misery, in this little state alone. All owing to bad Government and bad laws.

An Irish Christmas

Christmas passed off with rather less than the usual amount of gaiety, owing to the great poverty of the masses at the present time. But the miserable, fighting, brutish Irish found money enough to get as drunk as usual. And about a dozen of them got their heads cracked and bunged up in a grand fight down the street at a rum hole. What a miserable race they are. Lower, meaner and uglier in every way than the miserable Digger Indians of California. And to think they have the controlling power in this, my beloved country, makes me look with foreboding to its future. They are no more fit to exercise the elective franchise than so many baboons. I cannot be anything but a Native American in politics as long as I live.

Protect Yer Pile!

12/ 26 - It was very cold yesterday and this morning commenced snowing and now (noon) the ground is covered with its arctic mantle. This is the first snow of any account this season. The whole conversation nowadays is of course upon business topics, the panic etc. And many are the anecdotes told of its effects upon nervous men of capital. For instance, an hombre of rather limited ideas of these banking institutions, but who nevertheless had, by some means, been induced at some previous time to invest his little amount in bank stocks, became rather restless and anxious concerning the safety of his pile. And after standing it as long as possible, he at last rushed for the People's Bank and struck a trade with the teller for his stock, selling it by the way at 5% below market price.

"How do you want your money Mr. Green, in the specie or bank bills?" Says the teller. "Oh, hang the difference so I get my pay," was the reply and accordingly the amount was counted out to him in bills on the bank. Mr. Verdant Green counted them over anxiously, examining every bill and ascertaining that it was all right, he drew a long breath and with an appearance of great relief, crammed the bills in his pocket and exclaimed; "There, now durn the bank, let her bust and be durned to her. I, me out of the scrape." Again, an Irishman a short time before the suspension of the specie payment, came into the New England Pacific Bank and demanded the specie for about $200 in bills of the bank.

"What do you want of the specie," says a gentleman standing near, who was at that time doing a big business entirely on credit. "What do I want of the spacy?" Says Pat, "Do yer suppose I want this rag money nowadays, when all the durned banks are about to bust, bad luck to em." "Well but my friend," says Mr. Oily, "the specie will be a great inconvenience to you to carry about your person. And besides you are liable to be robbed in these times if it is known that you carry about with you such an amount." "Be dad I know it, shure I don no what to do with it now I have it," said Pat And Pat looked at the mass of silver he had been paid in, "sure now Mr. Oily, what wud you do?" "My old friend," says Oily, "would it not be better to let some good, sound businessman have it to keep for you and then you know it would be safe and also would bring you in some $12 a year interest?

Now I have no particular use for money now. But to accommodate an honest old friend, as you are, I don't know, but I would do the job for you to accommodate you." "Give me your hand Mister Oily, shure you was always the poor man's friend, take it and be Howly Ghost. I'll sleep the sounder for knowing me money is in safekeeping and not in the durned Whig Banks, bad cess to em." The transfer was made, Mr. Oily received the $200, gave Patrick his note payable on demand and Pat left the bank with a light heart. For he had turned the nasty rag money into specie and had invested it where it would fetch him a good income. Meanwhile Pat had no sooner left the bank when Mr. Oily passed the specie back to the cashier, took up a note for $150 that fell due that day, left the balance on deposit and in less than a month made one of the worst kind of failures -- assets zero dollars, liabilities $50,000 or something near that style.

As to Mr. Whig-hating Pat, he has been drunk on fighting whiskey ever since. Has beat his wife and children regular every day and been just as regularly cleaned out himself every night. He has finally come to the conclusion that he would have been full as well off if he had not made that run on the bank.

Note: 2 pages appear to be torn out of the journal after this page.

Enjoying Society

12/29 - About noon yesterday the weather moderated and the sun came out warm, the snow began to disappear, but at night it came on frosty again as ever. This morning the weather was warmer and during the day had a slight fall of snow, not enough however to make good sleighing. Our family spent the day with Eliza, this being the fifth anniversary of her wedding. Had quite a pleasant time. Last evening called on Mrs. Charlie Lawton and enjoyed the call very much, she is a noble looking woman and excellent company. May her path through life be strewn with the flowers of love, her prospect ahead be one of joy full anticipations, is the heartfelt wishes of her friend DA Jenks. Tonight, it snows again. But not fast enough to ensure much sleighing.

Troublemakers

12/30 - The weather as usual of late looks rather snowish. The political world is all excitement owing to the aspect of affairs in Kansas Territory. They have crowded the free state settlers into war and bloodshed again. Walker of Nicaragua has been arrested by a US Man of War and he and all his men been brought back prisoners. Truly he has a hard road to travel and must be very anxious to acquire a name of questionable renown, to persevere as he does in his raids upon that miserable country of fleas and other vermin. He made great threats of what he would do if he was molested, but after all was said, he surrendered without firing a gun.

Note: 2 pages appear to be torn out of the journal after this page.

Weather & Correspondence - January 17, 1858

Yesterday it rained all day and had very much the appearance of one of our old California "49 rainstorms. They say here that there never was so mild a winter as this has been thus far. There has been but two or three light snowstorms and I believe the thermometer has not run as low as zero yet. In fact, most of the time it has been from the 20° to 30° above. I received two letters and eight papers yesterday from California. One letter from A. Harris, one from J.G. Douthitt of Yreka and the papers from Edgar W. Potter of same town. They say they have had a fine open for winter up to date (Dec 6th). On Friday evening I attended a lecture at the Catholic Church in this place. Subject, the old Catholic monks by Father Quinn of Connecticut.

1/28 - Never in the memory of the oldest inhabitant did we ever have such weather here as now. Everything wears the aspect of spring, the grass is green, flowers in a few places have made their appearance and the buds on the trees begin to swell out in their spring fullness. Thermometer stands 60° in the shade.

1/29 - Rather unpleasant today and it looks as though we might have a snowstorm soon. Have written two letters today, one to E.W. Potter the other J.G. Douthitt of Yreka California. Today's paper says, in reference to business prospects, that although we all hope for better times still, to our vision, all is darkness ahead.

Note: A page appears to be torn out of the journal after this page.

Sleighing Pawtucket Pike

2/21 - It commenced snowing yesterday and continued all night. And this morning we have about 6 inches on the ground, enough to start the sleighs out. Evening ~ we have had a very pleasant day and the sleighs have made their appearance in great numbers.

2/22 - Tiptop sleighing on the Providence Pike and well improved by the owners of fast nags.

2/23 - Went out onto the pike this afternoon to see the sleighers. The track is not as it might be, but it furnishes tolerable fair sleighing and the opportunity thus (for the first time furnished this season) is well improved by all, whether they are the owners of a 2-40 nag, or one whose speed will not come down to anything less than 5-80 or thereabouts.

Pomfret, Connecticut

2/25 - Started yesterday at noon for this place by the Hartford Railroad. After passing through numerous factory villages (all or mostly all stopped at present) we arrived at the junction of Plainfield. Here we exchanged cars and after passing through Central and Danielsonville we arrived at Daysville, the termination of my rail ride. Hiring a team, I started on for a ride of about 5 miles to Mr. Averill's. Arrived just after dark and was warmly welcomed by the family. Found a great many of the guests had already arrived, for be it known that the occasion of my visit was to witness the marriage of my friend William Collar, a student of Amherst to Miss Hannah Averill, our host's daughter.

The wedding in the evening passed off very quietly and with but little of the usual loud and boisterous mirth ~ owing in great measure no doubt to the entire exclusion of all wines and other Life and Mirth generating liquids. It was a regular old-fashioned Puritan wedding. The couple were joined together in the holy bands of wedlock and the guests were expected to kiss the bride, congratulate the groom, eat their cake and disburse by 10 o'clock in the evening. Today arose early and went downstairs, found all hands assembled at family prayers. After breakfast Bride and Groom, together with the guests from abroad including myself, tumbled into two lumber wagons prepared for our reception and started off on a visiting tour, to friends in the vicinity. Spent the day very pleasantly, visiting with the farmer friends of the bride, but was not all flattered by the notice they appeared to take of my personal appearance, owing to my California appendage ~ i.e., my pet mustache.

2/26 - Last evening was passed very pleasantly at a brother of the bride's, a Mr. Sharp, and after a pleasant moonlight ride of about 2 miles we arrived at Mr. Averill's and soon retired for the night. This morning all was hurry and confusion about the house in the excitement of packing up certain trunks, carpetbags, band boxes etc., previous to our departure. But by 10 1/2 o'clock all were ready and we started for Daysville. We arrived at Plainfield alright and found we were obliged to wait over four hours for the Providence train. Fortunately the ladies found out that there was to be a meeting of the Teachers Institute and they availed themselves of the opportunity thus offered, to pass away these long four hours. At 6 1/2 o'clock we arrived at Providence and after considerable trouble with the baggage, we arrived home.

The Weather & Economy Begin To Thaw

2/28 - This is the last day of winter and the sun shines out warm and bright as ever it did in spring. For the last three days it has been quite warm, and of course our sleighing has disappeared. Thermometer stands at 3 o'clock 48°. Have not attended church today.

3/1 - The first of spring opens with a rainstorm and the snow is fast disappearing. Thermometer stands at noon 43° in the shade. As to business matters, they are at a standstill as yet, with but little prospects of an immediate improvement. But a few of the thread manufacturers have started up their mills and some few of those in the cotton prints, other branches are trying to start the wheel of business but make but slow progress. As to other matters political I shall not attempt to keep run of them at all.

3/2 - Snowed all night and this morning we have about six inches upon the ground but as the ground was soft, we shall not get much sleighing out of it.

3/3 - Cold as blazes today.

3/4 - Ditto ~~ Ditto

3/5 - Very cold today and clear. Life in this town this winter does not afford many charms for a man of an active temperament like mine and furnishes but little suitable food for journalizing. Everything has a dead and laid out appearance, not at all to my liking. But I must stand it I suppose for a while, whether I like it or not.

Fouch's Lazy Fortune

3/6 - Saw a Mr. Mayberry last night who has just returned from California. He says my old partner Fouch and his brother came on with him on their way home. He furthermore says they had about $3000 apiece. Just my luck, now they have made this out of my old claim since I left there last July. Now I don't know if it is all right -- but I'll be damn_d if I believe it is. Here I worked night and day on that same claim, month after month for a mere pittance. Worked harder than they ever did, still I could not make anything out of it. But as soon as I quit it, the claim commenced paying from $300-$500 per week. And now here am I, not worth a bung town copper and they, my lazy partners, have come home with a fortune. Just my luck. What is the use of my trying? I give it up.

3/6 - A year ago today I sat in my smoky cabin, resting my wet and weary limbs after a hard day's work, all alone by myself on my claim. My partner being too lazy to work himself and not liking to get as wet as he would have been obliged to in sluicing, had told me if I wanted to work on our claim I might do so, but he would not. Ambitious to succeed in acquiring wealth, I toiled on all alone and succeeded during the flood in getting our ground all stripped off the top or refuse dirt. After this we went to work and setting our sluices, we commenced washing up our dirt that I had stripped. We toiled on with but poor pay up to 1 July when I, for reasons stated at the time, sold out my interest and left for home...

Note: Pages appear to be torn out of the journal after this page.

Sacred Sticks & Stones

3/30 - Another beautiful spring day. In the morning took a walk with a friend on the Massachusetts side of the town. Our travels of the morning were overground and through streets and lanes made sacred to me by the memory of other days. For years I have not trod this ground before and every tree and almost every stone looked to me like old familiar friends. These same trees, years ago, had witnessed much of my joy. For many a moonlit evening have we passed along under their wide spreading branches. Whispering to one another our joyful anticipations of future bliss. Here upon such an evening had we stooped beneath the cool refreshing shade of such a tree, to while away the precious moments, in a heavenly converse and again here upon this rock, how often had we sat together, to rest and pass away the time. Every stick and stone is sacred to me.

In the evening visited a married female friend and by 10 o'clock was at home and abed again and another day was worried through with.

5/31 - Like a lamb full of gentle mildness, this last day of spring takes its departure. Bless God the giver of the rose as well as of the thorns, of fair and love inspiring days, as well as foul. Bless him that he has sent us the rose with the thorn, that our days here on earth are not all cloudy ones. That the sunshine of happiness does occasionally burst through the clouds of misery that overcast our earthly horizon.

My Last Resting Place

6/1 - Arose this morning at 4 o'clock for an early walk. Rambling around, I finally found myself in the Old North Providence Burial Ground where I spent an hour or so pleasantly and I trust profitably. The old spot is rather crowded but there is still room there for many of the children of our old mother Pawtucket and may my last resting place be either there or in the vicinity of this, my home.

Pawtucket Weather

6/2 - Yesterday was cloudy with occasional showers of rain but today is bright and warm and everything looks lively and soul inspiring. Last evening after watching the course of a balloon set up in Providence until nearly dark, I went to see the panoramic painting of scenes in Italy now on exhibition in Pawtucket. Liked it very much. Today Sallie has gone to Newport with some of her friends to attend the Sabbath School Convention there in session.

6/3 - Another fine day, warm and beautiful. Yesterday sent two papers and a letter to E.W. Potter of Yreka.

6/4 - Warm and pleasant weather today. Nothing of any importance to journalize today. Business prospects are improving.

6/5 - A most beautiful day. In the afternoon attended church.

6/7 - Fair weather today.

6/8 - Clear fine weather, very warm.

6/9 - Fair and quite warm.

6/10 - Warm and sultry.

6/14 - Received a letter from J.G. Douthitt, answered it today.

6/15 - Saturday last it commenced raining and has continued to up to this time. And a fair prospect now for a long continuance of the same kind of weather.

This Rainy Hole

6/16 - I must say that this is the most disagreeable, damn, rainy hole I have ever seen. Rain, rain, rain day after day, week after week, aye months of it and in fact it's nearly all rain, snow or frost all the time. Have not had on average two clear and pleasant days a week since I've returned home. I am sick of it and want to leave this damp, moldy hole. Why under the heavens the old Puritans ever settled down here is more than I can conceive, for I swear it's the meanest climate in this world. A person starts out here in the morning dressed for summer weather and in less than an hour he has to hurry home to change his linen for an overcoat and fur cap. I don't believe this hole in the ground will hold me much longer, for I can't stand this everlasting drizzle.

July 4th, 1858 - Since my last, we have had very warm weather and as I write this the sweat is pouring from every pore. Passed the day very pleasantly at home. It is too hot to write much.

Having Regrets

7/28 - Received a letter from E.W. Potter today and have answered the same. I wish I had never taken his advice in coming home. Times in California, he says, are good, business lively and the season favorable for mining. Why could it not be arranged so as to give them a part of our rain and let us poor, moldy Yankees be blessed with a little of their pleasant clear sunshine? But this miserable world appears to have been given over to the spirit of contrariness and it never rains where it is most needed, but it pours down upon us here, where we have no use for it.

Drizzle Town

8/4 - Rain, rain, rain, an eternal rain, never ending, constant, unfailing daily drizzle. Who ever saw the light of this part of the world for unpleasant weather? For weeks past we have had our daily rain. First thing in the morning a sickly sunshine, next a drizzle, then a rainstorm. I would try to express my feelings upon the subject but cannot find words in the English language suitable for the occasion. If cursing were of any use, I think I have done enough of that to turn all blue. If we could have on an average one whole day of 24 hours fair weather in a month, I think we could stand it if all the rest of the month was rainy ~ but this having all rain and no shine is rather binding on me.

When I first arrived in this moldy place a year ago it was raining. Day after day, it continued to rain and they said about here that it was the equinoctial storm that had set in rather early. Well by the time this was over with, winter set in and we had with a cold mild winter ~ that is, it was not cold enough to freeze a man to death if he did not venture away from the stove ~ but it still continued to rain pretty much all the time (occasionally snowing to give us a variety) until spring set in with its April showers of a week's duration. After this came the May storm and we have a little more rain. This was immediately followed by the June storm, which held on to us till dog days set in, with a little more rain. We are now enjoying our dog days rain and I suppose by the time we are out of this, the equinoctial storm will set in. So that between them all, the inhabitants of this weeping part of the world are likely to have water enough.

And all that surprises me is to see how they can distinguish the difference between the storms ~ that is I don't see how they can tell where one ~ say the May ~ storm ends and the June storm commences. For to me, they are all alike and appear to run into and connect one with another, as well as the separate links in a chain. The somewhat celebrated John Phoenix says of Oregon (whose winters by the way resemble this rainy climate) that it rains so much there that the children are all towheaded, their hair having bleached out in the constant rain. I wonder if that is the occasion of there being so many towheads raised in this section?

Oregon - The New Eureka?

8/5 - What shall I do to pass away the long dreary day? And after I have dragged through with this, the same question arises in my mind tomorrow and so on. Day after day, week follows week, and still the same question arises with the days return. Truly this life of idleness unfits a man for life. He (if of an active turn of mind) becomes unfit for social life, a curse to himself and to all connected with him. Always uneasy, never contented. Such is my life here at home. Is there no escape from this? I know not which way to turn. I lay awake nights trying to think of some occupation to take up my time, some way whereby I may by constant, strict attention to my business, not only employ my mind and body, but may be enabled to do so advantageously. But thus far without success.

Business in this part of the world received such a check last winter that it will require years to recover from its disastrous effects. Although manufacturing is improved a little since last winter ~ yet it is not what it was years ago and the great cry still is "nothing to do". The discovery of gold in the British possessions north of Oregon has caused a considerable excitement, especially in California where at least 25,000 have left for this new Eureka. Many are leaving here for these new diggings, but I am not disposed to follow them in their mad rush for this cold, savage and inhospitable country. I am afraid that those there this winter will suffer much from famine, cold and cruelty by the Indians of the country. Time will tell. No, I do not wish to emigrate to a colder climate than this, when I move again it will be to a warmer sphere I think.

The Beginning Of Hostilities

8/5 - By the last steamer from California we received the news of a fracas onboard one of the coasters, between the chief of the Rogue River Indians, who was a prisoner onboard and several of the crew, whereby several were wounded by this desperate savage. It is to be hoped that this may be his last fight. He is now a prisoner, having been sent down to headquarters in California for trying to induce his tribe at the US reservation in Oregon to raise and revolt. This last scene in his life reminds me of scenes in Oregon during the war with his tribe in "55 and it may be interesting in time to come to refer to these early trials of the settlers of Northern California and Southern Oregon, many of which I was an eyewitness of.

John and Sam, two brothers, jointly governed the tribe. John was styled the War Chief and Sam was called the Peace Chief. In the month of July 1855, a Mr. Peters of Humboldt Creek in California was forced into a fight with a party of John's Indians, Mr. Peters lost his life in the affray. This was the first link in the chain. Then followed the cold-blooded massacre of McKinney's Bar on the Klamath River, also in California. The victims of which were hardly cold in their graves before two citizens of Rogue River Valley, who were on their way to Yreka with produce for sale, were murdered upon the Siskiyou Mountain. Their property destroyed and their cattle wantonly shot down in their yokes.

Not sated with this wanton and atrocious crime, for which the slightest palliation cannot be found, even in the savage and brutal customs of Indian revenge and reprisals. These murderers march down to Cottonwood Creek and shoot down a miner peaceably engaged at his work and severely wounding his companion. The loss of so many innocent lives and the shedding of so much innocent blood was more than could be borne. Every exertion of Captain Judah and the officers of Fort Lane to ferret out and punish the guilty were fruitless. All traces of their whereabouts seemed lost, until a trail was discovered by citizens of Rogue River leading off the Siskiyou Mountain to Butte Creek. Taken with the previous discovery of the Humbug Klamath Volunteers, clearly pointed out the fact that these systematic and continued outrages had been planned and carried out by Indians who went from, and came to, the reservation at Fort Lane.

Old Chief Sam who had remained at the reservation with a few of his men and who refused to take part with his tribe in the war now fairly commenced, confessed that bands of Shasta and Applegate tribes, aided by discontented spirits on the reservation had, against his council, long been secretly making preparations for hostilities and have large quantities of provisions stored away in the mountains. When the citizens of Rogue River Valley therefore turned out to search for and punish the Indians whose hands had so often of late been died in innocent blood, they but adopted a course that was forced upon them. The first encounter with these savages was upon their trail at Butte Creek, from whence they escaped to the reservation. They thought their plans had been so secretly carried out, that no suspicion was entertained against them by the officers at the fort and they counted upon their protection. But murder will out and justice was upon their tracks.

They were again attacked on the eighth and 30 of them killed. One of the volunteers May Lupton, was severely wounded. He was carried to a house to have his wounds dressed. That night the house was attacked by the Indians and the noise of firearms and pelting of bullets against the sides of the cabin so excited him, that he jumped from his bunk to take part in the affray. But the blood gushed from his wound and in a short time he was a corpse. The next morning the Indians appeared at Evans Ferry, numbering about 80 warriors and commenced a fearful massacre. It is not known precisely what number of men fell victim at the ferry and on the road there, but the number is set down as 20.

Mrs. Wagoner was the first woman killed by them. On Monday night Miss Sarah Pellet, the celebrated temperance lecturer, had delivered an address in the vicinity and had stopped overnight at Mrs. Wagoner's. On Tuesday morning Miss Pellet left and Mr. Wagoner accompanied her some distance down the road, to behold a most heart-rendering scene upon his return. The red skins, after killing every white man on the road, reached Wagoner's house just after a large pack train passed. The Packers noticed that there was an unusual number of Indians in sight, and from their sullen manner became suspicious of them and kept looking back at the house. Presently flames began to burst forth from the barn and the screams of Mrs. Wagoner were heard from the house.

The word was passed to cut loose the packs and try to save the mules by flight, which was quickly done. There is no accounting for the Indians allowing these men to escape, unless it was because they were anxious to feast their fiendish appetites with the blood of the helpless inmates of the house and feared their prey might escape by flight if they delayed to attack the train. Just as the men had succeeded in freeing the mules of their loads, the Indians had finished their fiendish work and were upon them. But they succeeded in making their escape with all of the mules but one. Mr. Wagoner returned in time to see his buildings still on fire. But suspecting what had happened, took a circuit around by a neighbor's house, where he learned of the outbreak. When he reached his home, he found the buildings burned to the ground and the bones of his wife and child buried beneath the smoking ruins of his house.

Near Wagoner's, the Indians attacked the house of Mr. Harris. When they began to gather around, an Indian who had frequently stopped there and always been well treated by the family came boldly into the house with his gun. Mrs. Harris said to him "You surely are not going to help murder us?" "No," says the Indian, but immediately turned and shot Mr. Harris who was coming in the door, who fell mortally wounded. Just then the little girl, 10 years old, received a wound in the arm from a shot fired from the outside, as she ran into the house. This left Mrs. Harris in a most trying and horrible situation. And the heroic manner in which she conducted herself surpasses any recorded case of female courage in times of old. Her husband lay upon the floor dying. And a large party of infuriated savages without, stood ready to rush in and finish their bloody work.

Mrs. Harris pushed the Indian who had shot her husband out of the door and closed it after him. The floor was covered with blood from the wounds of her dying husband and wounded child. Mr. Harris, before dying, instructed her how to load and fire an Allen's revolver. This she loaded and fired and thus kept the Indians at bay for awhile. Night came and she watched for an opportunity to escape. The Indians withdrew out of gunshot, to induce her to come out, so they could pursue and take her without danger to themselves. She took advantage of this and fled into the brush with her little girl. Her pistol balls had given out. But by continuing to load with powder, and the constant firing, she managed to keep them from charging into the bush. The morning arrived at last and she was rescued by a party of mounted men, before whom the Indians retreated.

These are a few facts concerning the wars of this old Chief John. If I were to relate all that I am knowing to of his and his tribe's cruelty, it would fill this book to overflowing. These were but the opening scenes of the war of "55. On Monday morning we had our engagement with them at Butte Creek and what I have related all transpired in the following 24 hours.

I'm Lost

Note: A page appears to be torn out of the journal after this page.

… home to me with so much force that I am induced to repeat down here as my own feelings upon the subject. "Believe one who knows. The man of civilization who goes back to the savage state throws away his life; his very mind becomes like the dyers hand, subdued to what it works in." I have dropped out of the ride of life and progress in my nine years seclusion and struggle as I may, I cannot retrieve the time lost. The present age knows me not, I have lost my place in it. The thoughts, feelings, habits all around me, seem strange to me. I have been pushed out of the line of march and can never fall into step again. In society, in business, in domestic life, it is all the same. Trial after trial has taught me the truth of this. I am indeed too late.

DA Jenks

Atlantic Telegraph & News

8/15 - The all-absorbing topic of conversation at present is the great Atlantic Telegraph. On the 4th of August, Mr. Cyrus Field says that by and with the assistance of the supreme being, he succeeded in landing the American end of the cable. All now are anxiously awaiting the arrival of the first dispatch from England which is to be from Queen Victoria to our President James Buchanan, upon the receipt of which we throughout the length of the land are to have one grand celebration. The Mormon War is over, without a drop of blood being shed, I believe. The Fraser River gold excitement appears to have been one grand humbug and present appearances indicate a great amount of suffering there amongst the crowd of mad gold adventurers.

At home here, as to news, our new stone bridge over the Black Stone River is slowly progressing towards completion and bids fair to be an ornament to the town. Aside from this, there is but very little building going on (or up) here this season. All are crying up hard times and to an outsider like myself, seeking for business opportunities, I should judge that they were about right in their cries. It seems to me impossible to find anything to do here. Would to God it were otherwise.

Dexter Brothers Explosion

8/16 - Was awakened this morning by the explosion of the boiler of the steam mill (Dexter Brothers at Pawtucket). The building took fire but it was finally saved with the loss of all the machinery in the lower story, a great quantity of stock. Two persons badly injured by the explosion.

Slatersville

8/17 - This afternoon took the cars for this town and arrived at Millville in the rain, here I took passage in the little miserable coach that runs from Millville to Slatersville. And after a jolting ride of about 2 miles was at last, to my great relief, landed at friend Horace Beach's residence in time for tea. Was somewhat amused in the coach by the conversation of a fellow traveler, a resident of Slatersville. A perfect specimen of the inquisitive Yankee, as he is portrayed upon the stage. We two were the only passengers. And I could see by his movements, long before he spoke, that he was very anxious to open conversation and at last he broke out with;

"I say, huntin for a job?"
No Sir, I am not.
"Darned lucky for you, for this is the meanest place in creation for a poor man. Stranger in these parts haint ye?"
No sir, I use to pass through this town quite often in my youth.
"Ha, haven't been here lately then, live in Providence?"
No Sir.
"Massachusetts man maybe?"

No Sir.

"Going to stop over in Slatersville?"

Yes Sir, I am.

"Ha, all fired poor accommodations for travelers here, where are you going to stop?"

I thought some of stopping where night overtook me.

"Yas, spose so, where'd you say you come from?"

Didn't say.

"Well I declare, you are a queer chicken."

And finding he could not pump me, he went on and gave me his own history, his trials and tribulations, how he had been abused by the rich and mistreated by the poor. And upon the whole, I must say he gave the residents of this town a rather hard name.

Conquering Self-Doubt

8/27 - I have just finished a very interesting book entitled 'This, That and the Other'. And in the perusal of it have found many gems of thought, many new ideas, beautifully expressed. It shows in many places the force of the human will and the Authoress thinks there is no such thing as failure to one who exercises his power in full force. To me there is one good result in reading such works, that is it points out to me wherein I am deficient. I know that in this respect I am so. I am lacking in a sufficient amount of self-confidence. I have not force enough, am doubtful of my ability to accomplish. I must conquer this feeling before I may hope to accomplish anything in this world.

Autumn Blues

9/1 - Since last Sabbath we have been blessed with fine weather. May it long continue the same. This the first day of autumn came in as lovely as a lamb, bright and clear, with a warm sun and light and refreshing breezes from the sunny south. The all-absorbing thought with me is what shall I do for a living? What business shall I engage in here? In vain I worry my brain thus far for a solution of this problem. All the available avenues to wealth seem shut out from me. I am very anxious to engage in some respectable paying business, but as yet have seen no opportunity to do so with any prospect of ultimate success. May I succeed in soon doing so, or I shall die of that miserable complaint called by us the 'Hip Po, or Blues'.

Discontented Wanderers

10/1 - Another long and weary month has passed and now dull, dreary, soul oppressing winter begins to make its appearance. John Young, my friend, my school mate of other days, has returned from California and together we have revisited the old spots around town. We have talked of old times, of old friends, of old scenes, until we could talk no longer. He says this does not appear to him like home and he is now ready to return to California, satisfied that the home of other days has passed from him forever. Thus it is. One after another return, but few are satisfied to remain here, and but few are aware of the secrets of this discontent. But to one of the initiated, it is no mystery.

Note: Pages appear to be torn out of the journal after this page.

Blackstone Bridge Jollification

11/4 - Today has been set apart to celebrate the completion of the new stone bridge over the Blackstone River at this place. This bridge which has cost the state $12,000 and the towns of North Providence and Pawtucket each $1500 more apiece, has been all summer in building and is now finished, and accordingly, we are to have a grand jollification over it. But alas for human foresight, we could not ensure a fair day and who could get up much enthusiasm in a cold rainstorm. But the day has come and so had the invited guests, or a part of them at least. And our brave boys and firemen were anxious to "train" and so, in spite of the rain, we were bound to put it through and we did. But Lord deliver us, twas mighty uphill work. But with the assistance of a plenty of inside wetting, we managed to do it.

11/6 - Rain and wind as usual. No danger of the inhabitants of this section of the world ever being obliged to wear goggles to defend their eyes from dust. I should think it would be impossible for the dust to ever blow here, even if it should happen to clear off at some future time for a day or two. No wonder they have the potato rot here, it's enough to rot most anything.

Society's Luxuries

11/10 - Tonight attended the opening of the Fair of the Baptist Society. It was a perfect jam, and the ladies have met with a most decided success. It is seldom that I pass a more agreeable night or enjoy myself better than I have tonight. A plenty of good and lively female company is a luxury to me, which I know how to appreciate.

11/13 - Tonight is the closing one of the fair of the Baptist Society of this town. This fair was got up by the ladies of the First Baptist Society of this town, to raise means to paint and otherwise beautify their place of worship and they have succeeded in raising upwards of $700 by the operation. For the four nights that it was open, the hall was crowded with the fair and beautiful ladies of this town and everything passed off pleasantly and very agreeably to all concerned. As for my part, it was a treat to be witness to such an array of female beauty as was here presented to view. And all the proceedings were conducted with so much modesty and proper decorum, that it could not fail to please the most fastidious.

The Providence Fire

11/18 - Last evening took tea at Uncle Steven Benedict's. He was the fortunate winner of the silver tea set at the fair last week and the small party was to celebrate the occasion and to introduce for service the new set. We spent the evening very pleasantly. This morning learned that Howard's Block and the Museum Building in Providence that was destroyed by fire on the night of the 15th, was not to be rebuilt at present. If this should be the case, it would be more of a calamity to the city then was at first apprehended. For the two buildings were two of the best in the city and in Howard's Hall being destroyed, the city lost the only decent one it possessed. But there are many rumors of Howard's intentions and no one knows the truth of any.

Note: Pages appear to be torn out of the journal after this page.

My Birthday ~ December 2nd

Yes, yes here it is again, how swiftly fly the years of late. Soon, aye very soon, I shall be knocking at old age's door. 31 years ago today, I made my first entry into this world of bitter disappointments. It seems hardly possible that I have thus far run my course through life. I have nearly reached the halfway house assigned to man in this life's racecourse. I can look back to the time when I was anxiously longing to leap ahead into manhood's estate, when I should assume my place amongst men and leave my childhood far behind. But now how gladly would I take the backward step, were it allowed us so to do. But I look around me and find that disappointment is the general lot of all. So take heart, oh faint heart and push on. For mine is but the common lot of man.

Pike's Peak Or Bust?

12/4 - Have just finished a letter to Loren Jenks of Boston, Ionia County Michigan, respecting his property here. I am anxious he should write and let me know the reason of his long delay in forwarding an affidavit from his Uncle, an article actually necessary for me to have before I can close the sale for him. Nothing of importance to write today. The weather is as usual stormy. Have a very strong inclination to go to Kansas, to see if it is possible for me to find any business there. The reports from the new goldfields at Pike's Peak continue very encouraging and if they should continue so through the winter, I think I must try my hand at the business once more. But Quien Sabe what the prospects may be by spring, I hope they may be brighter than now.

I cannot lay idle much longer. It is worse than folly to pass away my best days in idleness as I have been doing for a year past. No, no, push on and have the pleasure of knowing whether success crowns your efforts or not. That at least you tried to deserve success. And so, as I do not see any possible prospect of engaging in business at home, why of course I must go where the chances are better and where I at least have better opportunities than I have here. I have no desire to engage in mining again if I can help it and therefore shall endeavor to find some other occupation if possible. If not, why then I can try mining. Confident that I have as much practical knowledge of gold placer mining as anyone in Kansas. But time alone can tell. Man proposes, but God disposes.

There's No Going Back

12/8 - Rain, sleet, hail and frost is the order of the day. For the past week we have had miserable weather and it still continues to hold so. John Young left us for California in the steamer that sailed on Monday the sixth. He probably will make California his home for the future. Having returned to the home of his youth, to find his place filled by strangers. He has now returned to the home of his adoption, satisfied that he must now settle down contented with his lot in life. Or if that is not possible, he must at least try to be so. For with him as with all others he has learnt that in this world there is no going back. As he has 'made his bed, there he must lie'. It was impossible for him to return and find the place he had left, or to resume with his former life here at home.

Note: A page appears to be torn out of the journal after this page.

Note: At the top of this page is a sketch of a hand pointing to the text: "Wrote to EWP today also sent 4 papers."

Praise The Living - January 3, 1859

This morning at about 7 o'clock Henry C. Reed committed suicide by shooting himself through the head. He has been Depot Master in this town for many years and since his death, we hear that he was very much respected by all men. Why wait until after death before you praise the aspiring and worthy young? If the public had shown any of this great respect for his worth whilst living, probably his life might have been spared. For public esteem goes a great way toward dissipating the horrors. Henry had followed another friend (H.B. Balcolm) to the suicide grave, and they say there is no known cause for his committing the act. Well, I know something of the frame of mind a man must have to contemplate such an act. Death is sometimes preferable to life.

Blew, Snew & Stuck

1/4 - What an awful storm we have had today. It blew and snew and the devil knows what it didn't do. The snow is about a foot deep on the level, or it would be if there was any level. The railway trains are having a good time today. The Boston train arrived in the cut across the bridge this morning and there it stuck until 3 o'clock this afternoon, when they succeeded in hoeing about. The Worcester was no better off, having stuck hard and fast between here and Valley Falls. But towards night four locomotives and a snowplow succeeded in butting and tearing their way through and I suppose will have cleared the track to Worcester before night. This is the biggest snowstorm I have seen for years.

Shoveling For Dollars

1/5 - Today the sun shines out as bright as ever sun shone, and all Pawtucket nearly are out shoveling snow. That snow ordinance passed by the Town Council, whereby all property owners are obliged to clear the sidewalks in front of their estates of snow within four hours of the abatement of the storm or laid themselves liable to a fine of a dollar an hour, is a hard one on me this morning. And I think that the less land a man has here on such a morning as this, the better for his nerves. We unfortunately have 200 feet front on High Street. And as the sidewalk is about 7 feet wide and the snow a foot deep, according to my reckoning, I had to move about 1400 feet of snow in four hours. Oh, how my shoulders ache.

Old Bill & My Cousins

1/6 - Another bright and sunny day and I have improved the opportunity offered for a sleigh ride on a pleasant day and harnessed up Old Bill, who has not been out of the stables for over a month, and started for Seekonk and Sally Fairbrother. After much trouble and tribulation, I arrived there and found them all well. Took dinner and about 3:00 PM started on my return. The road was horrible over half-bare ground and the rest 6-foot drifts. In the evening took cousins Amelia and Delia out for a ride and should judge from appearances they were much pleased with the ride. Poor girls, they are two pretty girls as anyone ever owned for cousins and it is a pity that from poverty, they should be compelled to live so close.

Mysterious Undergarments

1/7 - Aye, aye, here we are again all sposh, slosh and drizzle. Not contented with the snowstorm, we must now suffer a second infliction worse than all. This morning set in rain, moderated to a drizzle and closed with a blanket like fog that is so warm and thick that a person breathes it like mush. That is, his breath seems thick and to sum it all up it is "damned disagreeable". The sleighing is going and the sposh is a foot deep. Oh lord, but it is perfectly awful to wade from here to the Post Office through such a porridge, and what a figure the women cut today in the street. There goes one, both hands full of hoops, her arms extended out at right angles, her dress up to her knees, showing all the fine needlework underneath and displaying undergarments, which of course are a mystery to me.

1/8 - This morning pedestrians "have a hard road to travel" in every sense. For last night it cleared off cold and this morning the sposh of that yesterday is frozen into ten thousand little pinnacles and hummocks of ice, making very rough and slippery going.

Drawings For My Friends

Today I finished the last of a set of pen and ink sketches of scenes in California, with which I have busied myself this winter. They are intended to serve as gifts of remembrance to my friends here at home. The set consists of the following pictures.

A View of Yreka
2d Warner's Pass
3d San Buenaventura Valley
4th San Luis Harbor
5th Lagoon Crescent City
6th Acapulco Mexico
7th Sierra Nevadas
8th Pawtucket from our chamber windows.

Note: 2 pages appear to be torn out of the journal after this page.

1/11 - Yesterday was the coldest of the season and some say I have not seen as cold weather for many years in this town. Last night the thermometer stood at 10 o'clock 10° below zero. This morning it stood when I got up at 11° below and continued quite cold until noon when it moderated and now at 5:00 PM it is snowing quite fast. Have kept to my room pretty much all this week, owing to the weather. Have finished another California picture today, the mouth of Fall River. It is so dark, I cannot write anymore tonight.

Tolerably Coolish

1/12 - Snowing today and the thermometer down to 2° above zero. This season, or rather the weather for the past few days, is the subject of general conversation at present. On Monday last the thermometer stood as follows.

At Portland 17° below zero
At Ellsworth 20° below zero
At Frankfurt 40° below zero
At Bangor 26° below zero

This is enough to show that we had pretty tolerably coolish weather here.

1/13 - Weather has moderated and today a man can turn out without fear of freezing. The sleighing is first rate and everybody (nearly) are improving it.

Note: A page appears to be torn out of the journal after this page.

Who's Next?

1/14 - Rains today and a good prospect of a long continuance of the same. This is a beautiful climate, beautiful country and contains a beautiful race of inhabitants. Another man got tired of living here and last night took poison and stepped out. His name was Captain Baker. Judson Hutchinson, of the celebrated family of singers, also become disgusted with the things of this world and tied a rope around his neck and choked himself out of the world and all his troubles at Lynn, night before last. So, they go. Suicides are becoming fashionable. I wonder who will go next. Quien Sabe? Mi amigo, or yo.

1/15 - Today is quite warm with the usual heavy damp. I never saw such a changeable climate as this is. Four days ago, and the thermometer run down to 17° below zero. Now today it is up to 45°. Our sleighing is fast disappearing.

1/16 - Last night I slept with the windows open, an open room being far more comfortable than a close one, such is the great change in the weather. Today the sun shines out bright, but we have a raw wind from the northwest and the thermometer is down to 40° at noon. Mary McDonald is to be buried today. Received no news from Yreka this mail but got a paper from Mr. Harris, the San Francisco Bulletin.

Lonesome Wanderers

1/16 - In The Bulletin, I found an article respecting returned Californians which soulfully corroborates what I have so often affirmed respecting the wanderers feelings upon his return, that I must make a few extracts. He says: "A feeling prevails almost universally among people who have not been east since emigrating to California, that it is necessary for them to pay a visit home and that such a trip will be to them a source of unmitigated joy" … "but it is a fact that those who go quickly return, disgusted with their travel and glad to get back" and why is this? "They are taken with an epidemic called homesickness and yearn once more to behold the scenes of their childhood. They picture to themselves their old home, just as they left it… they naturally imagine that their absence has created a gap in their former circle, that is still open. They long to go back and resume their place and fill this gap which they think will be an easy matter." But what is the result of all this, how terminate these bright daydreams?

"Arrived home, the wanderer finds all is changed. The young are grown up and married, the youth have become staid men of business and the middle aged have become old, many are dead. All is changed. But the change that is more keenly apparent than all others is in the feeling of old friends toward themselves. They are not forgotten, they have not faded entirely from the affection of those who love them, but they cannot hide from themselves that they are not now a part of the society. They are in one sense strangers; they belong to a different time and place and of secondary consideration to those who once looked to them as dearest and nearest friends. Their former position has been taken by others. The gap which their absence occasioned has long ago closed up. And they discover that their old friends have managed to live without them, with the same content and comfort as they formerly did with them.

Therefore their old home, that they have long been in the habit whilst in California of talking about as preeminently their home, they now find is no longer a home for them. The scales drop from their eyes, the illusion vanishes and quickly the melancholy conviction comes upon them, that their old home has passed away forever. They now learn that the links of affection must be kept bright, by constant use and attention. During the wanderer's absence, they have become rusted and weak. The potent hand of time has healed up the wounds caused by separation years ago and although it causes a pang to realize the fact that our first home knows us no more as one of its own, still few there be that are desirous of reopening the scarred seam.

The visit of the returned Californian therefore to his old home does not turn out as full of pleasure as he anticipated. He tries to convince himself in some cases that he is enjoying himself hugely, but if the truth be told, most of them hardly place their feet upon eastern soil before they begin longing to return, and this feeling increases as time passes." Well now I have made extracts enough from this article to show that I am not alone in my views and feelings. No, would to God it were otherwise. That we could resume our places of old in the hearts and affections of our old friends, would that we could again resume our places in the old society of other days, that we could again live over the days of our youth, but no. All, all is changed.

How many times have I said it? John Young came home and hoped to resume his place in society, he hoped to find the gap made at his departure, but he (as will all others) found that he was too late. It had healed up and the places that knew him once, knew him no more. Home had disappeared and after a few short months vain search, he returned to the home of his adoption. Such is the fate of all wanderers, myself included.

1/17 - Is a warm but foggy day. There is to be a grand party tonight at Tales of Central Falls.

1/18 - Clear but cold. In the evening went over to Starkweather's Hill to see the crowd who were there coasting. Beautiful, clear and moonlight evening.

1/19 - Another warm day with a clear sky. Harndon's Express was robbed last night in Providence. In the evening received a call from Mr. and Mrs. Lawton.

I Must Go

1/20 - Thick and hazy but warm. Nothing of importance to communicate. Am weary and heartsick, feel lonely and friendless. And tired of life as I see it and I am almost tempted to follow the example of Reed, and rid myself of this miserable existence.

1/21 - Hazy disagreeable weather. Am low spirited as usual today and oh how sad I feel to think that I must (aye must) leave these, my only friends, so soon. Oh Father, Mother, Sisters dear, if you but only knew how it wrings my heart to be again compelled to leave you all. I, who have tried the world before and know how heartless it is, how little sympathy one meets abroad. I know what I am about to lose, but the sacrifice must be made. I can no longer live upon you. I must do for myself. You cannot support me thus. I rob you by living thus and I must leave you and seek my living abroad. I cannot find a situation here. I must go where I can. Would to God I could settle here with you, but fate has decreed otherwise, and I must obey. God be with you and sustain me.

Sunday evening - Is a clear but cold day. As usual all hands have gone to church this afternoon, leaving me at home to take care of Eddy. During the week we have had much stormy weather and the snow has disappeared, causing quite a freshet in the Blackstone, sufficient to stop all the factories yesterday.

Thackery's Virginians

Received the February number of Harper's Monthly last night and I have been reading it today. In this number of Thackery's Virginians he makes one of his heroes to say; "If I am unhappy tis not your fault nor perhaps mine. Tis fate you see; tis the having nothing to do; I must work;

and how George? That is the question." What on earth is there for me to do at all I say. That's what makes me miserable.

1/23 - And I am in the same predicament. In fact, I find that in many cases or points, I am like this young man. He was one of two sons of a Richmond Virginia family, the younger son. He was brought up to a life of idleness "unfitted with a trade", he spent his younger days in idleness in the expectation of inheriting sufficient wealth to support him without labor. But whilst away from home he discovered that his wealth was all a dream. His former friends deserted him. He became unhappy of course and he must find relief from some source and where should he look for it? His unhappiness caused his brother much misery of course and he fears that the cause may lie with him. But Harry derrys it in the words I have quoted. And like him, I say I must work. But what on earth is there for me to do?

Like him, I am very anxious that my friends at home should know and understand that it (my uneasiness) is not occasioned by any lack of affection for them. But is merely the result, aye the natural result, of a life of idleness upon a man who has been often disappointed in life. I must work and I have not been able to find as yet any work that I could do. Therefore I am unhappy, even here at home where all that I hold dear in life reside. My mind must be exercised and took from brooding over bad luck of other years. It is not their fault by any means, nor mine entirely, but I have been unfortunate and am apt to brood over it.

Being Content

1/30 - Sunday Evening. Another week has passed away and I am still eating the bread of idleness, but my life of idleness is drawing near its close and soon, very soon, I must bid farewell to friends and kindred and again commence my roving, homeless life in the new and almost unexplored regions of the far west. The Rocky Mountains must be my home for years to come and the rough, half-civilized inhabitants of our frontier states and territories my sole companions. Like the savages of those distant wilds, I must be content with the rudest fare. Glad to get the rudest cabin to shelter my head from the storms of winter and the sun's fierce rays in summer.

But "life is but a dream at the best" and I who have suffered so much in times past, need not fear for the time to come. Contented I shall be, if when old age draws near and I shall be drawing near the close of this unhappy life, I may then be allowed to close my eyes here at home. None but the Wanderer knows the worth of a home. Home, the scene of our childhood, the place where we were born and passed the first few years of youth, seems always dear to man. Be it ever so inhospitable, be it ever so humble, let it receive us ever so coolly after our long absence, even when our early associates turn from us, as from strangers. Let them all treat us ever so coolly, still it is home and as such will always be cherished and be held dear by the man of feeling.

1/30 - In time to come then, if God sees fit to spare my life I hope to be enabled to settle down here and surrounded by scenes never to be forgotten. Under the roof of my father's house, in the shade of trees planted in youth, then grown old and moss covered with age, like myself. I may then hope to pass from this life. Happy in the consciousness of that peace of mind, of that rest to the weary, that has been denied me in manhood's days, but which I hope to enjoy in the second youth, common to all men, old age.

Farewell then old Pawtucket. May but few of your sons ever know the bitterness of heart that has been my lot. Gladly would I have passed the remainder of my days here at home, but ye would not that it should be so. 10 years ago and I was then, as now, preparing for a long voyage from home. 10 years ago today and I was spending my last Sabbath at home previous to my departure for the land of gold, California.

I Dreamed Of A Different Life

And now after a long absence from home and a short visit to the scenes of my youth, I am again making preparations to launch my barque upon life's troubled sea for another voyage of uncertain duration. God only knows my feelings at this time. No permanent abiding place. For me, there is no loved one to partake with me of life's burdens and joys. No wife to mourn my absence or to greet one upon my return.

February 6, 1859
I'm alone, all alone though I rove,
Through the cities thronged street,
There are none that I love,
No kind smile do I meet,
I hast through the crowd,
All unheeded, unknown.

But "God's will be done" we must all travel the road that fate has fore ordained we should pursue. And if mine is a solitary lonely one and is full of difficult gaps to cross and high precipitous mountains to pass, why I must not flinch but continue on to the end. But oh, what a different life had I pictured out for myself years ago. From my youth up, have I envied those who have been enabled to live at home, surrounded by friends, with their families around them. And the height of any ambition has been to find a paying business at home. To marry and settle down, here in old Pawtucket. In my younger days when all looked bright before me and I was much given to castle building, and looked forward to the future as to the consummation of all my hopes and aspirations.

In those days I was not ambitious to acquire great wealth, as most youths are. No, the height of my ambition was to get into business for myself. So that I might be enabled to build myself up a humble home here in this country town. Where I might, with my wife, live happily at home contented with my lot in life, so long as I had a wife to share my lot and a little cot to shelter us. But this was denied me and I left home. And for years I was a wanderer, homeless and almost friendless. And for many a long weary year I lived thus, and the only hope left me was that in time I might return, enabled to gather around me these long wished for comforts of a civilized life. At last I returned, still hoping that now I might find what I had so long been seeking, a cot in the valley I loved where I might pass the remainder of my days in that social happiness, in the company of some loved one that I had so long for.

But alas I find that it is not so to be. Others can find such homes, but there is none for me. God forgive me if I do wrong, but I cannot help the feeling of envy I feel as I visit others of my young associates and find them enjoying the happiness of their homes, surrounded by their wives and children, happy in each other's society and then contrast their lives with mine. But no such fate is mine. In vain I look for these pleasures here and I am compelled again to resume my wandering life.

About My Journal

2/13 - Another Sabbath evening has made its appearance and I am alone again. God bless the dear ones here at home I cannot be with that much longer. My time draws near. Last week I completed a job upon which I have been busily employed for about 10 days. I have been copying into a new book my old scraps of a journal of "49-50 and part of the year of "51, preparatory to starting out on my new trip to the Rocky Mountains.

My journal would not be of any interest to anyone else, I know. But in years to come it may be a source of instruction to me. To look over my past life, where I have day by day noted down my feelings, my hardships, trials and tribulations. In old age it may serve to while away the long wintry evenings, to again read over my travels in search of happiness and wealth. At any rate, it is a source of relief at times to (in absence of all confidential friends) thus turn to these blank pages and with pen and ink converse with an imaginary confidant. And another thing that has induced me to keep it up, is that in the savage life I have led I troubled to think that I was losing all tastes for writing, all taste for corresponding.

In fact, I was afraid of becoming like the half-civilized beings with whom I was obliged to associate. And in self-defense, I was obliged to do something to keep alive in my breast a taste for civilized life, to keep me from becoming entirely lost to all sense and knowledge of better things.

Daniel A Jenks

Goodbye Pawtucket

Eight more days and I leave my home again. Probably, this is the last time I shall write in this journal before my departure. And I would say to all friends; "Hope for the future." Although compelled again to bid adieu to home and all its attractions, let us hope that it may be for the best. I do not start out expecting to accumulate a fortune, but I pray that at least I may succeed in making a good honest living. An honest one it must be, for I wish not for money obtained otherwise. I cannot write. My heart is full to overflowing. Goodbye all and send us a speedy reunion, is my prayer.

2/20 - Sisters, mother, father dear, always bear in mind that although I am a stern and disagreeable companion at home, still I have a warm heart, one that feels as acutely as ever son or brother felt for friends at home. I cannot help it if I am so disagreeable, it is my nature so to be. I may possibly have had cause enough to sour anyone's disposition. I think I have, but as I said before, I am alright inside.

I love you all and I want you all to know and believe it and it grieves me much to think that you appear to doubt it. If God ever gives me an opportunity to, I'll prove it to you.

Daniel A Jenks

Daniel Jenks Gold Rush Journal Volume 4: 1859-1860

AD 1859
Daniel A Jenks of Pawtucket RI

"Is not a man from his birth doomed a pilgrim to roam,
O'er the world's dreary wilds, whence by fortunes rude gust,
In his path, if some floret of joy chanced to bloom,
It is torn and its foliage laid low in the dust."

~~~~~~~~~~~~~~~~~~~~~~~~~~~~~~~~

"When man expelled from Eden's bowers,
A moment lingered near the gate,
Each scene recalled the vanished hours,
And bade him curse his future fate.

But wandering on through distant climes,
He learnt to bear his load of grief,
Just gave a sigh to other times,
And found in busier scenes relief."

1859 DAJ

~~~~~~~~~~~~~~~~~~~~~~~~~~~~~~~~

Pawtucket

February 28, 1859 - Having made all due preparations for my trip westward, I this morning visited my most intimate friends at home and bid them a long adieu. At 12 noon I took my seat in the cars at Providence and was soon underway for the far west. Goodbye now to friends near and dear. Goodbye father, mother, sisters dear, farewell all. May God keep and help you during my long absence. Arrived at Worcester a little after 2 PM and by 4 o'clock was again seated in the cars bound to Springfield and Albany. At about 10 o'clock we reached the ferry and were soon landed on the opposite shore at the New York Central Depot.

CENTRAL PART OF PAWTUCKET, LOOKING UP MAIN STREET.

St. Louis

3/3 - Arrived here this morning. Taking a berth in a sleeping car at Albany on the night of February 28, I awoke the next morning in western New York and arrived at the suspension bridge near the celebrated Falls of Niagara about noon. Had a fine view of the rabid river and of the falls above, crossed the bridge on foot and took dinner at the railway station on the British side. We soon left here and traveled all day through a miserable looking country but was surprised to find such large towns, where I expected to find a perfect wilderness. About 9 o'clock we reached the ferry opposite Detroit, Michigan. We had an excellent supper on board the ferry and were soon after landed at the Depot in Detroit.

I secured a berth in a sleeping car and turned in for the night and slept soundly until morning, when we awoke at Michigan City where we breakfasted. Thus far our road has been first rate, with good accommodations and gentlemanly Conductors. In fact, I never saw so good accommodations as we found on the Canada Road. About 11 in the forenoon, I stopped at Calumet to intercept the morning train from Chicago for St. Louis, by doing so I saved about 12 hours detention at Chicago. About 11:30 we took the cars on the Illinois Central Road and were again whirled along on our rapid way. A more desolate, lonely, dreary days ride I never had than this 2nd of March down through Illinois across this prairie country.

As far as the eye could see, naught but the same treeless, low, level plain of black mud, with here and there a small miserable cabin and occasionally stopping at a miserable little town inhabited principally by low Dutch and Irish families. The soil may be rich, no doubt it is, but I would not live there for the whole state. After fasting from early morn until dark we finally made out to get a miserable supper at one of the stations, after which we poked along in the dark and ran at about a 15-mile gait. And in the evening, we arrived at Mattoon where our car was switched off on to the St. Louis and Terre Haute Road. We had no sleeping cars on this road and I was bumped about from post to pillow. Half-drunk Hoosiers all the long night, over the worst road I ever saw and was truly thankful when we arrived in the morning opposite St. Louis. Crossing in the ferry we were soon landed, per order, at the Planters House St. Louis early this morning. Where I was glad to avail myself of the opportunity offered to wash up, change clothes and get a good meal of victuals.

3/3 - Planters House - The hardships and trials of railway traveling are in a great measure done away with on roads that have introduced the new sleeping cars. And with the exception of my days ride on the Illinois Road, I felt no inconvenience nor wearisomeness from my long ride. This town presents a lively go-ahead appearance and is destined to be a large city. The house where I have stopped is a tip-top one and has the best Clerk I ever met. I tried in vain to find Miles Moies, and was forced to come to the conclusion that I was more anxious to see him then he was to see me. Paid $12 dollars for my passage onboard steamer Carrier for Kansas City Missouri some 400 and odd miles up the Missouri River.

She was to sail at 4 PM, but owing to the superstition of her Captain, who was afraid to start on Friday, we did not leave the levee until after 12 at night. We had a horseshoe nailed up over the saloon doors for good luck and I suppose now that all these precautions have been taken to ward off bad luck, we may rest assured of a safe passage up the river. My roommate, a young Virginian by the name of Farr and myself went this evening to hear the Old Folks concert at Library Hall. Found a crowded hall and were much pleased with the entertainment.

Onboard Steamer Carrier

3/8 - About 12 o'clock Friday night we backed out from the levee at St. Louis and started on our trip up the Missouri. We have on board about 100 passengers. Most of them western men, bound for Pike's Peak and the gold mines of the Rocky Mountains. And a hard, ill-looking set they are. Whiskey appears to be their staple article of diet, and euchre, poker and other games their principal accomplishments. A set of St. Louis gamblers are bleeding them very freely and already many of them have paid dearly for a sight of the elephant. Three card Monte and Chuck-a-Luck are spread out for their benefit in the saloon and the Pike's Pukes and Posies bite readily at the bait.

What confounded fools they are, but they must learn sometime and the sooner the better that they have no chance to win against such odds. We have had warm and beautiful weather thus far and the farmers in some places are plowing the ground to prepare the soil for spring planting. Some difference between this and the climate at home, where now all is covered with the winter coat of ice and snow. The banks of this river present but little to interest a stranger and if I were to form my opinion of the state by what I have seen of it in my voyage of the river, it would be a very unfavorable one. As we have seen but little else than Cottonwood flats on the one side and limestone cliffs on the other, with only an occasional wood chopper's hut, with its small clearing and its group of half-civilized, ragged and uncouth towheaded inhabitants.

An occasional village - called a city - and the numerous wood stations are all there is to break the dull monotony of travel on this river. But they tell me that in the interior there is a fine country and inhabited by all together a different race of beings. "Powerful lot of heathen in this yere country, haint they?" Says a specimen from Hoosierdom to me tonight, as he gazed upon a group of the half-civilized wood choppers at a wood station where we had stopped to wood up.

Kansas City

3/10 - Arrived here about noon six days from St. Louis and took up my quarter for the present at the Eldridge House on the levee. Bid goodbye to friend Tarr with regret, as I have found him to be a first-rate fellow. But as he is bound to Leavenworth, where he has a brother in business, we had to part. Altogether I have enjoyed my trip first rate and was a little sorry to be compelled to stop here alone, a perfect stranger, but I must expect to put up with many such scenes for the next two years. And if I can but succeed in my efforts to make enough to accomplish the object in view, I will willingly suffer the trials and hardships that I well know are in store for me.

3/13 - Sunday today and I have been busy all day copying from my memorandum book the foregoing pages. Friday last was as unpleasant a day as I ever witnessed. The wind blew a perfect hurricane all day and I kept in the house, having a terrible cold. A Michigan lawyer (Mr. Hall) who I got acquainted with here, advised me to buy a box of Bryan's Pulmonic Wafers for it. I did so and today I am as well as ever. Saturday Mr. Hall and I took a walk over to Wyandotte, a rival town 2 miles distant in Kansas. A short walk from our hotel and we crossed the state line into the territory. We soon came to Goose Creek, a little muddy stream about 20 feet wide, where we found an enterprising but very ragged specimen of Missourian had established a ferry.

His boat was long enough to reach within 8 feet of the opposite bank. Hall asked him why he did not run out a plank from his boat to the opposite shore and thus save the trouble of hauling his boat across? "Wall I allow to do it, some these yere days, but I'll be dog yearned if lumber ain't so scarce. I kernt afford to now. But stranger, if you just hearn me, this yere run haint no small shucks of a stream in the springtime." We paid him his half dime and jumped ashore and soon came to the Raw River which we ferried and were landed in Wyandotte. This is a new town, laid out by speculators to rival Kansas City below. Much money is being spent in both places to secure a large town, but for the life of me I cannot see where the business is to come from to pay for all this outlay.

We caught a down steamer here and sailed back to Kansas City free of cost. Today two more steamers have arrived here, loaded down with men bound to Pike's Peak. Every boat comes up loaded with adventurers for that region. Last night I received a letter from Mrs. L. Jenks, who was then in Illinois on her way with her husband to join me here, en route for Pike's Peak. I have my doubts of the stories that are afloat respecting the gold stores that are found out there, but I have started and would not back out now if I knew it was all a humbug. I never would have started if I could have lived at home and now, I must not go back. Live or die, sink or swim through, I will not go now if certain death were on the way.

I wish though to record this, my earnest belief for future reference, and that is that these stories of great gold deposits in western Kansas have grown from a very slender foundation and have been magnified by interested parties on this river into their present state of brilliant prospects, for the purpose of starting a rush of emigration westward to create markets and purchasers for their livestock and produce. I hope I may be disappointed in this, but I doubt it very much.

3/20 - My friend Loren has not arrived as yet and I am growing very uneasy here in this dull town, alone and a stranger as I am. I received a letter from him during the week and he was then at Chillicothe in this state and expected to be here sometime during the week. But the roads are terrible muddy, and I expect he finds it so where he is. We have had miserable weather this past week. One day it would blow and rain, the next it would be pleasant and warm, and then by night it would haze up in the west and rain and blow again. This is a great country for mud and let it rain a day and it becomes so terrible muddy as to almost stop all travel.

In fact, let two men meet here in town from different portions of the surrounding country and the first question asked is "How's the mud out your way?" "Waul we have a right smart chance ont roads are powerful bad, but I allow we are as well ont as our neighbors, how is it out your way?" The rush of gold hunters still continues and the boats from below arrive daily, crowded with the Pike's Peak adventurers. May we find it say I. But I am not very sanguine of success. But however, it does not in the least discourage me, for I must go on. For me, there is no back track to take.

Novelists, romancers and storytellers generally may say as much as they please of the beauties of western life, life on the prairies etc. etc. But it has no charm for me. So, no, give me society, give me town life by all means and if I had the means I would never live away from home - the east is the place to enjoy life. But alas poor me, I never could live there because I had not the means. I do not live in this wilderness from choice, but to accumulate money to enable me to live by and by at home. I feel as sad at parting from friends as anyone ever did, but I have learned to hide my grief from other's eyes and consequently have the reputation of being coldhearted.

Colonel Milton McGee

Yesterday and today, we have been blessed with beautiful warm weather. Was somewhat amused yesterday to see in front of this house the old and somewhat vulgar saying "It is impossible to make a silken purse of a sow's ear, verified." Colonel Milton McGee, a ferocious border ruffian of olden times, a leader in the proslavery and Free State difficulties in Kansas. A Colonel of border ruffians but the richest man in this town, owning 240 acres in the heart of this young but growing city. The proprietor of what is called McGee's Addition, making a fool of himself whilst drunk, surrounded by a gang of levee workmen, lifting and otherwise showing off his strength to the admiration of the gaping crowd of low Irish. "You just bet Old Milt is some on a lift. I'll bet $50 I can out lift any white man in this yere town. I, Old Milt McGee say it. My name is Milt McGee by the eternal, hoop, hi, yah." etc. etc.

And the crowd would laugh to see his tomfoolery and he would strut about and look the world defiance. Judge Cato, another illustrious personage, a Judge who has immortalized his name by his in-just and iniquitous decisions in the Kansas difficulties and who is now boarding here, was also present. A looker on at these feats of his fellow laborer's strength. This town was the grand hotbed of slavery during the Kansas difficulties and this house where I am now stopping was deserted then because the mob had threatened to burn the "d__d abolition house to the ground." But how changed their tone. Then the levee was crowded with armed men who swore no Eastern Man should come up this river. Now all their best efforts are put forth to attract them to this town.

The right must and will prevail and they know it, though now my life would not be worth a pinch of salt if they knew I was writing this here. But the day for these one-idea men is fast passing away and soon the Yankees will have possession of this, as well as the towns above. Slavery in Missouri is destined to be short-lived. Speaking of McGee, a bystander remarked, "He just keeps drunk about all the time now, just to drown his conscience. He has been an infernal villain, and many is the Free State man he has murdered in cold blood." But to change the subject. I have just finished two letters for home, one for Sallie, the other for Billy Reed. In Sallie's I have endeavored to explain to her the whys and wherefores of my uneasiness whilst at home.

She never knew me aright; she has formed an erroneous idea of me and I am afraid thinks me coldhearted and careless of home and friends and I have in my letter endeavored to set her right. To Bill, I have sent two papers and written him a letter concerning our reports from Pike's Peak and the gold mines. No later news from my partners and I cannot imagine where they are all of this time, for I should think they have had ample time to reach here before this.

3/24 - Yesterday upon calling at the Post Office found a letter there from friend Loren, informing me of his arrival in town and stating that he was encamped about a mile out of town on the Santa Fe Road. Accordingly started out and found his camp. Was introduced to his wife Lissy, his brother Jud, Charlie Upham & Dan Keedwell who are to be our traveling companions. Found also one other team who are to travel with us owned by two brothers from Illinois by the name of Nebo, Norman and Jesse. Today we were very busy purchasing our provisions etc. etc. At night having got all aboard, returned to camp to be ready for an early start in the morning. It seems old-fashioned to be in camp again.

Camp 1: Shawnee Springs - March 26, 1859

This morning turned out from my blankets spread on the ground, as fresh as though my bed had been of down. Lissy soon after made her appearance and breakfast having been dispatched, we got the cattle up and rolled out on the road. Passed through Westport and about noon camped at the springs. And now that we are on the road, before we go any further, let me introduce my traveling companions. First, Loren is an old California friend of mine. We have both seen some hard times before and camping out is nothing new to us. He returned from California soon after I left there. Went home to Michigan, got married to a young schoolmistress about 18 years of age and intended to settle down there for life. But became restless and taking the Pike's Peak fever wrote to me that he was going out, invited me to join him and now here he is with his young wife on the road.

His brother Judson is a perfect specimen of the Mountaineer of the Rocky Mountains. In the year of 1852 Jud and Loren started out from their home in Michigan to seek their fortunes. Jud being 16 and Loren 18 years old. Arrived at the Missouri River, they hired out to a Teamster who was about starting out with a train loaded with supplies for Fort Laramie. After the usual hardships attending a trip across the plains, they were finally hemmed in by snows at Ash Hollow. The expedition becoming short of provisions, an extra express was sent out on foot to try to reach the fort to get assistance. Jud and two others volunteered for this service. They traveled on through the snow for days, until their feet became badly frostbitten and their provisions giving out, they started to return to camp.

But by this time, Jud gave out and could go no further. And his companions not much better off, left him to his fate. As they expected never to see him alive again. For nine days he sustained life by crawling on his hands and knees from his nest in the snow and grubbing for roots. On the ninth day he heard someone hallooing and he answered them, they proved to be a party sent out in search of him from the camp. He was drawn back on a sled and his life was spared. But he was crippled for life, having lost all of his toes and most of his fingers. Since then, he has lived in the mountains, most of the time at Bent's Fort, until last summer. He having heard of Loren's return from California, went home to see him. He has lived so long out of society that he is unhappy in it and is far more happy now that he is once more on the road, than he was at home.

Another one of our mass is Charlie Upham. A long-legged, gaunt Yankee about 22 years old who Loren picked up at his home in Michigan, where he was clerking in a small country store. He is a good natured, easy-going sort of a fellow but perfectly useless about camp, being as ignorant of this sort of a life as any other Greenhorn. The other member, Dan Keedwell, is an Englishman, bullheaded and going to Pike's Peak because he wants to see the "bloody country", he says. He was reared on a stock farm near Bristol England, came to this country about three years ago, has traveled up from place to place pretty much all over the States and now wants to see the wilderness, he says.

We six of us are in company, we have a good three yoke ox team loaded down with provisions, about a ton in all. And with Lissy on top of the load, whilst we trudge along on foot. At night our tent is pitched, and we vacate the premises while Lissy gets into bed and then we turn in ourselves. Rather close stowing for a man and his wife and four big buck men to sleep in one small tent, about 10 feet in diameter. But we all manage to get along without much crowding, although Charlie says if he had known how small a compass he was compelled to sleep in, he should have tried to stint his growth and taken about a foot off of each leg, so as to have kept his feet inside of the tent nights. For in spite of him, they get stretched out under the tent every morning.

Slept first rate last night, Lissy is busy all day baking cakes and bread. Myself and the other boys have been busy all day getting out a lot of spare ox bows, tent poles, pins, etc., preparing for our trip, for we soon will be where there is no timber and we must prepare all these things before we start. Fine day for us. Just above us on the road stand the remains of the Old Shawnee Mission Church, the former rendezvous of Buford's Company of border ruffians. A very bloody spot during the Kansas war. Many a man has here been compelled to give up not only his property but in many cases his life even, on this spot. Often during that time were the inhabitants near here awakened by the death shrieks of some poor unfortunate, who had fallen into the hands of these desperados.

Last night was an awful one. It commenced raining and blowing about 10 o'clock but we all lay still in our tent, in hopes that it would stand the blast, until about 2 AM. Lissy cries out that the water is a foot deep in her bed! About this time one of the windward guys gave way and down came the tent and by this time we were all wet to the skin. I crawled out from under the wreck, it was pitch dark excepting when it lightened. Pretty soon another flash discovered Lissy crawling out. Her night clothes sticking close to her skin, looking like a soaked ghost. We flew around, got the tent up again and crawled into it to try and weather it out until morning. Planting ourselves around the tentpole, wrapping ourselves in wet blankets, we tried to gather warmth by huddling close together. Thus, we passed the remainder of the night till break of day.

Loren told me to keep Lissy warm and he would try to build a fire. After a long time he succeeded in getting a light blaze, but little warmth. During the day it continued to snow, rain and blow from the northwest a perfect hurricane, and in vain we endeavored to create a fire sufficient to give us a little warmth. Shiver and shake was the order of the day. Loren succeeded in getting Lissy over to a squatter's cabin nearby, where she was made comfortable. After this we succeeded in making the tent more comfortable by building a small fire in the middle of it, and laying close to the ground, we escaped the smoke in measure. Towards night the storm abated and by the assistance of a bottle of whiskey we passed the evening very pleasantly.

Boots froze and all hands chilled through, but a clear day is before us, though cold. Ice made one quarter inch thick last night. Have to lay here another day to dry our blankets and clothes. Everything is wet through and froze stiff this morning.

Camp 2: Cedar Creek - 3/30

Sun rose clear, but cold. We soon had a fire and breakfast cooked, struck the tent, loaded up and rolled out to make a new start. Traveled over a rolling prairie for about 7 miles, came onto a creek and stopped for dinner. Here we met another team bound to Pike's Peak, a company of seven men from Ohio. Santa Fe mail passed us here bound to States. After dinner we traveled 10 miles further and camped on Cedar Creek.

Camp 3: Hickory Point - 3/31

Were turned out last night by cattle breaking loose. Cold and clear this morning. Feel perfectly fresh this morning after my 17 mile walk yesterday. Traveled 10 miles this morning to Cherry Creek, where we nooned. After dinner we made 12 miles more to this point where we stopped for the night in a pretty grove of Hickory. Our noon rest was at Black Jack, one of the Kansas battlefields where Old Brown cleaned out a proslavery party who had left Missouri to capture him. This whole country is almost destitute of wood, all that is seen is the small groves on the banks of the creeks, about from 8 to 12 miles apart. The country between these creeks is a low rolling prairie with very rich soil, thinly settled as yet. This grove is full of camps of Pike's Peakers, about 100 altogether.

Camp 4: Willow Spring Creek - 4/1

This morning was quite cold but clear. Ice made last night. Cattle strayed away last night, we did not find them until quite late in the day. Drove about 10 miles and, it looking like a storm, we drove off the road about a mile to a little low bottom, where we were well sheltered in case of the storm and would have a plenty of wood.

4/2 - Stormed all night and today is very cold, wet and windy. We lay here all day trying our best to keep comfortable. We were fortunate in selecting this for our camp, for we are protected here by the timber from the awful cold northwest winds that blow across the prairie.

Camp 5: 110 Creek - 4/3

Today I believe I have suffered more than I ever did before in the same length of time. This morning was very cold but clear and we hitched up early for a long drive. The understanding was that we were to drive 12 miles to Rock Creek and noon, then drive 13 more to this place to camp, as there is no wood on the road here for 25 miles. I pushed on ahead of the teams and reached a log cabin, which proving to be a Mail Station, I sat down and wrote a short letter home, then started on again. Overtook and passed our teams and arrived at Rock Creek, waited up for our teams to come up for dinner. By this time, it commenced blowing and it's snowing again. There was no chance to build a fire, for there was not a stick as big as a pipe stem in the whole country.

In vain I stamped around, I felt I was freezing. I was hungry and tired but there was no rest for me. I must go on to shelter somewhere.

So on I pushed. As far as I could see on every side was the same dreary waste. As I proceeded on my way, the storm increased in violence.

Sunday April 3d 1859

It was with the utmost difficulty that I kept on my course, as the wind was dead ahead and the snow almost blinded me. At times I would lay down in a rut or gully to gather strength, to again renew my strife with the elements. I came very near losing the road several times and I knew if I did, my death was almost certain. At length I caught sight of a cabin and made for it, but I found it was deserted. And whilst I was looking around for means to strike a fire, I heard a cowbell in the distance way ahead. This gave me new courage and I pushed on again and soon reached the creek, where I found a little settlement of squatters. By this time, I was nearly chilled through and very hungry, having walked about 25 miles on an empty stomach.

I walked into the first cabin I came to and asked the landlady if she could get me a supper. "Faith an do you think this is a tavern?" She says. I explained to her my situation and she immediately relented, and soon I was made extremely happy over a supper of ham and eggs. And didn't I do it justice? In about two hours our teams came along, and we drove down into the heavy timber at bottom, where we soon had a rousing fire. The snow was scraped away, our tent pitched and we camped for the night.

Camp 6: Burlingame - 4/4

This morning everything froze stiff. Ice made one inch thick during the night. Our boots and coats were like so many boards and Lissy's dress needed no hoops this morning to make it stand out. But by noon we got thawed out and packing up we started on again, and traveling for 6 miles we came to Switzer Creek where we camped for the night. Across this creek is the town of Burlingame. Thus far our course has been through a rich agricultural country but thinly settled as yet, but soon bound to be a thickly populated district. We have had very unpleasant weather but have all enjoyed good health. Ice has made every night thus far.

Camp 7: Dragoon Creek - 4/5

Ice one half inch thick this morning and Charlie growls very much about his long legs, which insist upon crowding his feet outdoors every night, much to his bodily discomfort. Made 12 miles today and just stopped for the night on this lovely creek. Our boys caught several trout tonight in the creek, which Dan says are nearly as fine as the trout of Old England - but not quite so fine flavored. These with a brace of hare that Dan shot tonight made us a tiptop supper. Lissy says she begins to sort of like this way of living, if it "weren't so horrid cold at times." As for me I have not forgot last Sunday's scrape as of yet, and "shan't" praise this sort of living until I see more of it.

Camp 8: Elm Creek - 4/6

This morning very high wind and quite cold again but we rolled along and nooned at Bluff Creek. After dinner, drove about 8 miles further and came to this creek where we camp for tonight. As I said before, our road (the old Santa Fe Trail) takes us over a bare rolling prairie and the only timber one sees is on the banks of the creeks, which are from 8 to 20 miles apart. So in traveling we have to make one of these creeks every night for wood and water. Therefore, if we come to a creek at 2 PM we have to stop there for the night, if it is too far to drive to the next. Then too, as soon as one strikes the timber he is protected from the severe northwest winds that most constantly blows on the prairies at this season of the year.

Camp 9: Council Grove - 4/7

This morning was clear, and we had promise of a fine day. Reached this place about noon. Here we made what few purchases of articles we needed, as this is our last chance. This point is 150 miles West of Kansas City, the most western town and may be considered the outpost of civilization in this direction. Here we met the first wild Indians, they were Kiowas. Here I sent two letters home. We met the outward-bound mail here, but no letters for me. This mail is carried from here to Santa Fe in coaches drawn by mules, but the driver is more of a gentleman on this line than most others. All he has to do is to sit on the box and hold the lines and a man rides a mule by the side, who does the whipping and hallooing.

In addition to the passenger coach, there is another which follows on behind as a tender. This carries the provisions, cooking utensils and grain for the animals. They drive 50 miles and change mules until they get out 200 miles, then drive 100 and change from that on. Jud found several friends here, mountaineers from the Rocky Mountains. In the afternoon we drove about 8 miles further to a creek but poorly timbered, where we camped for the night. Loren traded off one of his horses for two cows at Council Grove and the two Nebo boys took in a passenger for Pike's Peak. He looks like a hard case and has been a soldier. Awful cold tonight and mighty little wood to be had. Soldier says it's nothing to what we will see after we once get out where there is no timber at all.

Camp 10: Prairie ~ West of Council Grove - 4/8

Tonight, we are encamped on the open prairie for the first time, with not a tree or bush in sight. We dug holes in the ground and by piling on weeds and setting them on fire we succeeded in cooking a sort of a supper. After which we soon rolled up in our blankets to keep warm. The soil this side of Council Grove begins to look less inviting in every way. We had an arrival in camp about dark. An old man, at least 75-year-old, in a thin coat and a straw hat, with a carpetbag slung on an axe over his shoulder, came trudging along and asked permission to lay down by our tent for the night.

We asked him where he was bound, "Pike's Peak," says he. What not alone, on foot and without either blankets or provisions? Asks I. "Oh yes," says he, "I think I'll manage to get through somehow, never you mind me." We tried our best to prevail upon the old fellow to turn back, but no sir he was going on. We gave him his supper and he crawled under the lee of the tent, though I can't see how he could sleep, it was so cold that with all my blankets I suffered. We are now fairly in for it and must from this do without wood, at least most of the time. Dan says, "Darn the bloody country that can't furnish wood enough to make a toothpick." "Oh you dry up," says the soldier, "if you don't like the country, why in thunder don't you leave it?"

This stopped Dan's growling for the time.

Camp 11: Cottonwood Creek - 4/9

This morning by 4 1/2 o'clock we turned out all hands to gather dry buffalo chips, ox chips, weeds and dry grass to make a fire and at last succeeded in half cooking our grub. Though our slap jacks were well peppered with the dust of buffalo chips and ashes before we succeeded in baking them. About 7 o'clock we got underway and traveled until we came to a pond of rainwater where we nooned. After which we continued on over this sea-like barren waste till night when we reached this creek, having walked for 30 miles today. Here we found a little timber and building a good fire, we made a square meal once more. Found quite a collection of teams here all bound to Pike's Peak.

4/10 - Lay by here today, commenced our regular guard duty today. Our train consists now of three wagons, the Ohio boys have joined up here. My guard today, each man has to take his turn on duty. Two men are on at a time, they have to stand all night once a week to guard the camp and cattle from the Indians. From my notebook, I make the following extract. Mother, father, sisters dear, as upon this pleasant Sabbath Day I lay out here on a mound of this vast prairie, our cattle in full view in front, my horse grazing at my feet, made fast by his lariat to the horn of my saddle, upon which I lay stretched out in the tall dead grass.

My thoughts are with and of you, how you would look if you were to see me now. And what are you doing just now, whilst I am thus occupied? Oh, Father in Heaven protect you and spare your lives, for all my hopes of earthly bliss lives centered in that sacred spot called home. And how are you occupied today? Do you ever give one passing thought to one who thinks of you as one near perfect? God bless you all and spare our lives to meet again. Alone though I be, far from the civilized world, still your spirits follow me and bare one company. A man is never alone who has such friends on earth, no matter how distant they may be.

Camp 12: Turkey Creek - 4/11

Last night I stood guard all night and an awful time I had of it, I like to froze. We carried buffalo chips and kept the fire up until we had drained the country of its supply and then we had to flee to our blankets in spite of us. Twas awful cold to be sure. Traveled all the forenoon over the prairie until we came to a frog pond, where we nooned. Buffalo chips for fuel again and a frog pond for water, and you may imagine what our dinner was. After dinner we went on to this little muddy stream, making 22 miles today. Buffalo chips for fuel again, not a tree or bush to be seen in today's travel.

Camp 13: Little Arkansas Creek - 4/12

This morning at 4 1/2 o'clock we were routed out by the guard, gathered a sufficient quantity of barnyard fuel and got breakfast. At 6 o'clock were on the road again. After passing over 13 miles of the same dreary dead prairie, we halted by a quagmire and got dinner. After dinner went on crossing several dry creeks and by sundown reached this small creek where we found a little timber, the first we have seen this side of Cottonwood Creek. Fine day but windy. This little stream is called a river but is but a very small specimen of one. Saw the first prairie dogs here, a species of ground squirrel.

Camp 14: Chavis Creek - 4/13

This morning we made an early start and had not proceeded far before it commenced snowing and blowing in true 'Norwest' style. Wrapping ourselves in blankets we strode, endeavoring to keep warm by fast walking. Three of us left the teams and went on ahead. Had got about a mile in advance of the teams when we were hailed by a stranger who had left his teams to go off the road to hunt. He had killed a buffalo and wanted us to haul it into camp for him. Waited for the teams to come up to accommodate him, then pushed on again. About 11 o'clock we reached this creek about 10 miles from our last night's camp. We were delighted to find a plenty of timber but no water, the creek being perfectly dry. But stop we must, for Lissy says; "Oh dear, I know I'm freezing." And the balance of us felt it, if we said nothing.

So water or not, we determined to stop. About a mile below the road in the heavy timber we found a rude log cabin built by the U.S. Mail Company as a station house for their men, in case of just such a storm as this. We took possession at once, flew around and soon had a rousing fire. And I do think I never was so happy in my life as I was in this cabin after I commenced thawing out. The contrast between this and our condition out on the road was so great, that I felt perfectly happy. 17 of us slept in this hut tonight and thanked Fortune for favoring us so much. For I do believe if this storm had caught us on the prairie, it would have been all day with some of us.

You good people at home who live a civilized life and have homes to go to when it storms, who probably never in your life knew what it was to have Old Mother Earth for a bed and the heavens for a covering, can form no idea how pleasant it seemed when we first struck a fire in this rude hut. But it would have astonished you to have seen our crowd pitch in to the buffalo steak that the stranger brought in. We had it in all shapes, fried, boiled and baked and for once we got a belly full. Such a time as we did have. 16 men and one live woman, young and pretty at that, all hived up in a hut 10 feet square.

Lissy says, "Isn't this nice?" "You bet," says soldier stranger, "Allows his fellows haint got much the start on him by driving off and leaving him behind." After supper the ground in the hut is covered with our bedding, our muddy boots are taken off and we spread ourselves around as best we may, to take up as little room as possible.

The cold raw northwest wind roars through the timber, the snow

Charis Creek. Camp 14th

continues to sift through the slab roof but what care we, for we are housed once more and can laugh at Old Boreas. And laugh we do and a right pleasant evening we pass in this old hut away out in the wilderness. All of us a few weeks ago were strangers to one another but now fast friends. For aye, it is impossible to ever forget one's traveling companions on such a trip as this. Dan, our John Bull, says he don't know but it's fun for us to live like darned injins, but if the Good Lord forgives him for this time, he never will so tempt fate again, sir.

Camp 15: Plum Butte - 4/14

Ice a plenty this morning but a prospect for a fair day. Started on the road again about 7 o'clock and nooned at Cow Creek. During forenoon we crossed a very pretty creek with timbered banks and saw my first buffalo. Saw my first cactus plant today also. This Cow Creek is the most western Mail Station. Found lots of Pike's Peakers camped here. After dinner, rolled out again. Country now begins to look more barren than ever; the rich black soil is exchanged for sand and alkali soil. At sundown we came to the foot of these low hills which, owing to the almost dead level of all the surrounding country, have been dignified by the name of Buttes (or peaks) although they are not over 100 feet in height. Here we found a little quagmire and as it is the best camping ground the country affords us, encamped for the night. Dung for fuel and a frog pond for water again, consequently not much of a supper tonight.

These buttes are two low, sand hills that rear their ugly heads above the barren waste around and serve as landmarks as they can be seen for miles and miles over this desert-like waste. Buffalo are very abundant all around and from these buttes I could look off for miles around and the whole country appeared to be alive with them. Our boys have all been hunting down today but have not succeeded in bagging one as yet. Cold raw wind tonight and our blankets are sought at an early hour, for that is the only chance to get warm.

Camp 16: Arkansas River Great Bend - 4/16

Here we are at last, having reached here about 11:00 AM. Last night we had another awful time of it. During the night the gale increased to a perfect hurricane and about midnight, down came the tent. "Oh dear," says Lissy, "I'm wet through and through, what shall I do Loren?" "All you take care of Lissy and I'll see what I can do with the ___ tent," says friend Loren. But in vain were his efforts to make it stand, the wind was so strong. So we all crawled under our blankets and laid and soaked till morning. In the morning we found it to be impossible to start a fire as our barn yard fuel was altogether too moist to burn well. So we were obliged to go without our breakfast, or nearly so, as all I had was part of a cold flapjack that I picked up in the road where it had been rolled in the sand all night, after our tent blew over and our affects had been scattered by the winds.

The morning sun brought no abatement of the storm. And hungry, wet and shivering we rolled out for a better camp. 8 miles further brought us to the river, where we found protection from the cold winds under its banks, where we soon had a rousing fire and breakfast cooked. During the day we were joined by about 75 more Pike's Peakers who drove in and camped alongside of us during the afternoon. And they came near burning us out, having through their carelessness set the prairie on fire. At night Jud and I went up the river about a mile to Bent's Camp, where his train is encamped on their way to the States.

Camp 17: Arkansas River - 4/17

Last night Jud and myself spent with Bent's train. Jud found all his old associates of the fort at the camp. The Wagon Master was an old friend of his and was very kind to me. They are laying by here for grass to start before they proceed on their road to the States, loaded with buffalo skins and wolf pelts, their principal articles of trade. John the

Wagon Master says we must keep a good look out for the Comanches, for they are plenty on the road and we all know what their disposition is. The country here is very barren, poor soil and but little timber. The river is about one quarter of a mile wide and about 4 feet deep, with a quicksand bottom. Buffalo, antelope, geese and duck are very plenty.

4/18 - Moved up the river and camped again to give our cattle a little chance to feed, as they have been on short allowance since we left the States. Came near being bit by a rattlesnake this morning whilst out after the cattle, but escaped by chance and killed the varmint. John - Bent's Major Domo - made me a present of a fine buffalo robe and a pair of moccasins yesterday, which I mean to keep if possible, to remember the giver. Extract from my notebook. Last night the wind wound down at sunset and we had a calm, beautiful moonlight evening but quite cold. The Prairie was on fire below us on the opposite side of the river and presented a grand sight from our camp.

This is my guard today and I write this stretched out in the tall dead grass out on the prairie about a mile from camp, where I am guarding our cattle whilst they feed. Occasionally a large gray wolf will make its appearance, trotting along in search of a dead carcass or grub of some sort. But upon spying us off he goes at a two forty gait, glad to get off with merely a view of us. Buffalo and antelope can be seen feeding in the distance whilst numerous flocks of brant, geese and duck are constantly passing overhead. This forenoon it is quite warm and pleasant with a fine southerly breeze...

I had written this much when, whir...whir...whir... went a rattlesnake close alongside of me. I killed him and secured his rattles, nine in number.

Camp 18: Pawnee Fork of Arkansas River - 4/18

Early this morning we broke up camp and traveled on till noon when we drove onto the prairie and got dinner without water, after which we drove on till the dark and reached Ash Creek, but found it dry. Continued on till about midnight before we reached this creek, making in all about 30 miles drive without water, over a dry, level prairie. About 9 AM we reached Allison's Ranch, a trading post for the Kiowa Indians. It is situated at the junction of Walnut Creek and Arkansas River, has a strong house and corral built of walls set endways in the ground, forming a safe defense against Indians. Leaving the fort, we continued on for 20 miles to Ash Creek, passing the U.S. Mail Company who were camped by the side of the road getting dinner. They had two passengers bound to Santa Fe.

Met several bands of Indians during the day, also a surveying party were on the way to the States, having been driven from Pawnee Fork where they were building a mail station by the Kiowa Indians. At noon we stopped the train to rest the cattle and get a bite for ourselves, but had no water. After this, we continued on our weary way over this dreary waste, the country looking most desolate. And passing Pawnee Rock at sundown, reached Ash Creek by dark. Rested our team until the moon rose, about an hour, when we reached here about midnight where we found a plenty of water but no wood. Two of our boys came in just as we reached camp with a load of buffalo steak, which they had killed, and we soon had a rousing fire of buffalo chips and a good supper of buffalo steak prepared. A more dreary, desolate, lonely day's travel we have not had than today's has been, with little or no grass, no water, not a tree or bush to be seen, with the exception of a few Cottonwoods on the banks of Ash Creek.

This Pawnee Fork has been the scene of many Indian massacres and is undoubtedly bound to be of many more before this wilderness becomes settled by Whites.

<< Yreka Dec. 2d 1859 >>
Since I was there last spring, the S. J. Mail Company was attacked by the Kiowas and all but one of the company were killed, their horses taken and coaches burnt.

Also, several parties of Pike's Peakers have been murdered since then at this spot.
DA Jenks

Camp 19: Chief Little Mountain - 4/19

Morning fair. Finding it to be very poor feed at our last night's camp, and as our cattle begin to show their hard fare, we broke camp and moved on up the creek about 6 miles to better feed, where we camped for the day. Found here plenty of wood. During the day our camp was visited by several Indians and amongst others by Little Mountain, a Kiowa Chief. They wanted us to give them provisions, but we begged to be excused and at night they left us, surly and mad. This Chief had hung on his neck a golden image of our savior, which he had robbed some Catholic Church of in New Mexico in one of his many forays against that people.

In parting, he gave us to understand that we had better give him what he demanded or take the consequences.

Camp 20: Desert between Arkansas & Pawnee Fork - 4/20

Last night after dark we could hear a grand powwow amongst the Indians away off down the creek. They were singing and dancing, beating their stretched antelope skin drums, hallooing and yelling and in fact, making a "devil of a din." As soon as Jud heard it he says, "Boys get up the cattle and be quick about it if you don't want to have a fight, for as sure as you are born we must fight or run for it now. Those red devils are preparing for a fight, sure." So we got the cattle up and started as silently as possible out onto the road again. Traveled all night and all of the day till night before we stopped. Tonight we are camped on a dry gulch waiting for the moon to rise to start again, for we have had no water since we left the Pawnee Fork.

Camp 21: Arkansas River - 4/21

Reached the river about noon today almost froze. Having driven our teams and walked 75 miles across a barren, treeless, waterless desert in 36 hours. Pretty good time I take it, for an ox team. The first 30 miles we made in 14 hours from Pawnee Fork, our cattle not having a drop of water until then. At this place we found a hole full of rainwater and this relieved us some. Last night, after a few hours rest and the moon having arisen, we resumed our flight across the desert. Moon rose about midnight, but it brought a northwest snowstorm with it. We pushed on against the wind and sleet all night, nearly froze and the morning sun brought us no relief.

I thought I should perish with the cold and fatigue but pushed along and by noon we reached the river, where we found a little relief from the cold blasts by creeping under the rocky bluffs. But there was no timber here and the dry buffalo chips were anything but dry today. So we were compelled to go without fire, and I certainly never suffered so much from cold before. This desert we have just crossed is "cut off", that is the Arkansas River at this point makes a long sweep southward and by cutting across we saved 40 miles travel. It is a barren tract, not a tree or shrub to be seen, almost perfectly level and with little feed at any time and none at all at this season of the year. Truly it is a hard road to travel. Carcasses of oxen, mules and horses line the road. Had it not been for the storm we should have suffered for water, but as it was, we got a sufficient to sustain life from the pools in the road.

Camp 22: Arkansas River - 4/22

At noon we hitched up and drove on up the river about 6 miles and camped again for the night. Last night was bitter cold and as we have no fire, of course we suffered. Ice made over one half inch thick last night and this morning the river is full of drift ice. What an awful desolate looking country is this. Not a tree or shrub to be seen, naught but the same dead level prairie as far as the eye can see. You can form some idea of the country from the fact that for a distance of 350 miles (from Pawnee Fork to Fontaine que Bouille Creek) there is not a single tributary. This shows you what a sterile country it is and further, for over

200 miles traveling up this river you will not see a single tree or shrub. The same dreary view is always present, vast plains, low sand hills, the sluggish river of quick sands to your left, the desert-like plains on your right and the everlasting prickly pear seems to have monopolized this country as its own.

Wolves, prairie dogs, owls and rattlesnakes are its sole inhabitants, save occasionally a band of red skins who visit the road for the sake of plunder. The buffalo, who have left the plains around thickly strewn with 'chips', are now seldom seen above this point of the road. What travelers through this country would do were it not for these chips I do not see, for there is no wood and that is a very essential thing on such a trip where a man has to board himself. Our cattle begin to show their bad fare and we are obliged to make short drives for their sake.

Camp 23: Arkansas River - 4/23

Made 13 miles today and camped. Last night was another cold one. A train of Mexicans bound to Santa Fe came along this morning who stated that instead of taking the cut off that we did at Pawnee Fork they came around by the river. They passed through an Indian village of over 400 lodges and were considerably pestered by them, but finally got through without a fight. But they considered us in good luck in escaping them as we did. Passed the ruins of US Fort Atkinson this morning, the former scene of many an Indian fight according to Jud's account. Dry barnyard fuel in abundance tonight. Good feed for our cattle and baked duck for supper. What more can we ask?

Camp 24: Arkansas River - 4/24

This morning we rolled out early at daybreak and traveled about four hours and stopped for breakfast on the banks of the river with plenty of grass, chips, etc. Lay here till 2 PM. After dinner our road took us up off the river onto the high prairie. Ascending the molehills to our right, we crossed several wide ravines and came out onto the wide prairie. Here, for miles upon miles lays spread out the most level land I ever saw. A 36-mile racetrack might be lain out here and the horses would always be in sight all the way round. We kept on over this high prairie for about 8 miles when the road took us down onto the river bottom again where we camped in good feed. The Santa Fe Road crosses the river where we nooned. We are now on the road to Bent's Fort.

Camp 25: Arkansas River - 4/25

This morning being my watch, I got our party up by 4 o'clock and in half an hour we were on the road again. Our Ohio and Illinois friends swore they wouldn't stand it any longer, twas out of all reason they said, starting out so early in the morning and they'd be 'dod rotted' if we might not go it alone for all them. So we left them and went it alone. During the night the strong wind we have been 'blessed' with nearly ever since we left the States, increased to a gale and has continued to blow during the day as I never saw the wind blow before, anywhere. Cape Horn itself want a circumstance. All day has it blown a perfect tornado, dead ahead, making it almost impossible to either travel or lay by on this accursed desert, where there is neither timber nor hills to shelter one.

Clouds of sand fills the air and hides the sun from view. Clouds as black as thunderclouds made by the drifting sand. It flies by us, it fills our eyes, our mouth, we breathe it in every breath and our faces and hands bleed from a thousand little wounds occasioned by this sand tornado. By noon it had become truly awful and we searched in vain for a gully, a ravine or hole, anything to protect us from the storm. But in vain we searched, the country is as level as a barn floor. At 2 PM we were obliged to stop, we could not make headway against it any longer. We drove down to the river and turned the cattle loose and throwing ourselves into the grass, we lay low to avoid the wind as much as possible. Towards night we dug a hole in the ground about 5 feet deep and cooked our supper in that.

Camp 26: Arkansas River - 4/26

The gale continued during the night. Loren endeavored to pitch the tent during a lull in the storm at sundown, succeeded in getting it set and he and Lissy turned in. Dan and I concluded to try our luck in the wagon. So stowing the cargo in the after part, we made a nest forward where we could curl up for the night. Just as we had finished our arrangements and were congratulating ourselves on having secured a shelter, I heard the old tent, rip, rip and down she came. All in a heap, split from end to end. "Oh dear," says Lissy, "What shall I do? I'm awful cold." Come in with us Lissy says I, by sitting in my lap we can make room in here.

So in she came and thus we passed the night, four of us cooped up in a place in the wagon about 4 feet square. Jud and Charlie slept in the hole we dug to cook supper in. As for Jud, it don't make much difference to him where he is, he is used to hard fare. But Charlie's long legs were awfully in his way again last night. He says he will be 'Gaul Darned' if he was put up for this kind of business. As to sleeping on the ground with the clouds for a cover lid, or eating flapjacks on a windy day when they become sick with the dust from the buffalo chips fuel, that's alright enough. But when it comes to sleeping in a well, 3 feet across with a bedfellow, he says that is more than he bargained for. "You see, my legs must have room." Towards night the wind died away, we made about 16 miles today. Country very barren, sandy and poor grass. Same dead level waste, nothing to break the dull monotony of the view.

Camp 27: Arkansas River - 4/27

This morning we were called up by the guard at 3 1/4 o'clock, and by 4 o'clock were on the road. Ice made last night, fine frosty atmosphere this morning but the sun rose bright and clear. Wolves and coyotes very plenty about camp of nights, but other game is very scarce. Have not seen a buffalo since we left Pawnee Fork. Country is very level, sandy and barren. Not a hill or ravine a foot deep to cross all day, grass scarce and no timber. River as ever, wide and shallow, dotted here and there with little sandy islands. Many of the emigrants who have overtaken us complain of the Kiowa Indians having robbed them at Pawnee Fork. Did not trouble us that way, because they didn't catch us. Made about 8 miles by 9 o'clock and camped for breakfast.

Whilst preparing our meals two dirty, ragged specimens of humanity made their appearance, coming down the road. They came into camp and we gave them breakfast after hearing their story. It appears that they and 11 others started out from Leavenworth last February on foot for Pike's Peak taking the Smoky Hill Fork Road, intending to foot it through. They traveled about 600 miles west before they begun to give out. By this time their provisions had given out, their trail was no longer visible, and they struggled on for three days without water. They then struck south to strike this river and these two were all that reached it. The other 11 perished on the way. We fitted them out with provisions, and they resumed their journey homeward. They had lived for days on roots and what they could gather on the prairies, and expect to beg their way back to the States from the emigrants on the road. They say that very many must have perished on that route.

What fools we all are to be sure, us gold hunters. Here on this road are thousands now on route to Pike's Peak who have sacrificed their all to fit out for this trip. Some with handcarts, some with wheelbarrows, some on foot - begging their way along from the teams on the road. Made 18 miles today and camped in poor feed at night.

Camp 28: Aubrey's Crossing - 4/28

This morning we turned out in the rain by 4 o'clock, got our cup of coffee and continued on our winding way. Traveled until about 11 o'clock when we camped for the day, owing to the rain having made but about 10 miles. Country begins to look more hilly, grass scarce and road sandy. Occasionally a tree to be seen now on the opposite bank of the river and on the islands in it. For the first time since we left Pawnee Fork, we have a wood fire tonight. On the opposite bank there is a tribe of Comanches encamped, there are about 30 lodges of them. They are sulking around our camp tonight but do not venture in. We are on our guard and if they attack us, they will find us prepared for them.

Camp 29: Arkansas River - 4/29

Last night we turned in to our wet blankets rather apprehensive of an attack before morning from our Comanche neighbors, but the night passed by and the morning came without the loss of either our property or scalps. But we were not disposed to tempt fate by longer delay then possible, so long before daybreak we were on the road again. Sun rose clear and we traveled on till 9 o'clock before we found feed for our cattle and here we stopped for breakfast. We passed Comanche Camp before day broke. Made 20 miles today and camped at the mouth of a dry creek about 8:00 PM. Plenty of wood tonight and grass good today, has been the first warm day we have had on the road. Passed Black Butte during the afternoon, a singular cone-like hill of slate rock about 50 feet in diameter and about 30 feet in height. Went onto the top of it and found several Buffalo skulls which had been used as records by other visitors, being covered with names in pencil mark. My guard tonight and had a devil of a time herding our stock.

We reached camp late and before we got supper it was dark, so when we went out to look after the cattle they were not to be found. We hunted and traveled till 2 AM before we found them and then they were within a quarter of a mile of camp. This night guard business is an awful bore, and besides, is not as safe as it might be. To say nothing of the chances of being popped at by Indians, it is anything but pleasant to hear the rattlesnakes buzzing around your feet in the night.

Camp 30: Cold Spring Camp - 4/30

Started out at 3 1/2 o'clock this morning and made about 10 miles, when we drove off the road about a mile to feed and water near a clump of Cottonwoods. Cold Spring Camp is the name of the spot and it is the most desolate looking spot I have seen for some time. It is nothing but an alkali marsh for miles around, the ground being white with the poisonous stuff. About noon the old northwest wind made its appearance again accompanied by clouds of sand and alkali dust, this was finally followed by rain, in torrents. We pushed on through it all for we might as well travel as lay by, where we have neither shelter from the storm or fire to warm us. In vain we hunted for some material for a fire and we trudged along wet and shivering all the afternoon in the vain hopes of reaching someplace where we might find wood and feed for our cattle as well as water.

At dark we were compelled to camp on the riverbanks, without either grass for our cattle or wood for ourselves. One ox gave out during the afternoon, laid down in the road and we were compelled to leave him there to die. Raw pork for supper tonight and a bed in the mud was our portion. Dan and I waded the river to try and find some fuel on that side but did not succeed. Shivering with cold, drenched and just soaking with the rain, hungry with fasting and tired out with our 20 miles walk today, we spread our wet blankets on the driest place in the mud and crawled into them for the night. In the night it cleared off cold and our blankets were froze stiff.

Camp 31: Arkansas River - 5/1

This morning I lay in my nest until the sun rose and then turned out, all steaming. Blankets, boots and everything froze stiff and the hair of my head white with frost. And here, a sore that has long been festering came to a head. Jud and myself had an out and out, rough-and-tumble, fight. He has for some time past, presuming upon his long acquaintance with the road, been very overbearing towards us Greenhorns, as he styles us, and has at various times used language towards me that I will permit no man to use. He commenced again this morning and I put a stop to it in the most effectual way. His sort can't rule me. Now it has passed by, I feel no regret that I pursued the course I did with him. Our difficulty delayed the train till noon.

We then drove on up the river about 6 miles, came to timber and good feed and stopped for the night. I intend to draw out from the crowd as soon as possible to avoid further trouble. I cannot submit to abuse from any source, much less from an inferior in every sense. Loren and I understand one another, and he says, "Dan you are right. Jud is my brother, but you are my friend and I feel as much for one as the other. To avoid all the trouble, you and Jud must separate, I suppose." We have now reached the point on the river where we shall have a plenty of wood, feed, etc. And the country has changed, its flat surface has become more hilly.

Camp 32: Bent's Fort - 5/2

This morning started on ahead of the teams and reached the fort about 10 o'clock. This fort is 545 miles from Kansas City, we have been 32 days traveling time in coming this distance. Since we struck the river this side of the cut off, our road has been near its banks all the way. The prairies are very sterile, nothing growing in many places excepting sagebrush and different species of the cactus. From the point above mentioned to where the Santa Fe Trail crosses the river it is 27 miles. The distance from there to this fort is 150 miles. Here we first strike timber on the banks of the river.

The fort is built of cobble stone in a rectangular shape, about 125 feet long by 100 wide and 14 high. Has two entrances, one upon the north and one upon the east and is altogether a strong fortification for the purposes for which it was built. We found a tribe of Comanches encamped on the bottomlands to the east of the fort and only four men at the fort, which was pretty well cleaned out, we having met the train belonging to it at the Great Bend on the way to the States.

I stayed here an hour or two, by this time our train came up and we went on about 8 miles further and camped for night in good feed. Jud and several others have stopped behind at the fort. To have a spree, I suppose. Am preparing to pack a horse and go on ahead of teams, as I can travel this way much faster than the teams go. I am sick of ox team navigation and this trip will do me for my lifetime, I think. Horned horses may do for farming but they "haint" just the thing for traveling.

Camp 33: Chief Ten Bears - 5/3

This morning started early, our road took us up a low hill onto the prairie, cutting off a bend in the river. From here we caught sight for the first time of the snowcapped peaks of the Rocky Mountains, away off in the dim distance. Traveled 10 miles to the river where we stopped for breakfast. Whilst at breakfast, Chief Ten Bears and another Comanche rode into camp from below stating that they expected their whole tribe to come in here from above during the day. About noon, just as Dan and I had finished our preparations for packing, we heard an awful clatter on the other side of the river and we soon saw the advance guard of the tribe come rushing into the river. On they came like a flood, big bucks with their hideous faces daubed up with paint, riding their meddlesome ponies, long files of squaws leading ponies loaded down with their camp plunder, trailing their lodge poles behind them.

Papooses without number and of all sizes, from the infants lashed in a sack and slung between the poles, to the young bucks just able to straddle a pony. On they came, fording the river and pitching their camp right around us. Our horse being packed, Dan and I started off and our train soon followed, all being anxious to leave this neighborhood as soon as possible. We made (Dan and I) 20 miles that afternoon and all the afternoon, as far as we could see off the river on the opposite side, this tribe was still a coming, strung out for miles and miles along the trail. There must have been several thousand of them and they had at least a thousand head of horses.

Dan and I have packed on Loren's horse 10 days provisions, our blankets, cooking utensils, etc. and in company with two western men with a hand cart, are pushing ahead for Puebla. A little settlement of mountaineers at the mouth of Fontaine que Bouille Creek, a tributary of the Arkansas. Tonight, we camped at the mouth of a dry creek. The country today has been sandy, rocky and hilly with little or no grass, excepting a little occasionally on the river bottoms. Our teams are far behind and we expect to make an average of 30 miles a day. Our fellow travelers of the hand cart are very anxious to see the promised land, are very sanguine of success and have implicit faith in all the newspaper stories respecting that country. Which is more than I can say for myself.

Camp 34: Arkansas River - 5/4

We lay in our blankets this morning till daylight after enjoying one whole night's rest, which is more than I have done for weeks before. About sunrise our teams passed by our camp, they having started at 3 1/2 o'clock in the morning. We got our breakfast and packing the horse we soon overtook them and passed them, continuing on we overhauled the Ohio boys and passed them. About 9 o'clock passed the ruins of Bents Old Fort, now deserted. About 10 1/2 o'clock we were compelled to flee to a Cottonwood Grove on the banks of the river to escape the hurricane that was filling the air with clouds of sand. Lay here till nearly night before the wind went down. Yesterday afternoon as Dan and I were trudging along, we met two men driving a yoke of oxen. They belonged to Bent's Fort.

The young man stopped me. I had a short conversation with him and we then separated. Loren told me this morning that he camped with them last night and said he was from Pawtucket and his name was either Buffington Pierce or Pierce Buffington and he had forgotten which. That he knew me by reputation but hadn't seen me for years, and consequently didn't recognize me. I'm sorry I didn't know this at the time I met him. Country this forenoon is sandy and rocky with poor soil and but little grass. About 4 o'clock we packed up again and travelled over a hilly road until 9 o'clock before we reached the river again, when we camped in a sage thicket for the night.

Camp 35: Arkansas River - 5/5

Left camp about six this morning and had traveled but a few miles before we met the advance guard of disappointed, returning, Pike's Peakers. The first we met were on foot. Soon after, we commenced meeting teams of all kinds; mules, oxen and horses, hand carts and go carts. On they roll. And a more disappointed crew, or longer faces, I never saw. Curses both loud and deep were showered by them upon the originators of this ___ humbug. And now, how have the hopes of the sanguine fallen. Looks of blank dismay stare you in the face on every side. Teams are stopped, a vote is taken whether they shall go on and see for themselves, go back, or go to California.

Some turnabout and take the long, weary backtrack. Others split up their companies and whilst some go on, the balance return to the homes they never ought to have left. But worst of all many, aye very many, have neither money or provisions to take them back. And what to do, they cannot tell. Truly it is a sad sight to see strong men weep as they think of their families at home and their situation here. I being ahead of my team and not knowing how this news may affect them, intend to lay by for them to come on. I cannot go back, that is certain. And I am bound for California now. We are camped tonight on the river bottom a mile from the road in a Cottonwood Grove with good feed. Our handcart man has concluded to take a loaf of bread in the morning and start back for Illinois. He is a man of about 45 years old and he cries like a child as he talks of his situation.

Camp 36: Handcart Man & Boney - 5/6

This morning our Illinois friend of the handcart shouldered his blankets and started on his long and weary homeward road. "It's all fired hard," says he, "to go back to Polly in this fix. I mortgaged my little farm to raise the means to start out here. Had to give my note for $300 to raise $150 and it, bearing interest at the rate of 2% a month. I'll never get clear of this infernal scrape if I work all the balance of my days." Another fellow called Boney, his companion, accompanies him. Was somewhat amused at a remark he made once on the road. It had rained all day and at night we had no fire, so we had to turn in to our blankets wet and cold.

Boney had but one pair of blankets and as he was as thin as a June shad, he said the cold winds fairly whistled through his ribs. The first thing in the morning that I heard was a sort of a war hoop from Boney. He awakened the whole camp by his yells. What the devil is the matter, asks someone. "Why when I woke up and found myself alive, I had to jump as high and yell as loud as I could to find myself on this side er Jordan. Oh Lord but I was powerful cold though." Another one of his company owed him a small sum of money and he wished for a settlement. Finally, the debtor agreed to give him an order on his father in Missouri for the amount. "Yer mought as well give me an order on a jay bird tother side er the Wabash as that," says Boney.

Dan and I concluded to remove our camp to some point nearer the road, so as to be able to see our teams if they should pass. So we packed up and drove about 6 miles further and camped in a grove on the bank of the river, in full view of the road.

5/7 - Lay in camp today, Dan and I all alone waiting for our teams to come up. Our Pike's Peak trip is up and now we are to prepare for a still longer one, to California. Rather than go back to be laughed at, I'll try old California again. Ours is a very pretty camp where we now lay. A grove of Cottonwoods shelters us. Free from underbrush, the level river bottom being covered with the new crop of grass just springing up. Geese, duck and brant are plenty in the marsh below, whilst the gobble of wild turkeys reminds us of Christmas feasts at home. Our little tent stands out in bold relief in its groundwork of green, forming a very pretty picture as viewed from the road.

Teams of emigrants are almost constantly passing to and fro. Some energetic fellows pushing forward to Pike's Peak to see for themselves whether they have been humbugged or no. Others, satisfied of that fact are homeward bound. Have many times thought of the singular fate of an individual I saw with Bent's train when we met it at the Great Bend. Amongst others, I saw one whose face showed him to be a white man but whose appearance every otherwise was decidedly Indian. I asked the Wagon Master who and what he was. He told me that he was a Comanche captive that Colonel Bent had bought from that tribe.

He was stolen from his parents in Texas years ago, when he was a little boy and had grown up with their tribe, had lost the knowledge of his mother tongue and had become in everything but features a perfect Indian. He must have been about 50 years of age and in his tastes and inclination was as much an Indian now as any of his red skinned friends. His only companion with whom he was on terms of intimacy in the train, was a Cheyenne Indian that traveled with them as hunter for the party. By the way this Cheyenne was a brother-in-law to Colonel Bent, he having married a squaw and his children are all half breeds.

These mountaineers are a singular race, singular in their tastes and habits, almost as wild as the tribes by whom they are surrounded. They become so habituated to the life that, they are never easy in any other station and many of them are well educated men and of good families at home. At night our train has not made its appearance as yet. If they do not come on tomorrow, I shall go back to meet them. We are but a few miles below the mouth of the Huerfano, a tributary that puts into this river on the opposite side, from the south.

Camp 37: Charley Autobees' Trading Post - 5/8

This morning our teams hove in sight, our Ohio and Illinois friends of the forepart of the trip were with them again. We found our party intend to go on to Pike's Peak at any rate. And if that in fact proves a failure, then most of us intend to cross the country to California. Lissy says she can't go much further, she has traveled far enough with an ox team. Reached the Trading Post at the mouth of Huerfano at noon kept by a mountaineer by the name of Charley Autobees. Found the inhabitants much excited by the news of the murder of an Arapaho

Indian, brother of a Chief of that tribe. He was murdered by a Mexican for his pony and the Whites fear the tribe will retaliate upon them. After dinner drove about 8 miles and camped.

Camp 38: Arkansas River - 5/9

Today we moved on up the river to near the mouth of Fontaine que Bouille and camped. Our cattle are very much reduced in flesh and some are very foot sore and we shall have to lay by somewhere to let them recruit. Nothing but man can stand this trip, he with his iron will outlives all others of the animal kind. Loren and wife, Jud and Charlie propose stopping here on this creek at least for this season. They intend to put in a crop and trade with the Indians and emigrants. I would not stop here for all the wealth of Pike's Peak. There is a little collection of mud huts and log cabins at the mouth of this creek, inhabited by Mountaineers and Mexicans and called by some the Puebla. By others since the gold humbug, Fountain City. Near this place Loren intends to squat.

Camp 39: Fountain Creek 5 Miles North of Pueblo - 5/10

At last, we have left the river and are now steering north. We have followed up this river from where our road first struck it 380 miles. For most of that distance it runs through a perfect desert. A few miles above here it enters the mountains and runs through narrow canyons. From Bent's Old Fort to this point there is a narrow strip of beautiful bottom lands, fit for farming. But once off of this narrow strip you strike the sterile plains, fit for nothing on earth but its present inhabitants, the prairie dogs, wolves and coyotes. From Bent's Fort up, the banks are lined with groves of Cottonwoods. But from that point down there is scarcely a tree or shrub. We drove into Puebla about 10:00 AM and remained there till about the middle of the afternoon when we drove up to this point to feed and camped.

Puebla as I have said before is inhabited by two or three dozen Mountaineers and Mexicans and about a dozen Mexican women. It is situated at the foot of the Rocky Mountains and the snowcapped peaks are in close view from the town. San Cristobal to the south is near Santa Fe but is in plain view from here. Pike's Peak is a few miles to the north. A very dissipated but talented brother of Governor McDougal of California lives here, or rather exists here, for it is not living. Another, a Mr. Shaffner and Mr. Wilson, two well educated men, are wearing out an existence here. "Oh," they say, "we have lived in the mountains so long we don't feel at home anywhere else. Society has no charms for us. Here we are free to do and act as we please, are freed from all the restraints society imposes upon one."

They are living illustrations of the saying, "I had rather be a king amongst hogs, then a hog amongst kings." Wilson told me that McDougal, who appears to be king here, had traded with an emigrant for two 10-gallon kegs of whiskey about 10 days ago and he had kept the little Hamlet drunk ever since. Everything is free to those they like and as they took a fancy to us, we were on the free list. Lissy left us here and Loren secured as good a cabin as there was here for her to live in, until he locates somewhere for himself. About dark she gave birth to a boy and there was a grand drunk came off in honor of the event. This is the first native born white child in the Pike's Peak country and its name is Dan Jenks. What an awful honor to be sure.

Camp 40: Fountain Creek 10 Miles North of Pueblo - 5/11

Lay in yesterday's camp till noon then hitched up and went up the creek 5 miles further and camped. Soil is poor and sandy, producing little else then sagebrush, greasewood and cactus. To our left lies the Pike's Peak range of mountains, on our right a long stretch of low sandy hills and desert plains, covered with the usual productions of the country, sagebrush and prickly pear. On the banks of the creek there is a little seed and timber of the Cottonwood species. What a country to settle in.

My namesake, owing to its not being able to bear up under its great weight of responsibility in assuming the name, I suppose, quietly slipped its hold upon this world and returned to_to_to Heaven, I suppose. At least, it died. And where it went to, I'll leave for others to decide.

Camp 41: Independence Camp ~ Fontaine qui Bouille - 5/17

We moved up here last Thursday to a fine grove of Cottonwoods and good feed. And here we have lain ever since, recruiting our cattle and preparing for our overland trip to California. I have bought Loren's wagon and we have divided our provisions and tomorrow we bid him goodbye. He is preparing to form it here and Lissy is to remain at Puebla until he builds a cabin for her here. Dan, our John Bull, is to go on with me and drive my team for me. The Ohio boys and our Illinois friends are to go to California with me. During the past few days our boys have been out on a hunting expedition to the mountains. But they returned last night almost famished and without any game.

Camp 42: Jim's Camp - 5/18

This morning early we got our cattle up, bid the boys a goodbye and rolled out again. This time for California bound. Kept on up the Fontaine que Bouille about 15 miles and stopped for dinner. Here we left the creek and taking the hills to our right we had a 12-mile drive without wood or water and didn't reach camp till 10 o'clock at night. This hole is a sort of an oasis in the desert, with good feed and water and plenty of wood for cooking purposes. Found the first pine here that I have seen on the road. We found here about 20 teams of Pike's Peakers encamped for the night. We were so late getting into camp we had to go supperless to bed, for it was too dark to hunt for wood or water.

Camp 43: O'Falley's Grave - 5/19

Drove about 12 miles this morning and came to the first fine timber we have seen on the road. In fact, it is the only patch of forest timber we have seen on the whole route. What little timber we have seen heretofore has been narrow strips of Cottonwood on the banks of the different watercourses. Here too the country begins to grow more hilly, the road being crossed by many little ravines and gulches with pine covered hills between. We stopped for dinner at Loring's Corral. It was built by Colonel Loring of the US Army who led a detachment destined for Utah a year ago. At this place we found a grave of probably one of his men. After dinner we went on about 6 miles further to our present camp. Here also is a grave of one of Loring's men.

Camp 44: Head of Cherry Creek - 5/20

This morning we drove about 10 miles and stopped for dinner in the open prairie hills and after a bite drove on to our present camp 4 miles further. Whilst driving along this morning a man rode up to us and asked if we had any whiskey aboard, we told him we had. "Well then," says he, "for the love of man let me have a little, for old Colonel McDougal is out here in camp and has the trembles awful." I drew a quart and went out to their camp and found old McWilson and Shaffner there en route for Denver City. McDougal swore I had saved his life by coming. The whiskey worked wonders, for very soon McDougal declared himself able to go on and we rode on to camp together. Found several parties prospecting for gold here but they were not very successful in finding it.

Camp 45: Lying Speculators - 5/21

Drove down the creek 10 miles and camped for the day. Passed through Russellville this morning, this is one of the prosperous mining towns we have heard so much of. There was a sawmill and about a dozen log cabins here, but the sawmill was stopped and the houses unoccupied. We saw but four men here, two were at the sawmill and two were prospecting the creek. This town speculation I reckon will prove a failure. They tried their lying games upon me here, but I was too old a miner to be caught with salt. I asked them where their diggings were. "Why in the creek anywhere," says they, "you can make from $3 up."

Yes, up a horn I presume all right. Do you ever find any coarse gold here? "Oh occasionally, I believe I have a lump with me now that I picked up yesterday," says one of them and he fumbled in his pockets and finally found a lump of amalgam gold weighing about $4, that from its dull appearance I would be almost willing to swear had been carried more than one year in a buckskin bag. Did you find that lump just in that shape yesterday, stranger? "Yes," says he. Well then allow me to tell you that I have mined in California nine years and this is the first time I ever heard of gold being found in that state. Old Dame Nature has been very bountiful to you, to gather all these fine particles of gold with quicksilver and then retort it for you.

He smelt a miner, turned on his heels and walked off to the mill. Fact is, there is a little fine gold found here almost anywhere, but I do not believe it will ever be found in paying quantities. I know it has not been found as yet. Speculators thought it was bound to be another California and pitched in to snake the most of it. They have been deceived. The mines have not turned out as they anticipated, and now they are bound to get even if possible. Their only chance is to keep up the excitement as long as possible and they resort to any means to accomplish this object. Here there is a sawmill and a town built, such as it is, and the prospectors are anxious to get people to settle here. To induce them to do so, they have employed these men to tell similar lies to those they spun out to me.

In the afternoon Bob Cornthwaite (one of our Ohio boys) and myself went out prospecting. We tried our best but could not raise a decent prospect, but became very near being frightened out of our boots by a catamount that sprung from a bush just ahead of us as we were walking down the creek.

Camp 46: Cherry Creek - 5/22

Fine weather we have now. This morning we drove about 10 miles and stopped for dinner. According to my idea of things in general, I should say this valley was much better adapted for farming than mining. This is as pretty a valley for farming as I ever saw. Our afternoon's drive was about 10 miles down the creek and the whole distance was a succession of beautiful, level bottoms of rich light soil. If gold is ever discovered in paying quantities, this valley will then be valuable and its settlers rich men. But it all depends upon the AU and that has not been found as yet. If one could but look ahead just one short year at this time.

God send all friends at home as pleasant weather, as light hearts and as good health as we now enjoy in this Rocky Mountain country.

Camp 47: Cherry Creek - 5/23

We moved down the creek about 2 miles to better feed. Then leaving a guard at our camp, the balance of us footed it down to Denver City. I found, as I expected, quite a collection of log houses, 50 or more maybe. There was not as large a crowd here as I expected to see, as many are leaving every day for the States. Those that were here wear very long faces, as the most sanguine fear that the bubble has burst. And the balance agreed that this has been the biggest humbug ever built on so slight a foundation. Much, aye very much suffering has been occasioned, but what care the speculators for that? I had a man pointed out to me who it was said had eaten of his brother's flesh to keep from starving on the Smoky Hill Route.

Camp 48: Denver City - 5/26

We have been encamped for the last three days on the banks of the South Platte near this city, tomorrow we leave here for Salt Lake City. I am satisfied now that there has been no paying diggings struck as yet and I see no reason to hope for any in the future. These speculators resort to all manner of expedients to induce emigrants to stay. But I have proven to my satisfaction that all of their stories of big strikes are lies and nothing else. I see no hope for their wishes ever been realized. This country has been prospected now a year and there has never been a single instance of success, not one, all the stories to the contrary notwithstanding.

In fact, some of the more honest of the merchants here have admitted to me that they have been deceived and now are trying to close out and leave here. Believing as I do, that there is no show here. I have invested what few dollars I have in a team to take me through to California. I have now a four-yoke ox team and a saddle pony and are now all ready for my start across the mountains in the morning. All who can, are leaving here as fast as possible. Those who have teams are selling off their cattle at from $10-$30 a yoke to get provisions to take them home. Others are building skiffs to float themselves down the Platte to the States. There are others who cannot procure even this means of conveyance and they wear dreadful long faces as they think of their situation.

Amongst this latter class I found one solitary poverty-stricken Pawtucket man who would gladly have returned to Yankeedom if he did but know how to accomplish such an end. I loaned him $10 on long credit, as he said if he had that amount he could make a start. One hears pretty hard talk here occasionally, as the excited Humbugged meet the Humbuggers. Thieves, Liars and Murderers are mild terms compared to some I have heard applied to the merchants here by the emigrants. On the 25th it commenced raining and came on so cold that I turned in to my blankets in the wagon before dark to get warm. And this morning woke up to find 6 inches of snow on the ground. By noon it had almost all disappeared before the warm sun's rays.

Every exertion is made by the townspeople to induce us to stay. But what on earth is there to induce a man to stop here? I cannot see. Our Illinois friends are taking passengers through to California from here.

Camp 49: Dry Gulch - 5/27

This morning after some trouble in gathering our herd of cattle, we at last got underway again. We have now 35 head of cattle in all. Our Ohio and Illinois boys and my team are traveling in company. We, all of us, speculated a little on beef stock and have a small band of loose cattle driving along in case we lose an ox. Passing through Denver we were followed down to the river by quite a number of its inhabitants, who tried to prevail upon us to stay. Crossed at the ferry, traveled about 6 miles and nooned on Clear Creek. Our herd is in tolerable good traveling condition, we have fine weather today and all are in first-rate spirits. And now that the season is so far advanced, we expect to have a pleasant time in traveling through the wilderness.

We expect to avoid the long bend to the north by Fort Laramie and the South Pass, by taking a mountain trail right direct for Fort Bridger. But this is a road but little travelled and we shall probably not see another team but our own until we get through. After dinner we moved on over a hilly grassy country for 7 miles to this little creek, where we camped for the night in good feed. Our road from here to Cache La Poudre Creek will run along the foot of the mountains in a northerly course. Arriving at that point we commence our climbing, so said our guide. We expect to see sights now in the way of traveling, for there are no ferries or bridges across the many streams we will have to cross.

1200 miles further to go, don't it look like an undertaking to make this distance with an ox team? You bet.

Camp 50: Mountaineer Creek - 5/28

Frosty nights but warm pleasant days thus far. Country today much the same as yesterday. Drove about 8 miles to a small, pretty mountain creek and nooned, good feed and little wood. Nelse and Albert, two Canadian boys traveling with the Illinois team, brought in an antelope this noon. After a rousing dinner of antelope steak, we drove about 8 miles to Boulder Creek. Found no wood here, drove on four miles further to a small creek where we found a plenty of willows for fire and camped for night. Found a party of mountaineers camped here bound to Pike's Peak. Country today a rolling prairie, Long's Peak is right abreast of us tonight.

Camp 51: Frosty Creek - 5/29

This morning I awoke early, my hair being white with frost for I have no tent now and sleep out in the open air. And getting our teams up we rolled out about 4 miles to another creek to get breakfast. Here we found plenty of wood and good feed for our stock. My pony is of much service to me and I find it very pleasant to mount him and canter away for miles ahead of the teams. Our road now has more to interest travelers then in times past. To our left for weeks past lies the rugged snowcapped peaks of the Rocky Mountains, whilst on our right the grassy hills stretched far away to the eastward and finally lose themselves in the vast level prairies that lie between us and the States. During the day we forded three rapid streams, the water nearly coming into the wagon bed. And having made about 19 miles today we at sundown reached this creek, where we camped for the night.

Camp 52: Cache La Poudre Creek - 5/30

Fine morning. After turning pony loose from his picket (where he has to be made fast nights, for pony and I sleep side-by-side in the tall prairie grass) I sat down to a good breakfast of venison steaks which Dan had prepared for us, before I turned out. Drove about 7 miles, came to a creek which we forded and camped for dinner. Long's Peak is behind us now and old Pike can just be seen in the dim distance. 7 miles further brought us to this roaring creek, this was too deep to ford in the ordinary way; besides it is very rapid. We managed to cross it however by driving a yoke of cattle across with a rope 100 feet-in-length tied to their yoke. Then, after they had landed, we whipped up and they towed us across by means of the rope, although we bounded about in the rocky stream like a leaf upon the wave. After we had landed one wagon in this manner, the rope was drawn back and another yoke of cattle sent across with it and another wagon hauled, landed 'tother side of Jordan and so on, till all were crossed.

We found here plenty of wood, water and grass - the three most essential wants of a campaigner. We also found here another village of mountaineers, mostly Canadian French with their squaw wives and half-breed children. The place is called by them The Colony, it consists of about a dozen rough log cabins and two or three buffalo skin lodges. Some of these old mountain men have large herds of stock with which they roam about from valley to valley, always at home wherever night overtakes them. Many of them have children 18 or 20 years old, who have never seen a settlement or town. They are happy as Lords and have the whole country for their own, leading lives similar in this respect to that of the old patriarchs of Abraham and Isaac's time.

Camp 53: Camp Windy - 5/31

This morning our road, instead of coasting along at the foot of the mountains as before, turned to the left here and took up the creek through a narrow ravine. Passing through this, the valley widened out and we came into a lovely wide bottom with tiptop feed. Here we found another family of half breeds encamped with a large herd of cows and horses. Passing through this valley our road led us off to the right, up over the hills following a little rivulet all the way. We are now for the first time fairly started into the mountains. To our left lies old Rocky, whilst on our right lies a succession of most singular looking hills appearing like rocky hills that have been cut into, leaving an abrupt face on one side and on the other a grassy slope to the prairies below. Most of the country we have passed through appears to be first rate farming soil.

Camp 54: Hunters Camp - 6/1

Yesterday afternoon we crossed a little divide, came down onto a creek and camped. During the night it was very windy and we had a poor camp for comfort. This morning we had some difficulty in finding the trail, which was a very blind one, but at last struck it, passed over a rocky, hilly country about 10 miles and nooned on a little rocky brook with but poor feed and little wood. After a hasty meal, we continued on over a rocky trail up this little valley about 4 miles to its head. Crossed a divide, came down a steep craggy hill, struck another brook, followed it up about a mile and found good feed and stopped for the day about 2 PM to give our cattle a chance to feed and rest, as our road has been a hard one today. We are now in what is called the Black Hills. Our boys are most of them out hunting this afternoon and I have busied myself in writing to Billy Reed.

Camp 55: Laramie Valley - 6/2

Last night one of our hunters, French Albert, failed to appear and this morning we laid by till noon before he made his appearance in camp. After dinner we hitched up and started again. Up, up, up. Hill after hill, we climbed the rockiest road I ever saw. In some places our wagons rolling off rocks 2 feet at a time. For about 4 miles we continued on in this way, then our road took us out onto a high-level mountaintop for about 4 miles, after which we descended into this valley where we camped for the night. This is a wide sterile valley, destitute of timber, with poor soil and few watercourses. The seasons must be very short here, as snow lays in patches all over the valley and the few bushes to be seen have not as yet leafed out. Cold and raw winds tonight.

Camp 56: Laramie River Valley - 6/3

Reached the river about noon. The banks are destitute of timber and during our forenoon's journey across the valley we found but little grass and no water. Red volcanic peaks are scattered all over the valley which produces little else then sage and greasewood bushes. Nooned on the riverbank, after which we forded it. The water coming up as high as our leaders' backs. It was a dangerous place to ford. After we had crossed, we traveled on across the valley in hopes of finding a decent camp. We kept on till dark before we struck a watering place and here we camped, without wood or grass. We have traveled today at least 25 miles and have seen but two trees on the route. This valley is as barren a place as we have seen. No wood, water or grass, excepting the riverbanks.

Camp 57: Pretty Creek - 6/4

We made an apology for supper and breakfast this morning and were glad to make an early start out of our miserable camp. Alkali ponds abounded throughout our forenoon's tramp. We have had bad roads today. During forenoon we traveled about 6 miles, came to a creek but no wood. Went on about 4 miles further came to another, but no wood, here we nooned. Bob and I went out hunting this forenoon, saw plenty of antelope but could not get near enough for a shot. After dinner drove about 6 miles further, crossed a rocky divide and came down into a lovely valley with a timber-bordered creek. There is not a tree between here and Laramie River. Plenty of good feed, splendid timber and a splendid camp tonight in a Cottonwood grove. We have called this Pretty Creek, knowing no other name for it.

6/5 - Our fellows have decided to keep this Sabbath and we accordingly lay by here today. Not only out of respect for the day but our cattle need it, after their last two days travel over bad roads on short feed. Washing, patching and mending appear to be the mania today and truly we need a day of rest occasionally for this purpose, for we are dreadful dirty and ragged to look at. Two Georgia teams that have joined us appear to be the only teams upon this road besides our own. My guard day today and I have the cattle to look after. Our camp is a picture to look at from the hill where I guard the stock. The white wagon covers, and tents of the Ohio boys peek out from the green foliage by which they are surrounded. The groups of men busied around the campfires, the snowcapped peaks around us, combine to make a very romantic scene of camp life.

Camp 58: Muddy Creek - 6/6

Drove about 10 miles this morning, crossing several streams of water each with more or less timber but poor feed, and at noon we found ourselves on the banks of a very rapid river. The banks were covered with big boulders and driftwood and little or no grass for our stock. We must now be on the very high land, as snow lies in big drifts all around us in this valley, which I think must be a tributary of Laramie River Valley. Laramie Peak can be seen from here away off to the northward, blue in the distance. All of these streams run northward, and I should say this was a gold bearing country here, for I never saw more quartz in my life. But if I knew it to be so, I would not stop in such a cold, barren, bleak and desolate spot for all its wealth.

Snow and last winter's ice can be seen all around us. I crossed a creek today on a bridge of snow and ice at least 6 feet thick. Saw a plenty of cactus plant today, proving to me that it is not in tropical climes alone that it thrives. In one place, I saw a ball cactus with full buds within 6 feet of the snowbank. We had some trouble in crossing this river as it was a perfect torrent, about 5 feet deep and full of boulders. But after much shouting and urging we got our train across, but not until we all got wet through. After crossing we climbed a steep stony hill, descended on the other side, crossed the head of a valley, ascended another hill and then came down onto this muddy creek and camped for night. We are now on the top of a very high chain of mountains, I can see another to the westward of us which appears to be still higher, judging from the amount of snow on it. Although there is no timber on the mountains here, away off to the south of us there is an immense forest of pines, but every tree is dead. It looks singular to see such an immense dead forest.

Camp 59: Cherokee Pass of the Rocky Mountains - 6/7

We made a fire of willows last night and got our supper. Frosty night but clear this morning. Drove down off of the mountain about 5 miles and came to another river where we nooned. Name unknown. Antelope very plenty this forenoon, we killed two. After dinner we forded this stream and drove on up the mountain about 5 miles and were obliged to camp right on its summit in the pass. Our wagons had to be chained to keep them in their places, the hillside was so steep. This pass is quite narrow with snow-covered mountains on each side of us. Off to our left lies the dead forest and away north and south we can see this range of snowcapped peaks stretch out, whilst in front of us lies the wide valley of the North Platte.

Around us beautiful flowers blooming in all the vigor of spring, within 6 feet of snowbanks 10 feet deep. Snow drifts in ravines many feet deep, level with the tips of Cottonwood trees in full leaf within a few feet of the snow. These are some of the strange sights one sees here today whilst antelope and black tailed deer crown the surrounding heights, looking down upon our camp with surprise to find that they alone do not inhabit this wild spot. Away in the west, across the Platte Valley, lies the dividing ridge between the waters of the Atlantic and those of the Pacific. Although that is the main ridge or chain of mountains, it is not as high as this ridge we are now on. At least we think so, from the fact that whilst this range is covered with snow there is none on the other.

It is quite cool here in camp tonight, but we found wood enough to make a rousing fire. In one thing I am disappointed, and that is I had an idea that the Rocky Mountain country was heavily timbered. But I find it is not the case. As none of the valleys have any and but few of the ridges.

Camp 60: North Platte - 6/8

We arrived at this river's bank just at dark and here we will have to build a raft to cross our wagons on, as the river is deep, wide and very rapid. We are encamped in a Cottonwood grove on its banks. This morning, having slept at an angle of 45°, was glad to turn out early. For in spite of the big rocks we placed at our feet to brace us against, we had to crawl up under the blankets several times during the night. Our road from camp down the mountain was a very rough one and at the foot of it we found a very ugly stream to ford, but by a good deal of persuasion we got our train across. And keeping on down the creek 7 miles, we camped for dinner in a sagebrush thicket. Here our road left the creek and for 10 miles took us over a dry sage covered plain of sandy soil, until we reached the river where we found a plenty of good grass for our cattle.

This valley in the heart of the mountains is a barren, sterile spot, producing little else then a crop of sagebrush and is about 40 miles in width. We found here our Georgia teams who left us a few days ago, they waited for us to come up to help them build a raft. My John Bull wants to know if I had any idea before what a devil of a big country this US was. "Why," says he, "there is room enough here for a world to settle." "Yes," says Georgia, "but if t'warn't no better sile than this yere, t'would be a powerful mean country for a poor white man to settle in, you bet."

We have great times out here in the wilderness of nights as we gather around the campfire and lay spread out in the grass, listening to Dan's arguments with the Georgians on the slavery question. Their arguments are powerful weak (to use a Georgia phrase).

Camp 61: Mud Creek North Platte Valley - 6/10

Yesterday we were busy all day building a raft. This forenoon we rafted all our wagons over and swum our stock across without an accident. After dinner we traveled about 10 miles across the valley over a barren, dry, clayey country covered with sagebrush, without either grass or water and by sundown reached a muddy stream where we camped for night. The above is from my notebook. Since then, upon our arrival at Fort Bridger, we heard that two days previous to our arrival at the river a company of seven men from Salt Lake City, attempting to raft the river, had all been drowned excepting one, who got ashore and made his way to Bridger. So you see, this passage was one of some danger after all.

Camp 62: Pine Grove Creek - 6/11

Drove about 5 miles, came to a small creek and watered our stock, then drove about 4 miles further to the foot of the mountains, found a small creek and stopped for dinner. This Platte Valley, lying between two lofty ranges of mountains, is perfectly destitute of timber of any sort, save on the banks of the river where we found occasionally a narrow strip of cottonwoods. The soil is very poor, being a clayey gravel, strongly alkalized and almost destitute of grass and covered with clumps of sagebrush. It is quite chilly, bluffs of sandstone running out in all directions and with but few tributary streams crossing it. About 17 miles west from the river our trail forked, and which to take we knew not. But as one bore due west and the other northwest, we took the first name, as that was nearest the course we wanted to steer.

Our Georgia teams took the northwest road, they thinking it to be the proper trail, so here we separated. After dinner we drove on the creek to near its head, crossed a low hill, came down onto another creek, followed it up a piece until we struck a grove of pines where we camped for night. During afternoon had a terrible gale accompanied with rain and hail. This camp appears to have been occupied for some time by a company of US soldiers, judging from appearances. We crossed two bridges this afternoon, probably their work also, as bridges are a scarce article in these parts. Found here good grass for our stock and plenty of wood for ourselves and we needed it too, as we are wet to the skin and it is very cold tonight. We are within about a mile of the highest point in this pass.

Here we are on a stream that finally empties itself into the Atlantic. One mile further and all the streams from that on find their way to the Pacific. This is the backbone of Uncle Sam's domain.

Camp 63: Summit Camp - 6/12

Whilst our friends at home are quietly seated in their cushioned pews at church, probably wondering where we are at this time, we spend the day on the summit of the Rocky Mountains. Crossing several low hills we struck a small stream running west, this is the first Pacific stream. We found a fine little patch of green grass at the foot of the first hill, where we nooned. We lay here several hours waiting for some of our men to come into camp, who went out after an elk one of them had shot. Whilst we lay here waiting, Dan and I climb to the top of the highest peak in this pass. From this point we could look off for miles and miles in every direction. As far as the eye could see was naught but bare Rocky Mountain peaks, apparently destitute of timber and all vegetation save the everlasting sagebrush.

Away to the south was a range of snow-covered mountains, but on this range, there was but little to be seen. An awful stillness reigned, not a sound was heard save a dull murmuring away in the distance, occasioned probably by some raging torrent afar off. Desolate, lonely and gloomy was the scene to me. Whilst sitting on a rock surveying this scene, I heard the report of Dan's rifle on the other side of the cliff. It was a species of pheasant he had shot, who was so unused to man's presence that Dan said he came so near him he could have knocked him over with a club. Probably few, very few men had ever visited this spot before, for recollect we are not on an old long-established road, but one that is seldom traveled by anyone. We made a pyramid of rocks, wrote our names on a rib bone we found, buried it beneath the pyramid and left for camp. I lost a knife, a parting present from a friend at home, on this peak.

I found our boys have returned during our absence with the carcass of a fine large elk. After a feast on elk meat, we hitched up and commenced our downward course. We soon found out that we were on a new trail which had probably not been traveled on by more than one or two trains before this. The road was full of sagebrush, we kept on. Down, down we went, following a little rivulet to where it emptied into a small creek. Followed this down through a narrow ravine until dark, when we camped in a perfect thicket of sagebrush. Made about 15 miles today. Tonight, we are completely hemmed in on all sides by steep mountains covered with sagebrush but no timber. Our wagons look like butchers' carts, we have so much meat hung around them.

The approach to this pass from the east is a very easy one, up a gentle slope not at all difficult for our teams. But from the west it is much worse, the ascent being much steeper. Were it not that a great deal of work has been done on this trail in grading the canyons sides, it would be impassible for wagons. This is some US Surveyors work and has been done within the year past.

Camp 64: Desolation Camp - 6/13

This morning we found our further progress stopped by the muddy creek. The surveying party had built a bridge here to cross their train on, but it has been washed away. The banks of the creek are nearly perpendicular and about 6 feet deep. We finally got a yoke or two of cattle across, then stretched our chains across so that by lowering the wagons down into the creek, our cattle on the opposite side were able to haul them up this perpendicular bank. During the day we crossed this stream in this way seven times, all the bridges having been washed away. But it was the worst place I ever saw a wagon hauled. We can now account for the US Camp at Pine Creek, the surveying party had to haul all their timber for these bridges from that creek - from 30 to 40 miles.

We kept on down this canyon until it opened out into a desolate sterile valley and finding no grass, kept on until dark. By this time, we were where there was no water. Our cattle have not had any feed since yesterday noon, so we kept on in hopes of finding either feed or water for them. We traveled on till 2 AM in the night before we found water and then "twas" but an alkali pond. But here we rested till morning, our teams nearly giving out. Ourselves weary, wet, hungry and cold. A more desolate spot there is not on earth than this. It is a valley of death, for there is not a healthy production here, even the water is poisonous for it is like so much lye. The hills and mountains perfectly bare of all vegetation, the valleys white with alkali, producing a poisonous weed and thickets of sage and greasewood. Not a living thing to be seen. Not a bird, no, not a fly even have I seen today.

Dan says this place is where the Great Architect of the Universe threw his waste materials after his creation of the world. I guess he is right for once.

Camp 65: Alkali Camp ~ Valley of Desolation - 6/14

We lay where we were last night till noon today to rest our worn-out cattle, then hitched up. Following this blind trail, we traveled on until dark over the same barren waste with neither wood, water or grass. At dark we rested until the moon rose, then about 8 o'clock started on again in search of water or grass. About midnight we struck a small creek of alkali water and little coarse grass. Here we stopped for the balance of the night. Country today is the same as yesterday. No grass, no water, no timber, mountains of clay and sandstone, perfectly bare of everything in the way of vegetation, valleys of sand and clay affording just a sufficient nourishment to keep the clumps of sage growing. Not a living thing to be seen, not even a snake. This place reminds me of descriptions I have read of the opinions of astronomers of the appearance of the Moon and other planets.

Camp 66: Bitter Creek ~ American Desert - 6/15

At daybreak we started on again in search of feed and decent water. Both men and cattle are sick from using this alkali water. Valleys looking like dried-up frog ponds, being perfectly level and coated over with sun baked clay, mountains of clay of all colors, ring streaked and striped. All around us fire red buttes, covered with singular looking volcanic rocks, coal veins from 3 inches to 3 feet in thickness and veins of mineral of some kind are cropping out on all sides. These are the views presented to us today. What a country. Passed over valleys and hills all day of this description, looking anxiously ahead from every ridge to see if possible we can discern Green River. Our flour is getting short and we at times fear we may not be on the right trail. Where we are, we know not. For we never heard of such a looking country as this. Sometimes as our road bears south, we fear we may be on a trail leading to some fort in the southern part of the Colorado desert. But we are in for it now, so we must push on, whether or no.

At night reached a little valley between the sand hills, where we found a stream of water not very brackish and tolerable good feed for our cattle. Dan says Uncle Sam may have an all fired big scope of country, but if much of it is it like this, no other country need envy him his possessions. "Lord but ain't this a mighty ornery country," says our Illinois chummy Norme. "No need of standing guard here, for I'll swear no injun ever visits these parts." Prickly pear, sage and greasewood are the only productions of this valley, save on the banks of the little creek.

Camp 67: Bitter Creek - 6/16

Started out about 9 o'clock, drove about 8 miles, found a little water in the creek which is nearly dry. Stopped here for dinner, watered our cattle from buckets, a tedious job. Water tastes like saleratus water. After dinner drove about 6 miles further, found a little grass on banks of creek and camped for night. Our cattle are getting very weak from want of feed and good water. No sign of the river yet, though we every day climb the highest mountains to catch a view of it, if possible. Oh, but it is a long dry desolate road. These everlasting clay valleys and sagebrush thickets.

What use can man ever make of such a country as this? If ever there was a Hell on earth, this must be the place to locate it. Bitter Creek, the mountaineers call it, and it is rightly named. It is a bitter one to us.

Camp 68: Bitter Creek - 6/17

Coal veins crop out here on all sides of us. This evening I climb a high mountain, as usual of late, to see if I could see any signs of the river. Whilst there I found a vein of coal 4 feet thick that burns well in our campfire. This vein is the largest we have seen. Drove 10 miles and stopped for dinner. no grass for our cattle. Saddling up my pony, I rode ahead to find feed. Found a patch about 2 miles ahead and turning my pony loose, I lay down to wait for the teams. After feeding about an hour, we rolled on again till sunset and we camped on the banks of the creek. At this point the creek runs through a deep channel and we had to water our cattle from buckets. Oh, how I long to get out of this barren country, for weeks now we have not seen a team but of our own train.

Camp 69: Bitter Creek - 6/18

This morning drove down through a canyon about 6 miles, found a patch of good feed and stopped for dinner. After dinner our road bore off to the right, leaving the creek for about 6 miles before it struck it again. One of my oxen gave out this afternoon and lay down to die, refusing to travel further. Found a patch of grass and camped for night on the banks of creek. Water is as salty as Lot's wife here. Only 14 miles today. When will we get out of this wilderness? If we don't soon, we never will get our cattle through, for they are about used up. They have not had a fill of grass this side of the pass and the water here physies them terribly. Our provisions are nearly out, as I have been furnishing others of our party who had run entirely out. We must reach the other end of this alkali desert soon, or we are done for.

Camp 70: Green River - 6/19

Hurrah boys, here is the long looked for river at last, sung out one of our men from the top of a hill ahead of us about noon today. We drove down onto a big grass covered bar on the banks of it and camped. At last, we have reached our long looked for camp. Pure water was a rarity for us, and we took long swallows as we lay down and drank from the flowing tide. Our cattle too seemed like to burst, so greedily did they fill themselves. We found out here that the trail we had traveled was one surveyed by authority of the government last year. It is one never traveled, on account of the scarcity of water and feed. It is 175 miles from here to the pass and if we had been one month later, we would have found by that time but one spring of water in that distance. Of course, if we had been caught there in that predicament, it would have been almost certain death. So we may thank Fortune that we traveled through it before Bitter Creek run dry.

Bridger's Pass was north of where we crossed and the road to it was the right-hand one where our roads forked in North Platte Valley. — See page or rather Camp 62 — Our Georgia friends who took the older Bridger Road, crossed the river two days ago. We found a ferry boat here, but the ferryman was drowned in ferrying the Georgia boys across. We found the boat in the possession of two Packers who traveled with the Georgians. They, knowing that we were behind, had taken possession in order to make a dollar or two out of us. We declined paying them, took possession ourselves and ferried our wagons across and swum our cattle. This River is about 80 or 100 yards wide. The valley is narrow and poor soil, red volcanic peaks surround it on all sides. We camped on the west bank of the river tonight. From this river to the Platte Valley there is not a tree, little or no grass and about one spring of pure water. A more desolate barren country it is hard to imagine.

On both sides of the trail and from the surrounding peaks, as far as the eye can see, presents naught but the same dreary aspect. Mountains after mountains rear their ugly heads, till the view is shut off in the dim distance by snowcapped peaks and not a green spot between upon which the eye can rest to vary the desolate scene. Once only I saw a hare in this valley, the only living thing larger than a mosquito I saw in this desert. And he was so unused to man's appearance that he had not learned to fear him. I was searching in an old volcanic crater for volcanic rocks and specimens for friends at home. Puss started from behind a sagebrush and stared at me. I threw a rock at it, but it merely dodged and did not run. I tried to catch it and it would run just far enough to keep out of reach, but it did not fear me enough to run away.

Camp 71: Hams Fork of Green River - 6/20

Owing to change of water I presume, I was quite unwell last night but am alright today. Some of our Illinois boys' passengers, who have run out of provisions, started on ahead on foot for Fort Bridger to try and procure provisions. Our road leaving the river took us up through a canyon onto the high lands above, from which we had a fine view of the surrounding country for miles. There is a range of snow mountains to the north and another south of us that shut off the view in that direction. About 12 miles from the river, we came down onto the Black Fork where we nooned. During our drive through the canyon this morning our boys shot 12 hares. After dinner we drove on up the creek 8 miles and camped for night in good feed. Mosquitoes are very plenty tonight, so have been the better part of the day. This river's bottom lands afford us good feed for our cattle, but off of these the country back is as barren as ever.

Camp 72: Black Fork of Green River - 6/21

The mosquitoes came near devouring us last night. Our Canadian boys left us to go on ahead this morning, they too are short of grub. This forenoon we lost our road but in beating about we finally struck a wide well-beaten road, the first we have seen since we left Denver City, which proved to be the Great Salt Lake Road to the States. We now felt as though we were out of the wilderness, where we had been journeying alone for so many days. We felt now that we were in sight of civilized life again and you at home can form no idea how much we felt to rejoice now that we were once more on a road again, where we were likely to meet with our fellow man occasionally. Traveled on up this road about 4 miles and camped for noon. This road is lined with carcasses of oxen, mules and horses, fragments of broken wagons, ox chains, wheel irons, etc. All going to show the hardships, trouble and trials of the US Army last year whilst on its way to Utah.

Our new camp was rather a poor one for feed. After dinner we drove about 7 miles and camped for the night on Black Fork. Crossed Hams Fork near its mouth this afternoon. Found here an old Mountaineer's camp, the old fellow has been in the mountains since 1812. He, the old patriarch, lives in a hide lodge which he moves about from place to place, whenever he sees fit to change his place of habitation. He is surrounded by quite an army of half-breed children and grandchildren, owns a large herd of fine fat cattle and horses, and is Lord of all he surveys. One of his sons, a fine looking fellow, rode along up the road apiece with us. He is about 24 years of age, says he never was in the settlements, knows nothing about how people manage who live where the houses are so thick. He couldn't see how people could be contented to be shut up in that way. Tonight, the mosquitoes are awful.

Camp 73: Black Fork - 6/22

At Hams Fork yesterday saw two brothers by the name of Stewart, who left Yreka California in May 1857 for the States overland. They had become fascinated with this free and easy style of living, had procured two squaws and set up housekeeping after the manner of the Mountaineers. They said they intended to lead a roving mountain life from this on. They had quite a herd of cattle they were attending and said this sort of life suited them first rate. Well, well there is no accounting for tastes. This morning traveled about 12 miles and stopped for dinner on Muddy Creek amongst a lot of Mormons, Snake Indians and Mountaineers.

The Mormons are families returning to the States and they are a sweet, pretty lot to look at. About four dozen young towheads to a wagon and the women - oh deliver us from their sort - dirty slovenly, barefooted, bedraggled, a nastier mess I never saw. The Snake Indians are cleanly compared to them. Here is another camp of Mountaineers and another flock of half-breed imps. This is a perfect hell for mosquitoes. About 4 o'clock we started out and traveled until 1 o'clock at night over a barren hilly country, before we struck water. At this point we struck Black Fork again about 4 miles below Fort Bridger and here we camped for the balance of the night. Found several California bound wagons encamped here. The mosquitoes are very bloodthirsty here and by this time I am covered with the sores occasioned by these terrible torments.

The air is full of them and we have to keep continually in motion to keep them from eating us up. I hope I may be _____ pardoned if I use any improper language now, for the temptation is great.

Camp 74: Bridger Fort - 6/23

Lay in camp until noon, I wrote two letters home during forenoon. And if my friends only knew what an undertaking it was to write, where the air is full of bloodthirsty mosquitoes as it was here, they would give me more credit for this act of friendship then they probably will, not knowing my situation. First, I closed my wagon as tight as the cover would admit of to keep the varmint out if possible, but in spite of all I could do they would get in. Besides it was as hot as Tophet and the sweat would roll from every pore as I wrote. About every five minutes, the mosquitoes would get so thick I would have to open the front and drive them out, then sit down and resume my writing for another five minutes and so on, until the job was finished. T'was an awful job.

After dinner went on ahead of our teams up to the fort. Found it to be quite a little settlement, consisting of about 20 fine log cabins for the privates' use beside the fort proper, which is a square stone enclosure similar to Bent's Fort. There were about 200 soldiers here at this time. The fort is pleasantly located on Black Fork, in a fertile valley surrounded by mountains. But it is a cold place in the winter. Last winter they run short of fuel and were compelled to burn up 150 Government wagons for fuel. One of the officers told us that there was a party of Mormons who had exacted toll of emigrants for crossing a government bridge between here and Salt Lake City on the East Fork of Bear River. He told us not to pay them if they were there when we crossed, as they had no right to collect a cent and had been driven from there several times by the soldiers. But as soon as the Dragoons left, they would come back again.

I don't think we will pay them much.

Camp 75: Silver Creek - 6/24

Yesterday our boys having procured what provisions they needed at the fort, we left about 4 o'clock, drove over a hill about 8 miles, came to a little stream of water and camped for the night. U.S. Mail coach drove through our camp about 9 o'clock in the evening, bound to Salt Lake City. Today we drove about 18 miles to this creek. During forenoon our road took us up over a large grassy hill to Muddy Creek, where we crossed and camped for noon on the top of a high mountain to avoid the mosquitoes as much as possible. Confound the pests, they give us no peace, they are an awful nuisance. Our road follows the ridge to the head of Spring Creek, then follows down this creek to the valley below and after crossing a low ridge we came down onto Silver Creek, where we found about 20 California-bound wagons encamped for the night. Indians quite plenty about camp tonight.

Camp 76: Head of Echo Canyon - 6/25

Mosquitoes are awful tonight; they fill the air. We breathe them in every breath, I never saw the like before and hope never to suffer the same again as I have today. Arrived at Bear River about 9 o'clock and found four Mormons well-armed on the bridge, who demanded $3 apiece for our wagons and $.50 a head for our cattle, before we could cross. We gave them just one minute to leave the bridge and told them if they were not gone in that time, we would ventilate them. They laughed but swore that we would catch hell when we reached the city. This is the place the officer at Bridger spoke to us about. We nooned on a big flat and whilst at dinner one of the Mormon thieves from the bridge passed our camp, bound to Salt Lake City I suppose. The country between here and Green River is as destitute of timber as the country on the other side, save a few cottonwoods on the water courses but the feed is first rate.

Camp 77: Echo Pass - 6/26

Last night we camped about 2 miles below the head of Echo Canyon, mosquitoes in swarms beset us. Today we moved down through the pass, which is about 18 miles in length, to where it (or the stream that runs through it) empties itself into Weber River. This pass is a narrow passageway cut through the mountains and is from 50 to 500 yards in width. A little stream of water winds its way through it and on each side the mountains rear their heads aloft, being from 600 to 1500 feet in height. Nooned about 10 miles from last night's camp. Good feed all the way through this pass. After dinner we moved on down the canyon, surrounded by scenery most grand. Noble old rocks by Nature's own hand reared their heads far above us on each side of the narrow defile. Within a mile or two of the mouth of the pass it becomes very narrow, say 50 yards in width. Here the mountains on each side are perpendicular walls of bare rock from 200 and 300 feet in height.

Here, in this well of a place, the Mormons made their stand last year in their celebrated war against the Government. Their ditches across the narrow valley, their big dams for stopping the water, their little fortifications on the heights above, were all as they left them a year ago. Every little projecting spur of rock along here had its nest-like fort of cobblestone from which their rifles were to pick off the soldiers in the canyon below, they being so far above were out of harm's way. If an army had been caught in this trap by surprise, they would have lost a great many men before they could have forced their way through. But as Uncle Sam was well informed of all their plans, he nor his officers would have never been caught in here, until he had routed the Mormons from the heights above. This could have been easily done from the higher mountains in their rear.

Camp 78: Dry Camp - 6/27

Last night we camped on Weber River just below the mouth of Echo Pass. This morning went on down this river about 3 miles to a bridge which we crossed and bearing off to the left up a ravine we crossed a hill at its head, came down to a little dry ravine and camped for the night. Not very good soil in Weber Valley where we traveled in it. The banks are lined with groves of Cottonwood.

Camp 79: Dragoon Camp - 6/28

This morning at sunrise we were on the road again, passed down into a deep valley which we followed up about 6 miles, then it turned to the right. We kept on up a creek bed to the top of the high mountain, the road all the way up the mountain being right in the bed of the creek, a rougher road I never saw. The whole road was lined with carcasses of oxen and mules and fragments of wagons. After reaching the summit we commenced the descent of the other side, it was an awful steep one. And some 4 miles down it, we nooned at the foot of the mountain. After dinner we went on down the creek about 4 miles and camped for the night at the foot of another mountain. This is the Bear River range of mountains. We found encamped here a company of Dragoons who are en route for the States escorting home about 20 children, the only survivors of the horrible Mountain Meadow Massacre.

A company of emigrant families about 150 in number were about two years ago, while encamped at the Mountain Meadows, attacked by a band of Mormons and Indians and all were barbarously murdered. Excepting these children, who they thought were too young to appear as evidence against them. But they were not so young. They knew and recollected the horrors of that night, at least some of them. God only knows why it is our government neglects to bring this band of murderers to suffer for their many crimes.

Camp 80: Salt Lake City - 6/29

Here we are at last at Mormon Headquarters. This morning we crossed the last mountain, another awful steep one. And keeping on down a narrow ravine about 10 miles we at last came out into the wide Salt Lake Valley, the city right before us. We drove down into the city, bought our provisions and drove out to the outskirts of the town and pastured our cattle. After which we took a turn around the city to see the sights. There is no timber fit for lumber in the country. Therefore 9/10 of the buildings are nothing more than mud huts, being built of Adobe or sun-dried bricks. Even their fuel has to be hauled up 20 miles over two mountains, the two that we crossed. The town is laid out in squares and every dwelling has a garden patch of about an acre. Streams of water run down on each side of every street for irrigating the gardens.

The church property, the Tabernacle, the President's house, with its numerous outbuildings and the general storehouse, or tithing house, are all well-built and enclosed by a high and substantial wall. There is one thing that all travelers notice and that is the great number of towheads around every house. It reminds a fellow of so many chicken coops, with the old motherly hen surrounded by her brood. I paid a visit to the printing office and had a long confab with its editor, he was surprised to hear I was from Rhode Island and from his numerous questions respecting its different towns, I imagined he might formerly have lived in that section. He was very anxious to know how the Eastern people felt towards the Mormons and I told him they had not a very exalted opinion of them. He laughed, said he supposed not, but says they were not as rabid as the Western people, who he very much disliked.

They are a queer set these Mormons and their leaders live a jolly life. I saw but a few pretty women here, I saw one or two though who were lovely to look at, sure. I have not time, space, nor ability to give a lengthy account or description of either the town or its people and this scanty description must suffice. I saw our Bear River Bridge thief in town, but he has not opened his head to us yet. Fact is there are too many Gentiles in this city now for them to play any of their pranks. The Mormons say Uncle Sam is a __ old dotard, for they have succeeded in having things on their own way and the longer he keeps his soldiers here, the better for them. For this army requires provisions, hay and grain. And who is to supply them and at good round prices too, but the Mormon farmers. Before the soldiers came, they had no market. Now they have a ready market at good prices for all they can raise.

Camp Floyd with its 2000 soldiers is about 40 miles south of here. Old Brigham was invisible to us, they say he seldom makes his appearance in the streets. The farmers' wagons that were coming and going out and into the city during the day were pretty well loaded down with livestock. In front would be the old patriarch, on each side of him a wife and the bed of the wagon would be filled with some dozen or two towheaded young ones. It is no uncommon thing here to see seven or eight children, all under four-year-old playing about a house, the daddy of them all looking complacently on as they fish about him.

According to Mormonism, a man can have as many wives as he can support. So when a farmer thinks his means will admit of it, he adds another room to his building and leads another wife home and installs her as mistress of the new room. Some of the farmhouses have been lengthened out so many times in this way, that they look like bowling alleys and the number of young ones around such a house is truly appalling to an old batch like myself.

Camp 81: Salt Lake Valley - 6/30

Not having any greater desire to prolong our stay in the city, where our expenses were considerable owing to our having to pasture our stock, we this morning started our teams on the road again. I, taking my pony with me, went up to the city and stopped till noon, then rode on to overtake the teams. Just outside of the city we came to a spring and pool of warm water just hot enough to make it comfortable for bathing. We off clothes and I plunged in and I never had as fine a bath in my life before. The water was very brackish and very buoyant, so much so in fact, that it was impossible to sink in it. This place is used for bathing purposes by the people of the city, and they have two days in the week when it is against the laws of the church for men to bathe in it. These days the pool is for the ladies use.

A few miles further at the foot of another mountain was another spring of hot, boiling hot, water. It was hot enough to take the hair all off of the leg of an ox who foolishly stepped in to get a drink. "Hell can't be far from this place," says our John Bull. Traveled till noon, overtook the Ohio boys, encamped for dinner by the roadside but my team was on ahead somewhere. Wishing to rest my pony, I stopped with the boys for dinner. A farmhouse stood near our camp, and I went to it for some butter. As I approach the house an old witch of an Irish woman came to the door and hailed me. "Come here honey," says she. "Come here, me boy. I want ye." Have you any butter for sale my good woman? "Aye, and a plenty of it, come in." So in I went.

It was a miserable dirty hovel. Like most of the others in the country, almost destitute of any kind of furniture. "Here take hold on this bed cord and lend me a helping hand dear honey, just set me bed up right," says the old crony, pointing to the bedstead that she was trying to set up. "An is it to California ye are going? An have ye a wife along?" I told her I was very sorry to have to acknowledge that I was forced to travel this wide world alone, not being blessed with a helpmate.

"Oh, and ye have no wife to tend ye when ye are sick and comfort ye when ye are weary, to do yer minding and washing and such like? An here in this nasty country if ye had lived here, ye would have had a dozen at least and the Lord knows how many children to bless ye in your old age. Aye, tis a pity ye don't stop here honey an my word for it, ye have wives enough soon." Has your old man any other wife, says I. "My old man is it? No, no the worse luck. He is too poor to support one an thin my old man an I have travelled this world alone, together and the good Lord willing, we will live an die as we commenced."

By this time the bed was set up alright, for all of this time I had been busy assisting the old woman in putting things shipshape. "God bless ye honey, for a kind young gentleman that you are and may the holy saints protect ye through the wilderness, an now here is the butter and help yourself." Taking a pound of it I bid her goodbye and left for camp much amused with my conversation with the old lady. As we passed by her door after dinner on our way she hailed me, again bidding me God speed.

About dark I caught up to Dan and my team where they were encamped by the roadside near a farmhouse. The country for 60 miles west of Salt Lake City is settled up and for that distance the road is fenced in by farms. On our right is a range of bald mountains, the road being just at their base, whilst on our left-hand the land slopes off to the Salt Lake, about from 1-3 miles distant from the road. All the intervening land between the road and the lakeshore is taken up and fenced in for farming purposes. About every 4 miles there is a creek or brook that puts down out of the mountains, emptying into the lake. All of these watercourses have been ditched and the water brought along the side hill in large ditches for irrigating purposes. I was surprised to find the country so well improved.

Every few miles you come to a little town like our little country towns at home and in fact this valley is better improved and thicker settled than any farming country I have passed through since I left New York State. The farmers are for a general rule mostly foreigners of the lowest class, although you will find occasionally a man of intelligence and worth located here. And where you find such a one, he is sure to be found wealthy in droves of fine fat cattle. Take them all in all, I found them to be the most independent and the most prosperous every way of any farming community I ever saw. They were all in easy circumstances as far as I could see and not only that, they appeared to be happy. Where we camped tonight, I went over to the farmhouse for eggs. This fellow had no less than four wives, each wife and her family of children occupied a separate room in the one-story adobe house.

I went from one to the other of these dwellings to see how this manner of doing business worked and for all I could see to the contrary, they appeared to get along quietly enough. Peggy had her suite of rooms that were her own individual property and Maggie, Polly and Madora had theirs. And if Peggy felt a little provoked with Polly at any time, she orders Mrs. Polly to vacate her premises and Mrs. Polly has to retire to her own 12-foot square. But Lord want there a host of towheads around? If this fellow keeps on, he will have at least 100 young responsibilities to look after by the time he is an old man. But the children learn very early here to take care of themselves.

Camp 82: Salt Lake Valley near Weberville - 7/3

Last Friday we drove up to a little creek where we found good feed near the road and camped. We have lain here now three days to rest and recruit our cattle. I have occupied my time in washing up a lot of dirty clothes, mending the same and in writing letters for friends at home. I have visited around amongst the farmers considerably in my searches for butter and eggs for our camp and we in turn have had many visitors in camp. Farmers' wives would visit us bringing eggs, butter and cheese for sale and we have had quite a pleasant time of it. If the women are as dissatisfied as we have heard through the papers they were, they have a good way of keeping these feelings of dissatisfaction to themselves. A more ignorant set I never saw, they actually believe in their foolish doctrine of Latter-Day Saints.

They say we should not judge of their country by the crops we see this year, for the wheat and other grain is nothing but volunteer crops. Last year, the Prophet Brigham told them they must flee from here and leave their homes, so as to not become prisoners to the wicked US Government. And they all left everything and retreated to the mountains in the south and there they stayed until He, the prophet, gave them permission to return last winter. So their farms were neglected and this year they have but little produce to dispose of.

They are awfully prejudiced against our Uncle Sam; think he is the fiend incarnate, sent upon the earth to torment the Saints. They say the earth is the Lord's in the fullness thereof. And as they are his Saints, it is of course perfectly right for them to take possession of the Lord's property wherever they find it. This, we are foolish enough to call stealing. But then of course, we have no right to complain if caught in the possession of any of the Lord's property, if his Saints take it away from us. These are the ignorant foreigners who talk thus. But there is another class (who knowing how easily such a class of people are led around by the nose) have joined this band of robbers for the sake of gain, who believe in Joe Smith's doctrines as much as I do.

These fellows are the leaders. They plan for the poor devils to work. And there is still another class, and these are the desperados of California and the States, who have joined the church and scruple not at taking life even, when it becomes necessary for them to do so to acquire gain. These desperados do the dirty work for the leaders. They are encouraged to join them for this purpose and if a gang of them joins a band of Indians and cut off on emigrant train for the sake of plunder, the leaders of this church are bound to protect them. For it would not do for them to desert them, for they know too much about the church affairs. To sum it all up in a few words, these three classes are governed by the following principals.

First the leaders are smart seminary men. They joined, or originated, this scheme for the purpose of money making. They held out great inducements to the poverty-stricken to emigrate here. They have succeeded in gathering together here many thousands of the lowest class of foreigners, who believe every word of the doctrine and who every year pay into the church (or the leaders' pockets, the same thing) one 10th of their income. It becomes necessary occasionally for the leaders to have a job of work done that they hesitate to entrust to the hands of this second class. And so they have encouraged the third class to emigrate. These are the horse thieves and murderers of Salt Lake. I have no doubt but this third class commit many crimes on their own hook, which the leaders would not sanction. But then they are, from interest, bound to shield them from Justice, if possible, whenever they are caught in the act.

Camp 83: Salt Lake Valley - 7/4

Moved on up the road about 8 miles crossing the Weber River, passing through Weberville and camped for the day on a little creek about 4 miles beyond the town. Have celebrated the day by running over hills and valleys guarding the stock. My guard day today. Hot as Tophet. Mormons stole an ox out of the herd today, in spite of me.

Camp 84: Salt Lake Valley near Willow City - 7/5

Passed through Ogden City this morning, crossed the creek and camped for breakfast on the opposite bank. After breakfast started on again but had made but a few miles when we were overtaken by the bridge thief, in company with Elder Richardson a Mormon leader and a Sheriff of this district. They ordered us to stop, demanding $8 of me and the like sum from the others for crossing the Government bridge at East Bear River. We were told by Richardson that it was useless to resist, for he could summons a posse sufficiently strong to take us if we did. He cursed at the Government, said he didn't care a damn whether it was a

Government bridge or not. If we wanted to go on, we must pay him his price or go back to Ogden.

We saw we were in a bad fix; we were not strong enough to fight the whole nation and we knew there was no use to appeal to the Mormon courts at Ogden for relief. If we undertook to carry the case up to Salt Lake City, we probably would be robbed of all before we could get away. So we very reluctantly submitted to the robbery. I told Richardson he and his church were nothing more nor less than a band of robbers. I twitted him of the Mountain Meadow Massacre, and he said he had never been so roundly abused before in his life. I told him I had paid him for the right to abuse him and intended to do so. All of this time we both had our hands upon our revolvers, and I intended to shoot him the first motion he made towards me. I never did want to shoot a man before, but my fingers fairly itched to pull trigger on him.

He knew he had no right to collect a cent from us and he also knew that he would have lost the suit if taken before a US Court at Salt Lake City. But he knew that we had rather pay him $8 and go on our way than to be detained here at a big expense and run the risk of having all our cattle stolen. We knew of a German doctor who crossed the bridge at the same time that we did and he got as far as Ogden when he was stopped and money demanded of him. He refused to pay, was arrested, tried before a Mormon Justice at Ogden, was beat in his suit, appealed to the US Courts at Salt Lake City, gained his case, came back to Ogden and found his cattle, wagon, provisions and everything stolen during his absence. He had to pocket his loss and his anger and procure a passage with another team to California.

And this is the way with this band of Highwayman, who have stationed themselves on the road between the Pacific and Atlantic states and rob all who pass through their country. And our Government dares not assert its right, and break up this den of thieves and murderers. After paying these Highwayman that Uncle Sam protects the tribute they demanded, we were graciously permitted to pass on. At night we camped near a cold spring about 3 miles east of Willow City. During the afternoon we passed another hot sulfur spring, as hot as fire could make. "What a God's blessing t'would be," says Dan, "if this thin crust that lies between Salt Lake Valley and Hell would cave in and let the Mormons all through at once. T'would be a short-cut home for them."

Camp 85: Brigham City
Box Elder Creek - 7/6

Last night just as we were getting supper, we saw a solitary foot traveler trudging along the road, a heavy budget slung across his shoulders. We hailed him, but he answered us in French. Our Canadian boys were called and through them he was brought to. I never saw a man more pleased than he appeared to be when he found that Al understood him, and he could converse with him in his native tongue. He told Al that he was bound to California. That he had served all through the Russian war in the Crimea. After his return to France, he received a remittance from a brother in California sufficient to pay his passage from Paris to San Francisco.

He started from home, reached New York and bought a ticket for California but his ticket was stolen from him in New York and he was left penniless in a strange land. He procured work there, earned enough to take him to St. Joseph Missouri and from there he shouldered his pack for a tramp of 1800 miles across the country, alone and on foot. He made on average 50 miles a day, reached Fort Laramie before his provisions gave out, obtained a new supply and reached Salt Lake City in time to splice out his supply of crackers for the trip through. He had now, he said, crackers enough to do him 18 days more. By which time he thought he could reach Sacramento. Here was an instance of perseverance for you.

This I suppose is the material that forms the French army. No wonder they endure so much or that they are so invincible. The old soldier was kept by us all night and he had at least one "square meal" on the road. We traveled on all day and at night camped about 2 miles beyond or west of Brigham City, a town of Dutch Mormons.

Camp 86: Warm Springs - 7/7

Last night we camped by the side of an Irish hovel and pastured our cattle in his field. Mosquitoes in swarms beset us all night long, in vain we build fires of wet straw to smoke them out of camp. They were smoke proof. Brigham City is the most western town in this valley and in a few miles travel this morning we passed "the fort", a palisaded house built as a frontier protection against the Indians. By the way, all of these towns are enclosed within a wall of mud or stone to protect them against any Indian attacks. After passing the fort we were then beyond the settlements again, as there is not a farm or house beyond it.

A few miles further brought us to Bear River. We ferried this stream and took dinner on the opposite bank. We met here a party from Yreka

California bound home to the States. I knew several of them and they were much surprised to meet me here. This river empties into Salt Lake a few miles from where we crossed it. After dinner we rolled on 4 miles further and came to Molad Creek. This creek is about a rod wide and very deep, but we found a bridge and crossed it. From here 4 miles further we crossed a sage covered plain, struck Warm Springs and camped on the side of a bald hill. The whole country is perfectly destitute of timber as far as you can see every way. Were met here by a party from California, bound to the States to see their families after an absence of long, long years. Salt Lake lies in the valley directly below us and from the hill where we are encamped, we have a fine view of the whole valley.

We have not had a stormy day now since we crossed the Rocky Mountains, this makes it much more agreeable for us who have to be out in all weather, whether fair or not.

Camp 87: Blue Springs - 7/8

Woke this morning wet to the skin, it having rained all night. Drove 40 miles across a hilly country destitute of timber of any sort and came to these springs situated in a lonely valley. Found the water very brackish, drove about a mile further and camped for the day and night on the plains without water, excepting what we could get from the ponds of rainwater. It has rained all day. Cold, wet and disagreeable in every way, we passed this dreary day. Goodbye now to Mormon-dom and its gang of land pirates, we are beyond your settlements now and once more in the red man's domains. Consequently, we consider ourselves much safer now, for the Indian is not half as much to be dreaded as these white savages of Salt Lake.

Camp 88: Deep Creek - 7/9

Cold, wet and shivering, we turned out this morning and traveled until noon in the rain before we reached this creek 16 miles from Blue Springs. Here we stopped for the balance of the day and night. The stretch from here to Bear River is 38 miles over a rolling grassy country with good grass, but perfectly destitute of either timber or water.

7/10 - Lay by here today. This little creek is about a yard wide and at least 10 feet deep, as usual perfectly bare of timber but plenty of good grass and sagebrush for fuel. This afternoon the sun made its appearance again and we were once more thawed out of our torpid state. We found a plenty of first rate ripe currants growing here.

Camp 89: Pilot Spring Camp - 7/11

This morning we traveled down a deep creek to its sink, about 6 miles. Here the creek disappears in a marsh. As we crossed this swampy place we were beset by millions of large horseflies, the air was full of them. We fought our way through them at last and a few miles further, over a sage covered sterile plain, brought us to Pilot Springs. Here we watered our stock, filled our water kegs and rolled on to find grass. Went about 5 miles, found good feed and stopped for the night on the plains. Made about 21 miles today. "What a dog yearned miserable country this yere is," says our Illinois friend, Norme. "Sagebrush, horse flies and mosquitoes appear to be all it can produce. But the good Lord knows thars enough on the productions, thick as they are."

Camp 90: De Casure Creek - 7/12

Sage covered hills to cross for 5 miles and then we reached Stony Creek, a rough and rapid little mountain stream of cold pure water. Here we filled our kegs, and rolling on for 5 miles further found a good feeding spot on the dry plain and stopped for noon to give our cattle a feed.

After dinner kept on across this valley for 7 miles further, struck this creek at the foot of the mountains and camped in a bottom, covered with grass 5 feet high. No timber here and none between here and Salt Lake City. The country all the way is hilly, bare, mountains and sagebrush valleys, with occasionally a spring of water, with a little grass in spots. This is the character of the country generally this side of Salt Lake Valley.

Camp 91: Mountain Spring ~ Goose Creek Mountains - 7/13

Very cold last night. Went on up De Casure Creek about 6 miles traveling through the wild rye, higher than our cattle backs. Here we nooned. Ripe currants a plenty on the banks of the creek. After dinner our road left the creek, crossing a barren valley to the foot of the mountain. Ascending this up a very rocky trail, we came out on the summit at Pyramid Rocks, a most singular group of mountain peaks. Here we struck the great overland road, via the South Pass. Following the Great California Road, we crossed a wide sterile valley to the foot of the mountains on the other side and camped by a fine spring of excellent water at its base. Indians rather too plenty tonight for comfort.

Camp 92: Goose Creek - 7/14

Very early this morning we were on the road again, to avoid the rascally Indians who hovered around our camp last night. Dan, my John Bull, is becoming rather too important of late. I told him this morning to find some other conveyance through, as soon as possible. He procured a passage through in another team and I got Al, one of the Canadian boys, to drive my team. We crossed the Goose Creek Mountains this morning at the highest, longest, steepest and worst mountain to cross we have as yet seen. Coming down onto the bottom lands of this creek we found the best grass and the best soil I have seen on the route, but no timber in the whole country.

As we were at dinner, seven or eight Packers came into our camp and asked us if we stopped overnight at Mountain Spring. We told them we did. "Well says they, you left there just in time, for when we passed there this morning there was about 100 red skins there, all armed, painted and mounted, who demanded provisions of us. We told them we had none and they searched our packs but found we had so little they let us pass. But they said they had intended to take a train of ox teams stopped there last night but when they reached there early this morning, they found they had left in the night." So we were right in our belief that they meant mischief.

I begin to pride myself upon my knowledge of these red devils, for this is the second time we have escaped from them by giving them the slip. The boys all laughed at my fears last night, when I told them we had to look out for these fellows, for I did not like their appearance and actions. But lucky for them they followed my advice and made an early start this morning. They don't laugh now. We found quite a number of California emigrants encamped here, recruiting their stock on the excellent feed this valley affords. After dinner, only drove about 5 miles up the valley and camped for the night.

Yreka - January 13, 1860

The above is from my notebook written from day to day whilst on the trip. After my arrival here, a train arrived at Placerville who brought the news of a train of emigrant families being attacked at Mountain

Spring about a week after I left there and nearly all were killed, several women and children were of the number. One of the women, badly wounded, was picked up and brought in. She says she has no doubt that the Indians were led on by white men. Their cattle were all driven off and their provisions, money, etc. were taken. My friends at home have probably read of the circumstance, as the account of the massacre was copied into the eastern papers at the time.

A detachment of US troops were sent out to the place from Camp Floyd to see if they could find the savages, but I believe they were unsuccessful in their search. No doubt this deed was the work of this same band of red devils from whom we escaped by leaving camp and a dangerous neighborhood, so early in the morning. Only a week after, they met this train and accomplished for them what they intended for us. All the Indians I have seen between here and Salt Lake affirm that they are Bueno Mormon, that is good Mormons. This is their first salutation upon meeting a company of white men. Clapping their hand upon their hearts they say, "Bueno Mormon me." Ask them if they are friends to the white man? And their reply is "No good, white man, American man no good, Mormon me good Mormon." Does not this of itself show that these vipers at Salt Lake have been active in prejudicing these savages against all white men but Mormons.

I believe the Mormons are the cause of all these Indian murders on the plains and I believe that the cattle driven off by them finally reaches the farmers of Mormon-dom at Salt Lake. Mrs. Shepard of the train attacked at Mountain Spring, says that some of the Indians had white hair. Those white-haired Indians were Mormon Indians, for none but these have hair of that color.

Camp 93: Rock Spring ~ Thousand Spring Valley - 7/15

Goose Creek Mountain is 5 miles down it by the road. Shoshone Indians rather too numerous to make it agreeable. We are all well-armed however and never off our guard, so there is no chance for them to take us by surprise or to steal our stock. This morning we drove on up the creek and nooned near its head, 18 miles from where we first struck it. After dinner, drove over a very rocky hill 12 miles to Rock Spring which we reached after dark. No feed for our cattle tonight. Made 24 miles today.

Camp 94: Thousand Spring Valley - 7/16

This morning drove down this valley 12 miles to a good spring of water and good feed for our cattle and camped for the day. Plenty of company tonight, found eight other wagons here encamped.

Camp 95: Thousand Spring Valley - 7/17

This is a wide valley surrounded by bare timber-less mountains, full of springs of pure water, salt water, alkaline water, mineral water, ice cold water and boiling hot water, all kinds of water ever heard of. Excepting cologne water. I have seen no spring of this sort as yet. Plenty of good grass in the valley. We moved our camp down the valley a few miles to a spring of good water and camped for the day. During the day a train of Oregon bound emigrants came in and camped alongside of us. There were 10 wagons of them. They are all family moving to Oregon to settle and are all related to one another. Amongst the lot are some four or five young ladies. As they travel our road as far as Shasta Valley in California, those of us who intend on going to Yreka will probably travel with them, for company's sake.

Camp 96: Head of Thousand Spring Valley - 7/18

This morning when we started out of camp, we had quite a string of teams, as our train with the Oregon teams made in all 18 wagons and about 180 head of cattle. We traveled through this valley all day and at night camped at the foot of a low mountain divide near an excellent spring of water. Plenty of slip-shot women around camp tonight, rather a tough lot to look at, regular corn-fed, pipe smoking, backwoods people, "You bet". Indians are skulking around in the sagebrush on the hills around us, probably watching for a chance to steal some of our stock, as we now are too strong for any tribe east of the Sierras to attack us in camp. But we keep a good guard around our herd and fear them not.

Camp 97: Head of Humboldt Valley - 7/19

Crossed the mountain this morning, came down into this valley and followed it down 23 miles and camped for night in good feed near a sound spring hole of good water. Our new friends the Oregonians are a queer set, the women are about as rough as the men in their language and manners, and the girls are as fearless as young wildcats. "Here you, fellow with the white coat, just give us a whiff from your fancy pipe, for I'll be dog yearned if I haint smoked this yere corn cob till it's near about gone up," says one of these fair damsels to me tonight. You bet I will, says I. Anything else I can do for you? "No, unless you are a mind to set down here and tend to this Tiger." Tiger is a name for salt-bacon, which she was frying for supper. I set down.

Camp 98: Humboldt River - 7/20

Jumped clear of all my blankets at one leap last night before I was fairly awake, by the report of a pistol close to me. Found out that the guard who were watching the cattle around the camp had shot at an Indian who had crawled up in the tall grass to a horse that was picketed near him and had cut his rope. And was in the act of springing onto his back when the guard fired. The shot brought blood, but Mr. Indian got off before we could secure him. But we saved the horse. After breakfast we rolled along down the valley, came to the river, crossed the two forks of it, drove on down the north side about 5 miles and camped in first rate feed for our cattle. Our Ohio and Illinois boys, who have traveled with me from the States thus far, leave us tomorrow as they are bound to Sacramento City.

Camp 99: Humboldt River - 7/21

Dan, Scudder and Jim Newlin of the Ohio team have joined me, together with Al the Canadian, to go to Yreka. The Georgia teams also go to Yreka, whilst the Ohio and Illinois teams leave us and go to Placerville. I travel with the Oregon train from this on. Our Ohio boys have concluded that we did not drive fast enough for them. And as I am too deeply interested in the stock trade to risk their lives by over driving, I prefer separating from them to running any further risk. So this morning we separated, although we travel the same road from here to Lassen's Meadows. These newfound friends, the Oregonians, are a pretty fair set, although very rough.

Their captain, a Mr. Howard Paris, and I are already pretty good friends. He is an old settler in Oregon. He emigrated with his wife from Iowa to Oregon in 1853 and settled in the Umpqua Valley. Last fall he left his wife in Oregon and went home to the States for his widowed mother. He passed the last winter amongst his wife's brothers in Kansas. This spring they concluded to move bag and baggage to Oregon, so they all hands joined in with Paris in his trip "across the plains".

The party consists of the following persons. First Mr. Paris, his mother and a grandson of the old lady's called Joe, in one wagon. Mr.

Jonathan Hodgson, wife and four or five towheaded young ones in the next. Mr. Enis Hodgson, wife and about the same number of responsibility in the next. Mr. James Hodgson, wife and half a dozen children in the next. Billy McCormick, his young wife a daughter of E. Hodgson's. A tall raw-boned specimen of humanity called Abe Jobe and the belle of the party, Miss Rachel, occupy the next wagon. This is a very loving team full, as Mr. Abe Jobe is very much in love with Miss Rachel and Billy is but just married.

The next in order comes a wagon occupied by Mr. Solomon Wade and family. His wife is a perfect tartar and snubs old Solomon awfully. They have two daughters of marriageable age and very much in need of a beau, also a son - a perfect brick. Next comes George Beaver's team. He and his pretty little wife, a daughter of James Hodgson's, appeared to be well mated. A perfect love match. Next in order, John Roton's team. He, his wife and a perfect swarm of squalling, dirty faced brats, hive in this team.

Last of all Nelse King and his wife Susannah, tall, slab-sided, barefoot, pipe-sucking, termagant and two orphan children occupy this team. The Brothers Hodgson are rank abolitionists and went from Iowa to Kansas during the troubles there to assist the Free State men. Old Nelse King was one of John Brown's lieutenants during the Kansas wars and he and his Susannah had to flee from their house to the prairies many a night for safety from the border ruffians. King was shot three times during the wars but always made good his escape. He is a hard old case. Formerly a Methodist preacher, once a member of the Iowa Legislature, he has become since his advent in Kansas one of the most profane men I ever listened to. He has with him two children whose father and mother were killed in one of the Kansas battles.

Our Georgia boys who have been taught to hate an abolitionist as they would the very "evil one", do not feel very contented in the company they are placed in. But they keep their thoughts to themselves. But we outsiders have a great deal of fun occasionally, when Old King commences (as he often does) to curse and rave against Old Buford's Company of Georgia cut-throats who went to Kansas to harass the Free State settlers there. "He's an all full ornery old sinner, haint he Dan?" Says one of them to me last night. "But taint no use to argufy with him, the old gray-headed sinner, he don't know no better. But Lord wouldn't I like to catch him in Georgy, wouldn't I make him skin it all back. You bet I would."

Now that I have introduced my traveling companions, let us roll out on the road again. We will find that this valley is shut in by high barren mountains on each side, the valley being from 4 to 8 miles wide. The river is very crooked and the valley, with the exception of the low river bottoms, the same sage-covered sterile soil we have traveled over for so many miles. But the bottomlands are covered with the rankest kind of grass, higher than our cattle backs, so that an ox 6 feet from the road is out of sight. We waded through this tall grass about 30 miles today before we camped for the night.

Camp 100: Humboldt River - 7/22

Tonight, we are encamped at the foot of a mountain we will have to cross to avoid a bend of the river. Women are scolding young ones, squalling, girls are singing and some of the men are cursing around camp tonight. It looks like a little town to look down from the mountains where I write this, into our camp. "Susannah, where the devil did you put my pipe," bawls Old King, "None of yer business, look for it yerself, don't you suppose I have enough to do, without keeping the run of your traps," is the mild reply of sweet Susannah. And look off yonder at the other end of the camp, out in the tall grass, see how fondly our six-foot lover Abe Jobe assists Miss Rachel to milk the cows. "Solomon Wade, do you come right here and help me cook this Tiger ef yer want yer supper tonight, and don't be foolin away yer time, loafing round where yer haint wanted," bawls out the lovely Mrs. Wade.

Camp 101: Humboldt River - 7/23

Ascending the mountain this morning we, by noon, reached the other side and camped for dinner on Willow Creek, a tributary of the Humboldt. After dinner we kept on down the creek about 3 miles to its junction with the Humboldt, then down the river about 4 miles to where the road again leaves the valley for the mountains. Here we should have camped for night, as there is a dry stretch of 18 miles over the mountains here. But we did not know it, so on we went and climbing the mountain we traveled on till 9 o'clock in the night, in hopes of striking the river again. But by this time it had become so dark we were glad to camp by a spring we found in a narrow rocky ravine, without feed for our cattle. Went supperless to bed tonight.

Camp 102: Gravelly Ford Humboldt River - 7/24

This morning early, we started on down a very rocky ravine and in about 9 miles made the river at Gravelly Ford, where we camped for the day. Passed a camp of US Dragoons in the ravine this morning. They were sent out from Camp Floyd to protect and assist the emigrants. They are to remain on this river during the summer. Who would be a soldier? They must lead a lonely life, stationed way out here in the wilderness. Some of the Oregonians who have run short of provisions applied to the officers for assistance and received quite a supply of flour and bacon. Old Mother Wade gave her Solomon a terrible blowing up for not begging a supply for them. But Solomon, who is a quiet sort of a soul, meekly answered her that he was too old to commence begging now, he'd never done such a thing in his life.

Camp 103: Humboldt River - 7/25

This morning early, we were on our weary way again. Ascending a low hill to our right, we again left the river to avoid another long bend 6 miles across the sandy hills and we struck the river again. Followed it down about 3 miles, took across another hill about 3 miles, then struck the river again where we nooned. After dinner we followed the banks of the river, avoiding a trail that bore to the right around by the foot of the mountains. We cut across over the miry, swampy bottoms and after a great deal of hard pulling, and more cursing by certain ones, we made out at last to find dry land enough to camp upon. This valley has been called by some the "Valley of Death", owing to its poisonous waters and the great number of cattle that die in passing through it. The river is strongly alkalized and the grass that grows so rank, it is anything but healthy for stock. Made 18 miles today.

Camp 104: Humboldt River - 7/26

Oh, the mosquitoes, the infernal mosquitoes, how very active and numerous they are in this Valley of Death. Last night we suffered almost death from these pests and Tan (my pony) hovered about camp, as though she thought her only safety lay in being near us. After crossing numerous sloughs and mud holes, we reached Strong Point where we watered our cattle and where we ought to have camped, if we had known the character of the road beyond. But we did not and we went on, and on, and on, again. Across a wide, sterile, sandy plain for 20 miles before we struck the river again. This was a trying time for man and beast. Our cattle waded through the sand and dust, their tongues hanging out of their mouths through thirst and the men were no better off. At last, we hove in site of the river again about dusk. I left the teams to follow on whilst I pushed on ahead, to sooner arrive where I could wet my parched tongue.

I reached a pond of red-looking water. I could not wait to reach the river but down I went and drank at least a quart, before I stopped to taste. Twas an awful dose. And although I took the chances of it killing me, I would not risk my cattle drinking it. So arming myself with a club, I beat them off as they, maddened by thirst, pressed on. About a mile further and we reached the riverbanks where we camped. But myriads of mosquitoes gave us no peace. We build fires all around our camp of the stinking greasewood, to smoke them out. But the only means we had to escape was to do without our suppers, lay down and wrap ourselves, head and all, in our blankets. Where we lay and sweat it out. Our cattle were driven nearly wild by their attacks upon them.

Camp 105: Humboldt River - 7/27

Early this morning we were on the road again which soon took us up onto the high prairie of the valley. For 15 miles we traveled over a sandy, barren plain, before we reached the river again. Here we camped for the night. Mosquitoes, gnats, rattlesnakes, sagebrush, greasewood, alkali dust, alkali water and alkali grass appear to be the only productions of this river valley. Bones of dead cattle, horses and mules line the road, whilst the little mounds often seen by the roadside show us why this valley has been called the Valley of Death. Old Nelse King fairly raves in his curses against these awful pests, the millions upon millions of mosquitoes that follow and hover about us day and night. Tonight, they are worse than ever.

Camp 106: Humboldt River - 7/28

This valley below Strong Point is not as good pasturage as it is above that point. Most of the valley this side being little better than a sandy desert with no grass, excepting on the bottoms near the river. And those are very small and badly cut up by miry sloughs and alkali ponds, being in fact but little better then so much swamp. At this point the valley is about 20 miles wide, with high barren mountains on each side. The road is very sandy and at this point takes a long sweep to the north to avoid the swampy land that lies in the bend. We drove about 10 miles around the bend and nooned where the road leaves the river for the sand hills again. We stopped our wagons in the road and drove our cattle about a mile down to the river for feed and water.

After dinner we drove over the sandy, rocky hills about 6 miles then struck the river again, drove down it about 4 miles and camped for the night. The Mail Road strikes the river at this point of the opposite side and there is a station opposite our camp, the first house we have seen since we left Salt Lake. We found also on this side of the river a trader encamped, who has come out from Honey Lake to trade with the emigrants. Made 20 miles today. Had a visit tonight from the Station Keeper on the opposite side of the river. Old King was anxious to know if there was any show for he and his Susannah to get a "straight meal" over there, in case they waded the stream. He "allowed, if there was any show to get his favorite dish of yellow-legged-chickens, with whiskey dip," he'd go over.

Camp 107: Humboldt River - 7/29

This morning we found ourselves surrounded by ponds and sloughs of alkali water, alive with mosquitoes, gnats, horseflies, snake, lizards etc. Altogether too lively for our comfort, so we were glad to make an early start. We kept on down the valley about 5 miles when we struck a sloth running northerly, which we were compelled to run around. This took us about 8 miles out of our direct course over a very sandy road. We nooned at the crossing of the slough. After dinner we ascended a sandy hill covered with loose rock making a very rough road. Traveled along this ridge a piece, then descending to the bottomlands, we continued down the valley about 5 miles and camped for the night. Made about 20 miles today.

Camp 108: Humboldt River - 7/30

We have lively times in camp nowadays. Paris and myself generally ride on ahead of the train (sometimes accompanied by the girls on horseback) and pick out a good camping place for night, looking out for the best feed and watering places for our stock. Finding a suitable spot, we unsaddle our ponies, turn them loose to graze (if the mosquitoes are not too numerous to admit of it) then we throw ourselves down in the grass, to wait for the teams to come up. After a while they begin to file in and drawing the wagons up in a line on the banks of the river, the cattle are unyoked as soon as possible and turned loose to pick their daily allowance of feed. Whilst a part of each company are thus occupied, the rest are busy collecting wood for the different campfires at the end of each wagon.

Soon our 15 fires are lighted all in a row and the cooks are busy preparing our suppers. Those who have women along are well supplied with cooks. But as for us poor California-bound batches, we have to do our own cooking, although we occasionally get a helping hand from one or the other of the girls. Supper cooked and stowed away; the night guard are called. They start out, collect the cattle and horses up, drive them up to camp where they generally lay down around our wagons until daybreak, when the guard turn them out again to graze. After the guard are sent out, we gather around our fires in groups and chat with the girls till bedtime, listen to stories of the great Kansas war, or perhaps some other train having camped near us for the night, we get up a dance by the light of the moon.

Anyway, such a camp as ours presents a lively romantic picture at night. The row of bright fires, the white wagon tops glistening in the background, the large herd of cattle and horses in the foreground and the groups of men, women and children gathered around the different fires or scattered around camp. The singing, laughing and gay talking of the men and the girls, interrupted occasionally by the squalling of some of the numerous tribe of young ones. Take it all in all, it has to be seen and heard to be appreciated. I must confess there is a romance, a wilderness about it that amply repays me for the many hardships and trials one endures on such a trip. In one word, I like it. At an early hour the fires are put out and men, women and children seek their pile of blankets spread upon the ground around and under the wagons, where we sleep as sound and awake in the morning as refreshed as though we had a bed of feathers to lie upon and a roof to cover us, lest it rain, snow or freeze.

No one ever knows what it is to have a cold. Although I have slept out on the open plain on this trip when of a morning, I would awake to find 3 or 4 inches of snow upon my blankets, and probably my hair on my head white with frost at another time. Still, I never enjoyed as good health before. But in vain my attempts at description of camp life, one must have experienced it to properly understand its pleasures or its hardships, for it hath both. "Get out of that nest, you miserable old batch, haint yer ashamed to lie there till this time er day and I have been and got breakfast already. Come get up and try my cooking this morning and see how a woman's cooking will relish."

This was my first greeting this morning as I awoke and found that one of my neighbor's girls of the next wagon to mine, had pulled the blankets from off of me to arouse me. She and her friends slept under their wagon and Al and I under mine, about 4 feet apart, so we were pretty near neighbors. I accepted the invitation of course, and took breakfast with them. But I must say that "tiger" is "tiger", even if it is cooked by fair women's hands. And although I have not a word to say against Rachel's skill in cooking, still my breakfast tasted very similar to others prepared by mine own unskillful hands. Didn't taste of woman at all. Drove about 20 miles today over a sandy, barren waste. Dust was so thick today that often-times one could not see his lead oxen if he (the driver) was sitting on the wagon box.

Camp 109: Big Bend or Lassen's Meadows - 7/31

Drove 21 miles today and tonight are camped in a perfect bog. We are surrounded by swampy, boggy meadows. Our cattle have to look out for themselves tonight, for it is impossible to herd them near us and they are wading about in the mud and water up to their knees, picking up their feed. Women bawling and children yelling, men cursing and girls giggling, as one after another tumble into bog holes knee-deep with water all around camp. Our drive today has been a hard one, part of the time over sandy, dusty plains, then from that, down onto the overflowed bottomlands where the mud and slime was at times knee-deep. Mosquitoes by the millions lull us to rest with their sweet music tonight.

Camp 110: Antelope Springs - 8/1

A hearty good riddance to the valley of death. This morning our road left the Humboldt River for good. After considerable delay this morning in hunting for our trail, which we knew left the river at the Lassen Meadows, we at last got started on the right track. Crossing a dry, barren, sterile plain to the foot of the bare mountains west of us, we found our road took us up a rocky ravine 12 miles, to where we found this little spring gushing out at the foot of a bare mountain. We found but a very limited supply of water here and not a particle of feed. Bare mountains all around us. I went on and off the road about a mile, found good bunch grass on the side of a mountain and moved our camp to this spot. Camped tonight without water.

Camp III: Rabbit Hole Spring - 8/2

This morning we started on without watering our stock, crossing a steep hill we came down into a wide, dry, sterile valley. Crossing it we passed on over another long rocky mountain, came down into a ravine, where I anxiously hope to find water, but no. We wound down through the narrow rocky defile, with bare rock mineral mountain ledges on each side. Came out at last into a dry, sandy sage covered valley and no water as yet. By this time my tongue felt an inch thick. I was on foot and way ahead of the teams. Pushing on through the sand ankle deep about 5 miles further, making 20 miles this morning. I at last reached these springs, most famished for want of water and awful tired. I found the spring to be nothing more then so many little bog holes, with a little very muddy, bad tasting water.

Our teams reached here about an hour after, our cattle most crazy for water. We went to work, dug out holes and in four hours we succeeded in getting them one bucket full apiece. But this did not begin to satisfy them. There was no grass to be had here and in fact we have not seen any today. Naught but sandy plains covered with sagebrush and bare mountains all around us. Have been busy all the afternoon dipping up water in tin cups as fast as it would boil up from the spring, to water our cattle, who stand around us lowing for more. At 10 o'clock the moon rises and then we push on to try and find a feeding place for our stock, who begin to look very hollow.

Camp 112: Warm Spring - 8/3

At 10 o'clock last night we resumed our flight across this desert. Gathering up our loose stock as we could find them and trusting to their following us in the darkness of the night, we started on again. I mounting my pony, rode on ahead. Rode all night and morning broke but still no water or grass. Laying down by side of the road making pony fast to a sagebrush, I slept in the sand until the teams came up. About 9:00 AM we came out onto a hard clay covered plain, 4 miles in extent. Here for miles upon miles you could look across this perfectly dead level floor of hard baked clay and not a stick, stone or straw of grass, not a reed to be seen as far as the eye could see. Nothing at all ever grew here, nothing obstructed the view for miles.

The whole valley looked as though it had been the bed of a lake that had filled up perfectly level with mud and then the water had evaporated. A more desolate, unearthly place cannot be imagined. All that broke the unevenness of the surface was the bones and carcasses of animals that have perished here. They arose like black islands from this sea of clay upon all slides. Crossing this plain diagonally, we came at last to a warm spring of alkalized water, too warm to bear your hand in it. Our poor worn-out cattle, most famished, tried again and again to drink this accursed liquid, but of course in vain. Their low, mournful groans were pitiful to hear, and how hollow they looked. Many of them their eyes far sunk in their heads, looked as though their time had come. They have not had a bite to eat since Monday night and but one bucket full of bad water.

Camp 113: Granite Creek - 8/4

We lay by for about two hours at Warm Springs to give our cattle a rest, then started on again. My poor Tan (pony) looked like a skeleton and was too weak to carry me, so I turned her loose to follow the wagon and on foot I pressed on across the same clay plain. By this time the wind was blowing a perfect hurricane, right in our faces, carrying clouds of sand and the dust before it. But we struggled on, passing every few rods carcasses of dead cattle and several times passing cattle not yet dead, left by the teams ahead of us. One after another, six of ours laid down to die and as yet none of mine had given out.

We kept on and at last about sundown we reached the mountains of the other side and found a little cove-like spot at the foot of the mountains, where we found a plenty of grass, plenty of water and protection from the awful hurricane that blew across the desert. Oh, how thankful we were that night when we set around camp after having our fill of water. Pure water, the best beverage on earth. Since we left Antelope Springs Monday noon, where our cattle got but a bucket-full of water apiece, until Wednesday night, they had traveled about 50 miles, night and day without a mouthful of grass and but one bucket full of water. Their cries, or rather moans, were pitiful to hear as they slowly dragged themselves along over this accursed desert.

And as the wind increased to a hurricane yesterday after noon, driving the alkalized dust in the clouds before it, it gave to our faces an unearthly yellowish look, that made us appear like so many ghosts arisen from the grave. This dust was so thick that it was impossible to see a rod ahead at any time. And as one after another of the oxen laid down to die, I thought it would be impossible to reach the other side alive. This desert must have been at some time a large shallow lake, that from some cause has run dry. For it is surrounded by high mountains, is at least 50 miles in length and from 8 to 20 miles in width, is as bare of vegetation of any kind as so much bare rock. Level as a lake's surface it, from the effects of the mirage, appears to be from a distance, a pond of water.

At its head a few miles above here, steam in large clouds arise from numerous large springs of boiling hot water. From these pools of boiling water, a person standing on their banks can look down through the water and see large fissures in the rock, through which this hot water boils up in torrents from the infernal regions below. There are also springs from which every few minutes an escape of steam from below sends the black mud up in torrents high in the air. It seems unearthly and makes one feel uncomfortable to be around such an infernal looking spot. Especially as you can feel the earth tremble every few minutes beneath your feet.

And one is mighty apt to ask himself the question; where he would be likely to fetch up, in case the ground he stood on should give way. Some of these holes in the ground are big enough to take our wagon in and they send out hogs heads a minute of boiling hot water, that runs but a few feet before it sinks again out of sight. We have driven our cattle into a mountain ravine where there is a little creek and plenty of grass to fill up once more, as they look like skeletons with hides drawn over them now. We are to lay by here for a day or two. We have plenty of company here, teams are arriving every hour of the day and night. How sudden at times, the change from want and misery, to gaiety, plenty and happiness.

For days past, just crossing this desert all were full of misgivings, fears and doubts. We suffered through extreme fatigue, loss of rest, want of water and through the fear of losing our worn-out stock. But now the danger past, secure in having plenty of feed and pure water for both ourselves and stock. All are full of life and ripe for frolic and as the night draws near, arrangements are made for a dance by moonlight on this grass covered oasis in the desert. Tonight, there must be at least 50 wagons collected here and over 300 emigrants. Amongst others, a company of German musicians on their way to California. Arrangements having been all made, after supper the musicians tuned their instruments, the couples formed on, and the ball commenced.

Our girls did their best and I never saw a livelier party anywhere than this one on the desert. It was a picture worthy of a painter's skill. In the background, the dark gloomy mountains hemmed us in. In the center our camp, encircled by its white top wagons and its numerous campfires, the busy ring of dancers and spectators of both sexes. Whilst to our left, the white, cheerless, almost deathly looking plain of the desert, glistened in the bright moonlight like a field of ice. Teams are coming in at all hours of night and day. Our cattle are filling up once more on good feed and we are willing to layover another day for rest for them.

Camp 114: Wall Spring - 8/6

This morning getting our cattle down from the mountains we hitched up and started on again. Passing by the hot springs at the head of the desert we passed around a point of a mountain and kept on down through a barren, desolate looking valley to deep springs where we nooned. This spring of ice-cold water boils up through a large seam in the rock, forming a basin at the surface about 10 feet across. Although there is no outlet to it, still it, like most other springs of pure water in this country, is full of fish. After dinner we moved on across another clay covered plain, smooth and as bare of vegetation as the surface of a lake of water, about two and a half miles. Then turning to the right, we left the road, struck across to the foot of a range of mountains.

About 8 miles further and came to a beautiful pond of ice-cold spring water, surrounded by first rate grass for our cattle. Here we camped for the night. This pond is situated in a sagebrush thicket, in a barren sandy valley. Is about 25 feet in diameter, a perfect circle, has no outlet or inlet but always remains level full, never stagnates and is no-one-knows how deep. Its banks are perpendicular, and the pond is raised some, a few feet above the level of the plain around, as it is on top of a little mound. This too is full of fish. One of our traveling companions remarks that either of the singular springs of which we have seen so many for a few days past, would be a fortune to any man if you could but own one anywhere near the civilized world.

Here are hot springs hot enough to boil in, close alongside of others ice cold.

Camp 115: Smoky Creek - 8/7

This morning early, we left our camp at Wall Spring and leaving the sage thicket under the mountains we once more rolled along over the smooth level surface of the desert. Hearing that water was scarce for some 20 miles ahead, three of us took shovels and rode on ahead of the train, to dig for it at a swampy place some 8 miles on our road. Crossing a barren country for this distance, we saw to our right about a half mile from the road a clump of green rushes (a sure sign of water). We rode out to it and soon had a well dug about 6 feet deep, which afforded us a limited supply for our stock when it arrived about noon. Here we lay by until sundown, watering our cattle. For it takes some time to water a band of about 160 head of thirsty cattle, at the rate of a bucket full a minute, and that was about as fast as we could get it.

At sundown the moon rose, and we started on again, traveled all night and at break of day Monday morning we reached Smoky Creek Camp about 5 miles above where we first struck it, the creek. About 8 miles from our new camp the road left the barren valley, and it took to the mountains on our right for about 4 miles. We crossed several sandy rocky hills when we came down onto this creek, which was dry where we struck it. We clambered on over rocks and stones over a very rough and dangerous road, up the bed of the dry creek for five miles when we came to a Trading Post located in a good meadow of fine feed, with a plenty of running water. Here we camped. During our night drive up this narrow canyon we many times came very near upsetting. And as to keeping the loose cattle in sight in the darkness of the night, it was impossible. We had to depend entirely upon their instinct and superior sight to find and keep the road.

Towards morning it clouded up and came on very cold, so that when we reached camp, my first move was to find my buffalo robe and blankets, spread them out on the grass and turn in for a good nap. Our Kansas preacher got drunk last night, and he and his Susannah were left behind on the road. Old King swearing that he would not drive any further until he had a nap. He is an awful hard case. "But you see Jenks," says he, "I used to be a decent man once and always was until I went to Kansas. I went out thar to preach to the heathens from the border states. Waul you see, I settled in Osawatomie. Old Brown was one of my neighbors, we were first rate friends used to like to hear the old fellow talk upon religious subjects. Well, the infernal border ruffians used to come over from Missouri and drive off our stock and occasionally kill a settler. I wanted to live a peaceful life, but they wouldn't let me and every time they made one of their sallies, I was sure to be a loser of 8 or 10 head of fine stock.

At last, they stole all I had but that stumped-tail cow, that you see yonder. And that night I lay in bed and I thought it all over, and finally turned over to Susannah and says I, Susannah I'll be ___.___ if I stand it any longer. Old Nelse King from this on means to play for even and you bet them d__d Missourians soon found out who Nelse King was. I'm even on em now ___ ___ them. And now I'm bound for Oregon. When I get thar I'm going to reform and be a decent man again."

We have laid by here for two days now to give our cattle who are very poor and weak a chance to rest and fill up a little on the good feed this camp affords. We now feel as though our long journey was near its end, California is but a short distance from us now and we are not so inpatient as we were to crowd ahead, regardless of our stock. Our camp is like a little town. All the bushes about our camp bend beneath their crop of washed clothes, children are squalling, girls are singing, boys skylarking, old women smoking their black pipes sitting around their campfires telling each other of their trials and tribulations whilst in Kansas. With music, singing, laughing and dancing, we passed away time whilst in camp. During the last 24 hours there has arrived here in camp

26 emigrant wagons, they have been coming in at all times night and day ever since we arrived.

Last night as I lay under my wagon rolled up in my buffalo robe, the air resounded with the laughter from a crowd of fellows dancing a stag dance. Keeping time with a fiddle from which a persevering youth of something over 6 feet in his stockings, known amongst our boys as the infant, was with much sweating, drawing forth that favorite air, called the Arkansas Traveler. What dancing! Twas awful to behold. But you see the boys (all strangers to us) were putting in their best licks before the girls, who were looking on. My attention as I lay here is divided between the dancers on my right and another group on my left around a campfire at the tail of the next wagon. Abe Jobe is there. Our 6 feet lover improving his time, making love most desperately to Rachel who, sad coquette that she is, laughs at him for his pains.

The infant, otherwise known as Ross Dugan, and Shanghai, alias Tom Bass, are a pair of over 6 feet boys who are partners and have traveled with us all the way from the North Platte. These two, together with Mike our wild Irishman and Shoemaker, a long-legged lean ghost of a Dutchman, are traveling with the Georgia boys. And take them altogether, they are as odd a whole lot as ever traveled in one team. This quartet: the infant, Shanghai, the wild Irishman, Andy Shoemaker have made more fun for us that I thought it was possible to see on this road. Take them and our fighting preacher from Kansas; who with a license to preach in one pocket, a pack of cards in the other and a brick in his hat and who swears with all round oaths that he can drink more, "burst head", play "keards better", out "swar" and "out fight any d__d white man on the road," and our team of originals is complete.

Camp 116: Honey Lake Valley - 8/10

I arrived in this valley about midnight, several hours ahead of our train. This morning we broke camp at Smoky Creek and in company with most of the teams encamped there, we started out on the road again. Leaving the creek bottom we crossed a very stony hill and in 12 miles we came to a spring where we found a little feed. Here we nooned. We had from here 17 miles to make before we reached another watering place, so we concluded our cattle would stand it best to travel it in the night. Accordingly, we laid by until sundown, then hitching up, we started out by moonlight. The road was very rocky, in fact it was nothing but a massive cobblestone. All night long we drove over these horrid rough roads and by sunrise our teams reached the valley. I followed the teams until I became chilled through, then mounting my pony I rode on ahead all alone and reached the valley in time to secure a good nap in a haystack, before our teams arrived.

Thursday morning. Our teams begun to arrive and our boys turning the cattle loose did not wait for breakfast, but hunting their blankets preferred sleep and warmth to victuals and drink. Some of our teams did not arrive until nearly noon today. For the first time since we left the Bear River Mountains we are blessed with a sight of timber. The mountains on the west side of the valley are covered with pines to their summits and this is the first heavily timbered mountain I have seen since I left the Rocky Mountains. Since we left for Salt Lake, we have not seen a single tree, not one, before today.

Camp 117: Honey Lake Valley - 8/11

Thank God we are once more in a land productive enough to bring forth a healthy growth of forest timber, a good grazing land and in a country inhabited by white men, with white hearts. There is a vast difference between the reception of weary travel-worn emigrants here and at Salt Lake. About 4:00 PM we hitched up and moved on up the valley to a creek which puts in from the north, where we camped for night. This creek is about 6 miles above the trading post, where we first struck the valley. Lassen Peak of the Sierra Nevada is in full view, head up the valley. We are once more "out of the wilderness" and are now very near our journey's end.

Camp 118: Susanville - Honey Lake Valley - 8/12

This morning early, we started on up the valley passing through a fine grazing country, dotted here and there with the "shake" board houses of the settlers. Until in about 12 miles travel, we reached the head of the valley, where we camped for the day, near a little town of log houses and stores, called Susanville. This valley is already filling up with settlers and is considered a fine country for stock raising. The land around the lake borders is first rate soil for farming purposes and already many farms are fenced in and improved. The mountains on the west side are covered with a heavy growth of pines, whilst those on the eastern side present the same barren aspect of all the country beyond them, between this valley and the States.

The advent of such a party of girls and women as were in our train, was considered of enough importance to warrant the inhabitants to get up a ball to honor the occasion. And accordingly, we all received invitations to attend a party this evening at the public house. I met here a Mr. Stone from Toddy Valley California, who was intimately acquainted with Cousin Newt Benedict of that town. I told him to tell Newt that he had seen a cousin of his at this place following an ox team, on his way back to the land of golden hopes and bitter disappointments. Also met a Deputy Sheriff here from Yreka, in pursuit of horse thieves from Shasta Valley. 12 o'clock midnight went up to the ball this evening and such a shaking down as the puncheon floor of that old cabin had tonight, was a caution to nervous people. The Arkansas Traveler was done up brown for once.

Camp 119: Mountain Camp - 8/13

For the first time in the whole trip, we today have traveled all day through a heavily timbered country. About 10 o'clock this morning we left Susanville, our road taking us up into the mountains over a stony country and after climbing 7 miles we came to a beautiful open glade and a spring of pure mountain water, here we nooned. After dinner, went on the mountain 5 miles further through the forest, came to a little rivulet and camped for the night. Glorious campfires we have tonight, for our boys seem as though they never would tire in their eagerness to gather wood enough, to once more have an old-fashioned fire.

After having traveled so long where nothing but greasewood and sagebrush could be procured for cooking purposes, I feel once more at home now that I am surrounded by these old friends, the giants of the forest.

Camp 120: Eagle Lake ~ Summit of Sierra Nevada - 8/14

Cold nights and fine warm sunny days we have now. This morning leaving our camp in the forest, we drove about a mile and came out into an open glade where we stopped about an hour to let our cattle feed. Then we drove on through dense forests of pine, cedar and balsam fir, with occasionally an opening of good feed and water until night when we reached this little pond of clean cold water, where we camped for the night. During the day we met two Packers on their way out to meet friends that they expected across the plains this season. They informed us that the Pit River Indians were murdering the Whites wherever they met them. And that only yesterday, as they stopped at a cabin in Pit River Valley, they found both of its occupants lying dead on the floor, they having been just butchered by these red devils. Let them try us if they want a good fight.

Camp 121: Indian Battle Camp - 8/15

Ice made last night about a quarter inch thick and pony caught a terrible cold. We are now in the worst Indian country in the world and our guard duty at night is anything but pleasant. Tonight, we are camped on a little creek, the scene of a murderous Indian attack at some previous time. For there are six graves here all in a line, with the name of the deceased and stating the manner of their death on the rude grave boards at their heads. Soon after leaving camp this morning we came to the forks of the road where the Shasta Road branched off. At this place was a grave with this inscription on the headboard "Ann Winkle Died Sept 5th, 1853", probably the heroine of the tale published in Hutchings California magazine of 56 or 57.

Passing on through the forest until noon, we then came out into a wide valley, where we nooned without water for our stock. One of my oxen were taken sick here, also a cow belonging to one of our party. After dinner we went on about a mile further to our present camp. Rock, my sick ox, was driven on into camp, but the cow was left to die. Out of our herd of 160 head of horses and cattle there are but a very few that could be driven much further, they are all pretty near used up. Even oxen that have been driven loose all the way are as bad off as any of them.

Nothing but man can stand such a trip. Dogs, horses and cattle all got footsore and are nearly ready to lay down to die before they got this far. But man with his iron will, braves it all and arrives at his journey's end in good health.

Camp 122: Spring Camp - 8/16

Last night my turn came again to stand guard. About 1 o'clock a soldier rolled into camp and requested permission to stop with us until morning. We told him to make himself at home after he had informed us that he was sent from Fort Crooks on Pit River to Honey Lake, after a company of US Dragoons who had been stationed there all summer. He further stated that the Indians had murdered many settlers in the valley this month and that Col. Adams of the fort was about to take his men out in pursuit of them.

~~~~~~~Note~~~~~~~~
Long Gulch Yreka Jan 26th, 1860

I may as well state here that after we passed through this country, the volunteers under Col. Kibbe had several battles with these Indians and took over 400 of them prisoner and carried them down into California and placed them on Mendocino Reservation. Another independent company of volunteers, formed of settlers in the valley, had an engagement with a band of them at Willow Creek and killed over 100 of them. All of these red skins were lurking about in these forests when we passed through there and probably were deterred from making an attack upon us owing to our having so large a number of men together and keeping so strict a guard at night. For at this very time, they were killing every settler they caught.

When we arrived at Willow Creek, we found a large band of them there, but we watched them closely and passed through safely. This I suppose was the same band that the volunteers a few weeks later, "wiped out".

~~~~~~~~~~~~~~~

Today we traveled 15 miles over a pine-covered mountain to our present camp by a small spring with good feed.

Camp 123: Pit River ~ Mouth of Willow Creek - 8/17

Ice again last night. Drove about 20 miles today, all the way downhill over a very stony, rough road. Indians are very plenty around camp tonight and not only plenty, but very meddlesome and ugly. I found one of them could talk the Chinook Jargon and through this barbarous language, I conversed with him. He said that his people were going to drive all the Whites out of the valley \\ "Oak, oke, mica, illahea wake mica licke Boston mitalache mica illahea. Alia mica mima luse higu Boston. Wake tilacom siwash. Nica tom tom hias cultus," etc. Which rendered into plain English is this.

This is my country; I don't want the Whites to live here. By and by I'll kill a great many of them. Your hearts are bad. You are no friends to the Indian.

Camp 124: Fall River ~ Opposite Fort Crooks - 8/18

Drove the Indians out of camp last night at dark, stationed a double guard and slept soundly all night. Caught my first view of my old friend of other days, the snowcapped Shasta Butte. After hitching up this morning we started on again, followed by a large number of Indians, until in about 5 miles we came to the ford. Here our Indian guard stopped and we crossed the river. And traveling across the valley for 8 miles further we came to Fall River, where we camped for the day. We are camped a few miles above the falls, where this river empties into Pit River.

~~~~~~~~~~~~~~~~*Note*~~~~~~~~~~~~~~~~
Maria you will recollect my drawing of these falls.
It is a correct picture of them.
~~~~~~~~~~~~~~~~~~~~~~~~~~~~~~~~~~~~

Camp 125: Near Fort Crooks - 8/19

My ox Rock died last night, having been bit by a rattlesnake at Spring Camp. I traded his poisoned carcass to an Indian for his bow and arrows. This morning we rafted our teams across the river and went on up to the fort, which is a collection of neat log cabins, situated in the pine forest on the banks of the river. Brindle, another of my steers, died this morning. Traded his carcass to a red skin for a mess of salmon. So they go. Two steers in 24 hours have I lost. If I was not so near my journey's end, I should have to go in on foot. But we are now on the Yreka and Red Bluff Road and consider ourselves once more at home. Our camp tonight is on the banks of a beautiful creek in the pine forest.

Camp 126: McCloud's River - 8/20

About 9 o'clock this morning we started on again. Traveling on over the hills and valleys, through dense forests of pine, balsam firs and arborvitaes of from 2 to 8 feet in diameter, we reached a little brook about noon where we halted for dinner. After dinner we traveled till 10 o'clock at night, before we reached McCloud's River. My guard tonight. Old Mother Wade took pity on my forlorn situation and about midnight, when she had prepared supper for her family, asked me to join them. "Waul Mr. Jenks I suppose we shall not have the pleasure of eating together again, as you are going to stop in Yreka. Why don't you go along with us down into Oregon, get you a farm, marry and settle down?"

I thought of Mother Sherman at home, of course she didn't want me to marry either of her daughters.

Camp 127: Near Pilgrims Camp - 8/21

Today we traveled till 2 PM, then camped for the day at the foot of the mountains dividing Pit from Shasta Valley. In coming down off of the mountain last night Al, who was driving my team, run into a tree and broke the tongue of my wagon. It seems as though my bad luck was coming to a head, now that we are so near our journey's end. Pony is so weak that he can scarcely bear my weight. And my cattle, what there is left of them, walk cross-legged through weakness. As for the Oregonians, their teams are in a worse plight than ours and one poor fellow has lost all but one ox and I had to loan him a yoke of mine to get his wagon thus far on the road.

Camp 128: Mountain House ~ Shasta Butte - 8/22

Passing the Pilgrim Camp House this morning, we climbed the mountain through the heavy forest all the way and camped for the night on the divide. Here we found another roadhouse and I found an old acquaintance in the landlord. He was an old friend of mine when I was in Yreka before and was much surprised to see me driving an ox team in from the plains. We camped about a mile from his house and I treated pony for the first time to all the hay and grain he could eat. Our boys saw two bears tonight, as they were out guarding the stock whilst feeding. Many of our Pike's Peak boys who were freighting through to California in some of the teams, have become inpatient and left us tonight to go on ahead to Yreka 40 miles from here.

Camp 129: E. Herd's Ranch ~ Shasta Valley - 8/23

Leaving the teams to follow on I mounted pony and rode on ahead. Arrived at friend Herd's about noon. He recognized me through the coat of dust and dirt that had been accumulating for the last five months that I have been on the road. "Hello old fellow, where the deuce did you come from?" I told him that I was a pilgrim, just crossed the plains. "Is that the latest style of pants in the States?" Says he, having reference to my pants which were minus legs below the knees. "But never mind your bloomer pants, come into the house. For I have an old friend of yours living with me who recognized you as you rode up and who says; "tell him to wash his face and come and see me." Who the ___ is it, I asked? "Miss Mary Pettis is living with my wife now," says Herd, "and I know she would like to hear through you, from home."

Upon hearing who it was, I apologized for refusing to visit the house before my train arrived and I could procure a suit of clean clothes. For I must say, I was anything but fit to make a call on the ladies in my present situation; unshaven and unshorn, dirty, dusty and ragged. In fact, I looked like all others when they first reach these settlements after crossing the plains. In about two hours the train arrived and camped by the side of the road. After a thorough scrubbing and changing of clothes, I went to the house and for the first time in five months, I sat down to a table in company with ladies. I had been so long used to eating on the ground that I did not feel at home in sitting down to a well-filled table, like a civilized man.

Camp 130: Shasta River California - 8/24

For the first time in five months, I had a roof to cover me last night. For five months let it be raining, snowing, hailing, freezing, or fair and pleasant, it was all the same. My bed was old Mother Earth and the heavens my roof. My trip is finished. I have suffered much at times, but I have also enjoyed myself and I do not regret that I took the trip across the plains. Never did I enjoy better health or feel more robust than now. Far from feeling in the least fatigued, I never was in better condition to stand it. I feel now as though I could travel on for years, as I have done for the past few months.

Our Oregon friends leave us here and at noon today I bid them farewell, promising to call on them at their new home in the Umpqua Valley at some future day. The old women and their barefoot girls did not know what to make of it, seeing one is so intimate with as well dressed a young lady as Miss Pettis has become. And Old Mother Wade asked me in a confidential manner, "if that are gal in the fine feathers up at the house was my sweetheart?" I told her she need have no concern upon that head, for Miss Pettis was engaged to be married to a gentleman in Yreka.

"Oh she is, hey, waul I didn't know, but never mind, good bye, be sure and come down to Oregon next summer an see us. By that time, we shall have a house up and our gals will look a heap more like white folk then they do now. An we shall all be so glad to see yer." After dinner we hitched up our cattle and drove across the valley to the river where we camped for the night. There are but three wagons in the camp tonight and we feel awful lonesome. We miss our Oregon friends.

Yreka City ~ Siskiyou County California - 8/25

Once more I am at home again, for a home it has become to me, though not as sacred as my home in the east. The home of my parents will always be nearest my heart. There I first saw the light and God willing, there I wish to close my eyes when death draws near. There I would have lived, but I went to the place of my birth and they knew me not. There was no place for me and nowhere in my travels have I been so coldly received as in that place that gave me birth, always excepting my own father's house. Almighty Ruler of the Universe, guide and protect the inmates of that house. For it contains all the friends I have left me, in that place I have so often loved to think of and call my home.

I found but little change in Yreka during my two years absence. Many of my old friends had left here and gone to the "States", but many still remained here. Squire Potter, my old Pawtucket friend, was here looking as young as ever, keeping Bachelors Hall. He invited me to share potluck with him and for the present I share his roosting place with him. My cattle I have sent out to a ranch, to see if rest and good keeping will once more stuff their hide and align their framework with good healthy beef. As for pony, who has done me such service on the road, I am determined she shall not do anything more this year. And if good pasturage can build her up again, she shall have the benefit of it.

Pike's Peak Expedition Mileage Chart

A few words now respecting the country through which I have traveled this summer. After leaving Kansas City Missouri, taking the Santa Fe Road through Kansas Territory, the distance from one camping place to the next was as follows.

110 Creek	Was	80 Miles	
Burlingame	Was	6 Miles	86 Miles
Dragoon Creek	Was	6 Miles	92 Miles
Bluff Creek	Was	21 Miles	113 Miles
Elm Creek	Was	8 Miles	121 Miles
142 Creek	Was	4 Miles	125 Miles
Council Grove	Was	4 Miles	129 Miles
Diamond Spring	Was	16 Miles	145 Miles
Lost Spring	Was	16 Miles	161 Miles
Cottonwood Creek	Was	20 Miles	181 Miles
Turkey Creek	Was	25 Miles	206 Miles
Little Arkansas Creek	Was	15 Miles	221 Miles
Little Cow Creek	Was	13 Miles	234 Miles
Cow Creek	Was	2 Miles	236 Miles
Plum Buttes	Was	12 Miles	248 Miles
Arkansas River	Was	13 Miles	261 Miles

Allison's Ranch	Was	5 Miles	266 Miles
Ash Creek	Was	22 Miles	288 Miles
Pawnee Fork	Was	6 Miles	294 Miles
Arkansas River	Was	76 Miles	370 Miles
Crossing of the Santa Fe Road	Was	27 Miles	397 Miles
Bent's New Fort	Was	150 Miles	547 Miles
Bent's Old Fort	Was	40 Miles	587 Miles
Huerfano Creek	Was	40 Miles	627 Miles
Fontaine que Bouille	Was	15 Miles	642 Miles
Independence Camp	Was	18 Miles	660 Miles
Jim's Camp	Was	15 Miles	675 Miles
Brush Corral	Was	12 Miles	687 Miles
O'Falley's Grave	Was	12 Miles	699 Miles
Head of Cherry Creek	Was	14 Miles	713 Miles
Denver City	Was	40 Miles	753 Miles

Pike's Peak Expedition Summary

This brings us to the end of our Pike's Peak expedition. As far out as Council Grove our road was through a fine agricultural country of rolling prairie, with creeks every few miles and timber-covered bottoms. Arrived at Howell Creek 236 miles out and passed the last house. After leaving this point the country becomes more barren and sterile. As far as the eye can penetrate, naught can be seen but the level treeless desert-like prairie. For nearly 200 miles there is not a tree to be seen. Following up the banks of the Arkansas River for 379 miles we crossed but one tributary affording any water at the time we were on the road.

Were it not for the scarcity of timber, the bottom lands on this river would be desirable spots for stock-raising farmers, for the soil is good and the rolling prairies afford a plenty of good buffalo grass. Arrived at Bent's Fort 547 miles out, where we first strike timber again on the river bottoms. We first strike the foot mountains at the head of the Fontaine que Bouille Creek. Crossing the South Platte at Denver City we coast along the post of the mountains, crossing numerous little mountain creeks, till we strike the Cache La Poudre Creek. Here we leave the old Laramie Road and bearing to the left take to the mountains. The distance from Denver City by our route to Salt Lake is about 500 miles, although I do not know the exact distance.

The whole route from Cache La Poudre through, is over rocky barren mountains and small sterile valleys not capable of being converted into farming lands. The country is very thinly timbered, there being no such growth of timber anywhere to be seen as our Sierra Nevada affords a few stunted pines and juniper cedars are about all a man will see. The dead forest near the North Platte Range was the most extensive forest there was on the whole route.

California Expedition Mileage Chart

Calling it 500 miles from Denver to Salt Lake - and I think it is all of that - it would make 1253 miles we traveled to this point. Therefore, from Kansas City to Salt Lake 1253 miles. From Salt Lake to:

Bear River	Was	80 Miles	1333 Miles
Moled Creek	Was	3 Miles	1336 Miles
Warm Springs	Was	4 Miles	1340 Miles
Blue Springs	Was	14 Miles	1354 Miles
Hensell's Springs	Was	11 Miles	1365 Miles
Deep Creek	Was	6 Miles	1371 Miles
The Sink	Was	6 Miles	1377 Miles
Pilot Springs	Was	10 Miles	1387 Miles
Stony Creek	Was	14 Miles	1401 Miles
De Cassure Creek	Was	12 Miles	1413 Miles
Pyramid Rock and Junction of overland road to States	Was	11 Miles	1424 Miles
Mountain Spring	Was	5 Miles	1429 Miles
Goose Creek	Was	8 Miles	1437 Miles
Head of Goose Creek	Was	18 Miles	1455 Miles
Rock Spring	Was	12 Miles	1467 Miles

Head of Thousand Spring Valley	Was	38 Miles	1505 Miles
Headwaters of the Humboldt	Was	8 Miles	1513 Miles
Forks of Humboldt River	Was	26 Miles	1539 Miles
Canyon on Humboldt	Was	76 Miles	1615 Miles
Story Point on Humboldt	Was	52 Miles	1667 Miles
Lassen's Meadows	Was	116 Miles	1783 Miles
Antelope Springs	Was	12 Miles	1795 Miles
Rabbit Hole Springs	Was	20 Miles	1815 Miles
Warm Springs	Was	15 Miles	1830 Miles
Granite Creek	Was	15 Miles	1845 Miles
Wall Spring	Was	20 Miles	1865 Miles
Buffalo Spring	Was	8 Miles	1873 Miles
Smoky Creek	Was	17 Miles	1890 Miles
Honey Lake Valley	Was	29 Miles	1919 Miles
Susanville	Was	18 Miles	1937 Miles
Mountain Camp	Was	12 Miles	1949 Miles
Eagle Lake	Was	13 Miles	1960 Miles
Pit River	Was	45 Miles	2005 Miles
Yreka	Was	110 Miles	2115 Miles

California Expedition Summary

This lands us once more in California. 2115 miles is quite a long road to drive an ox team, and most of the way through a country inhabited by naught but the red skins. I had no idea the road was so long myself, as I have never footed up the figures before today. And taking everything into consideration, I think we have made a quick passage. Our route is far from being the most direct one overland. For we first went a long way south to strike the Arkansas River, then we went as much too far north to strike the Humboldt and then again missed it and going down to Huntington Lake Valley. But in the condition our teams were in, we were obliged to travel the routes where water could be procured in the shortest drives.

For instance, from Salt Lake to California there is a road that runs direct across the country, saving nearly if not quite 150 miles less travel than by our road. But then the watering places are from 20 to 50 miles apart, so that worn out cattle never could make the trip. Instead of a great wide valley, as I expected to see between Salt Lake and the Sierra Nevada, I found the whole country was cut up and crossed in every direction by bare mountain ridges between which lay sterile alkali valleys. Producing nothing but fields of cactus sage and greasewood with but very little soil suitable for farming purposes and not a tree to be seen in the whole country.

Ascending these mountain ridges, you could see in every direction valleys glistening white with the alkali that was spread over their surfaces, like new fallen snow. Occasionally a cloud of steam arising from some one of them showed where a spring of boiling hot water gushed out from the parched earth from the regions of volcanic heat below. Bands of miserable, half starved, Shoshone Indians roam about these valleys and manage to keep body and soul together by hunting ground squirrel, meadow mice, snakes, lizards, anything that has either flesh or blood. I examined the game bags (they carry their game tied up in their rags about their loins) and as such a filthy collection of dead vermin I never saw collected for culinary purposes before. One old fellow had in his pouch, two snakes, five little gopher mice, four squirrel, two horned toads and about a dozen little fish he had caught in the Humboldt. His belly band was drawn so tight, it looked as though there was a great danger of his collapsing.

They are the poorest specimens of the Indian race I ever met. The Humboldt down, which we traveled some 270 miles, is a very crooked and deep extreme which, like some dozen or so others that empty into this great basin and have no outlet, are well supplied with fish. These form the staple article of food for the poor miserable red skins that inhabit the country. As soon as you reach Honey Lake the country changes, the soil becomes more productive, fresh healthy springs and brooks take the place of the alkali water of the "plains".

Mountains covered with dense forests of mammoth pines exchanged for the bare ridges of the basin and valleys. And open glades of meadow grass, take the place of the white, sandy, sage covered valleys of the desert just passed. Never was mariner, just returned home from a long cruise, more delighted with the first view of his native land than I was to once more behold the pine covered forests of old Sierra Nevada, after traveling so long over the desert-like waste between here and the eastern states.

Yreka - 9/12

This morning commenced work as Clerk for misters King and Green, merchants of this city. My wages are to be $75 a month and board. I have sold my wagon for $125 cash and one yoke of cattle that cost me $40 at Pike's Peak for $125, payable in three months note to draw 3% per month, until paid. The balance of my stock I have sent out onto a ranch to winter. Once more now have I started in to try and secure what so many succeed in doing here, a competency. Many a one commencing life as poor as I am have succeeded in their efforts to honestly accumulate wealth here, and why not I? The fault shall not be mine if I fail this time.

Yreka - 10/27

"Times are dull, money is scarce, and we must economize every way Dan," says my employers to me last night. "And we would not ask you to work for under wages, and we have to make a boy do our work." So, their meanness was the cause of my losing my place, as they found a boy that was willing to work for anything over "grub". He is a relative of King's I believe. And now I am out of work again, through no fault of mine, for they liked my way of doing business but could not afford to hire a good clerk. Their cash receipts during the time I was there never fell short of $100 a day and from that to $400. "Life is mighty onsartin," says Pike County, "one minute a man thanks as how he's alright and then agin he ain't so sure ont."

Yreka - 12/2

Tonight at home, whilst I am writing this in my daily diary, my friends are thinking of me. For they have met at my father's house according to an agreement on this, my birthday, to have a social, real old-fashioned, Yankee "sing". How I would like to peep through the red curtains from the piazza tonight and see the party assembled around the old piano. Make it ring Maria and as you sing "Home again", do not imagine that I ever ask myself "Do they miss me at home? Do they miss me?" For it's an assurance most dear to me, to know that you miss me and often-times wish I were there. "True love can ne're forget" and I know such is your feeling for me. May every happiness be yours, friends at home.

Yreka - 12/24

As I saw no prospect of obtaining steady employment at Yreka, I today bought a mining claim on Long Gulch and once more I'll try my luck in the mines and as they say, "look for a dollar where you lost one". I have concluded to seek for pay in the same gulch where I so long mined with poor success in my previous trip to California. My claim is about a quarter of a mile above my old claim of "57. As to mining for a living, I don't mean to do it. But if a person has little or no capital to commence business on, he must try some means to make "a raise", to get a start. As all other resources are shut off from me, I must try my luck in mining.

"Root pig or die."

Long Gulch ~ Near Yreka - January 1, 1860

My book is full, my journey o'er and now my friends at home, to you I wish a Happy New Year. Consider this as my new year's present to you. It would not interest others, but you I know will be pleased to read an account of my trip "across the plains". Just 10 years ago (February 1849) I first left home for a trip around the Horn. 10 years passed by with its many changes, its disappointed hopes, its few joys and many sorrows. Nearly 9 of those long years I passed away from home and friends, separated from all my nearest, dearest, and best friends. Living a secluded and companionless life, never having the benefit of social intercourse with society, seldom visiting, and never receiving visits.

I became at length (like all others who leave society and bury themselves in these mountain wilds, hermit-like) almost unfit to take my place amongst civilized beings and altogether lost in the refined society of the eastern states. Therefore, upon my return after nine years absence to the home of my youth, I was made to feel very sensibly wherein I was lacking. I was conscious of my want of refinement and polished manners and often times was made to feel, to say the least, very uncomfortable when in society. By my knowledge of my rough mountain way of saying things, that I ought not to have said, and leaving undone many things that I ought to have done.

Amongst a tribe of wild red skins, I would have been more at home than I was in a parlor filled with Pawtucket's fair daughters and I never had one half the fear of the former, as I had for the latter. For the safety of my scalp, I never trembled as I did through fear of being ridiculed for my mountain roughness of manners. Through fear and trembling I ventured into society and a band of Comanches never caused 1/10th part the dread to me, that I felt at the rustle of a silk dress. And the giggling of a party of handsome young ladies sounded more terrible in my ears, than the war dance and songs of the Kiowa Indians on the night of April 19th. But now it is passed away again, society and all its pleasures I have left far away in the east and shall I say "like a dog to his vomit" that I have returned to the mountains again. No friends, let us hope that it is all for the best. So mote it be. - Dan Jenks

Long Gulch ~ Near Yreka - 2/1

Friends at home, do not criticize my style of writing, my bad grammar or my spelling. For now, that I have finished this job of copying from my notebook an account of my trip "across the plains", I find many errors in spelling. But they have been made in the hurry and confusion occasioned by writing in a miner's cabin, crowded every evening by visitors, all talking, laughing, and joking at once. During my trip, I day by day wrote in a little pocket diary an account of our progress, description of the country and any incidents worth mentioning. After I moved down here last Christmas I commenced copying it into this book. All the time I had to write was evenings, after my days at work.

Such as it is, I present it to you sister Maria. And if it gives you one half the pleasure in perusing as it did me to write it for you, I am satisfied.

Yreka – from Long Gulch Mountain.

Daniel Jenks Gold Rush Journal
Volume 5: 1863-1865

Pioneer City, Idaho
January 20, 1865

Of all the barbarous middle ages, that
Which is most barbarous is the middle age
Of man: It is - I really scarce know what;
But when we hover between fool and sage
And don't know justly what we would beat
A period something like a printed page
Black letter upon foolscap, while our hair
Grows grizzled, and we are not what we were.

Too old for youth - too young, at thirty-five,
To herd with boys, or hoard with good threescore,
I wonder people should be left alive;
But since they are, that epoch is a bore;
Love lingers still, although t'were fate to wife;
And as for other love, the illusion's o'er;
And money, that most pure imagination,
Gleams only through the dawn of its creation.

Byron's Don Juan - Canto Twelfth 1-2

Yreka - September 23, 1863

It having been a long time now since I have written anything in my journal, I may as well go back to the date of my last entry. In the spring of 1860 I sold my mining claim in Long Gulch at a loss to me of over $400. Determined to find some other business to engage in, I cruised around Siskiyou County until fall when I commenced clerking for R. B. Handy Grain Merchant of Yreka. I continued in his employ at a salary of from $50 to $100 a month, up to last April. During this time, I was twice elected City Assessor of Yreka. The last time, although a known union man I was elected to fill the same office, although the city was strongly Democratic.

At last I left Handy's employment being unwell at the time and from that time on during summer, spent most of my time in the country fishing and hunting for amusement, also because I thought such recreation best for my health. About a month ago I first thought of taking a trip to Boise Basin Idaho. Bob Whittle, a Mountaineer with a squaw wife and two or three half breed children, was anxious to have me go with him. And as I was out of business at the time, I consented to do so. Idaho and its gold mines were attracting a good deal of attention at the time. Many were leaving Yreka for that place and Yreka merchants were anxious to find a direct route from Yreka across the country to that point, in order that they might compete with the Oregonians for the trade.

We knew it was but about 400 miles in a direct route from Yreka to Idaho and by the way of Oregon it was over 1000 miles. Therefore, if a road direct across the country could be found, we could successfully compete with Oregon for their trade. Consequently, when Bob and I talked of going across the country, several of our businessmen suddenly became very anxious to send out goods by me. We finally got all ready for a start and our party consisted of between 30 and 40 men, one woman, one squaw, several children and Bob's half breed daughter Caroline, about 12 years old. Robert Lehman sent out in my care two freight wagons loaded with 8000 pounds of freight in charge of one Shaw, owner of the wagons. He had his family along, also one light wagon loaded down with provisions for some 8 or 10 men he was taking out as passengers.

George Myers started out with a band of beef cattle (about 120 head) and 8 or 10 men as Drovers and two wagons loaded with about 3500 pounds freight apiece. A man by the name of Bryant joined us with six or eight men and a band of beef cattle. And last of all Bob Whittle, his squaw and daughter Caroline and myself. We the last-named party messed by ourselves. Bob was employed as guide and as we were mounted and had our grub on pack horses, we calculated on having a pleasant trip as far as we were concerned. As we could ride in two hours as far as the wagons could go in a day. We had plenty of time to fish and hunt on the road.

E. Herd's Ranch - 9/24

This morning having seen our two freight wagons off, Bob and I packed our animals and after bidding friends goodbye we started out of Yreka, the squaw taking the lead. My particular friend EW Potter Esq. accompanying us for several days trip out into the mountains for his health. At night we reached E. Herd's Ranch and were invited to camp here for the night, we did so. And unpacking our horses we camped just outside of Herd's fence, close by his house, 20 Miles from Yreka.

9/25 - This morning was aroused by Esq. Potter whose jolly face shown down upon me from where he stood by the side of my blankets, with a hat jammed full of hens' eggs. What he said was the result of a foraging expedition of his, in Elijah's barn. Four of our wagons had come into camp during night and after an early breakfast we started out. Bob esquire, squaw and Caroline started with the pack animals, intending to hurry through to Butte Creek and wait for the train at that point, as it is good fishing and hunting there, whilst I am to wait for the wagons. 6 miles from Herd's, at the foot of sheet rock, we found water and hauling our wagons about a mile beyond we camped 26 miles from Yreka.

Grass Lake Valley - 9/26

In the morning I left the wagons to follow on the best they could up an awful steep and sandy mountain. And I rode on to Grass Lake Valley at the top of the mountain, there to await the arrival of the balance of the train of wagons and loose cattle. I went around the lake or swamp to Herd's Dairy House, where he is doing quite an extensive business in that line. Herd is the only one occupying this valley. He herds his stock here summers but has to move out in the fall with his band of cows, as it would be impossible to winter here. This is the last house on our road and from here on we have to "go it blind" as the saying is. 10 miles today and no wagons in camp tonight.

9/27 - Last night George Myers and Bryant's party with over 300 head of beef cattle came in and camped. But the wagons have been all day coming in. During the night the cattle broke out of the corral and broke back for Shasta Valley and Meyers lost over half of his band by this stampede. Consequently, he does not feel justified in going on himself with as small a band and wishes me to act as his agent and take charge of his interests.

I agreed to do so upon conditions that I should have no trouble with his property on the road, but that his herdsman should tend to them and if we get through, I am then to sell them for him. At night we were joined by Maj. Green, with another heavy loaded wagon and four passengers.

Bob's Camp on Butte Creek - 9/28

At last we got fairly underway again this morning, the beef cattle were started out of the corral first and away they went on the run as wild as deer. The wagons follow on as best they can. I went on ahead, for I am anxious to join my own mess mates for the trip who are in camp at Butte Creek, where we go today. 12 miles over a rocky road brought me to Bob's Camp on Butte Creek and I was glad to find the shelter of our tent, as it was raining all day and a bitter cold wind. I also found our friend the Justice busy broiling venison ribs and the squaw just as busy jerking and smoking antelope hams. It is the opinion of the Squire that four mountain-trout boiled on the coals and a few boiled bones of a venison, taken with about a quart of coffee, strong enough to bear up a small sized boulder, is the best remedy for dyspepsia that he ever saw and I concur.

9/29 - Everything covered with ice this morning. One of Lehman's wagons broke down already. Shaw the boss Teamster surrounded by his wife and a half a dozen or so of towheaded children, all crying for and on account of the cold weather, seems to be half crazy. We finally arrange matters in this way. Shaw goes back with his family to Yreka again. He takes the broken-down wagon loaded with flour and beans, back with them and I am to look out for his interests also.

I am compelled to do this in order to save Lehman from further loss. We now have Lehman's 4000-pound wagon and eight yoke of cattle. Shaw, light two yoke wagon with Shaw's passengers. Myers two freight wagons and Myers' band of cattle and horses that I have control of.

Bryant's band of cattle and horses and Major Green's freight wagon and passengers; making a party of 30 men and Caroline who will go through if possible. Myers and Potter will go one more day's drive with us and then they go back to Yreka and Bob leaves his squaw amongst her people at Klamath Lake. At last, everything being arranged, we got the train started once more, leaving Shaw and family to find their way back to Yreka. 20 miles over a rocky, hilly road brought our party to Willow Springs, where we camped. Plenty of trout here, splendid fishing, good feed, etc.

Little Klamath Lake - 10/1

We lay over at Willow Springs all day yesterday waiting for Shaw's light wagon, it having broke an axle coming from Butte Creek. We begin to smell a very considerable quantity of trouble on account of these infernal freight wagons. We have got no time at this season of the year to fool away out in this country, if we don't want to winter here. The trout fishing in Willow Creek was excellent and Squire Bob and Dan Cash, one of Shaw's passengers and myself put in the day fishing with excellent success. During the day, one of Meyer's Teamsters shot an antelope and the camp was well supplied with game and fish. If it was only earlier in the season, I wouldn't care how long we were on the road, so I had plenty of fishing and hunting. But the season is so far advanced that we have no time to lose.

By night some of the men had got out a new axle for the Shaw wagon and it arrived in camp, and this morning we started on down Willow Creek. For 2 miles down this creek the road is good, here we left the creek and crossing a rocky hill came down onto Little Klamath Lake. We kept on around the border of the lake about 7 miles and camped in the rushes at the foot of a very rocky hill that we have to go over. No timber in today's drive, nothing but sagebrush for fuel. Good feed for stock and plenty of geese, duck and brant. Squire and Myers left us this morning to return to Yreka and Dan Cash joins our mess. I hated to see old friend Potter leave, we have messed and roomed together now for years and I hated to part with him.

Lost River - 10/3

Crossed rocky hill and in about 4 miles came down into an alkali valley. Traveled down about 4 miles and crossing a low sandy hill to our right, we came over into Tule Lake Valley. Here at the foot of this hill we turned to the left, leaving the old emigrant road to our right. And bearing off to the left across a sagebrush valley for about 4 miles, we came to Lost River. Keeping on up the bank of this dull, sluggish stream for about 4 miles we camped in good feed. As usual, we arrived in camp early enough to enable our mess to catch a good supply of fish. Which together with a sage hen and two duck shot by our Dan Cash during the day, furnished us a good supper.

10/4 - The wagons did not arrive in camp until about 12 o'clock last night and the loose cattle did not reach camp until this morning. Consequently, we had to lay over again today. This is mighty slow work the way we are traveling at present.

Chief Jacks of the Klamath Lake Indians - 10/5

Started again this morning, went 4 miles and came to Lost River slough. Crossed it and went 6 miles further over a level road up the banks of Lost River and camped in good feed, sage wood for fuel. Bob's squaw Matildy left us here for her home at Klamath Lake. She is a sister of Chief Jacks and he came in to our camp and stopped with us overnight and took his sister off with him this morning. The Klamath Lake Indians are the strongest and most warlike tribe we have in Northern California. They are very pleasantly located around the banks of this beautiful lake. Their country abounds with game in the lake and all of its tributaries are well-stocked with trout and whitefish, duck, geese, swan, pelican are found here in great numbers. And the timbered hills are well-stocked with deer, antelope, mountain sheep, hare, grouse, sage hen, etc.

Last May Squire Potter and myself were out here in company with Bob Whittle for nearly a month fishing and hunting, camping with the Indians in their Rancheria and enjoyed ourselves hugely.

Yarnee Lake - 10/6

Up the riverbank 4 miles over level road, then 4 miles across the foothills over a very rocky road, brought us again to the banks of the river. Here we leave Lost River to our right and bearing off across an alkali valley about 2 miles out, we struck a beautiful spring of water where we camped in good feed. To our left, about a mile distant, is another small alkali pond or lake which the Indians call Yarnee Lake or Spring Lake. As usual, Bob and myself got into camp about 3 o'clock but the wagons did not get in until about 10:00 PM. Myer's Dutch crowd seeing our fires out on the Prairie, took us for Indians and turned their wagons around and started back before they discovered their mistake.

10/7 - Bob and our little party of Packers (our mess) lay in camp until the wagons and droves of beef cattle were well along on the road and then we struck camp, packed up and started on after. Overtook and passed the train and camped about dark at a spring about 16 miles from last camp. Leaving our last night's camp, you crossed a wide dry valley about 8 miles to the foot range of the timbered hills. Here the old trail keeps up on the side of a very rocky hill, but a much better road could be made through the bottomland to the right, where there is plenty of water, feed, etc. After leaving this bottom we crossed several low rocky spurs for about a mile and a half and came down to our present camp.

Martin's Fork of Klamath - 10/8

After our loose cattle came in, we found that there was not water enough for the whole band and Bob started on with them after dark to find water, whilst I stopped behind to help the wagons on. Our wagons did not reach camp at all last night but were left strung out down the road back for 2 miles and their drivers came in with their cattle (loose) for water and feed. Some of them did not reach camp until after midnight. I firmly believe that we are bound to be snowed in for the winter out on these infernal plains beyond us. For at our present rate of locomotion, we never will get anywhere. To add to the fun of the thing, our horses stampeded last night. And tearing through our camp, away they went over the rocks and stones, making everything shake as they flew along. We got them all back in the morning however and started on once more.

And striking across a low hill came down onto a brook where the cattle camped last night, but they had gone on before we reached their camp. Here I left the old emigrant trail and bearing off to the left struck down into the valley of Martin's Fork of Klamath. Drove on up the valley to an Indian Rancheria where I found Bob, and where we camped and waited for the wagons.

10/9 - Lay over at our camp today to cut a roadway down to the river, so as to cross our wagons. By night we had succeeded in getting the wagons all across and they camped on the opposite side of river for the night, whilst the loose cattle camp at the same place as last night. Martin's Fork of Klamath is a beautiful valley and were it near a market, would be soon settled up. As it is now, the Klamath Lake Indians have full control of it. They are oftentimes troublesome to the emigrants passing through their country but to us they were very friendly, owing to Bob's influence over them. They consider Bob as one of the tribe. We hired one of these Indians to go out with us as far as Silver Lake, to introduce us to the Snake Indians as friends of the Klamaths. We gave him the name of Ned and he messed with Bob and I whilst with us.

He could not speak a word of English, but Bob's little daughter Caroline interpreted for us, as she is as much at home in the Klamath language as she is in English. Ned soon became a favorite with the whole camp, and many is the mess of 6 and 8-pound trout that we were indebted to Ned's skill in the use of the spear. For he was particular friends to our mess and was very anxious to have us come back next spring and live with him on Martin's Fork. Maybe it might be well to do so yet. Who knows?

Old Jones the Santa Fe Ox Driver - 10/11

After crossing the river kept on up the valley in grass belly deep to the stock, until we came to a fork. Forded this and turning to the right kept on up a wide grassy valley to running water at its head and here we camped for the night in excellent feed, wood and water. We are now traveling without a sign of the trail but depend entirely on Ned's guidance. He is a trump. We have in our party one Jones, an old Santa Fe ox driver as dark colored nearly as an Indian. Who is never so well pleased as when he has a party around the campfire at night, listening to his yarns of frontier life. He drives one of Lehman's wagons on this trip. If there is any one thing Jones is proud of, it is his skill with the rifle. And many is the long yarn he pins of his success with it on the plains.

Tonight, just before dark, our butcher wanted to kill a beef for camp use and soon had one selected out from the band and drove it on up to camp to kill. After getting it near enough for the purpose, they commenced shooting at it, but did not succeed very well in bringing it down. Jones, who had been looking on with big disgust at such shooting, suddenly grasps his rifle and marches out to the spot to settle the matter. At the same time cursing the infernal Greenhorns for torturing a dumb brute as they were. And deliberately raising his rifle to sight, with all the importance of judge of such matters and blazes away. And he hit an old stump tailed cow away across the valley, in the land at least a quarter of a mile off. Who, surprised at such a powerful sting in her rump, went off with the whole band bawling in a perfect stampede up the valley.

Just imagine Jones's feelings as the crowd burst out into one roar of laughter at his first trial of his skill as a marksman. He looked at the rifle, then at the steer before him and lastly at the crowd behind him. And throwing down his rifle, swore that he could skin, scalp and eat any "son of a __female dog__ that dar to kum out an try him on." He could "outshoot, out swear and lick any ___ man" that didn't believe him.

Trout Creek - 10/11

Lost five horses last night and was detained until nearly noon before we all got off. Then continuing along up the valley to a low sandy and pine-covered divide, we crossed it diagonally and came down onto a pretty, clear creek. Which we called Trout Creek, from the great number of beautiful large 3 and 4 pounders we caught from it whilst the wagons were crossing. Plenty of good feed here and about 9 miles from past camp. After crossing the stream, we came on to the old emigrant road again on a sidehill, the road was very rocky and sidling for about a mile, when we came down again onto a meadow on Trout Creek.

Here we found the band of cattle waiting for wagons to come up and the drivers all busy trout fishing. We told them to come on that night if the wagons got in in time, to a spring that Ned said was about 3 miles further on. And our mess pushed on over a rocky hill to the place where the spring ought to be, in a grassy valley to the right of the road, but the spring was dried up. However, we only had to cross a low rocky hill to our left and came down again onto Trout Creek, where our mess camped by themselves that night in good feed, with plenty of pine timber and excellent water.

After fixing up camp we started out fishing. And in less than an hour, Bob and I had 32 trout of from 1 1/2 to 4 pounds in weight and Dan coming in with a brace of grouse, we had a high old supper.

Beautiful Meadow Valley - 10/12

This morning our mess packed pack animals and started on over the hill again and struck the trail. Followed it over two low ridges and left it again at a dry creek, we taking the left-hand trail, followed around a ridge on a good trail until we came abreast of a beautiful little meadow valley. And leaving the wagons on the ridge, we took the cattle down onto the meadows and camped for the night only 4 miles from the last camp. This is a beautiful little valley, almost surrounded by pine-covered mountains and hills with excellent feed, water and all the other necessaries for a good camp. We saw plenty of deer sign, but no deer. The wagons all arrived on the ridge by night and we all camped together once more.

Licam Creek - 10/13

Started about 10 o'clock. Kept on up the little valley to near its head, crossed a sandy pine-covered hill and finally came out onto a little dry marshy bottom. Crossed this and wound around without a trail, over a very rocky and sandy table land, with no water for 5 or 6 miles. We came down into what our Ned says the Indians call Licam Valley or Lake, although there is not much of a lake here at present. Up this valley about a mile, we camped on a sluggish stream which we called Licam Creek. No wood but a few willows, plenty of grass for stock and any quantity of duck, geese, brant, etc. And the biggest, best flavored trout I ever saw, fared sumptuously tonight.

10/14 - Wagons did not arrive in camp last night but have been all day coming in. Consequently, we had to lay over again today. Curses are very frequent about this time on account of the wagons getting along so slowly. And it is as much as I can do to keep the party together on that account. It is no pleasant prospect to have to spend the winter out here and I don't blame the boys much for not wanting to do so. Our Teamsters were fortunate enough to find a little water in a hole out on the table land to the left of our trail, where they camped last night. We of our mess were busy trout fishing all day and had splendid success. Duck, geese and trout for every meal nowadays.

Spring Creek - 10/15

Crossed the wagons and stock this morning and keeping on the right of creek we passed over a grassy valley, leaving a bile lake to our left for about 4 miles, then crossed a low sandy pine-covered hill and came down into a dry grassy valley. Followed it down this valley about 6 miles and came to a creek, which we call Spring Creek. This creek boils out of a large deep spring at the foot of the hills and abounds with trout of large size and delicious flavor and empties, I believe, in Silver Lake. Spent an hour or two very pleasantly fishing after we arrived in camp. These trout and a brace of duck which Dan shot, made an excellent supper.

Silver Lake - 10/16

Today we crossed over the worst piece of road I ever saw in my life. Leaving Spring Creek we crossed the valley, entered the pines on the opposite side, crossed a low sandy pine-covered divide and struck the wagon trail once more. From here on, the road crosses spur after spur of the mountains. Some pine covered and all rocky as the "noted road to Jordan" is said to be. Crossing numerous dry gulches, where no doubt in the spring of the year there is plenty of water, but as dry now as a defeated politician's throat. For 20 miles this is the character of the road. Long and dreary hills, perfectly bare of all shrubbery, no water, nothing but loose rock and sand. About 16 miles from Spring Creek we came down into an awful canyon, almost impossible for wagons.

And crossing this we hurried on our pack animals and reached the banks of Silver Lake about dark. The loose cattle reached camp at 11 o'clock but as for the wagons, I knew there was no hope of their reaching here this night, if they ever do. Here Ned is to leave us and he has been burning signal fires ever since we came in sight of the lake, to call the Snake River Indians who live here so as to have a conference with them. It is awful cold tonight, and the wind sweeps across the lake in awful cold blasts, whilst to add to our comfort there is but little wood here.

Snake Indians - 10/17

Lay over at this lake today waiting for wagons. Snow squalls all day. Anything but pleasant prospects ahead, on account of being delayed so much by wagons. Ned and Bob went out on horseback today, to see if they could find any Indians to talk with. Rode about half-a-mile when Ned jumps down from his horse, starts a signal fire and presently Indians commenced popping up all around them in the sagebrush. They were Snake Indians and knew Ned. He told them that we were friends of the Klamaths and were going to travel through their country and if they troubled us in any way, the Klamaths would resent it as an insult to them.

They promised to see their Chief and if it was alright, they would come down to our camp before night.

Ned and Bob then returned to camp. And in the afternoon about a dozen of as mean-looking Indians as I ever saw came into camp and promised Ned that their tribe would not molest us. We then killed a beef steer and divided with them and they had a grand blowout on boiled beef bones and ash bread. Our wagons got along in today. One had an axle tree broken, another its reach, another lays out about a quarter-of-a-mile from camp right in sight, with one wheel off and the end of the axle splintered. They found a chance to avoid the canyon by going up its banks about a mile and crossing above it. They also found sufficient water for camp purposes at this point. They all swear terribly about the wagons, are afraid we will have to leave them.

THE LOST GOLD RUSH JOURNALS

Tornado Lake ~ You All Will Die - 10/18

I believe this is about as miserable a hole at this season of the year as I have seen yet. Here, laying on the banks of the lake, we are having a constant succession of tornadoes, some accompanied by rain, some by sleet, some by hail and some by snow. The wagons are not sufficiently repaired to go on as yet and I have to fight the whole crowd to keep them from abandoning them right here. It is no very pleasant situation for a poor devil to be placed in, as I have charge now of the whole train, with the exception of Bryant's cattle and Major Green's wagon, owing to the owners backing out of the scrape. At night we made a start and went around the lake 3 miles and camped again.

10/19 - Snowed this morning quite fast and was very cold. Nothing but sagebrush for fuel. Got the wagons started once more and then commenced to saddle our own animals. Tried to get an Indian to go with us but could not hire one for the whole train to undertake it. They say we will all die before we get much further, but I believe they lie. Overtook the wagons about a mile from camp, jammed fast amongst the rocks on the southeast side of the lake. On one of Myers, an iron axle tree broke square off. Lehman's heavy wagon down on its axle tree again. Myers' other wagon, a broken reach and Shaw's small one a broken axle tree.

And it's snowing and blowing equal to Cape Horn in midwinter. Passing the wreck of wagons, we pushed on with our pack animals and cattle to find level ground enough to camp upon. In about 5 miles came to where the trail leaves the lake and it strikes out across the desert. Here we struck a camping place down in the tall grass and waited for the wagons. Went back to the wagons, got Lehman's 4000-pound wagon up onto its wheels again and made a trip cart of Myers' iron axle tree wagon, and during the day made out to get some of them into camp. Owing to Myers' wagon having broken down, Bob and I have to pack our saddle horses and go afoot from this on, or lose a great portion of our grub.

Arctic Plains - 10/20

Lay over all day repairing wagons and fixing up pack saddles to pack some of our provisions. And it snowing and blowing equal to the Arctic regions and not a stitch of timber within 8 miles of us. A pretty foretaste of the time to come, I suppose.

Chalk Springs - 10/21

Ice made 1/2-inch-thick last night, making it very pleasant to be camped out on the desert! Started out onto the road today afoot to make a 90-mile tramp across a desert, without a drop of water. Very pleasant prospect ahead for the next 40 or 50 hours at least. God knows how much longer. Traveled along for 12 miles over a sagebrush alkali valley, came to Chalk Springs and found them dried-up. Continued on 30 miles further and camped on the side of a very rocky hill without water, grass or anything else but sagebrush, rocks and sand. We made ourselves as comfortable as possible by tying our horses to clumps of sagebrush, making big fires of sagebrush and trying to catch a few winks of sleep occasionally.

The band of cattle and horses had to be surrounded by a line of fires and all the Drovers were on watch all night to keep them herded together. As for the wagons, they were all night coming in. None broke down today, thank God. If they had, they would have been left.

Dog-Gone Mountain Springs - 10/22

Early in the morning we were underway again. And trudging along on foot, I felt mighty thirsty at times, but it was of no use to say a word now. In about 8 miles we came to Salt Springs, but no water could be found. 20 miles further over a barren rocky waste, with occasionally a miserable juniper cedar here and there, we came down into a deep wide valley where we were almost sure we would find water, but no. A few dried-up pond holes was all. 20 miles further for us across this valley of sagebrush and rocks and about 9 o'clock at night we struck the hills on the eastern side. Better yet, we struck a dried-up creek channel and we argued that here we would find water.

We kept on up its bed to near its head and at last gave up in disgust. Too tired to hunt further, we camped, unpacked our jaded animals, tied them to sagebrush, built a fire and lay down to rest. 90 miles on foot without water had made us willing to try a little rest. In about an hour one of our party came in from off the desert (for our mess was ahead). Where is the water was the first question? "Halo chuck," or no water says Bob. Hell is that so, I am nearly dead for a good drink. But whilst we were talking Tom's dog came into the fire, wet all over. "By the howly frost the dog has found water," says Tom McGrath. And you bet we soon followed the sagacious animal who led us to Mountain Springs on the side of the Mountain where we camped not 500 yards from our campfire.

10/23 - Last night after we had found the water through the assistance of the dogs and had watered our horses, we turned them loose to graze and built a rousing fire of sagebrush at camp, to encourage the poor devils along out of the desert. For from our position high up on the side of the mountain, our fire could be seen for 20 miles back on the road across the sagebrush valley. About 12 o'clock Tim Oldham, who was captain of the cattle band, rode in with the cattle and all night long our boys were coming in one or two a time. And towards morning the Teamsters commence coming in with their loose work cattle, having left their wagons out on the desert. Some 4, some 5 and some 15 miles out.

Poor fellows, they were all pretty well used up with their long dry march and when they first caught sight of our light, they swore that no lighthouse ever looked better to a boat crew of shipwrecked sailors than ours did to them. In the spring of the year there is water at the following places that are dried up now.

12 miles from lake is Chalk Springs,
38 miles from here to Salt Spring,
20 miles from here to Sage Valley, passing one or 2 pond holes and from here,
20 miles to Mountain Spring where there is a living spring the year around.

The road across this desert is, for first 20 miles, over an alkali valley full of sagebrush but no grass. You then find occasionally rocky hills to pass from that on until you come down into a sage valley. And across this valley the road is good for most of the way to Mountain Springs. Taken all together, a more miserable dried-up country I never saw. No danger of Indians here, they can't live here and a country must be infernal poor where a Snake Indian can't live. In getting our band of cattle together today we found that about 1/2 of the band, not finding the water last night, had broke back and we sent out two men to overtake them and drive them in again. From our camp we can see their dust away out about 15 miles on the desert. Jones' wagon broke down again about 7 miles out on the desert and tomorrow I am going out to throw off about 2000 pounds of freight, for we can never haul the whole load through.

The Wagon Rescue - 10/24

This morning, taking two men with me and tools for the purpose, we went back on foot and found the wagon down on its axle tree again and fore axle badly splintered. We went to work and unloaded it, got it up on to its wheels again, raised in the high box and left over 2000 pounds of freight piled up there for the benefit of the next traveler on this route. Most of the freight was barrels of pickles, weighing from 400 to 500 pounds apiece and as the wagon has upset and been crippled so many times, we were obliged to throw away a part in order to save any of the freight. I can't imagine how any old Teamster should have been such a fool as to start out into a new country, where there was no road for over 400 miles, with such a load. Especially at this season of the year.

And if the owners lose every wagon, it will be no more than they deserve for their foolishness. The whole train has been delayed by them and through this delay we may yet lose every head of cattle we have. For it is too late in the season to be fooling away time out in this country where there is not a stick of timber for hundreds of miles. And let but one foot of snow fall, and we would lose not only all the wagons but all the cattle and stand a mighty fine chance of losing what is infinitely more valuable to us, "the number of our mess"; i.e. our lives.

Crooked River Valley - 10/25

Got another start this morning and crossing several low sandy hills for about 12 miles, came down into Crooked River Valley. Found good feed for stock and plenty of excellent trout for ourselves in the stream.

10/26 - At this point of Crooked River is a small stone fort or breastwork, where a party of cattle Drovers fortified themselves against the Indians last fall, after losing over 400 head of cattle and nearly all their horses. Leaving here in the morning we kept on up the left bank of the river about 12 miles and camped at the mouth of a canyon on a fork of the river. We have traveled back today on the left bank about the same distance we came down yesterday on the right. If we had come straight across, we would have saved at least 18 miles travel but we followed some other fool's track that had preceded us, and this is the result.

10/27 - Only made 3 miles today up the creek and camped at the foot of a high hill that we have to cross. Excellent feed for stock, plenty of wood for ourselves and duck, geese and sage hen for supper.

Harney Lake Valley - 10/28

Crawled up the hill this morning and winding around on its ridge we came to a strip of pine timber once more. 8 miles further over a rocky road through sagebrush country, we descended a rocky hill to a spring at the head of a long valley, since called Harney Lake Valley. This spring use to be called the Malheur Spring by travelers.

10/29 - At this point the blind trail that we have struck and occasionally followed since we left Yreka, bears off to the left over a high range of mountains and goes into these settlements on John Days River. Down the valley there is a very blind one that can be seen occasionally along in spots that leads to Malheur River, this we want to follow as far as practical. Accordingly, we kept on down the valley about 10 miles and camped in good feed. Water in holes along the creek bed.

10/30 - Snow squall this morning. Awful cold wind. Traveled on down the bottom about 6 miles, crossed a ridge about 4 miles and coming down onto the creek bottom again camped.

10/31 - Badger roasted before the fire. Duck broiled on the coals and sage hen fried, was part of the bill-of-fare this morning. I felt very loath to leave our quarters this morning in the dried-up bed of the creek, where the overhanging willows protected us from the bitter cold winds that blew this morning, but we had to do it. And starting on down the bottom we traveled about 10 miles, with no water. Here we left the grassy valley and for 13 miles further we pushed on over a sandy sagebrush country, until about 10 o'clock at night we found a pond of alkali water and camped. Ice on the pond was an inch thick and it's snowing like Siberia, and nothing but miserable grease wood for fire. Awful cold, miserable camp.

The Dead Sea - 11/1

Snowing this morning, wind bitter cold and ice an inch thick and no fuel but the miserable little grease wood bush. Lay over here waiting for the cattle band to come up as we have not seen them for two days. They came in tonight. This has been an awful day. Snow, hail and wind, bitter cold and no fires but the miserable apologies for ones made from grease wood. Parties are out today ahead hunting for the trail. Right abreast of us is a large lake of muddy alkali water that must be 20 miles across it. The waters are bitter as Sodom and a more dreary, miserable view I never saw. This is Harney Lake, and the old fellow is not at all complemented by naming it after him, or at least I should not be. It looks more like the Dead Sea than any place I ever saw.

11/2 - Lay over again today, trying to find a route around the lake. Pleasant today.

Camp Five Shirts - 11/3

Another snowstorm today. Starting out this morning to make our escape to a more sheltered spot. But we soon found ourselves headed off in nearly all directions by a perfect labyrinth of swamps, sloughs, mud holes and dry creeks. We have had no trail at all for the last two days' travel. The snow squall shuts out from view all the surrounding country and we are completely befogged as to which course to take to get out of our difficulty. To sum it all up, we are completely lost as to our future route or present position. Constantly on the alert for an Indian attack, whose presence in our immediate vicinity we are every morning made aware of, by unmistakable signs around our camp.

And in addition to this, our knowledge of the near approach of winter and in the daily presence of their forerunners in the shape of snow squalls, hailstorms and ice from 1/2 to 1 1/2 inches thick. our situation is anything but pleasant. But variety is the spice of life and if we get too high seasoned to keep upon this trip, why what's the difference? It all goes in to fill up our life's destiny. We traveled on through snow, sleet and hail, a miserable looking crew as ever was seen, for about 7 miles. And finding a place that afforded the three main wants of a traveling community like ours, namely water, feed and fuel. We camped for the night in the bed of a dried-up creek, overhung by large willows. Where we could build our campfires protected from the winds that swept the valley and very thankful to be able to grin at one another across a respectable fire of good-sized willow logs.

To be sure, we lay between two holes of what had been water but now was ice. And it snowed "like all wrath", as Pike said. But what of that? We were sheltered from the infernal heart-cutting wind that had seemed to penetrate through my whole wardrobe of five shirts, which I had all on my back at this time.

Emigrant Trail Junction - 11/4

Struck out across the valley about 4 miles crossing innumerable mud holes and finally came to another creek of running water. We found an old crossing which we conclude must be the old crossing of the Fort Boise, Malheur and Eugene emigrant trail. We crossed and camped in good feed and plenty of good water and fuel once more.

11/5 - This morning, we of the wagon train started on down the banks of the creek to overtake the Cattlemen, who did not camp with us last night. The ground was covered with snow and it was impossible to see any trail. But I have found out since that, right here is where we lost the old Malheur Trail

Note: A page with a color drawing appears to be torn out after this page.

We followed on down the banks of the creek we had camped on for about 4 miles when we reached the place where the cattle had camped the night before, but they were already gone on. We followed their trail across the valley in an easterly course, crossing numerous sloughs, swamp holes and dry ponds. And about dark we struck an old trail at the foot of the mountains on the eastern side of the valley, bearing nearly a due north course. We drove the band of cattle about a mile off the road, or trail, up to the foot of the mountains where we found water and feed and camped. It was about 9 o'clock at night when I reached camp and as to the wagons, I did not know where they were.

11/6 - No signs of wagons this morning, don't know where they are. Would never have found camp last night myself, had it not been for the signal fires built on top of the hill by the Cattlemen. We are in a perfect fog as to our course to get out of this dilemma. Mountains all around us, no trail to guide us and a constant wrangle amongst us as to our best course to steer from here. At dark tonight one of our men rode into our camp and said the wagons were camped about 4 miles from us up the valley. Plenty of Indian sign around to add to the interest of our present situation.

11/7 - Sent out men this morning to see if there was any show to get the wagons out of this, for I am bound to bring this train of wagons through if it is possible, in spite of all obstacles. Like all other undertakings of this description, there are conflicting interests at work here. Bryant who owns a band of beef cattle and has seven or eight men, wishes to leave the wagons to their fate and push ahead to save his cattle.

But I wish to get the whole train through if possible, now that circumstances have thrown the whole concern on my hands, with the exception of Bryant's and Green's interests.

The Cattle Heist - 11/8

Last night Caroline, Dan Tesh and myself had just got fairly asleep in our little tent, leaving Bob out in front at the camp fire, when we were aroused somewhat suddenly by a stampede of horses right through camp. There was a great commotion all at once around camp and a low whisper of Indians. We turned out immediately and our first efforts were to find the horses. About one half of the crowd volunteered immediately and we started out in the dark and finally found them all, but a mare belonging to Bob. Doc Franklin, an old ignoramus from Missouri (formerly), played a very conspicuous part in this part of the program.

He came very near getting shot in his hurry to get away from our camp. Bob having taken him for an Indian in the dark as he attempted to mount his favorite sorrel mare in the chaparral where he had found her. Another one of our fellows was very much chagrined to find out after he got back to camp that his double barrel shotgun was not loaded at all. But quiet once more settled down around our camp and it was a question in our minds whether the Indians had occasioned the stampede of horses or not altogether. Bob insisted that it was Indians and nothing else. And as Bob was the only one that was out a horse, we did not deny it might be possible.

After the balance of the horses had been once more securely picketed and all hands but the guard had turned in, we heard Bob's mare, who had left her colt in camp, crying as mares will from the top of the mountain for her colt. Bob and I started out again in search of her but we did not find her. But this morning we found, by tracking her up, that we must have been within good arrow shot of where she undoubtedly stood at that time. And why her Indian did not see fit to plant an arrow into us at that time is, as the Spaniards say, a case of "Quien Sabe". Moccasin tracks all around camp this morning, showing plainly that we have a plenty of scalp-loving, red-skinned neighbors. This morning all were anxious to leave here and we finally got started when, lo and behold about 40 hand of our best beef cattle were missing. Presently men ahead came riding back and said that the trail ahead showed plainly that our missing cattle had been driven off by Indians.

And to judge it by the tracks, there must have been 40 or 50 Indians. Here was another very pleasant sensation. Well, we concluded as they appeared to be going the same way as ourselves, we would follow on to next water and there camp and try if we could not overtake Mr. Indian on the trail with light horses. Accordingly traveled about 8 miles, passing through a gap to the east and camped on a creek with good feed.

Cattle Rustlin' Indians - 11/9

Last night after we had all arrived in camp and secured everything as well as possible, we commenced preparations for an Indian hunt. All hands were busy, baking bread, running bullets, cleaning rifles, muskets, pistols etc. for an early start. About 12 o'clock midnight I had just barely got asleep in my blankets propped up between the sacks composing our packs, when I heard a rush of our horses by our camp. I jumped up and found our horses had stampeded again. We rallied out and found them all and once more made them fast and cursing from the bottom of our hearts the infernal Indians, lay down once more to try to catch a few hours' sleep. At 4 o'clock we (sixteen of us) were all ready and we started out on the trail of our lost cattle.

We tracked them over hill, up valleys and over mountains until dark, when we found them. But the Indians had left and we succeeded in getting back all our cattle without a fight. The Indians had taken them around over the rockiest hills in the country. And taking a circle around had crossed the creek again where we were camped, not a half mile from our camp above us. They probably crossed at this place about midnight at the time of the stampede amongst our horses, then taking them along back into Harney Lake Valley, they expected to dodge us in case of a pursuit. But we stuck as close to their trail as bloodhounds and followed them so closely that they were all obliged to forsake their plunder and find hiding places for themselves.

We found the cattle within a mile of where they were stolen from and they have probably been run over 40 miles before they made the circuit, in the 30 odd hours they were in the hands of the Indians. We got back to camp at dark again and once more made preparations to go on again in the morning if our red skin neighbors do not stop us.

11/10 - No trouble with the Indians last night, excepting finding a cow with an arrow shot into her side this morning. We saved the cow however and Mr. Indian did not make anything by this operation. Traveled on down the creek valley about 10 miles and camped again in good feed. This creek is probably one of the forks at the head of the Malheur River, although we are not positive of this. Good feed but no running water in the creek. The only water we have is from holes in the bed of the creek, which are all froze over with ice an inch thick. More snow tonight.

11/11 - Kept on down this creek for about a mile further, where we came to a creek of running water coming in from the south. We crossed this and bearing off to the right we crossed the high mountain and came out onto a high table land. Continuing along over this rocky, barren waste, we finally halted for the night on the mountaintop. And driving our cattle and horses down into a ravine to our left, we camped for the night. The Cattlemen and our mess camped in the ravine and the wagon men camped with the wagons on top of the hill.

11/12 - Last night was bitter cold and the wind, snow and hail seemed to chill our very heart's blood. About midnight, old Bryant who was on guard commenced hollering, Indians, Indians boys, turnout, the infernal Indians are all around us! And although it was terrible weather outside of the blankets, we turned out in a hurry. For most of us preferred freezing to death to being murdered in our blankets. But we saw no sign of Indians and after going around the cattle and finding all right, we turned in again to tried to gather a little warmth from our wet blankets. This morning however, we found that Bob's colt, the colt of the mare the Indians stole from us on the night of 7 November, was missing and this accounted for our Indian alarm.

The Indians who had stolen the mare has followed us thus far and bringing the mare within sight of our campfires, she called for her colt. And the colt having heard the call, of course started for the mare. So the Indian was rewarded for his enterprise by the gain of a colt in addition to his other plunder, and succeeded in creating quite an excitement in the white man's camp. The country is covered with snow and ice this morning and an awful cold wind to face. We finally got the packs lashed onto our pack horses and started on and beat our way through snow, sleet, hail, rain and the bitter cold winds over a rocky, sterile, miserable-looking country all day long until just before night. We came to the other side of this strip of high table land and could see through the driving snow a big valley way down below us.

We halted for a time to see what show there was to get the wagons down this very steep and rocky hill into the valley below. But we finally concluded that we would trust to luck and let them get down the best they could. And we clattered away over the loose rock and, slipping and sliding along, we finally reached the bottom and camped by a spring in fair feed.

George Wasson's Grave - 11/13

Another snowstorm last night. The wagons all slid or tumbled down the hill during the night and we are all together once more. There is no trace of a trail from here and we have prospecting parties out to find out what course to steer from here. Found the grave of one George Wasson of Yreka who died July 14th, 1863 near our camp. The grave had been opened probably by Indians and the skull laid on the edge of the grave. For Wasson was with Boles, Dains and Doc Bruny's expedition that started out of Yreka on a prospecting expedition last May. Lay over here today.

11/14 - This morning we got started once more on our route. From the top of the mountain back of our last night camp, we can see a long range of snow mountains in a northeast course from us. As this is about the course we want to go and as we have no trail to follow, and also because we think that these mountains are on the other side of Snake River, we struck out in that direction through sagebrush plains and over rocky hills until night, when we camped without either water or feed on a sidehill. A little water about this time of night would be very acceptable if a fellow could get it.

Lost In Indian Country - 11/15

This morning we started out early and in about an hour's ride found water down in a deep gulch to our right, and taking the cattle and horses down, we camped for the day. The wagons had to be left back on top of the ridge about a mile from our cattle camp, all excepting Shaw's light wagon with his passengers that came down into the bottom to our camp. After getting breakfast we started out prospecting parties to see what the prospect was ahead for the next day's drive. We went down the creek we were camped on about a mile and here we found the biggest canyon I ever have seen up to this time. The little creek pitched off into a river at least 1000 feet below us, that run in a northwest course.

This river, as far as we could see for miles, runs in a canyon of perpendicular banks of rock from 1000 to 2000 feet deep. It was the grandest, wildest scene I had ever witnessed. The mountain banks of perpendicular walls were of all colors, seams of green, read, gray, brown and all intermediate colors were all blended together. And if anyone having the gift of painting could but transfer this one scene to canvas, it would be equal to any painting of wild mountain scenery in existence. A rabbit could hardly cross this canyon, of course our wagons could not, and we were compelled to look down the river for a road out of our present difficulties. I knew if we could only get down this river to its mouth, we would be alright. For I was positive that it was a tributary of Snake River and it matters very little to us whether it is the Malheur or Owyhee. Either one, by following down their banks, would take us to Snake River Valley.

Great times in camp now. Every night some of our boys, who have about as much of an idea of the geography of the country as they have of the Moon, swear we are all lost and are as liable to go to Salt Lake as anywhere else. Some swear this is the Humboldt, although this stream runs northwest, and Humboldt runs southwest. Still, they swear, "Tis the Humboldt," and they know it and blast you what do you know about it. But old Bryant surprised me more than all the others when he asked with all seriousness, what Bob's private opinion was whether we were on the north or south side of the river before us. And old Bryant is a man that thinks what he don't know upon any subject, it is perfectly useless for any man to learn.

Between the fears of some of Indians, others of being caught out on this desert by deep snows and the others of being lost entirely, we have very lively times in camp.

Owyhee River - 11/16

Lay over again today to try to find a route for the wagons. Saw a light in the sky right east of us last night, which is either the reflection from the lights and fires of a town or big Indian camp, don't know which. Also found plenty of evidence white men have been in this neighborhood quite recently, a scrap of Sacramento Union newspaper and a bundle of blank bills of sale of mining claims, also boot tracks in the sand. All of which encourages us to believe we are nearly "out of the wilderness". Another sign is not quite so encouraging, plenty of fresh moccasin tracks prove to us that our red skin friends are always near us, although never visible to the eye. They appear to take a great interest in our personal welfare. But having a proper care to their own safety, never show themselves.

~~~~~~~~~~~~~~~NOTE~~~~~~~~~~~~~~~~~

We have since found out that the light spoken of in the sky to the eastward, was the reflection of the fires at Booneville on Jordan Creek in the Owyhee mines, about 20 miles distant on the opposite side of the river. The river before us was the Owyhee. And further, that we were at this very time in the worst Indian country in the whole territory. They have repeatedly made raids on Jordan Creek and stole hundreds of horses, mules etc. and murdered many men during the winter.

~~~~~~~~~~~~~~~~~~~~~~~~~~~~~~~~~~~~~

11/17 - Broke camp this morning and started on down the river. We had not made a half mile when Shaw's light wagon broke an axle tree. And as we have not seen a stick of timber for the last 100 miles big enough to make an axle tree of, we had to leave it where it was.

Threatened as we are daily by snow, Indians and the prospects of losing everything, we cannot afford to lay by too long to save a wagon or two, especially as we have no road to follow and don't know how soon we will be obliged to abandon everything to save our own lives. We made about 10 miles over a rocky, sagebrush desert and camped without water.

11/18 - Packing our horses, Bob and I started out early to get to water as soon as possible, leaving the wagons to follow on as rapidly as they could. 25 miles over an infernal dry, hilly, sagebrush country finally brought us after dark to water in the bed of a deep canyon that puts in from the west and seems to shut us off from any further progress in this direction, at least with the wagons. And how the deuce the wagons will ever get down this far is hard to tell. If we get out of this scrape, it will be the first wagons that ever came down this river valley on the north side.

Camp Lost Hope - 11/19

Prospected the route ahead this morning. We found an Indian trail running down the canyon and following it down through a narrow, rocky place we came to another worse canyon than the one we just left. And we came to the conclusion that it would be perfectly useless to ever try to get the wagons any further down the side of the river. I started back to stop the wagons from coming down into the canyon at all and riding back 10 miles found them camped at the top of the hill. I told them they would have to go back up the valley and try to find a route where they could cross the river higher up.

They threatened to leave the wagons where they were, they were not going to stay out in this infernal hole to be froze to death. Some did leave and commenced making preparations to pack their provisions on their backs to try to foot-it-out to settlements somewhere. Finally, I prevailed upon the Teamsters to stick to their wagons. And we started down the canyon with the work cattle, to get them to water for they have not had a drop for two days. The band of beef cattle are to go down through the canyon and get into Snake Valley as soon as possible, so to try to save them at any rate, if we have to lose the wagons.

11/20 - Lay over today making arrangements to divide our party. The Drovers of course stay with the band of cattle and must pack what provisions they need from this on until they get through. There is a great deal of cursing about the wagons and most of the men would leave them were it not for the idea that they have that we are entirely lost, and they are afraid to start away from their only show of getting provisions to eat. The Drovers can only take provisions enough for themselves and refused to feed them if they leave the wagons. So they are obliged to stop behind, though very much against their wishes.

11/21 - Last night about 10 o'clock old Major Green came down from the wagon camp and said the devil was to pay up there, that the men with the wagons had all made up their minds to abandon everything, take what provisions they could pack on their backs and follow the cattle at any rate. I tried to get men to volunteer to stop back with me from amongst the Drovers, but only succeeded in getting one, Yankee Johnston. I promised to give them all the back pay of the cowards who were running away, but twas no use. I could get but one man to join me. I then offered Bob $100 to stop with his horses and pack us out, if we did have to leave the wagons eventually. And he agreeing to this, we started back about midnight with our packs and reached the wagon camp about 3 o'clock in the morning.

It was a bitter cold night, and I could not blame the boys so much after all for not wishing to stay out in this second Siberia any longer than they could help. We found that we could raise (all told) a dozen men that agreed to stay with the wagons as long as Bob and I would. The balance skedaddled in the morning to follow the cattle down the canyon. After breakfast, we started on the back trail. And I must say I never was so loath to travel a road as I was this, but I was bound to do my best to save this property entrusted to me. We are to get back as quick as possible to the springs we camped at November 16. And after seeing the wagons all started back on the road, Bob and I packed up our pack horses and pushed on to try and reach them by night, for it is 35 miles without water.

We passed the wagons and pushed on until about 9 o'clock at night but could not find the camping place, as it was snowing hard and dark as Tophet. Consequently, we were obliged to wait for morning where we were. And making the horses fast, we rolled ourselves up in our blankets and tried to keep warm.

This Infernal Hole - 11/22

Sun rose clear but very cold weather this morning and everything covered with snow. After a breakfast of frozen bread and raw bacon, we started out and found our old camp of November 16 in about 1 1/2 miles, where we camped. Waiting for wagons to come up. About noon a small party came in with a part of the work cattle to get them to water, having left the wagons out about 10 miles on the road. We found at this camp one of Myers' beef cattle shot in two places by the Indians. We killed it for beef for our crowd and commenced "Jerking" it. For God only knows when we may get into the settlements. Towards night two of our wagons got into the old camp on top of the hill about a mile from us and drove their cattle down to our camp for feed and water. They left Lehman's and Tanahill's wagons about 10 miles out on the road and the little one broke an axle tree about 4 miles out.

11/23 - This morning sent two men back with work cattle to get Lehman's and Tanahill's wagons into camp. Whilst Bob and three others start out with three days provisions to try to find a route out of this infernal hole, by trying to find a ford across the river higher up. Meanwhile we at camp continue to jerk beef.

11/24 - Thank God no snow yet for if but one foot falls and lays on, we get these wagons no further. Meanwhile we are kept busy all day packing grease wood, sagebrush and the remains of Shaw's small wagon into camp for fuel, for there is not a tree within 40 miles of us as I know. Indians make their presence known every morning by the unmistakable sign of moccasin tracks all around camp, but no attack as yet. Lehman's and Tanahill's wagons arrived in camp tonight on top of the hill, the wagons are camped up on the hill about a mile from us. And Caroline and one of Shaw's passengers by the name of George McCartin and myself, occupy our tent in the ravine amongst the cattle and horses.

Of course, if Mr. Indian makes a raid upon us, we alone will be the ones to suffer from the attack. For the horses are picketed around our tent every night and everyone knows (that knows anything about Indians) that horse flesh is their greatest temptation to make an attack. And why they have left us so long free of attempts of this kind, is a mystery to me. Of course under the circumstances, I don't sleep very sound and worried as I am by constant fear of the winter's snow catching us out here and Indian attacks, I am nearly worn out.

11/25 - Still waiting in camp for our road prospecting party to return and report. Very cold this morning and every prospect of snow very soon. Indians prowling around camp all night, but no attack as yet. At dark our road viewers returned and report that the first night they camped near Wasson's grave. Next day they started out to hunt road and were approached by Indians and tried to talk with them but were not successful in this effort. They found a big Rancheria of them in a canyon of the mountains about a mile from Wasson's grave and they appeared to have plenty of horses, mules and cattle. Afterwards circled around for about 75 miles in all, but could find no wagon route out of the valley, but the way we came in. And after three days hunt returned to camp.

As the last resort, we all concluded that we must go back once more to the canyon where the beef cattle went out. And if possible, to get the wagons through to try and get somewhere ourselves before we are snowed in. For it will be impossible for us to live here, where there is no fuel but the miserable grease wood and the sagebrush. The mountains we crossed on 12 November are now covered a foot or two deep with snow. So we must go ahead. Whether or no, there is no choice.

Here Again Canyon - 11/26

Snowed again last night, beautiful prospect ahead of freezing to death out on this infernal route. Lay over one more day getting wagons ready for the trip back once more to the canyon. This will be the third time we have crossed in this stretch of country in our endeavors to get the wagons down out of these awful mountains. Very lively times these, for a poor devil that is nearly dead with the rheumatism and laying out exposed to snow, bitter frosts and awful cold weather and no boots on his feet. And not a stick of timber within 100 miles of me large enough to make a spoke for a wagon wheel.

11/27 - Snowed and blowed all day and was miserable cold but we all got started on the back track for the canyon once more. We of the pack train leaving the wagons to follow as fast as possible, push on and about 10 o'clock at night we reached our camp of 18, 19 and 20 in the canyon. Where we soon had a rousing fire of sage wood. And we needed it too, for we were chilled through. The wagons are to follow on as fast as possible. And when they arrive here, we will try our best to get them up on the opposite side. But if we fail in that, we are then to "cache" the loads, leave the wagons and make our way in on foot the best way we can. For it has become rather a desperate ease with us and we want to save our lives anyhow.

11/28 - Lay over today waiting for wagons to come up. Pitched our tent in a warm place amidst plenty of sagebrush and intend to lay here until we decide whether the wagons are able to make the effort to get through or not. Ice, snow and a bitter cold wind all day.

Dorris' Drovers from Siskiyou - 11/29

Still laying in camp waiting for the wagons to come along. At night we were surprised, delighted (I cannot express how happy we were) to see a party of white men ride into our camp. They were the first strange faces we have seen for 57 days. They proved to be a part of the Dorris Company of Drovers from Siskiyou, bound to Boise with a band of 300 head of beef cattle. They left Siskiyou October 18 and followed our trail all the way. And old Dorris swore he would have followed it, "if it led plumb into __ the dark regions we read about ___". We were mighty glad to see them.

You who never were in a like situation could have no idea how beautiful even an ugly face looks if it is white, under such circumstances. And the best our camp afforded was set out for their refreshment. They say our wagons will be down here tomorrow. One poor fellow Charlie Umber (one of ours) was so overjoyed to see other white men that it set him nearly crazy, as he had about given himself up for lost.

11/30 - Lay over again today, waiting for wagons. Dorris also lays over as his provisions are in a wagon that is with ours, trying to get down to our present camp. At night the wagons all got into camp about dark.

12/1 - This morning lightened up our three remaining wagons by taking 1000 pounds freight on our horses to pack up on the opposite bank of the canyon, so as to enable the wagons to get through if possible. Bob went with the pack horses and I remained in camp. At night Bob returned and reported that the wagons had got through the canyon safe and were camped at the foot of a high hill.

12/2 - The wagons passed on down through a canyon yesterday, over the rockiest road a wagon ever was hauled over, before they came to the hill they have to climb on the other side, which is considerably steeper than any Gothic roof ever yet made. Here they camped for the night. We with the horses did not move our camp yet. During this day they succeeded in getting them all to the top of the hill on the opposite side, after a great deal of useless swearing and useful labor. But it was an awful job, and I don't believe wagons loaded with freight were ever hauled over such an awful road before.

12/3 - Our wagons camped about 5 miles from us last night, on top of the mountain on the other side of the canyon. This morning Bob and I packed up to go on and overtake them, followed by Dorris' band of cattle. We reached the wagon camp on top of the hill about 10:00 AM and lo and behold, they were all in camp yet. We soon found out the reason. For the Indians (those harmless devils that all the old grannies in the east have so much sympathy for) had come in during the night and run off 19 head of their work cattle. Of course, this put a stop to our further progress unless we could get the cattle back. And we determined to do so if possible.

The Indians Pick A Fight - 12/4

An Indian fight and a capture of six horses and nobody hurt on our side. Yesterday when we arrived at the wagon camp and found the work cattle gone, we unpacked and soon had a volunteer company of 12 men from our fellows and from Dorris' camp. In less than an hour we were on their trail on foot and tracking them over hill and valley all day. At last, just at dark, Lee Bird (one of Dorris' men who was of the party, a half-breed Cherokee by the way and a tip top mountain man) came back and whispered us to be cautious, as the Indians were down in the canyon just before us and probably this was their camping place. We accordingly moved along in the dark as cautiously as possible over the piles of loose rock, until we came to a point of the hill where we could look down into the canyon before us.

Away down below us in the bottom of the narrow gorge, we could hear the red skins urging the poor old worn-out cattle. We lay still and presently they stopped, and two fires were built. We knew that we had them, if they were not too strong for us. We held a consultation and it was finally decided that four of our boys were to start out and try to get down into the canyon about their camp, the other eight of us were to get in down below them and coming up, attack the camp and take them by surprise if possible. Everything worked first rate. We of the attacking party made our way over rocks, brush and steep cliff-sides so quietly, that Mr. Indian never mistrusted a foe was near. We finally about midnight had crawled on hands and knees up to within 20 feet of where at least a dozen great strapping red-legged devils lay sprawled out.

Around their wigwam fires, we could see the cattle all around their camp. We arranged ourselves behind a clump of willows and just as we had got all ready, a great big buck of an Indian raised up to replenish the fire. We let him do so and as the blaze from the fire shown out, his quick eye must have caught sight of us, for he straightened up. But that instant we fired and such another stampede I never heard. They broke into the willows to make their escape up the canyon and those that lived to get that far were met by a volley from our fellows above. And they broke then for the sides of the canyon and the loose rock came clattering down the sides of the hills for a half hour afterwards.

Their camp was right in a thicket of low willows, and it being very dark I do not know how many we laid out, if any. But eight men having a dead rest within 20 feet of them must have done some execution. And from the way one old devil coughed, I don't think he could possibly live long. It was awful cold, and my fingers were so numb it was almost impossible to reload my rifle. Still, we dare not build a fire, but went to work and gathered up the cattle. We found nine head left (by the way we came to where they had killed several of them whilst tracking them up). We also found six horses picketed out back of their wigwams, which we confiscated immediately. After getting the cattle together we ransacked the Rancheria and found one baby, which we wrapped up warmly in deer skins (I have wished ever since that I had brought it off with me), also one number one rifle, a great quantity of bullets, caps, some powder and lots of skins.

After getting our plunder all together we started back to try and get back to camp. We finally halted about a mile from the Rancheria to wait for morning. And I believe these few hours were the longest I ever saw in my life. For we were nearly froze, still were afraid to build a fire on account of the Indians, we had no blankets, no grub and were obliged to lay all in a heap to keep warm. At last day broke and we started back and reached camp about dark, fully satisfied that we have learnt the devils of this desert the difference between robbing emigrants from the old states and Californians. A red skin had about as leave loose his life as his horse, and we have got all the horses that band had.

I made half a horse by this expedition, as we divided the horses between us, and Bob and I have one between us.

12/5 - Last night had all the camp out about midnight by a false alarm from one of the guard of Indians. This morning started once more and traveled over a very rocky, hilly route until night and camped in good feed, but no water.

12/6 - This morning Bob and I with our pack animals, together with Dorris' band of cattle, started out ahead of the wagons to get to water as soon as possible. Drove all day over an awful hilly rough country making about 20 miles, when about 9 o'clock at night we came down into the river bottom where we camped.

Out of The Wilderness - 12/7

Bob and another went back to the wagons this morning to assist them through and to let them know how near they are "out of the wilderness" of mountains we have been so long pent-up in. We lay over to wait for them. Rained all day, river is froze over with ice from 4 to 8 inches thick in places. We feel now as if we were out of our troubles, if the wagons only get in. And if they do, they will be the first ones that ever came down this river valley on the north side. No doubt we are in Snake River Valley now and the temperature is altogether milder than anything we have seen for some time.

12/8 - Still laying over waiting for wagons to come in. Rained all night. This morning two of our fellows went out down the river on horseback to see what the prospect was ahead. At night they returned saying that they had been to Boise Ferry on Snake River. That it was but about 10 miles below us and that this was the Owyhee River we were camped on. And further that the ferry man had told them that our Cattlemen, when they arrived in the settlements, had told such a dismal story of our being lost, that the Commander at the Fort had sent out a company of Dragoons to hunt us up and help us in. But unfortunately, they had gone up the Malheur, consequently we had never seen them.

12/9 - Wagons arrived in camp all last night. And this morning we started on once more. And after riding about 10 miles, our eyes were gladdened first by the sight of a good broad road and next by the sight of a log cabin, the first we have seen for about two months and a half. The road is the Old Emigrant Road from the eastern states to Oregon and the cabin is the Ferry House at the mouth of Boise River at old Fort Boise. We camped here and truly grateful are we that our troubles are over, for the last two months nearly has been awful trying to a man's nerves.

Old Fort Boise - 12/10

Lay over here today about a mile from the ferry. Old Fort Boise is now nothing but a mass of adobe ruins. But there is a Ferry House on the spot and a good ferry. During the day Doc Franklin, one of our Cattlemen, came into camp and said that he had just returned with the soldiers send out to our assistance. He had volunteered to go out with them when they left Fort Boise. The new Fort Boise is 40 miles up Boise River, near the foot of the mountains and is quite a collection of good strong substantial stone houses. A new town has sprung up near the fort called Boise City.

12/11 - Took us nearly all of this day to cross our train over the ferry and at night we went on up Boise Valley about a mile and camped.

12/12 - Traveled on up the valley about 5 miles and camped again, having lost one of our pack horses this morning. The wagons went on ahead. Bitter cold weather.

12/13 - Snowed all night and this morning everything is covered with ice and a bitter, bleak wind blowing up the valley. Tried to make ourselves as comfortable as possible in camp today, did not move.

12/14 - Started out this morning and went to carry on 15 miles from last night's camp. Passed several log cabins during the day, of the pioneer settlers of Boise Valley. The wagons all arrived in our camp tonight and we found Dorris' band of cattle here. Snowing again tonight.

Junction House ~ Boise Valley - 12/15

Packing up this morning we hurried on as fast as possible all day, until at about dark we came to the Junction House in Boise Valley, 9 miles below Boise City. Here we stopped for the present and for the first time for near three months, I had the pleasure of sleeping under a roof.

Junction House - January 1, 1864

Have now got fairly settled down for winter quarters, the wagons have all got in. I have disposed of enough of their freight to pay off the hands and have sold part of the beef cattle and intend to stop here until warm weather. For I have had enough rough usage for the past three months to do me for a while. Boise is only 9 miles from us and plenty near enough for me to do business in from here. I found our Cattlemen camped about 2 miles above us when we arrived here. They had no trouble in getting in after they left us on 22 November.

2/1 - Junction House Boise Valley - Still contented to stop at this roadside house after our previous hard times, this seems like a haven of rest to us. Have disposed of most of the cattle and all of the goods there is a market for here at present. This valley is nearly all taken up for farming purposes and the settlers are all busy improving their farms. Boise City bids fair to be a lively little town and will undoubtedly be a good business place one of these days. But I don't like this climate and do not believe I would like to live here.

3/1 - Junction House - Have sold all of our cattle and sent off the Herdsman according to orders from Mr. Myers, with the net proceeds of the sale to Yreka, to report to Myers. Lehman writes me from Yreka that he is coming up in the spring with a stock of goods and wishes me to find a good place to open business and wishes me to go in with him. As I have no other business on hand at present, I shall take a trip out to South Boise shortly to look at that country and see for myself what the prospects are out there. Owyhee is spoken of as a very promising camp for business, but that depends entirely on the silver lodes. I prefer South Boise.

Boise City - 3/17

This morning in company with one James Anderson, formerly from Missouri, but more lately from California, I started for South Boise on a business prospecting tour. We have each a saddle horse and I have a pack horse to pack our "traps", or in other words our "grub", blankets and cooking utensils. We have something like 100 miles to go, which would not take long if it was good traveling all the way. But although the grass on the plains and the hills around Boise City looks green and everything wears the appearance of early spring, still they tell me that 50 miles out I will strike snow 2 feet deep. We bought our outfit of provisions at Boise City and started out.

3/18 - Last night camped about 5 miles from Boise City. This morning ferried our horses across Boise River and went about 10 miles further and camped early.

3/19 - Packed up this morning and following a narrow trail all day over hills, mountains, valleys and canyons, at length stopped for the night in a miserable cold, bleak spot by the side of a little creek.

3/20 - Snowed all night and half froze as we were, we packed up to try and find some more sheltered spot to camp in. About noon we came to a deep canyon called Syrup Creek and camped.

3/21 - We lay over here today waiting for the weather to moderate, glad to find a shelter from the cold snowstorm where our horses can find something to eat and we ourselves find firewood enough to keep warm by. For firewood is a great necessity out in such weather as this. This creek is called 45 miles from Boise City. There are several camps of men laying here, all waiting for the weather to moderate before they go on. For from this time, we will have snow from 1 to 3 feet deep they say between here and South Boise settlements. In one camp I found four men, all old "49 Californians, still on the hunt for gold. Being a "49er" myself, I was well received in their camp.

3/22 - Still snowing and blowing and still laying over at Syrup Creek. Plenty of new arrivals in camp today, all fortune hunters bound to South Boise.

3/23 - Lay over again today, for the same cause.

The Horse Chase - 3/24

This morning Jim came into camp, said the horses were gone and without stopping to get a bite to eat I rolled out of my blankets where I had been trying to keep warm, and started out to track them up if possible. We came in sight of them about 2 miles from camp and hurried on through the snow and mud to overtake them. But like "paddy" celebrated flea, when we got where they were, they were not there. We tracked them until nearly dark, over hills, mountains and valleys at least 20 miles, occasionally getting near enough to see them way ahead, but could not overtake them. About this time, I felt like consigning all horse flesh to the author of all trouble on Earth.

But here we were, 20 miles from camp and no breakfast inside of me to buoy me, and still more beautiful prospects ahead of having to camp out, without even blankets to keep us warm and the temperature very close to zero. And my curses on the horses was not very loud, but deep. Jim and I held a consultation about this time as to further operations. We were 20 miles from camp, twas awful cold, we had no blankets and I had not had a mouthful to eat all day. What was it best to do? Let the horses go to the "Auyvel" and try to get back to camp by walking all night? I could not think of that, for I was awful tired now and must have rest before I could go back. Besides my bowels yearned powerfully for some kind of nourishment, even "boiled owl", as tough as it is said to be, would have been acceptable.

Finally, we concluded to go on after the horses and the first creek we struck that had timber on its banks we would camp and try to keep warm and rest by the side of the fire for the night. Accordingly, we pushed on until about an hour after dark we struck a creek where there was a plenty of cottonwood and willows. And in searching around the bottom we came across a squatter's shanty, deserted. This was right to our hand. We pulled down part of the roof for fuel and building a fire in the center of the hut we lay down one on each side of the fire, where we lay until morning, excepting having occasionally to get up and tear away more of the roof to replenish our fire. It was an awful cold night and our slumbers were not quite as peaceful as some we read about, but it was better than none.

3/25 - This morning at good fair daylight, we struck out on the trail. Bound to find something to eat somewhere before long and as the confounded horses had taken us thus far towards Boise City, we had no doubt now they were on the way back to their old pasture in that valley. About 10 o'clock a.m. we reached a tent, which answered the purpose of inn. And the landlord told us we were then just 15 miles from Boise City. I told him we wanted something to eat, for we had had nothing for nearly 2 days. Accordingly, he rolled up his shirt sleeves and commenced his culinary operations and presently spread out before us on the ground a pile of flapjacks and fried bacon and a tin cup of coffee a piece, with at least a half inch of half crushed burnt coffee floating on the top. "Everything goes in this country" is a favorite saying and we were well satisfied to pay $1.25 a piece for this kind of a breakfast after our long walk and poor night's rest.

Jim after dinner went on towards Boise City after the horses and I stayed at the tent to wait his return. This place where I have stopped is kept by Bob Marquis esquire and is called the Stage House, in anticipation of the Overland Stage companies making a station of it when they commence running it to Boise City this summer. As it is a fair specimen of the public houses of this country, I have made a rough sketch of it on the opposite page. The principal building is made of sticks set upright in the ground and plastered between the sticks with mud. The roof is covered with brush and long grass and a blanket for a door. The cooking has to be done outdoors on a little sheet iron stove. But as the "grub" is very limited in quantity and quality, the kitchen has plenty of room for all purposes. For the same reason the table room is ample for all practical purposes, having the whole sagebrush valley for his guests to eat in.

3/27 - About 10 o'clock Jim returned from Boise City with the horses, having found them near there and we mounted and put off for our camp on Syrup Creek. The grass did not grow under our horse's feet as we made our way back and about 2 o'clock we reached camp once more. Found quite an increase to our party at camp, all waiting for a chance to get through to South Boise.

3/27 - Lay over again today on account of snow. We intend to start out now the first fair day, snow or no snow.

Wood Creek Hotel ~ Road to South Boise - 3/28

This morning Jim and I packed up our traps and mounting our saddle horses, we started out to climb the mountains ahead of us. Ascending the steep mountain on the opposite side of the creek, we soon came into snow but found a good trail. We kept on up a gradual raise to the summit, crossed it and came down into Eagle Valley. Kept on down this valley until we came to a fork of the stream that came in from the opposite direction. We followed up this to the divide, crossed through snow 4 feet deep and came down into what some call Dixie Creek Valley.

Passed through this and over a divide and came down onto Little Camas Prairie which was covered as far as we could see with snow from 2 to 3 feet deep. No timber on the road thus far and by this time it had commenced snowing very fast and an awful cold north wind blowing. We pushed on through snow, sleet, and wind across this prairie and at last caught sight of pine timber ahead and a prospect for a good fire at night. 10 miles across this prairie and we came to the steep banks of Wood Creek, so called on account of the timber on its banks and bottoms. Descending the steep mountainsides, we have at last reached Wood Creek and the change in the degree of temperature between this sheltered spot and the bleak Camas Prairie above us, was very acceptable to both man and beast.

We found here another of those public houses, so rare in this new territory. A rough log roof had been thrown together, covered with mud and grass, making a kind of a shelter for a poor devil obliged to travel this road. But as poor as the accommodations were, we were very glad to find them here. At least the landlord was very accommodating and kind, and that is more than you can always say for a landlord.

3/29 - Lay over again today on account of a snowstorm. And as poor as our landlord's accommodations at the Wood Creek Hotel are, they were very acceptable to us. For a good camp in a sheltered place well timbered, is a luxury to a man in this sagebrush country where timber is so scarce. And if the house be but a hut, it matters not, it is a shelter and that is one great point gained. I suppose by another year these pioneer landlords will have good substantial houses in these places. These present ones are mere temporary affairs for the present time. During the day a drove of beef cattle, a pack train and several prospectors arrived in camp.

THE LOST GOLD RUSH JOURNALS

Happy Camp - 3/30

This morning having a clear sky, we packed up and started on once more. After fording several streams and traveling all day through snow from 2 to 3 feet deep, we reached the last crossing of the South Boise River about dark, 6 miles from Happy Camp in the mines. In making this crossing, pony made a wrong calculation as to its ability to find the best ford and the consequence was that pony and I found ourselves swimming. We scrambled out but it was so awful cold by this time that I would have made a very good model for Dumas Ice Statue. I drove the pony on ahead and walked from here to Happy Camp. Arrived at this mining town, we found the snow 3 feet deep. And as my clothes were frozen stiff, I told Jim that we must get somewhere where we could make a rousing fire.

We accordingly broke down the hill into the bottom which is well timbered. And unpacking and tying our horses up to trees, we soon had a hole dug in the snow big enough to pitch our tent in and a rousing fire of pine logs in front of it, by which we soon got supper and I got warm enough to turn into my blankets for the night. This camp does not look very prosperous just now, as the winter's snow is too deep to allow the miners to work at present.

3/31 - Sent our horses out to a ranch 16 miles out on South Boise, for it is impossible to feed them here. Everything is buried in snow and a few "flat broke" miners hang around the two or three stores of the town. No very brilliant prospects for business here at present, I don't like it. Up above the creek is a place called Rocky Point, I shall go up there tomorrow and look at that. That, say they, have rich silver mines at and around Rocky Point, but not one of them have a two-bit piece to buy a drink of tarantula juice whiskey.

Rocky Point - 4/1

Went to Rocky Point today, 6 miles from our present camp. I don't like it. The mines may be as rich as Washoe, but there will be but little money in circulation this year. Snow is from 3 to 4 feet deep. Thermometer down every night to a very close neighborhood to Zero. Millionaires worth millions in quartz lodes, but "nary a cent" in their pockets to buy the salt to season their flapjacks. I believe I will not locate in this part of Idaho. I returned at night to camp and having found a Packer who promised to pack my blankets out to where my horses are ranched, I told Jim that I should return to Boise in the morning.

4/2 - Having seen my blankets packed, I started out alone. After bidding Jim goodbye, on my return to Boise City, it commenced snowing again about the time I started and by the time I reached the place where I got my dunking on my way up, it snowed so fast that the Packers concluded they would go no further that night. We found a cabin empty and went in and took possession for the night. We were joined about dark by a Mexican pack train and we all turned in together.

Like so many pigs in a stye, we were perfectly happy to think we had such fine quarters for the night.

Syrup Creek House - 4/3

This morning sun rose clear and cold. Old Zero must have been very near to us at sunrise. After breakfast I started out on foot ahead of the train and sliding along over the crusted snow, I soon overtook a poor fellow loaded down with blankets. He was a Californian from Humboldt Bay, where he had left his family about a year ago to come up to Idaho to make his fortune. Like ninety out of every hundred, he was unsuccessful and was now tramping back to try and get home again. We traveled along until about noon when I found the ranch where my horses were. I told the Californian that if he would wait till morning, I would give him a horse to ride as far as Boise City. And we stopped here for the night.

4/4 - Saddled and packed our horses (me and Californian) this morning, and by night we were out of the snowy regions of South Boise once more and stopped at Syrup Creek House, where we camped so long, from the 20th to the 28th of March.

4/5 - Started out again this morning and by 2:00 PM reached the Stage House 15 miles from Boise and stopped overnight. Found some 30 or 40 prospectors here, all bound for some new humbugging, new excitement out on Woods River. There was a great many old Yrekans in the crowd, I hope they may strike it.

Boise City - 4/6

Two of my horses strayed off last night hobbled and consequently, Californian could ride no further. Pony was soon saddled, and I struck out for Boise City. I found my horses on the way in and driving them before me, I reached Boise City about 4 o'clock. Found Wall Lawrence the landlord of Junction House in town, who told one that Lehman had arrived and was waiting for my return at his house. After dinner I started on down the Boise Valley to his house and arrived about dark, found Lehman there and was glad to get home once more myself.

4/7 - The Junction House, a view of which I have given on the opposite page, is situated in Boise Valley about 9 miles below Boise City. And it derives its name from the fact that it is located at the junction of the Payette and old Fort Boise Roads. The landlord at this time is Wall Lawrence.

~~~~~~~~~~~~~NOTE~~~~~~~~~~~~~

January 1, 1865 - Since the date of the above, this house has become somewhat noted from the fact that Wall Lawrence has since then been murdered by his father-in-law. And his brother, known as Pony Lawrence who took the house after his brother's death, only survived him about a month, when he too was murdered by a hired hand.

4/8 - Today went up to Boise City and secured a place to store Lehman's goods when they arrive, for he expects them every day now. I shall go into partnership with him as he wants me to and try it for a year at least and see whether it pays or not. I do not like Boise City very well for our business, situated as we are, short of funds. But just now do not see any other very flattering opening. Boise City is a good place enough, if there was only money enough amongst the farmers to pay for what they want. But it is all credit amongst them and to sell their goods a man must wait until they harvest their crops next fall.

4/17 - Our teams not having arrived as yet, Bob started this morning for the Basin, intending to visit the four principal mining towns there to see if the prospect is not better up there for business. For we do not like the appearance of things down here.

4/20 - Bob returned last night, having visited Bannock, Centerville, Placerville and Pioneer City. He says all kinds of business is over done in all these places. But thinks that situated as we are, we can do better at Pioneer than here and accordingly we forfeited the $20 that we had paid down to bind the bargain when we rented the store here. And Bob started out with one of our trains that had arrived during his absence for Pioneer, whilst I started for the Payette to leave letters there to inform our other two Packers of our whereabouts. I took dinner at the Junction House and after that rode on over to the Payette Ranch. Here is where Bob made arrangements with the Packers to leave letters, to post them where to come to with their freight. The Payette Valley is a similar looking valley as the Boise. Both rivers run nearly parallel and empty into the Snake, about 16 miles apart.

Shaffer's Ranch - 4/21

Having left my letters with the landlord I started out this morning up the Payette Valley on the Placerville Road. The road for almost all of the day was a very good wagon road. About noon I stopped for dinner at a very good house, where they set a very fair table. After dinner rode on up the river valley until I came to a horseshoe bend, here the road leaves the valley and commences climbing the mountains. Just at dark came down into a narrow gorge and found Shaffer's well-known Ranch or hotel, it was crowded full of passengers and travelers bound to the mines.

4/22 - Left Shaffer's this morning in company with the stage passengers who are obliged to go in on horseback from here in, as the wagon road is impassable at present. The road for about 6 miles runs up the bed of a creek most of the way, as the ravine is so narrow there is no chance for a road on either side. About noon we reached Placerville and found it to be quite a lively town and much larger than I expected it was. Found several old Yreka acquaintances here and one from Pawtucket Rhode Island. Stopped overnight here.

Placerville - 4/24

Lay over at Placerville yesterday, sent my horse back to Shaffer's to ranch him for the present, intending to foot it over to Pioneer, distant about 6 miles from Placerville. Taking it easy, I reached our place at Pioneer about noon and found Bob had secured a store for our use. It was a rough old affair, no floor, no shelves, no ceiling, no chimney, nothing but a hewn log house, which the owners only asked $900 for. We could not rent anything for less than $150 a month and I suppose we will have to buy the shell, as poor as it is and pay the price for it. Bob has already sold some seven or $800 worth of goods and well he has, for "He bet" no two fellows ever started into business here under worse circumstances. Bob has about $700 and I about $300 and we have to raise immediately $3000 for freight and $1200 to fit our store up.

This will keep us rustling for a while I reckon, to make everything work smooth and that too in a country where neither of us are known. There is one thing I don't like about this place and that is the class of inhabitants, they appear to be all Irish. And as today is Sunday, they are out in full force and the streets are full of them. Drunk, noisy and quarrelsome as usual with them, and cheers for that infernal traitor Jeff Davis is a regular thing with them.

Pioneer City Idaho - 6/1

We have now got our store fitted up, shelves in and floor down, all on "tick". The house we have bought at $900. $400 down and $500 in two months. One train has arrived, and we expect the other daily. Business opens very fair, although prices are too low here, considering the cost of getting goods here. There is more competition here than in any place I ever was in and our Oregon traders don't seem to consider their time as of any account in calculating profits. They come in ragged and dirty, with their cayuse pack trains, pitch a tent and sell their goods at too small an advance on prices to leave any profit for a man that pays freight.

6/1 - Pioneer City Idaho - Still alive and that is pretty good luck for this country, where these rapscallions don't seem to care anymore for a man's life then they would for a partridge's. I don't know how many have been shot or cut to pieces here, but the graveyards begin to be pretty well stocked. Mostly violent deaths. About a dozen fights a day is our usual number of a Sunday. After getting their sins pardoned at so much a head by the French Priest located here on a Sunday morning, our amiable Irish friends devote the balance of the day to drinking toasts to Jeff Davis and fighting it out on their own hook.

Hog 'em - 7/1

I have changed the heading of this page to correspond with my feelings. Hog 'em was the name originally given to this camp by the disgusted miners of surrounding camps. But our immaculate legislature last winter, who met at Lewiston, didn't like the sound of the thing so they christened the town Pioneer City. But Hog 'em is too appropriate a name. And in spite of acts of legislature, this town is better known all over the territory by its original name than by its legalized one. Our politicians may try their best, but people will call it Hog 'em and the people are not far from right.

For I must say, as a general thing, this is the most appropriate name for it. I never before lived in a town where there was so many "gentleman of Irish extraction", compared with the population of the same. And where the majority are of this class, one can imagine what society is. I am already sick of it and wish to get away but cannot as yet, on account of business. I never in all my life was so disgusted with a place as I am with this. Drunken, quarrelsome, fighting Irish fill the streets every night and Sunday is their carnival hurrah for Jeff Davis and "dom" the Yankee abolition Lincolnites, is heard on all sides after they have succeeded in getting their sins of the previous week pardoned by the Priest at church.

On the opposite page I have given a view of our store in Hog 'em and its surroundings. The characters in the street are pretty fair representations of the Milesian population that so strongly preponderates here. Whiskey, beef and flour is all they need and plenty of it. Especially the former article. The old rapscallion and his son in the foreground are regular customers for whiskey. The other three can be seen any day in our streets, either they or their counterparts.

7/4 - During last month I spent a week out on the Payette River trout fishing in company with three friends, all old Yrekans, and enjoyed the change much from the close confinement of store keeping in Hog 'em. The Payette lies some 2000 feet lower than this camp and is a very rapid stream at the point where we struck it, about 8 miles from here. It abounds with fish. And camping out under a big pine tree on the banks of the river and feasting on trout and whitefish right fresh from the river, was a luxury that I enjoyed hugely. We returned in time to see how our amiable Milesian fellow citizens celebrate this National Day, where they have as strong a hold as they have here in Hog 'em.

Not a national flag was to be seen in town. The only flag staff in town belongs to the Wells Fargo Company express office and their agent is a New York copperhead. He probably thinks the "butter is thicker in this locality of the copperhead slice of bread, than on the patriots". Consequently, he could not think of raising the ever-glorious stars and stripes today, for fear of offending his Milesian friends. Who by night (as usual) were all drunk and making right hideous by their howls and cheers for their favorite chief, Jeff Davis - Number 1.

8/1 - Hog 'em - These gold mines were first discovered (I believe) by a party of miners, prospectors who came into this valley from the Payette for what is now known as Grimes' Pass. When they came in here the whole country was full of hostile Indians and as they struck a fair prospect in the bed of the creek and banks, they concluded to stop. But to enable themselves to do so with safety to themselves, they were obliged to build a palisade fort. This was in the early fall of 1862. After fortifying themselves they started a party out for Warren's Diggings for provisions. And 4 miles above here on this creek, right at Grimes' Pass, Mr. Grimes was killed by an Indian. This creek and the pass through the mountains received its name from him.

On the opposite page is a view of this pioneer fort as it looked when I first came here last April. But as it is situated right over good diggings in the bed of the creek, it is fast disappearing. The timbers making excellent firewood, and by another season not a vestige of the old fort will be left, as undoubtedly the ground will all be worked out. Grimes is buried right on the divide, in the pass through the mountains called after him. He sacrificed his life in his restless desire to find new mines. But unlike many others whose names are not known, his has given names to localities here that will cause his to be remembered.

9/1 - Hog 'em - I copy from a paper the best description of these miserable Snake Indians I have seen. These Indians are queer people. They do not go a continental __ cent on houses, but are passionately fond of red ribbons and plug hats. They roost on the highest hills where their campfires are visible through the stilly night, reminding one of the signal fires which blaze up in times of blood and terror. We seldom hear

of a Snake dying of cold, although his shanks are most always bare. And his roof, even when it is cold enough to freeze the handle off a white man's face, is the broad canopy of Heaven.

He digs a hole in Mother Earth or crawls under a sagebrush and builds a small miserable fire in the hole or under the bush. And when the hole gets comfortably warm, takes a dozen or more half breed "pups" and papooses and flings them in promiscuously. Nor does he care which of the two species suffers the most pain. Who would be an "Injun"? And a miserable race they are to be sure, but they have been the cause of untold misery to poor immigrants in years past. Whole companies of emigrants have been massacred by them in Boise Valley in years passed. One in particular, which took place about 25 miles below where Boise City is now located, known as the Ward Massacre is too horrible in its details to relate particulars as given by a survivor.

10/1 - Business is dull and a miserable prospect ahead for winter. With the stock of goods we have on hand we are obliged to stay here through the winter, to take advantage of the rise in the spring of the year. Everyone that can are making arrangements to leave here for the lower country to winter and return in the spring. A great number of the miners have made from $4000 to $20,000 for their summer's mining operations. One party of Irish went by the store a few days since with a packhorse loaded with over 300 pounds of gold dust. They nearly all got drunk before they left town "of course".

11/1 - Snow and frost and bitter cold nights have already made their appearance. The first snow fell about the middle of last month and has been gradually accumulating ever since. Most of our "skedaddlers" have left and the saloons, public houses and many stores are closed up for the winter. Hog 'em is desolation and it reminds one of a graveyard or city of tombs, to walk up its deserted street. Where now is the music that used to be heard in every saloon? Where are the graceful hurdy girls that used to "dance all night till broad daylight"? And the echo answers, gone below.

12/1 - Awfully, awful cold weather. Thermometer either below zero, or a snowstorm. Pine wood disappears in our stove like ice cream in a California sun. Time has lost all value, we all have more of that body on hand then we know what to do with. And all hands here are willing to sell out their interest in the next four months and take the natural chances on their living through it. The next novelty of this kind that I try, will be a trip to the North Pole. For a man that can stand life in Hog 'em during winter has a free pass for any arctic region on this small globe.

Hog'em - January 1, 1865

On the next page I have endeavored to give some idea of the

miserable condition of the poor devils that are obliged, owing to sundry circumstances, to winter in this desolate place. A few poor, unfortunate "hombres" try to imagine themselves enjoying life by experimenting on Norwegian snowshoes to kill time. But when a man has to climb out of his chimney in a morning to shovel the snow away from his door, before customers (what few there is left) can get in and the thermometer down to 20° below zero. I think that nothing but an Eskimo could properly appreciate such fun.

2/1 - Hog 'em - Still buried in snow, the town looks dead as a deserted ruin. Time drags along very slowly, it is the most lonesome, tiresome and longest winter I ever experienced. I never wish to pass another winter here.

3/1 - Hog 'em - Snow 6 feet deep on a level, thermometer from 2° to 27° below zero in fact, every night that it does not snow. And no more prospect this morning of winter ever breaking up than there was last December. Over 4 1/2 months now since we have seen bare ground and a fair prospect of it being two months more with such weather.

Idaho City - 7/11

This morning I start for Idaho City on my way out of this infernal country, as poor as I entered it. With the pleasant thought that once more I have failed to realize my expectations of realizing money enough to enable me to join my friends at home. I have tried earnestly to win the prize, but it was not to be won. Trade in this country is overdone. We sell our goods at small profits and take our pay in gold dust at $16 per ounce, that is not actually worth $13. Still, we are obliged to do this or leave the country. And I prefer to take my chance somewhere else in this broad world than to live in this miserable hole and furnish provisions to such a miserable set of Irish secesh for nothing.

On the 18th of May last, Idaho City was almost entirely destroyed by fire and my partner and myself both thought that this would be a fine opportunity to close out our stock. Accordingly, he took the most of it over there and I remained at Hog 'em to collect outstanding accounts and to dispose of our house. The goods we sent over that I expected to dispose of for at least $6000, somehow only netted us about $2000. Lehman says they fell short and prices were very low, I could not see how it was. My eyes were somewhat opened when I found that he had gone into business over there with another man and our stock had been sold principally to this new firm of Lehman & Solero. Some might think that possibly this had some connection with the low prices of the goods brought.

I have a faint suspicion that my former partner of German extraction would steal if he saw a good opportunity ever since that time. However, the deed was done, there is no one here. And I came to the conclusion that this country is not very well adapted for a man that prefers to live an honest life, if possible. Accordingly, I sold the store building and lot that cost us over $1300 for $200 and started once more to try my fortune somewhere else. Poor as a church mouse, but out of debt and comparatively happy of that account. But with the unalterable determination never again to allow any Dutchman living to get the start of me in winding up any business affairs that I may be interested in. I don't know where I shall go to, nor what I shall do. Neither do I care much. I have not money enough to travel a great ways but I am going somewhere where I can make an honest living in a decent way if possible. Anywhere but here.

Placerville ~ Idaho Territory - 7/15

Left Idaho City on the 13th by stage and passing through Centerville reached Placerville in the afternoon and lay here waiting for the stage for the lower country until this morning. Centerville and Placerville are both as dead as Pioneer City and are dragging out a miserable short-lived existence. Property is worth little or nothing. The mines are worked out already and the buildings that caved in with snow last winter have been allowed to remain as they fell, a monument for the time of the owner's folly for investing his time and money in such a country. I leave here this morning.

Weather Record - Winter 1864/65 Pioneer City Idaho

DATE		INCHES OF SNOW	BELOW ZERO
Oct 27	Snow Fell	1	
Nov 4, 5 & 6	Snow Fell	5	
Nov 8	Snow Fell	3	
Nov 15	Snow Fell	3	
Nov 24	Snow Fell	2	
Nov 25	Snow Fell	4	
Nov 27	Snow Fell	5	
Nov 28	Snow Fell	5	
Dec 1-3	Snow Fell	2	
Dec 4	Snow Fell	14	
Dec 5	Snow Fell	10	
Dec 9-10-11-12-13	Snow Fell	12	
Dec 14-15	Snow Fell	2	
Dec 19	Below Zero at 6AM		11
Dec 20	Below Zero at 6AM		8
Dec 25	Snow Fell	26	
Jan 1	Snow Fell	1	

THE LOST GOLD RUSH JOURNALS

Jan 2	Snow Fell	1	
Jan 3 & 4	Snow Fell	2	
	Carried Up	98 Inches	

DATE		INCHES OF SNOW	BELOW ZERO
Jan 11	Below Zero at 8AM		12
Jan 12	Below Zero at 8AM		12
Jan 13	Below Zero at 8AM		12
Jan 14-15-16	Tolerably Warm	1	
Jan 17-18-19	Snowing	7	
Jan 20-21	Thawing		
Jan 22	Below Zero at 6AM		18
Jan 23	Below Zero at 6AM		24
Jan 24	Below Zero at 6AM		25
Jan 25	Below Zero at 6AM		27
Jan 26	Snowing	1	
Jan 27	Snowing	2	
Jan 28-29-30-31	Moderate		
Feb 1	Snowing	5	
Feb 2	Snowing	3	
Feb 3	Snowing	1/2	
Feb 3	Below Zero at 6AM		10
Feb 4	Below Zero at 6AM		18

Feb 5	Below Zero at 6AM		14
Feb 6	Below Zero at 6AM		11
Feb 7	Below Zero at 6AM		11
		20 1/2 Inches	

DATE		INCHES OF SNOW	BELOW ZERO
Feb 8	Below Zero at 6AM		3
Feb 9	Below Zero at 6AM		2
Feb 10	Below Zero at 6AM		3
Feb 11	Below Zero at 6AM		2
Feb 12	Snowing	2 1/2	
Feb 13	Moderate		
Feb 14	Snowing	8	
Feb 15	Snowing	12 1/2	
Feb 16	Snowing	1	
Feb 17	Snowing	3 1/2	
Feb 18	Snowing	2	
Feb 19	Moderate		
Feb 20	Snowing	1	
Feb 21	Snowing	1/2	
Feb 21	Below Zero at 6AM		10
Feb 22	Below Zero at 6AM		11

Feb 23	Below Zero at 6AM		14
Feb 24	Moderate & Snowing		
Feb 24	Snowing	1	
Feb 25	Below Zero at 6AM		11
Feb 26	Below Zero at 6AM		8
		32 Inches	

DATE		INCHES OF SNOW	BELOW ZERO
Feb 27	Snowing	21	
Feb 28	Snowing	4	
March 1	Below Zero at 6AM		8
March 2	Below Zero at 7AM		24
March 3	Below Zero at 6AM		9
March 3	Afterwards Snowed	4	
March 4	Snowed	21 1/2	
March 5	Snowed	14 1/2	
March 6	Snowed	7	
March 7	Snowed	2	
March 8	Below Zero at 7AM		22
March 9	Snowed	4	
March 10	Snowed	6 1/2	
March 11	Snowed	2	

March 12	Snowed	2	
March 13	Snowed	2	
March 14	Snowed	5 1/2	
March 15	Snowed	2	
March 16	Snowed	1	
March 17	Below Zero at Sunrise		7
		99 Inches	

DATE		INCHES OF SNOW	BELOW ZERO
March 18	Snowing	2	
March 19	Do	3 1/2	
March 20	Do	3 1/2	
March 21	Snow, Sleet & Thawing Weather		
March 22	A little rain		
March 23	Do _ _ _ Do _ _ _		
March 24	A little more snow	1/2	
March 25	Frost night & Warm day		
March 26	Do _ _ _ Do _ _ _		
March 27	Do _ _ _ Do _ _ _		
March 28	Do _ _ _ Do _ _ _		
March 29	Do _ _ _ Do _ _ _		
March 30	Do _ _ _ Do _ _ _		

March 31	Do _ _ _ Do _ _ _		
April 1	Do _ _ _ Do _ _ _		
April 2	Snowing	3 1/2	
April 3	Freezing nights, windy days		
April 4	Do _ _ _ Do _ _ _		
April 5	Do _ _ _ Do _ _ _		
April 6	Do _ _ _ Do _ _ _		
April 7	Below Zero at 6AM		4
		13 Inches	

April 8	Frosty, cold day		
April 9	_ _ Do _ _		
April 10	Freezing nights, warm days		
April 11	Freezing nights, warm days		
April 12	Freezing nights, warm days		
April 13	Snowed	3	
April 14	Wet, cloudy weather		
April 15	Rain, misty Do		
April 16	Snowed Wind NW	1/2	
April 17	Do	1	
April 18	Flurries of Snow		
April 19	Flurries of Snow		

June 16	Snowed all night		
	Number of Inches	4 1/2	
	Snow during season	22 ft 3 inches	

Thermometer was below Zero at times from 2 to 27 from Dec 19th to April 7th. Long term of cold weather. March 4th the settled snow lay 8 1/2 feet deep in town on a level.

Umatilla Landing - 7/18

Arrived here tonight. On the 15th we reached the Payette Ranch on the Payette River. At 2:00 AM getting aboard the stage we went on down the Payette Valley to the crossing near Snake River. Here we kept on down the Snake River Valley to the Weiser, crossed it and continuing on down the valley to Old's Ferry, we crossed the Snake and here the road leaves the river. From here on to Burnt River Station, where we stopped for the night. On the 17th started out again at 2:00 AM and crossing a hilly mountainous country, came to Powder River Valley for breakfast. From here on to Grand Honda Valley to dinner and from there to the top of the blue mountains, where we stopped for the night at a good house built in the heavy forests that covered this range of mountains.

On the 18th started on again and after traveling over a good road along the ridge of the mountain, came out about noon into the big barren looking valley of the Columbia and reached Umatilla about 3:00 PM. Umatilla is not a very lovely place to look at, situated as it is on a sandy treeless desert on the banks of the Columbia. But the town does a lively trade forwarding goods to the Idaho country. I found several old California friends here in business.

7/19 - Umatilla - Lay over here today waiting for a boat down the river.

Dallas - 7/20

Arrived here tonight. The sail down the Columbia today was very pleasant to me, as I have not seen a steamboat since February 1859. We sailed down the river until we came to the first rapids. Here there is a small town built for the accommodation of the river travel and here we take the cars for the Dallas. The Dallas is a very pretty town and seems more city-like than any place I've seen since I left Yreka. The buildings on the principal business street are well-built and the hotels are excellent. But businessmen feel rather blue at the prospect for some years to come, owing to the mines of Idaho having given out.

Portland Oregon - July 22, 1865

Arrived here last night. Met the Speaker Colfax party at the Cascades as we came down the river. Portland is a fine city. I like the appearance of the town very much, but I can't help wondering why it is that there is no town built up on the Columbia that would take the river trade away from here. For now, the ocean steamers come up the Columbia to the mouth of the Willamette and then up this last river to this city. All goods and travel then for the upper country, have to be reshipped on the river steamers and go back again down the Willamette to its mouth and then on up the Columbia, making 25- or 30-miles extra travel up and down the Willamette, for the Portlanders benefit.

THE END

Author's Note

This was the last entry Jenks made in his journals. In the reading, we can glean that he was disappointed by the fruits of his long labors to find wealth in the American Wilderness. We know Daniel died a bachelor on February 8, 1869 and was laid to rest in Pawtucket, though few other details about his life from that period are known. Jenks was survived by both parents.

"It is later than you think," wrote the poet/adventurer Robert Service. He too, had been drawn from a life of ease and security to the gold-rush-fueled boom towns and the harsh environs in which they sprang up. And likewise, Service discovered no cave or stream streaked with vast veins of gold. But the man's life is treasured still today because of the words he left behind, through the chronicle of life's struggles and joys he put to paper for posterity.

It's about the journey, as the saying goes, not the destination. How many of us go through life never straying beyond the borders we set for ourselves? If our Daniel Jenks had soon found the thing he claims to have been seeking (gold), would he have gone on to call those countless experiences and interactions his own? Perhaps not. It may be the man became all the richer for those extraordinary years he lived.

We are certainly the richer for them.

Larry Obermesik

Acknowledgements

Elizabeth J. Johnson - Pawtucket History Research Center

US Library of Congress
https://www.loc.gov

Jenks Journal images courtesy Pawtucket Public Library
https://www.pawtucketlibrary.org

History Colorado
https://www.historycolorado.org

Heritage Alliance of Pawtucket
www.heritagepawtucket.org

Siskiyou County Preservation Society & Museum
https://www.co.siskiyou.ca.us/museum

Pueblo County Historical Society
https://www.pueblohistory.org

Daniel Jenks portrait courtesy US Library of Congress

US Library of Congress: Journals of a Pioneer Argonaut, Daniel Jenks
https://www.loc.gov/rr/program/journey/jenks.html?loclr=blogpic

US Library of Congress: Daniel Jenks Collection
https://lccn.loc.gov/mm2012085772

Fountain Valley Historical Society
https://www.fountaincolorado.org/residents/about_fountain

Cover Artwork & Book Layout
http://www.iamkerrywatson.com/bookdesigns

Dedication

To Betty Johnson.
Without her tireless efforts to preserve the Jenks Journals
for posterity, this book could not have been written.

Annotation Notes

To improve its readability, the Jenks Journals were organized into topical sections. When Daniel changed topics, a new section was created. With few exceptions, if Jenks wrote a title for a section, it was used. When he didn't, titles were created using the text in the journal entry, or some variation on those words.

Years before the U.S. Library of Congress purchased Volumes 4 & 5 of the Jenks Journals, they bought 20 Gold Rush era drawings which they also attribute to Daniel Jenks. Those drawings were not in the Jenks Journals, they were drawn on a separate artist's sketch pad. Since the dates on the Library of Congress's Jenks Drawings are in-line with the Jenks Journals themselves, they have been included in this book at the appropriate location in the timeline.

The Jenks Drawings fall into 3 categories; drawings within the journals, drawings acquired separately, and drawings that remain unaccounted for. A comprehensive list of Daniel's drawings, and their origin, is outlined in this book's index.

Index

1

110 Mile Creek 400, 527

A

Abe Jobe 494, 496, 512
Acapulco, Mexico 335
Aches, Dr. 288
Alban, John 299
Albin, John 298
Allen, William 11
Althouse Mine 199, 205
Andrews, Asa 11
Andy Shoemaker 512
Ann Winkle 518
Arkansas River ... 411, 412, 414, 416, 417, 418, 419, 420, 421, 422, 423, 424, 426, 428, 430, 431, 434, 436, 527, 528, 529, 533
Arnold, Henry 11
Arnold, Obadiah 11
Ash Creek 414, 528
Ash Hollow 396
Atkinson, John 9
Atlantic Telegraph 362
Austin, Horace 8
Autobees, Charley 435
Averill, Miss Hannah 348
Averill, Mr. 348, 349
Azores Islands
    Faial 14, 16, 19, 20, 26
    Orto 15, 16
    Pico 13, 15

B

Babcock 156, 158, 167, 168, 169

Baker, Ebenezer 10
Baker, Ezra 10
Baker, Orrin 10
Balcolm, H.B. 370
Barker, Jack was from Holt's Bottom 236
Barque Velasco Crew
    1st Cook James Griffin 12
    1st Mate Tom Sayce of Providence 8
    1st Steward James Gerrybine .. 12
    2nd Cook Dwight Newport 12, 82
    2nd Mate Isaac Nickerson of Pawtucket 8
    2nd Steward James Micklejohn 12
    Captain Giles Spencer of East Greenwich 8
    Larboard Watch - Bliss 12
    Larboard Watch - Joyslin 12
    Larboard Watch - Patt 12
    Larboard Watch - Plunkett 12
    Starboard Watch - Dyer 11
    Starboard Watch - Hicks 11
    Starboard Watch - Leister 11
    Starboard Watch - Manchester 11
    Starboard Watch - Stetson 11
Barque Velasco Passengers
    Allen, William of Central Falls .. 11
    Andrews, Asa of Providence 11
    Arnold, Henry of Woonsocket . 11
    Arnold, Obadiah of Providence 11
    Atkinson, John of Providence 9
    Baker, Ebenezer of Pawtucket . 10
    Baker, Ezra of Pawtucket 10
    Baker, Orrin of Pawtucket 10

Baxter, Nathaniel of Pawtucket 11
Bonney, William of Pawtucket 11
Bowen, Harvey of Pawtucket 9
Brown, Elisha of Providence 8
Burgess, John of Central Falls .. 10
Burt, Leander of Providence 11
Cady, James of Gloucester, RI .. 11
Capron, Sanford of Lonsdale ... 11
Carter, Hiram of Pawtucket 10
Chase, William of Pawtucket 8
Cleveland, Henry of Pawtucket . 8
Cooke, Cyrus of Pawtucket 9
Cushman, Henry of Pawtucket 11
Dexter, Paul of Providence 9
Ellsbree, Shirley of Valley Falls... 9
Fales, Louis of Blackstone 10
Fish, Frederick of Providence .. 11
Fisher, Luther of Thompson, CT. 9
Fletcher, Abraham of Providence 9
Graham, Samuel of Pawtucket 11
Hathaway, William of Pawtucket 11
Horton, John of Pawtucket. 9, 54, 66, 74, 78
Humes, George of Blackstone . 10
Ide, Herbert of Attleborough 9
Jenks, Daniel of Pawtucket ... 2, 8, 324
Jenks, Nelson of Smithfield 9
Johnson, William of Pawtucket . 8
Kelly, William of Blackstone 9
Lambert, Jonathan of Providence 10
Leonard, Samuel of Central Falls 8
Maxey, Levi of Providence 9
McCarty, James of Central Falls 11
McCormick, Thomas of Pawtucket 10
Messinger, Alfred of Providence 10
Moury, Spencer of Pawtucket . 10
Mowry, Winsor of Woonsocket. 9
Murry, George of Providence .. 10
Nurse, Lucius of Lonsdale 8
Page, James of Providence 10
Parsons, William of Fairfax, VT 11, 16
Perrin, Orrin of Thompson, CT ... 8
Perry, Davis of Pawtucket 10
Perry, Hiram of Pawtucket 10
Pierce, Francis of Rehobeth 10
Pierce, Silas of Pawtucket 10
Randall, Charles of Providence 11
Read, John of Providence 8
Read, Leonard of Pawtucket 9
Read, Tom of Central Falls 9
Rett, Francis of Blackstone 9
Reynolds, Allen of Pawtucket 9
Reynolds, Jeremiah of Providence 8
Richardson, Charles of Pawtucket 9
Saunders, Thomas of Pawtucket 9
Sayles, George of Blackstone ... 10
Sears, Abraham of Pawtucket ... 8
Shephard, William of Providence 9
Shephardson, Nathaniel of Hopkinton, RI 9
Skinner, Christopher of Attleborough 11
Smith, Benjamin of Johnston ... 10
Smith, James of Pawtucket 10, 31, 53
Taylor, Allen of Olneyville 9
Templeton, John of Pawtucket 10, 54, 66
Whipple, Welcome of Cumberland 10, 74
Williams, Henry of Providence .. 8
Winn, Freeman of Pawtucket 9
Young, John of Pawtucket .. 9, 54, 66, 74, 78, 365, 369, 377
Bass, Tom 512
Baxter, Nathaniel 11

Beach, Horace 363
Beaufort, James 277, 278
Beaver, George 494
Ben Rogers 168, 169
Ben Wright 256
Benedict, Ellen 342
Benedict, Mrs. 255
Benedict, Steven 367
Benicia 332
Big Oak Flat 90, 91, 108
Bigler, John 243
Billy McCormick 494
Billy Reed 394, 449
Bird, Lee 591
Bitter Creek 461, 462, 463, 464
Black Butte 425
Black Hills 449
Black Jack Battlefield 399
Black Legs 125, 126
Blockhouse 265
Bloody Point 298
Blue Devils 311, 313
Bob Cornthwaite 442
Bob Whittle 543, 544, 551
Boles, Mr. 319
Boling, Mr. 137
Boney 432
Bonney, William 11
border ruffian 393, 397, 494, 511
Boston 3, 4, 5, 17, 18, 23, 25, 39, 53, 121, 155, 219, 244, 339, 368, 370, 520
Bowen, Harvey 9
Bowie knife 90, 138, 145
Brannan, Sam 141
Brown, Elisha 8
Brown, John - Abolitionist . 399, 494, 511
Bruin, Mrs. 103, 134
Buchanan, President James 362
Buckeyes 314
Bucklin, Elisha 8
Buffalo
    chips 407, 419

skins 412
Burgess, John 10
Burlingame 402, 527
Burt, Leander 11
Butchers 179
Butte Creek .358, 361, 545, 548, 549
Byzer, Mr. 310

C

Cache La Poudre Creek445, 447, 529
Cady, James 11
California Ballot Box Stuffers
    Duane 287
    Mulligan 287
    Yankee Sullivan 281, 286, 287
California riots 293, 297
Calumet 387
Canton 333
Cape Horn ..3, 13, 27, 28, 30, 32, 33, 34, 47, 56, 67, 312, 421, 564
Capron, Sanford 11
Captain George's Troops KIA
    Collins 266
    Kennedy 266
    McCarten 266
    Olney 266
Captains
    Capt. Baker 374
    Capt. Buchanan 283
    Capt. George 139, 263, 266
    Capt. Goodell 220
    Capt. Hayes 264
    Capt. Jordan 299
    Capt. Judah 277, 358
    Capt. Kilcorn 266
    Capt. Martin 268, 298
    Capt. O'Neil 262
    Capt. Smith 257, 278, 282, 294
    Capt. Snow 139, 140, 142
Carter, Hiram 10
Cascades on the Columbia 266
Casey and Cora 281, 287
Casey, James 286
Cash, Dan 549, 550

Cassius Clay 186
Cato, Judge 393
Chace, Nelson................................. 8
Chalk Springs 565, 568
Charles Edes 196
Charley Autobees 435
Charlie Upham.................... 395, 396
Charlie, Sinister 145
Chase, William................................ 8
Chavis Creek sic Jarvis Creek 408
Cherokee 132, 299, 453, 591
Cherokee Pass 453
Cherry Creek...... 167, 399, 440, 442, 443, 528
Chilean Camp 85, 108
Chili
    Concepcion City 42
    Talcahuana 38
Chinaman 242, 283, 284
Chinese 30, 73, 74, 77, 78, 79, 82, 84, 85, 99, 108, 110, 112, 138, 142, 242, 243, 244, 269, 280, 291, 292, 333
Chinese Camp.73, 74, 77, 78, 79, 82, 84, 85, 99, 108, 110, 112, 138, 142
Chinook 520
Chuck-a-Luck 389
Clark Ranch................................. 209
Clark, Dan 209
Clay, Cassius 186
Clay, George 196, 211
Cleveland, Henry 8
Cold Spring Camp 425
Cold Springs House..... 199, 200, 214
Colfax, Speaker........................... 633
Collar, William 348
Colonels
    Col. Bent 434, 435
    Col. Buchanan 294
    Col. Milton McGee................. 393
    Col. Wright..................... 282, 289
Colton, Dave 322
Connecticut 347, 348

Constable 297
Cook, Frank................................. 138
Cooke, Cyrus.................................. 9
Cooper......................... 16, 120, 250
Cornthwaite, Bob 442
Cosby, Senator 322
Council Grove 403, 404, 527, 529
Cow Creek 263, 411, 527
coyotes 75, 309, 423, 437
Crabb, Mr. H. 327
Crescent City 196, 202, 203, 204, 209, 223, 256, 266, 373
Crescent Valley........................... 204
cribbage.............................. 124, 311
Crimea 482
Crown Rogers Company Express 174
Curry, Governor.......................... 267
Cushman, Henry 11

D

Dallas 299, 633
Dame Fortune 316
Dame Nature 21, 149, 312, 441
Dan Cash..................................... 549, 550
Dan Clark 209
Dan Keedwell..................... 395, 397
Dan Tesh..................................... 575
Daniel Jenks 1, 3, 148, 303, 312, 346, 362, 385, 415, 437, 538, 541, 635, 636, 637, 639
Dave Colton 322
Davis, Jefferson . 308, 613, 615, 616, 617
Davy Jones' Locker 337
Deacon G.J. Jenks 341
Denver 286, 440, 443, 445, 466, 528, 529, 531
Depot Master 370
depredations 184, 254, 262
deprivations 310
Deputy Sheriff Millhouse............ 290
desert 411, 416, 417, 419, 421, 436, 438, 439, 462, 464, 465, 479, 499, 505, 506, 507, 508, 509,

529, 534, 564, 565, 567, 568, 581, 584, 593, 632
desperados......... 116, 288, 397, 479
Dexter Brothers Explosion 363
Dexter, Paul.................................... 9
Diego Ramirez Island..................... 30
Digger Indians 315, 343
Doc Franklin 575, 595
Dog Creek House......................... 330
Don Neptune............................... 334
Dos Amigos Hard Ship 56
Douthitt, Isaiah G 341
Douthitt, J.G. 346, 347, 353
Dr. Aches 288
Dr. Kane....................................... 315
Dr. Randall.................................. 297
Dragoons 139, 402, 472, 527
Drawings In Journals
   1852 - Charlie's Restaurant, Marysville 151
   1852 - Digger Indian Camp 149
   1852 - Fouch's Hacienda, Long Gulch.................................. 171
   1852 - Johnson's Ranch 167
   1852 - Leonard's House, Yreka 170
   1852 - My Log Cabin Home ... 153
   1852 - Shasta Butte 156
   1853 - Babcock & Jenks, Yreka 180
   1853 - Cold Springs House..... 201
   1853 - Crescent City 194
   1853 - Saved by an Englishman 183
   1853 - Winter Cabin 178
   1854 - Long Gulch Cabin, Yreka 229
   1854 - Shasta & Volcano Butte Shasta Valley..................... 233
   1856 - Barque Velasco off Faial, Azores 301
   1857 - Shasta Butte 303
   1863 - Grass Lake Valley 528, 529
   1863 - Harney Lake Valley 583
   1863 - Silver Lake................... 563
   1864 - Bob Marquis' Stage House 598
   1864 - Fort Hog 'em from Pioneer City 618
   1864 - Walt Lawrence's Junction House................................. 610
   1865 - Winter Life in Hog 'em 621
Drawings Separate
   1859 - Bent's Fort 428
   1859 - Cache la Poudre Creek 448
   1859 - Camp 100 Humbolt River 492
   1859 - Camp 23d Arkansas River 420
   1859 - Camp 90 De Casure Creek 486
   1859 - Chavis Creek Camp 14th 410
   1859 - Cherokee Pass Rocky Mountains 454
   1859 - Cottonwood Creek Sunday April 10th 1859 406
   1859 - Independence Camp .. 439
   1859 - Mountain Camp Sierra Nevada.............................. 516
   1859 - North Platte................ 456
   1859 - Pretty Camp Rocky Mountains 434
   1859 - Shasta Valley from Long Gulch Mountain................ 538
   1859 - Sunday April 3d 1859 . 401
   1859 - The Dessert................. 418
   1859 - Yreka from Long Gulch Mountain 539
Drawings Unaccounted for
   1859 - A View of Yreka 373
   1859 - Acapulco Mexico 373
   1859 - Lagoon Crescent City .. 373
   1859 - Mouth of Fall River 373
   1859 - Pawtucket from our chamber windows 373
   1859 - San Buenaventura Valley 373

1859 - San Luis Harbor............ 373
1859 - Sierra Nevadas............. 373
1859 - Warner's Pass 373
Dugan, Ross 512

E

E. Clampus Vitus 289
Echo Canyon 470
Edes, Charles 196
Edgar Potter 328
Eldridge House 390
election... 53, 75, 282, 307, 308, 322
Elizabeth Jenks .. 391, 395, 397, 398, 402, 403, 408, 409, 412, 422, 435, 437, 438
Elk Camp House 214, 215
Ellen Benedict.............................. 342
Ellsbree, Shirley 9
Emigrant Road 595
Emigrant Trail 573
England...... 111, 130, 155, 292, 297, 301, 344, 362, 397, 403
Englishman . 114, 127, 137, 182, 397
Enis Hodgson 494
Evans Ferry 359
expedition ... 22, 125, 169, 307, 327, 396, 439, 529, 545, 579, 593
Express of Rhodes and Company 258

F

Fairbrother, Sally 371
Fales, Louis 10
Fall River 337, 373, 521
Ferry 75, 87, 137, 319, 359, 594, 595, 632
Ferryman 173
Field, Mr. Cyrus 362
filibuster 307
fire 5, 74, 75, 76, 81, 94, 96, 152, 170, 187, 188, 191, 195, 196, 199, 203, 205, 206, 208, 214, 217, 218, 227, 234, 239, 254, 263, 266, 267, 271, 272, 277, 292, 298, 310, 311, 312, 314, 315, 325, 332, 360, 363, 367, 398, 399, 400, 401, 402, 404, 405, 407, 408, 409, 412, 413, 414, 417, 418, 424, 425, 432, 446, 453, 461, 482, 483, 498, 501, 515, 553, 561, 565, 567, 571, 572, 573, 574, 575, 581, 582, 589, 592, 593, 601, 603, 606, 618, 619, 623
Fish, Frederick 11
Fisher, Luther 9
Fletcher, Abraham.......................... 9
flood 151, 152, 316, 351, 429
Ford, Pat 168
Forts
  Fort Atkinson 419
  Fort Boise............... 573, 595, 609
  Fort Bridger.... 445, 456, 465, 468
  Fort Crooks 519, 521
  Fort Jones 277
  Fort Lane 222, 275, 276, 278, 282, 358
  Fort Laramie 396, 445, 483
Fountain City 436
Fountain Creek .. 418, 430, 436, 438, 529
Frank Cook.................................. 138
Frank Rogers............................... 321
Franklin, Doc...................... 575, 595
Free State 393, 394, 494, 495
free trade 340, 341
Frenchman 57
frog pond.................. 407, 411, 461
Frontiersman.............................. 166
funeral 32, 116, 140, 188, 318

G

Gamblers 65, 117, 127, 286
General Cosby 298
General Wool 254, 264, 273, 277, 288, 299
George Beaver............................. 494
George Clay 196, 211
George McDougal...................... 437

George Myers 544, 546
George Peters 322
Georgia 451, 455, 457, 464, 493, 495, 512
Gerrybine, James 12
God 3, 15, 18, 64, 67, 78, 80, 96, 105, 111, 115, 128, 158, 182, 253, 261, 267, 273, 295, 299, 300, 308, 324, 338, 352, 362, 369, 376, 378, 380, 381, 382, 383, 384, 386, 407, 443, 472, 476, 482, 514, 525, 565, 586, 587
gold .. 1, 3, 34, 39, 44, 50, 51, 62, 66, 74, 77, 79, 82, 86, 97, 98, 106, 107, 108, 110, 112, 121, 125, 126, 128, 140, 161, 194, 203, 222, 223, 225, 231, 238, 262, 356, 362, 369, 381, 389, 391, 392, 394, 424, 436, 441, 442, 452, 543, 599, 617, 619, 622, 635
Gold Mining
    claim 78, 80, 88, 103, 109, 110, 112, 118, 130, 131, 132, 136, 223, 226, 228, 229, 230, 232, 233, 237, 242, 249, 255, 295, 297, 301, 316, 317, 325, 326, 327, 328, 329, 341, 350, 351, 536, 543
    drifting . 4, 16, 36, 56, 62, 63, 152, 208, 244, 246, 248, 249, 253, 295, 300, 301, 307, 311, 316, 317, 418, 421
    prospecting 34, 54, 63, 86, 92, 97, 167, 168, 173, 180, 251, 262, 315, 339, 345, 353, 365, 369, 374, 411, 442, 536, 560, 565, 580, 588, 594, 603, 611, 617, 619, 622, 633
    sluice 223, 225, 316, 317, 323, 324, 325, 326, 329, 351
Golden Era 271
Government 249, 256, 264, 275, 276, 278, 289, 342, 469, 471, 478, 480, 482
Governor 116, 267, 282, 287, 288, 294, 437
Governor Curry 267
Governor Johnson 282, 288
Governor McDougal 437
Graham, Samuel 11
greasers 242, 327
Green River . 462, 464, 465, 466, 470
Green, Major 549, 564, 585
Green, Mr. Verdant 344
Greenhorn 396
Griffin, James 12
Grizzlies 76, 81, 82, 83, 84, 103, 133, 135, 138, 314
guide 4, 185, 445, 525, 544, 574

H

H.B. Balcolm 370
Haines, Mrs. 255
Hall, Mr. 390
hallooing . 90, 95, 215, 218, 396, 404, 416
Hamilton, Sam 334
hanging ... 31, 40, 113, 158, 173, 202, 293, 498
Hardscrabble Creek 201, 202
Hardscrabble Mountain 210
Harney Lake Valley 570, 577
Harris, Mr. 250, 360, 375
Harris, Mrs. 250, 360
Harry Lockhart 319
Hathaway, William is now immortalized 191
Hathaway, William of Pawtucket . 11
Hawkeyes 314
Henry C. Reed 370
Hickman 258
Hickory Point 399
High Street 371
Highwaymen 116, 268, 301, 482
Hiram Woods 186
Hodgson, Enis 494
Hodgson, Jonathan 494

646

Hog 'em 615, 616, 617, 619, 620, 621, 622, 623
homesickness 375
Hoosiers 314, 388
Hopkins 289
Horace Beach 363
Horace Greeley... 275, 276, 277, 321
Horton, John 9, 54, 66, 74, 78
Howard Paris 493
Humboldt Creek 112, 357
Humboldt River . 492, 493, 495, 496, 497, 498, 499, 500, 501, 503, 532
humbug 50, 362, 391, 431, 436, 443
Humbug Creek 86, 88, 108
Humbug Klamath Volunteers 358
Humes, George 10
hung ...23, 66, 68, 89, 108, 113, 126, 132, 140, 141, 142, 277, 281, 287, 297, 299, 415, 459
hunger 58, 111, 179, 182, 224
Hutchings California 518

I

Idaho . 541, 543, 607, 608, 613, 615, 622, 623, 624, 626, 633
Ide, Herbert 9
Illinois Central Road 387
Illinois River 198, 199, 216, 218, 263
Ince, Miss 334
Independence Camp 1, 438, 528
Indian 58, 83, 92, 93, 95, 96, 98, 120, 132, 158, 159, 160, 161, 162, 166, 169, 184, 185, 187, 189, 190, 204, 217, 218, 219, 220, 243, 248, 250, 251, 252, 253, 255, 258, 263, 265, 268, 269, 275, 276, 277, 278, 279, 282, 283, 294, 298, 315, 320, 358, 360, 415, 419, 434, 435, 436, 483, 484, 489, 492, 518, 520, 521, 534, 554, 557, 564, 568, 572, 574, 575, 576, 577, 578, 580, 581, 582, 584, 587, 591, 592, 617

agent 294
buck 187, 188, 190, 217, 277, 314, 397, 592
burial 219
Chief 90, 91, 92, 218, 219, 276, 320, 357, 358, 361, 415, 429, 436, 551, 562
country ... 95, 162, 166, 217, 250, 251, 279, 315, 518, 582
Great Spirit 188
massacres 415
Medicine Woman 187
red skins 120, 168, 170, 184, 185, 190, 199, 204, 217, 218, 251, 254, 258, 264, 266, 268, 269, 275, 283, 292, 293, 301, 321, 359, 419, 488, 519, 533, 534, 537, 592
reservation ... 248, 249, 276, 278, 357, 358
retrial 204
squaws.. 187, 188, 235, 243, 244, 252, 274, 275, 314, 320, 429, 467
war 189, 253, 258, 269
Indian Chiefs
Chief Cyprianna 91, 92
Chief Jacks 551
Chief Lalakes 320
Chief Little Mountain 415
Chief Lou Terior 90
Chief Ten Bears 429
Chief Typsee 276
Our Indian Chief 218, 219
Indian Tribes
Arapaho 435
Blackfeet 255
Cheyenne 435
Comanche 413, 424, 427, 537
Coos Bay 265
Coquille 264, 265
Deschutes 299
DeShute 299
Kiowas 404, 415

Klamath Lake 551, 554
Modoc 191, 293
Pit River 189, 518
Rogue River Valley................ 183
Shasta 187, 189, 190, 191
Shoshone....................... 490, 534
Snake River 467, 554, 561, 617
Tyhee John's band 294, 295
Irish 278, 343, 387, 393, 475, 483, 613, 615, 619, 623
Isaiah G. Douthitt 341

J

J.G. Douthitt 346, 347, 353
Jack Barker was from Holt's Bottom 236
Jacksonville.79, 88, 89, 98, 100, 102, 105, 109, 110, 111, 122, 123, 127, 128, 131, 132, 136, 179, 198, 205, 220
jail157, 270, 280, 281, 286
James Beaufort................... 277, 278
James Casey 286
James King................................. 280
James Richards 333
jargon 36, 189, 243
Jefferson Davis .. 308, 613, 615, 616, 617
Jenks, Daniel.......1, 2, 3, 8, 148, 303, 312, 324, 346, 362, 384, 385, 415, 437, 538, 541, 635, 636, 637, 639
Jenks, Deacon G.J. 341
Jenks, Elizabeth . 391, 395, 397, 398, 402, 403, 408, 409, 412, 422, 435, 437, 438
Jenks, Judson J... 395, 404, 412, 416, 419, 422, 426, 427, 428, 436
Jenks, Loren S. ... 368, 392, 395, 396, 398, 404, 412, 422, 427, 429, 430, 436, 437, 438
Jenks, Nelson................................. 9
Jew 216, 218

Jim Savage's Camp aka Garrote .. 88, 90, 97, 98, 101, 107, 108
Joaquin 68, 69, 97, 243
Jobe, Abe................... 494, 496, 512
John Alban................................. 299
John Albin................................. 298
John Bigler................................ 243
John Brown - Abolitionist.. 399, 494, 511
John Bull.....108, 242, 410, 438, 455, 475, 487
John L. Stevens........................... 334
John McDougal........................... 116
John McGill................................. 196
John Phoenix 356
John Roton 494
John Wesley Prowers 412, 434
Johnson, Governor 282, 288
Johnson, William 8
Jonathan Hodgson...................... 494
Jones, Old.................................. 557
Judges
    Judge Cato 393
    Judge Lynch 89, 115, 116, 117, 158
    Judge Peters 322
    Judge Robinson 322
    Judge Terry ... 284, 288, 289, 297, 300
Judson J. Jenks .. 395, 404, 412, 416, 419, 422, 426, 427, 428, 436
Junction House ... 596, 597, 609, 611
jurors 89, 131, 256, 321

K

Kanaka Creek.............. 122, 129, 136
Kane, Dr...................................... 315
Kansas 289, 346, 368, 369, 388, 390, 391, 392, 393, 394, 397, 399, 403, 427, 493, 494, 495, 501, 510, 511, 512, 527, 531
Kansas Territory 346, 527
Keedwell, Dan 395, 397
Kelly, William................................. 9

Kentuck 113, 311
kidney disease 325
King, James 280
King, Nelson 494, 499, 511
Klamath Lake 320, 549, 551, 554
Klamath River 196, 205, 276, 357

L

Lafayette House 247
Lambert, Jonathan 10
Laramie Peak 452
Laramie River 450, 451, 452
Lawton, Mrs. Charlie 345
Leavenworth 390, 423
Lee Bird 591
Lehman, Robert 544
Leonard, Samuel 8
levee 74, 388, 389, 390, 393, 394
Lewis, S.R. 299
Library Hall 389
Lieutenant Warman 298
Little Arkansas Creek 407, 527
Lockhart, Harry 319
loneliness 54, 309
Long Gulch. 176, 223, 226, 237, 239, 273, 300, 301, 341, 519, 536, 537, 538, 543
Loren S. Jenks 368, 392, 395, 396, 398, 404, 412, 422, 427, 429, 430, 436, 437, 438
Los Angeles 297
Lune, William 8
Lupton, May 359
Lynch, Judge . 89, 115, 116, 117, 158

M

Major Green 549, 564, 585
Maloney 288
Man of War 57, 63, 65, 336, 346
Manzanilla, Panama 334
Marshal of the Vigilants 288
Marshal Richardson 281
Mary McDonald 375

Marysville .. 148, 150, 153, 156, 157, 158, 171, 172, 177, 268, 270, 331
Massachusetts 341, 351, 363
Maxey, Levi 9
May Lupton 359
Mayberry, Mr. 350
McCarty, James 11
McCormick, Billy 494
McCormick, Thomas 10
McDonald, Mary 375
McDougal, George 437
McDougal, Governor 437
McDougal, John 116
McGee, Milton 393
McGill, John 196
McGuries 333
merchants . 105, 119, 151, 171, 234, 240, 245, 285, 287, 295, 321, 323, 444, 535, 543
Merry Christmas 308, 309
Mesdames
    Mrs. Benedict 255
    Mrs. Bruin 103, 134
    Mrs. Haines 255
    Mrs. Harris 250, 360
    Mrs. Lawton 345
    Mrs. Wagoner 255, 359
Messinger, Alfred 10
Messrs
    Mr. Averill 348, 349
    Mr. Boles 319
    Mr. Boling 137
    Mr. Byzer 310
    Mr. Cyrus Field 362
    Mr. Frank Young 174
    Mr. H. Crabb 327
    Mr. Hall 390
    Mr. Harris 250, 360, 375
    Mr. Mayberry 350
    Mr. Peters 357
    Mr. Potter 241
    Mr. Shaffner 437
    Mr. Sharp 349
    Mr. Tirgin 140

Mr. Verdant Green 344
Mr. Wagoner 250, 359, 360
Mr. Wilson 437
Metropolitan Theater 334
Mexican..56, 58, 68, 89, 95, 98, 106, 107, 108, 125, 142, 160, 196, 211, 215, 322, 333, 436, 437, 607
Mexico..57, 106, 107, 307, 327, 335, 373, 415
Michigan 368, 387
Michigan City, Indiana 387
Micklejohn, James 12
Miles Moies 388
militia 287
Millhouse, Deputy Sheriff 290
Miners 268, 291
Misses
    Miss Hannah Averill 348
    Miss Ince 334
    Miss Sarah Pellet 359
Mississippi 117, 342
Missouri, Missouri River 388, 396
Missourians 226, 289, 511
Mister Oily 344
Modoc country 298
Moies, Miles 388
Monte Dealer 286
Mormons....340, 467, 469, 470, 471, 472, 473, 474, 480, 482, 483, 489
Mother Earth.....13, 35, 60, 301, 409, 524, 619
Mountain House 164, 275, 523
Mountaineer 395, 446, 466, 543
Moury, Spencer 10
Mowry, Winsor 9
mule road 201
mule train 196, 207
murder 68, 84, 99, 107, 113, 114, 115, 117, 120, 125, 132, 139, 142, 211, 218, 270, 274, 275, 276, 280, 281, 285, 286, 297, 320, 321, 359, 360, 435
Murry, George 10
Myers, George 544, 546

N

Narragansett Mining and Trading Company 3
Director Horace Austin of Central Falls 8
Director Leonard Walker of Sesconk 8
Director Nelson Chace of Providence 8
Director Robert Taft of East Greenwich 8
President William Roberts of South Scituate 8
Secretary William Lune of Pawtucket 8
Treasurer Elisha Bucklin of Pawtucket 8
Vice President Laban Wade of Woonsocket 8
Nelson King 494, 499, 511
Nevada 298, 514, 517, 529, 533, 534
New England 111, 130, 292, 297, 301, 344
New Mexico 415
New Year 79, 111, 223, 239, 307, 308, 309, 537
New York..39, 44, 51, 64, 67, 68, 69, 77, 137, 168, 273, 321, 334, 336, 337, 341, 342, 386, 387, 477, 482, 616
New York Tribune............... 273, 321
Newport, Dwight.................... 12, 82
Niagara Falls 387
Nickerson, Isaac 8
Nigel, my best friend 254, 295
North Platte453, 454, 456, 464, 512, 530
Northern California 357, 551
Norwegian 310, 622
Nurse, Lucius 8

O

Ohio... 186, 399, 406, 421, 430, 435, 438, 442, 445, 451, 475, 493
Old Bill 371
Old Boreas 6, 410
Old Jones, the Santa Fe Ox Driver 557
Oldham, Tim 568
Oregon 156, 158, 176, 196, 197, 198, 238, 248, 249, 251, 253, 254, 255, 257, 258, 262, 264, 265, 266, 269, 273, 278, 283, 289, 293, 294, 299, 301, 356, 357, 490, 491, 493, 511, 522, 525, 543, 595, 613, 633
Oroville 331
ox team 232, 236, 397, 416, 428, 435, 444, 446, 488, 515, 523, 533

P

Pacific Coast 307, 331, 333
Packers 72, 174, 197, 214, 222, 265, 293, 359, 464, 488, 517, 553, 607, 611
Page, James 10
Palmer, Cook and Company 284
Panama 57, 334, 335, 336
Paris, Howard 493
Parson Stratton 322
Parsons, William 11, 16
Pat Ford 168
Pawnee Fork 414, 415, 416, 418, 419, 423, 424, 528
Pawnee Rock 414
Pawtucket 3, 8, 9, 10, 11, 31, 32, 174, 209, 237, 334, 338, 341, 342, 347, 352, 353, 355, 363, 366, 371, 373, 381, 382, 384, 385, 386, 430, 444, 526, 537, 612, 635, 636
Pellet, Miss Sarah 359
Perote 186
Perrin, Orrin 8
Perry, Davis 10
Perry, Hiram 10
Peters, George 322
Peters, Judge 322
Peters, Mr. 357
Phoenix, John 356
Pierce, Francis 10
Pierce, Silas 10
Pine Grove 457
Pit River 189, 319, 320, 321, 518, 519, 520, 521, 532
Placerville .. 298, 488, 493, 611, 612, 624
plains ... 45, 146, 232, 236, 396, 419, 436, 438, 484, 485, 489, 493, 503, 504, 518, 523, 524, 534, 537, 539, 554, 557, 580, 599
Planters House 388
Platte Valley 453, 456, 457, 465
Plum Butte 411, 527
plunder 220, 243, 419, 429, 479, 577, 578, 593
Pocahontas 322
politicians 285, 301, 615
politics 308, 343
Port Orford 256, 265, 277, 294
Portland, Oregon 265, 266, 374, 633
posse 290, 480
Post Office 89, 372, 395
Potter, Edgar 328
Potter, Mr. 241
prairie 281, 329, 387, 399, 400, 403, 404, 406, 407, 408, 412, 413, 414, 418, 419, 420, 429, 437, 440, 446, 447, 499, 529, 603
President James Buchanan 362
prisoner 115, 141, 157, 186, 255, 267, 290, 293, 357, 519
proslavery 393, 399
prostitutes 291, 292
Providence Journal 342
Providence Pike 347
Pueblo, Colorado 429, 436, 437, 438, 636

Puritans 354

Q

Queen Victoria 362
quick sands 419
quien sabe 99, 103, 368, 374, 576

R

R. Woodward 332
rancheria 298
Randall, Charles 11
Randall, Dr. 297
rattlesnake 413, 521
Read, John 8
Read, Leonard 9
Read, Tom 9
red devils 90, 185, 218, 249, 254,
    257, 263, 264, 265, 266, 319,
    416, 488, 489, 518
Redding Springs 161
Redwoods 203
Reed, Billy 394, 449
Reed, Henry C. 370
Rett, Francis 9
revolver 113, 127, 145, 223, 250,
    290, 360
Reynolds, Allen 9
Reynolds, Jeremiah 8
Rhode Island. 69, 109, 112, 332, 341,
    473, 612
Richards, James R. 333
Richardson, Charles 9
Richardson, Marshal 281
roadhouse 75, 166, 174, 523
robbers 224, 258, 270, 285, 286,
    479, 481
Robert Lehman 544
Roberts, William 8
Robinson, Judge 322
Rock Creek 400
Rocky Mountains 380, 383, 389, 395,
    404, 429, 437, 446, 453, 458,
    484, 513
Rogers, Ben 168, 169

Rogers, Frank 321
Rogers, Z. 319
Rogue River
    Indians 357
    massacre 256
    reservation 276
    valley 169, 170, 183, 185, 248,
        249, 251, 257, 262, 265, 358
    war 273, 299
rogues 66, 82, 143, 281
Ross Dugan 512
Roton, John 494
Rough and Ready 199
Ruis 297
Russellville 441

S

S. J. Mail Company 415
S.R. Lewis 299
Sacramento
    city 161, 172, 331, 493
    river . 68, 159, 160, 162, 173, 330,
        332
    street 282, 284, 333
    valley 146, 151, 159, 190, 205
Sailor Diggings 199, 205, 265
Sally Fairbrother 371
Salmon River Mountains 168
Salt Lake City 443, 456, 469, 470,
    473, 476, 481, 483, 486
Sam Brannan 141
Sam Hamilton 334
San Bruno House 334
San Buenaventura Valley 373
San Francisco .. 44, 52, 62, 65, 68, 71,
    78, 140, 143, 144, 147, 258, 284,
    297, 317, 332, 333, 334, 375, 482
San Francisco Bulletin 375
San Francisco's Long Wharf 140
San Jose Road 334
Santa Fe 404, 414, 419
    mail 399
    road 395, 421, 527, 528
    trail 403, 427

Saunders, Thomas 9
savages 188, 249, 266, 283, 292, 320, 358, 360, 380, 484, 489
Sayce, Tom 8
Sayles, George 10
scalps 83, 177, 189, 264, 424
Scotchman 86, 270
Sears, Abraham 8
seasick 5, 7, 45, 61, 313, 334
Seattle 255
Seekonk 371
Senator Cosby 322
Shaffner, Mr. 437
Shanghai 282, 333, 512
Sharp, Mr. 349
Shasta
    butte 156, 161, 189, 285, 330, 521, 523
    city 161, 162, 163, 171, 174, 330, 331
    river 189, 222, 245, 251, 524
    road 186, 518
    valley..... 196, 222, 264, 283, 491, 515, 522, 523, 546
Shawnee Mission Church 397
Shawnee Springs 395
Shephard, William 9
Shephardson, Nathaniel 9
Sheriff 126, 131, 281, 286, 290, 291, 292, 293, 322, 480, 515
Shoemaker, Andy 512
shore ballast 334
Shylock 322
sick.. 5, 7, 13, 31, 59, 67, 78, 91, 156, 170, 181, 182, 187, 188, 193, 226, 227, 271, 272, 273, 276, 292, 314, 320, 325, 354, 422, 428, 461, 476, 518, 615
Sierra Nevadas........................... 97
Silver Lake................... 554, 560, 561
Sinister Charlie 145
Siskiyou...... 197, 222, 235, 248, 276, 293, 358, 525, 543, 589, 636

Siskiyou Mountain 197, 248, 276, 293, 358
sketches................................... 372
Skinner, Christopher.................... 11
slap jacks 312, 405
Slatersville 363, 364
slave state 308
slavery 75, 308, 329, 394, 455
Smith, Benjamin 10
Smith, James 10, 31, 53
Smoky Hill Fork Road................ 423
Sniktaw............................. 321, 323
soldiers .. 40, 41, 257, 258, 269, 277, 278, 282, 457, 469, 471, 474, 595
solitude...................... 160, 313, 314
Solomon Wade 494, 496
Sonora ... 83, 85, 100, 106, 117, 126, 139, 140, 142, 327
Sonora Herald............................ 139
Sons of Bacchus........................ 247
Sons of Temperance........... 246, 247
Southern Oregon................. 294, 357
Speaker Colfax........................... 633
specie 226, 340, 341, 344, 345
speculators 204, 391, 443
Spencer, Giles.............................. 8
Squaws for guns 251
SR Lewis.................................... 299
St. Louis 339, 387, 388, 389, 390
starvation ... 177, 183, 256, 262, 339
starving............................. 339, 443
steamer 44, 68, 74, 146, 205, 266, 282, 337, 357, 369, 388, 391
Steamers
    Atlantic 332
    Belle 266
    Carrier.................................. 388
    Central America.................... 336
Steven Benedict 367
Stevens, John L. 334
Stockton ...68, 71, 73, 74, 77, 82, 99, 106, 108, 117, 133, 138
Stratton, Parson 322
Sullivan, William 329

Sullivan, Yankee 281, 286, 287
Sydney 100, 101, 130, 131, 132, 141, 158
Symmes Hole 311

T

Table Rock 219, 220, 251, 274
Taft, Robert 8
taxes 308
Taylor, Allen 9
Teamsters 83, 100, 248, 396, 548, 549, 560, 568, 569, 585
Tehama 159, 160, 172, 173, 331
temperance 246, 247, 359
Templeton, John 10, 54, 66
Terry, Judge .284, 288, 289, 297, 300
Tesh, Dan 575
Texan 89, 90, 96, 132, 153, 311
The Bulletin 287, 375
The Colony 447
The Earthquakes 247
The Express 258, 317
The Fourth of July. 35, 234, 289, 354
The Humbugged 444
The Humbuggers 444
The Mountain Brow 138
The Providence Fire 367
The Sabbath .42, 104, 246, 269, 353, 365, 381, 383, 406, 451
The Yreka Fire 170
thieves 116, 282, 285, 323, 336, 470, 480, 482, 515
Thousand Spring Valley 490, 491, 532
Tifft 237, 240
Tim Oldham 568
Tirgin, Mr. 140
Tom Bass 512
Tom Walker 282
Tower House 175
towheads 356, 467, 473, 478
Trapper 162, 314
traveler 165, 199, 213, 217, 249, 264, 266, 274, 301, 363, 364,
419, 430, 446, 473, 482, 569, 570, 612
treaty..170, 252, 254, 274, 275, 282, 283, 320
trial 91, 112, 114, 122, 131, 141, 146, 157, 198, 237, 272, 281, 286, 288, 293, 295, 362, 557
Trinity Mountains 192
Trinity River 164, 165
Tule Lake 298, 550

U

U.S. Mail Company 319, 408, 414, 469
U.S. Mail Station 400, 411
Umpqua River 265
Uncle Sam ..236, 249, 257, 264, 278, 458, 462, 471, 474, 479, 482
Upham, Charlie 395, 396
Utah Territory 340

V

Valley Falls 9, 370
Vancouver 258, 267
varmints 81, 82, 192, 413, 468
Victoria, Queen 362
Vigilance Committees 141, 143, 157, 280, 281, 284, 285, 288, 297
Vigilant Fort 288
Vigilants 157, 281, 282, 283, 284, 285, 287, 288, 289, 300
villains .139, 140, 143, 242, 243, 281
Vitus, E. Clampus 289
volunteer army 301
volunteers 57, 84, 120, 169, 170, 177, 183, 184, 220, 249, 254, 258, 263, 264, 266, 267, 274, 276, 278, 282, 293, 294, 298, 299, 301, 358, 359, 478, 519, 520, 585, 591

W

Wade, Laban 8
Wade, Solomon 494, 496

wagon massacre 294
wagon road 205, 274, 330, 611, 612
wagon train 573
Wagoner, Mr. 250, 359, 360
Wagoner, Mrs. 255, 359
Walker, Leonard 8
Walker, Tom 282
Walla Walla 282
wanderer 253, 375, 376, 382
war ...48, 57, 76, 169, 183, 186, 191,
    198, 204, 214, 220, 236, 248,
    249, 251, 252, 253, 254, 255,
    258, 264, 268, 269, 273, 278,
    279, 282, 284, 287, 294, 295,
    299, 346, 357, 358, 361, 397,
    432, 471, 482, 501, 538
Warman, Lieutenant 298
warriors 220, 294, 298, 359
Washington 144, 286, 308
Wells Fargo 616
What Cheer House 332
Whipple, Welcome 10, 74
whiskey 150, 161, 211, 234, 299,
    345, 398, 437, 440, 500, 607, 616
White Indians 83
White Wolves 189
Whittle, Bob 543, 544, 551
wildcats 81, 442, 491
wilderness ... 93, 271, 329, 387, 393,
    397, 410, 415, 445, 455, 463,
    466, 476, 497, 502, 514, 582,
    594, 635
Willamette Valley 278
William Collar 348
William Hathaway is now
    immortalized 191
William Sullivan 329
Williams, Henry 8
Wilson, Mr. 437

Winkle, Ann 518
Winn, Freeman 9
wolf pelts 412
Woods Creek ... 84, 86, 98, 106, 108,
    112, 136
Woods, Hiram 186
Woodward, R. 332
Worcester 370, 386
Wormer 168
Wright, Ben 256

Y

Yamhill County 294
Yankee 42, 52, 57, 58, 128, 231, 243,
    281, 286, 287, 311, 363, 396,
    536, 585, 616
Young, John 9, 54, 66, 74, 78, 365,
    369, 377
Young, Mr. Frank 174
Yreka.. 161, 163, 164, 166, 167, 168,
    169, 170, 174, 183, 185, 186,
    189, 190, 191, 194, 196, 204,
    205, 220, 222, 223, 234, 235,
    236, 237, 241, 245, 246, 253,
    258, 260, 261, 263, 264, 268,
    269, 270, 271, 280, 285, 289,
    293, 297, 307, 318, 319, 320,
    321, 322, 324, 327, 328, 329,
    330, 341, 346, 347, 353, 358,
    373, 375, 415, 467, 483, 488,
    491, 493, 515, 519, 521, 522,
    523, 525, 526, 532, 535, 536,
    537, 538, 543, 544, 545, 548,
    549, 550, 571, 579, 597, 612, 633
Yuba River 331

Z

Z. Rogers 319

TheLostGoldRushJournals.com

www.ingramcontent.com/pod-product-compliance
Lightning Source LLC
Chambersburg PA
CBHW030900080526
44589CB00010B/83